Wimpole

Wimpole

Architectural drawings and topographical views

David Adshead

First published in Great Britain by The National Trust 2007.

Text copyright © David Adshead.

Design and layout copyright © The National Trust 2007.

Designed by Fetherstonhaugh Associates
www.fetherstonhaugh.com

The moral rights of the author and photographers have been asserted.

All rights reserved. No part of this publication may be reproduced, stored in a retrieval system, or transmitted, in any form or by any means, electronic, mechanical, photocopying, recording or otherwise, without the prior permission of the copyright holder.

ISBN-13: 9781905400560
ISBN-10: 190540056X

A CIP catalogue record for this book is available from the British Library.

Reproduction Fotolito Raf

Printed and bound by Lito Terrazzi Firenze, Italy

The Publisher is committed to respecting the intellectual property rights of others. We have therefore taken all reasonable efforts to ensure that the reproduction of all content on these pages is done with the full consent of copyright owners. If you are aware of any unintentional omissions please contact the publishers directly so that any necessary corrections may be made for future editions.

www.nationaltrust.org.uk

All images © The National Trust/Geremy Butler unless specified below. References are for catalogue numbers:

Ashmolean Museum, Oxford (11-14);
Bedfordshire & Luton Archives Service (84 & 85);
The Bodleian Library, University of Oxford (15, 25-27, 29, 30, 31, 33, 74, 75, 199);
The British Library (18, 28, 38, 43, 56, 66, 99-101, 139, 148, 200, 201, 203, 204, 223, 228, 239, 240);
Trustees of The British Museum (23);
Cambridgeshire Archives Service (221, 233, 274, 283-292);
The Syndics of Cambridge University Library (65, 190, 222, 224, 232);
Collection Centre Canadien d'Architecture / Canadian Centre for Architecture, Montréal (154, 158, 170, 184);
The Trustees of the Cecil Higgins Art Gallery, (17, 21, 22);
Christie's Images (227);
The Frances Lehman Loeb Art Center, Vassar College Art Gallery, Poughkeepsie, New York (155);
NTPL/AC Cooper (34, 193);
NTPL/Angelo Hornak (192, 248, 252);
NTPL/Brenda Norrish (229, 231, 262, 264, 265, 267, 269, 271, 273, 293, 307, 308, 316, 318);
RIBA Library Drawings Collection (86, 87, 88, 89, 238);
The Royal Collection (235);
The Trustees of Sir John Soane's Museum (6, 7, 9, 10, 16, 53-55, 103-111, 113, 115-123, 125, 131-133, 138, 140-153, 156-157, 159-169, 172-183, 185, 188, 189, 210-219);
Sotheby's Picture Library, London (226);
Society of Antiquaries of London (45);
Staffordshire Record Office (81);
State Hermitage Museum, St. Petersburg (92-96);
Tate Museums, London (19-20);
V&A Images, (2, 42, 76, 171, 186, 187, 198)

Contents

Foreword	6
Author's preface	7
Acknowledgements	8
Wimpole in the seventeenth century	10
Abbreviations and conventions	12
The Catalogue	13
Yorke Family Tree	140
Bibliography	141
Notes	148
Appendix	155
Index	157

Foreword

This is an auspicious publication. The National Trust is the custodian of a very large collection of architectural drawings and archives, spread across its varied properties, or deposited with family papers in the relevant regional archive offices. A research project funded by The Paul Mellon Centre for Studies in British Art is already underway to list all architectural drawings and eventually to put them on the web. David Adshead has gone one step further, by gathering together and cataloguing all the drawings and designs associated with Wimpole, whether in Trust ownership or elsewhere, such as the Royal Institute of British Architects or the Sir John Soane's Museum, interpreting them with the existing archives. I cannot recollect that this has been done for any other country house. It is very enlightening and he is to be congratulated.

John Harris

Author's preface

In 1992 Gervase Jackson-Stops (1947—95), the National Trust's then Architectural Adviser, curated an important exhibition, *An English Arcadia*, that celebrated nearly four hundred years of garden design and architecture.[1] The exhibition travelled to the United States of America and Canada in support of the Stowe Landscape Gardens Appeal and, fittingly, included eleven drawings and engravings of that greatest of British eighteenth-century gardens. While the designed landscapes at Wallington, Northumbria and Cliveden, Buckinghamshire were represented by eight drawings apiece, Wimpole, Cambridgeshire, with fifteen, topped the league table.

The choice of drawings was no doubt influenced by survival, significance, visual appeal, and the contribution that each one made to the chronology and compass of the exhibition. With drawings selected from some forty properties now in the care of the National Trust, that those from Wimpole accounted for more than ten per cent of the total provides some indication of the importance, interest and quality of the drawings that remain at the house and which chart the development of the gardens and wider landscape there. This is as true of those that describe the architectural evolution of the Hall and its ancillary and estate buildings.

It is perhaps appropriate, then, that the present catalogue, published by the National Trust with the Cambridgeshire Records Society, and generously supported by the Leche Trust, should be among the first of what it is hoped might be a series of property-based studies of the architectural, topographical and decorative drawings that, with honourable exceptions, remain, relatively unknown, in the collections of the National Trust.[2]

Initially innocent of their number, I suggested that the scope of the catalogue should be extended beyond a consideration of the drawings at Wimpole to include all design and record drawings for Wimpole, wherever their present location. Between 1740 and 1894 the Wimpole estate was continuously owned by the Yorke Earls of Hardwicke but during the previous hundred years it had changed hands with remarkable regularity and for this reason the documentary record is widely scattered. I underestimated quite how long it would take, in stolen moments, to delve in archives, libraries and, more recently, into the world of electronic resources, to track down the component parts of the 'omnium-gatherum' I had imagined. Inevitably there will be drawings and documents that have been overlooked but it is hoped that this publication may help to flush them out from the undergrowth and will prompt others to correct or amplify what follows.

The analogy between palimpsest, a manuscript in which the original text may be over-written on any number of occasions, perhaps partly erased in the process, and complicated, multi-layered, architecture in which successive building campaigns have altered but not wholly eradicated what went before, is perhaps now rather hackneyed. If ever that parallel were valid it is surely so in relation to the Hall and Park at Wimpole where a careful reading of either one reveals the vestiges of ideas overlain, one on top of another, which reflect in a rather remarkable way changing taste in English architecture and landscape gardening during a three-hundred-year period from the mid-seventeenth to the mid-twentieth century. This process of creation and partial destruction is made all the more interesting because the *dramatis personnae* reads a little like an architectural roll of honour, and includes, amongst lesser names, such celebrated figures as James Gibbs, Sir James Thornhill, Charles Bridgeman, Henry Flitcroft, Sanderson Miller, Lancelot 'Capability' Brown, James Essex, James 'Athenian' Stuart, John Soane, and Humphry and John Adey Repton.

In his analysis of Wimpole Hall, Eric Parry suggests that it is this history of constant metamorphosis of building and landscape, the story of the struggle of successive architects to adapt the existing fabric to meet the new requirements of their clients, each generation building on but not entirely destroying the foundation laid by the previous one, which makes a study of Wimpole such an engaging exercise for architect and historian alike.[3]

In the first of his 1927 articles on the house, Christopher Hussey admits that Wimpole presents 'to the student of architectural history, a nest of problems'.[4] As the bibliography reveals, it has subsequently received a good deal of scholarly and popular attention—not only was a compellingly thorough history of the estate published by the Royal Commission on the Historical Monuments of England in 1968, but it has been the subject of no less than nine articles in *Country Life*, while specific aspects of its story have been the focus of at least five studies in *Apollo Magazine*. To a considerable degree Hussey's 'nest of problems' has long since been untangled, although fundamental questions about the seventeenth-century house remain unanswered.

I have not offered a revisionist interpretation here, rather this catalogue is intended to complement the existing body of work on Wimpole, not least the excellent guidebooks written by Gervase Jackson-Stops (1979) and David Souden (1991) which provide a narrative history of the estate and its successive owners.[5] The catalogue's main purpose is to make available in one place survey and design drawings and topographical views, whether or not previously published. In order to provide a context for the description and analysis of each drawing, and so as to enliven what might otherwise be indigestible factographia, I have included material gleaned from primary and secondary sources—exchanges, where they survive, between patron and client, accounts which might provide details of work undertaken or materials purchased, the sums expended and the craftsmen contracted, together with contemporary insights drawn from family correspondence and visitors' descriptions.

By and large the drawings have been arranged in a chronological sequence and have been grouped together, with a common introduction, if they appear to by one designer or office, are for a single project, or are of a particular type. In addition to the black and white illustrations reproduced in the body of the text, and the colour plates, a digital version of each photograph, viewable as a full-screen image, is also stored on the accompanying CD-Rom. While it is not ideal to consult both the pages of a book and a computer monitor simultaneously, by adopting this technology it is hoped that the perennial problems associated with comprehensive illustration—cost and space—might be addressed and a hybrid produced that offers at least some of the benefits of both conventional and on-line publication.

Acknowledgements

For my parents with love and admiration.

&

In Memoriam
† Anthony Paget Baggs, 1934—2006

The gestation of this catalogue has been elephantine. Its conception must have come shortly after Dr John Maddison, the National Trust's then Historic Buildings Representative for East Anglia, introduced me to Wimpole in the autumn of 1988. As his new assistant, with delegated curatorial responsibility for the property, its collections, buildings and landscape, I was given the opportunity to pore over the architectural drawings in the house, some framed and on display, others salted away and in a tantalising jumble. Under John's inspiring tutelage, the relationship between the paper world of inky possibilities and the corresponding realm of bricks and mortar, timber and plaster, began to fascinate me as it should have done when nearly ten years earlier as a student from the School of Architecture at Cambridge I had visited with my class to survey the dangerously decayed Chinese Bridge in the park. The exercise then was to design a replacement bridge, build a scale model and load it to the point of collapse; perhaps it was my limited grasp of structures that suggested a path away from the practice of architecture towards the study of its history. To John I owe a very great debt of gratitude. His publication in *Architectural History*, in 1991, of the architectural drawings at Blickling Hall, Norfolk, completed and published in a fraction of the time that this volume has taken, provided the real spur to my attempting something similar for Wimpole.

Gervase Jackson Stops's *tour d'horizon* of designs for gardens and garden buildings in the care of the National Trust served as a second inspiration and point of departure for my research into the history of Wimpole's complex evolution. Gervase's star shines brightly still, as does his legacy of research and publication on the architectural, decorative and garden history of the extraordinary properties in the National Trust's care, serving as a touchstone for future enquiry. A memorable whirlwind visit to Wimpole by Gervase and his friend and sparring partner John Harris, which included a de rigueur riffling through the architectural drawings, concluded with my photographing the pair, arm in arm, wearing on their heads contrasting lamb's-wool tea-cosies purchased from the shop, one black and one white; there was a tussle, I remember, to get the role of the black sheep first.

Sporadic work on this cataloguing project over a protracted period has meant the involvement of successive colleagues, whether based at Wimpole itself, the Trust's East Anglian regional office (now the East of England), or at its London office, and I am delighted now to have the opportunity to thank all those from the 'plashy fen' and 'the Great Wen' who have so generously contributed in one way or another to the venture. Gregory the Great's supposed quip "*non Angli sed Angeli*" seems particularly apposite to describe friends and colleagues from the eastern counties. Merlin Waterson, the regional director under whom I served for twelve years, inspired me in a host of ways and I am ever grateful to him for encouraging me to write for the National Trust, as he himself has done so elegantly over the years. At Wimpole, Graham and Olga Damant, and George Potirakis, provided friendship, hospitality and an infectious passion for the place. Both Graham and Mike Rooney, his successor as Wimpole's property manager, led local fundraising efforts to help meet the production costs of the catalogue. Ann den Engelse, the Historic Buildings department's saintly secretary, helped in myriad ways, as did Angus Wainwright, who shared with me his great knowledge of Wimpole's designed landscape, its planting history and archaeology. After working under his direction, as part of a volunteer team, to excavate the footings of John Soane's hothouse in the walled garden at Wimpole in June 1998, Angus awarded me, with the irony perhaps due an archaeologist manqué, an embroidered badge bearing a golden trowel together with a certificate announcing my qualification as a 'Troweller Grade IV'.

Other colleagues, past and present, who have given generously of their time – whether championing the publication of the catalogue, answering queries and pleas for help, reading and commenting on draft text, offering valuable insights, spotting howlers or helping to run to ground, and transcribing, primary material in a host of record offices and other repositories – include: Lucy Armstrong, Amanda Bradley, Hugo Brown, Emile de Bruijn, Sophie Chessum, Edward Diestelkamp, Anna Forrest, Oliver Garnett, the late Gervase Jackson Stops, Simon Jervis, Tim Knox, Alastair Laing, Marcus Lodwick, Lucinda Porten, Mark Purcell, Sophie Raikes, James Rothwell, Christopher Rowell, Francesca Scoones, Sarah Staniforth, Helen Vigors, Alexa Warburton, Richard Wheeler, Tessa Wild and Helen Wyld. I am also immensely grateful to Rachel Elwes, and Suzi Nelson, who transcribed a number of key documents. Other scholars from whose correspondence and advice I have greatly benefited include: the late Tony Baggs, Thomas Cocke, Mike Cole, James Collett-White, Sir Howard Colvin, Nicholas Cooper, the late John Cornforth, Ptolemy Dean, Roderick O'Donnell, John Drake, Nesta Evans, Patricia Ferguson, the late Donald Findlay, Richard Garnier, Keith Goodway, Ivan and Elizabeth Hall, John Harris, William Hawkes, Richard Hewlings, Gordon Higgott, Richard Holden, Olivia Horsfall-Turner, Simon Houfe, Peter Howell, Susan Jenkins, Jennifer Meir, Adam Menuge, Hugh Pagan, John Martin Robinson, Anne Rowe, Peter Willis, Christopher Woodward and Lucy Worsley. Editors of *The Burlington Magazine*, *Apollo*, and *The Georgian Group Journal* – Caroline Elam, Robin Simon, David Ekserdjian and Richard Hewlings – kindly accepted, and made invaluable editorial suggestions to, various articles that were to serve as building blocks for this book. David Souden, the author of the National Trust's 1991 guidebook to Wimpole, very kindly passed on to me his immaculate research cards, which have been of very great assistance in identifying source material that I wished to return to.

The staff of record offices, archives and libraries both in this country and in North America have been unfailingly helpful, none more so than those at Sir John Soane's Museum: Margaret Richardson and Tim Knox (past and present Curator and Director), Stephen Astley, Will Palin, and Susan Palmer.

Drawings by members of John Soane's Office account for nearly one third of those in the catalogue, and I am particularly indebted to Sue and Stephen for their expert help and kindness in acting as my dragomen at Lincoln's Inn Fields, and for reading and commenting on the text with eagle eyes and profound knowledge. Not least, Sue saved me from the schoolboy solecism of ascribing, in a moment of fading brain power, a group of drawings to a hitherto unrecorded draftsman, L.J. Fields. Thanks are due also to the other institutions and trustee bodies that have granted access to, and permission to reproduce, drawings or other material from their collections. A number of private collectors have similarly exhibited great generosity. One section of the catalogue was written whilst sequestered in John and Gabrielle Sutcliffe's beautiful house in Cambridge, and I am deeply grateful to them for entrusting it to me whilst they were abroad.

Without a handsome grant from the Leche Trust, and the support of the Cambridgeshire Records Society, it would not have been possible to get this publication off the blocks. The fees from a lecture tour that I undertook for the Royal Oak Foundation in the United States of America were also harnessed to the project.

With advice from Mary Goodwin and Andrew Bush, the conservators Julie Marsden and Chris Calnan have in succession ensured that the drawings at Wimpole are properly conserved and cared for, and in 2005 the National Manuscripts Conservation Trust generously awarded a grant to ensure this, providing the funds for the repair of drawings and their safe storage in archival folders and acid-free boxes, work that was undertaken beautifully by Sally Price. The photographs of the drawings in the National Trust's Bambridge Collection were largely taken by Geremy Butler and Brenda Norrish, in black-and-white and colour campaigns as funds permitted, while Hugo Brown and Alex Newson digitised them for inclusion on the CD. Mariana Sonnenberg and Alexa Warburton have undertaken invaluable picture research.

At the Cambridgeshire Records Society the editors Peter Searby and Dr Rosemary Horrox have in turn provided encouragement and an incisive editorial pen at just the right moments, and if the protraction of the book's production has tested their patience they have generously suppressed the fact. I consider it a great honour that the catalogue is published as one of the society's annual volumes. Gill Troup and Liz Dittner have both undertaken copy editing at different times, and Monica Allen compiled the index.

James Parry has steered all this, and the author, with considerable flair and enthusiasm, keeping me committed to and cheerful about a task which at times seemed Sisyphean in character. I could not imagine a better, more entertaining editor and project manager to work with. Patrick Fetherstonhaugh, of Fetherstonhaugh Associates, has produced an elegant design, juggling with images and text in order to achieve meaningful proximity for the reader, and has shown great patience as catalogue numbers changed, further footnotes materialised and additional paragraphs appeared here and there.

It is an abiding sadness that a number of friends and scholars have died during the period in which this catalogue has been written – I can only hope that they might have enjoyed it, though each and every one would have been able to suggest corrections and improvements. Gervase Jackson Stops I have already mentioned. In the months before John Cornforth died, in 2004, he spoke enthusiastically to me of his interest in James Gibbs's planning abilities and felt that Wimpole was ripe for reappraisal. Perhaps most of all I regret not having been able to show this volume, either in draft or final form, to the building archaeologist and architectural historian Tony Baggs who died in 2006 and who, amongst many other distinctions, was the chairman of the Cambridgeshire Records Society. As a young man he contributed to the peerless analysis of Wimpole published by the Royal Commission on the Historical Monuments of England in 1968, to which I have returned again and again. Many years later, I had the pleasure of visiting Wimpole in his company with one of his supervisees, Elizabeth Haylett. I very much admired his combination of self-effacing modesty, deep knowledge and generosity in teaching, and I offer this catalogue in his memory.

David Adshead, London

'An Extraordinary curious neat house' – Wimpole in the seventeenth century

Sir Thomas Chicheley (1614—99), the builder of the modern house at Wimpole, was born to one of the wealthiest land-owning families in Cambridgeshire.[6] Its patriarch Sir Thomas Chicheley (1578—1616) died only two years later, leaving his wife Dorothy (d.1644) to manage his affairs and succour their children. The younger Thomas came of age in 1635 and inherited his father's estates in Cambridgeshire and Kent and a few months later married Sarah (d.1654), daughter of a neighbouring landowner Sir William Russell, 1st Baronet of Chippenham (c.1575—1654).[7] Chicheley's position catapulted him onto a privileged path of preferment; in 1637 he became high sheriff of Cambridgeshire, two years later the deputy lieutenant, and in 1640 was elected MP for the county. It is with his architectural patronage that the following account of the Wimpole estate should logically begin, but a paucity of documentary material makes this difficult and necessarily speculative. Apart from an estate survey of 1638 (*No.1*) and an engraved design for a gate-screen, published in 1693 (*No.2*), no design drawings or views for Wimpole appear to have survived from the seventeenth-century.

Almost nothing is known of the circumstances of the design and building of Thomas Chicheley's new house, let alone its authorship, its history muddied by the eighteen-year-long disruptions of the three successive Civil Wars, and the political experiments of The Commonwealth and The Protectorate. The tantalising description of a bundle of architectural drawings lotted together in the 1813 sale of the library at Merly, Dorset as 'A large Parcel of Houghton, Wimpole &c., *by Sir C. Wren*' raises more questions than it answers.[8]

The manuscript notes of the local historian John Layer (1585?—1640) at least provide evidence that Chicheley's building works had either begun by or began in 1640. His notes were written for the purposes of a projected parochial history of Cambridgeshire which had it been published would have been the first such for an English county. Like Charles Dickens's Mr. Gradgrind, Layer was first and foremost interested in facts and, in the words of his biographer, the 'laborious descents of manors', but the occasional descriptions of contemporary conditions and topography that he allowed himself have proved rather more valuable.[9] In early variants Layer had described Wimpole as the 'old faire house'—presumably the gabled and moated manor illustrated on the 1638 survey (*No.1*)—but in what must have been his final draft he made a telling modification, noting instead that 'Thomas Chicheley Esq. Lord of this village, is now erecting an extraordinary curious neat house near the antient [*sic*] site'.[10] Layer died in 1640 before he could publish his papers and before the new house at Wimpole can have been very far progressed. What did he find curious about it? Had he seen drawings for the building which would have revealed it to be of a progressive plan type, a proto double-pile house with a central 'glide' on the cross-axis?[11]

It has been suggested that Chicheley spent some £40,000 on estate improvements between 1630 and 1640.[12] Did the start of his building campaign, then, follow on from expensive changes already made to the estate, park and gardens? Chicheley's works must in any event have been interrupted as political events unfolded, and relations between Royalist and Parliamentary factions soured.

What proved to be the 'Long Parliament' first sat in November 1640, but as a Royalist (and a ship-money sheriff) Chicheley must have found its work—which saw the restriction of the king's powers, the execution of Thomas Wentworth, the Earl of Strafford (1593—1640), and the imprisonment of Archbishop Laud (1573—1645)—increasingly unpalatable. He was disabled from sitting at Westminster in 1642, and instead answered Charles I's summons to the alternative parliament established, in January 1644, in the hall at Christ Church College, Oxford. We know little of Chicheley's time in Oxford, but it was there that he sat for William Dobson (1610—46), van Dyck's successor as Court Painter. In Chicheley's absence from Wimpole his children and estates were cared for by his father-in-law, Sir William Russell and by Sir William's son by his second marriage, the parliamentarian Colonel Francis Russell.[13] Sir William Russell's own estates were never sequestrated during the Civil War, either because he was cautious not to involve himself actively in the Royalist cause or because of his familial connections with Oliver Cromwell.[14]

On 24 June 1646, three weeks after the king's capitulation to the Scots at Newark, the Royalists surrendered Oxford; Chicheley was amongst the signatories. He appears to have been imprisoned at Kings Lynn with other 'Gentlemen of Cambridge' and in 1647 he was punished as a malignant and forced to pay a heavy fine. Chicheley's estate was valued at £1,100 5s 4d and he compounded on the Oxford Articles for £1,985 10s 8d.[15]

It is possible that the house Layer had seen under construction was completed quietly during these years, but the evidence of the Cambridge Hearth Tax returns may suggest that Chicheley's house was instead completed after the Restoration, with the return of his political and financial fortunes. The hearth tax returns for Michaelmas 1664 show that between this date and 1662, that of the previous, surviving, record of the levy, the number of hearths listed under Thomas Chicheley's name had increased from thirty three to forty, accounting for seven of the eight additional hearths in the parish of Wimpole.[16] The tax, which continued until 1689 when it was abolished by William III, took account of fire hearths, stoves, smith's forges and baker's ovens (though not private ovens) and, although initially done on the basis of self-assessment, was subsequently overseen by 'Chimney Men' who had the right to search houses for hearths.

It is not clear under what circumstances Chicheley lived until the Restoration, but it appears that, having paid his fines in a timely manner, he was free to continue living at Wimpole and in his London house in Great Queen Street. Nonetheless, placed as Wimpole was in one of the counties of The Eastern Association, and despite the advantages of his connections with the Russell family, Chicheley's activities must have been circumscribed. Family burials and baptisms continued at Wimpole's parish church, St. Andrew's, and in 1651, despite his straitened circumstances, Chicheley bought from the Wingfield family one of the remaining manors at Wimpole to have escaped Chicheley ownership.[17]

Thomas Chicheley's wife, Sarah, died on 19 January 1654, the same year as her father, and was buried in the new vault at Wimpole. Later that year, or possibly during the following, Chicheley married again. His bride was the Hon. Anne Savile (d.1662), the daughter of Sir Thomas Coventry, 1st Baron Coventry of Aylesbourgh, and the widow of Sir William Savile, 3rd Bt. of Thornhill, Yorkshire. In August 1644 Anne Savile had been the heavily pregnant heroine of the siege of Sheffield, and was thereafter considered a spy by Cromwell's faction.

Chicheley's new alliance can hardly have helped his position.

The possibility that Chicheley was his own architect has been given credence by his membership of the Royal Commission established in April 1663 to oversee the repair (as was then intended) of old St. Paul's Cathedral. Various committees comprising different combinations of commissioners met and reported during the following three years, and when, in November 1673, a new Royal Commission was set up with the brief of rebuilding the cathedral Chicheley was again invited. He found himself in the distinguished architectural company of Sir John Denham (1615—69), then Surveyor of the King's Works (though according to John Evelyn 'a better poet than architect'); John Webb (1611—72), Inigo Jones's pupil and executor; Edward Marshall (c.1598—1675), a master mason; Sir Roger Pratt (1620—85) (subsequently one of the three commissioners to oversee the rebuilding of the City of London after the Great Fire), and Hugh May (1621—84), then Paymaster of the King's Works. But the list of members was long and it remains unclear whether Chicheley was included because he had some standing as an authority on architecture, or instead as a representative of the City—which was perhaps his role at the laying of the foundation stone of Sir Christopher Wren's St Stephen's Walbrook in 1672. It seems as likely that Chicheley attended in an official capacity for in the second Royal Commission, the king lists Chicheley as 'Master of our Ordnance'.

Evelyn, a supporter of Wren's then-emergent plan to demolish the old cathedral, had ridiculed the opinion expressed by Chicheley and Pratt on the committee visit of 27 August 1666—only days before the outbreak of the Great Fire—that the lean of the old fabric was a deliberate 'effect in Perspective'. Pratt, with whom Chicheley sided in favour of the retention of Inigo Jones's work at St. Paul's, clearly knew Wimpole in some detail and when advocating the double-pile (in preference to the 'stately' but 'exceeding costly' courtyard plan), as the most commodious of house types, warned: 'inconvenience will likewise be in some measure found in all those forms which have any considerable juttings out, and for those which are small, they only serve to make a room within irregular, except they make a room by themselves e.g. at Mr. Chicheley's Hall, though that defect be hid above by taking it into a closet'.[18] But this reference hardly amounts to explicit approval of Chicheley's architectural ideas. Chicheley, whether or not a gentleman architect, was in any event a man of taste and visual discernment, and his son-in-law Richard Legh apparently 'consulted him on even the smallest and most trivial matters, down to the selection of a piece of furniture or suit of clothes'.[19]

As we have seen, Chicheley prospered after the Restoration: he resumed his county responsibilities and in 1661 was once more elected MP for Cambridgeshire; in the same year he was, with John, Lord Berkeley of Stratton and Sir John Duncombe, appointed a commissioner for the ordnance and in 1670, the year he was knighted, became master-general of the ordnance with a salary of £1,500; and in 1682 became chancellor of the duchy of Lancaster. He was a flamboyant member of the court and appears to have been close to the king. In September 1667 Samuel Pepys, who saw him as a high flyer, mentions his playing tennis with Prince Rupert and Captain Cooke – the master of the Tennis Court at Whitehall Palace – in the company of the king.[20] Chicheley was clearly interested in fine things and we know from the correspondence of Richard Legh that in 1666 he had a handsome Coach 'of crimson Damaske and but just made'; this he appears to have sold almost immediately buying instead 'Mr. Palmer's Chamber and all the Furniture in it. I was with him to witness the possession. It is a fine Chamber in Grays Inn and full of fine Curiosities, Pictures, tables, Stands and Cabinetts'.[21] In March 1668, Pepys describes going to dinner with Chicheley at his house in Great Queen Street, Covent Garden: 'A very fine house, and a man that lives in mighty great fashion, with all things in a most extraordinary manner noble and rich about him, and eats in the French fashion all; and mighty nobly served with his servants, and very civilly; that I was mighty pleased with it: and good discourse'.[22]

Relations with Richard Legh's family were extremely harmonious and 'presents were continually sent from Wimpole to Lyme, apples, grapes and fruit of all kinds, unobtainable in the cold Cheshire climate, the compliment being returned by cheeses, ale and brawns being dispatched from Lyme'.[23] Chicheley's fortunes, however, were to decline rapidly in the 1680s. Characterised by Baroness Newton as 'a hopelessly indifferent man of business', Chicheley was evidently living beyond his means, and although the sale of Wimpole was not completed until 1686, transactions for its disposal were under way as early as 1684. It has been suggested that George Legge, 1st Baron Dartmouth, exhibited great enmity towards him and sought to reduce his political power, a trend that continued after the accession of James II in February 1685 when a new guard inevitably took up the reins. In October 1685 Chicheley's daughter-in-law, the wife of his son Sir John, wrote to her brother-in-law Richard Legh:

> I had yesterday a very doleful letter from Mrs. Langley upon the old matters of Sir Thomas's misfortunes and necessityes how her poor husband is forced to come to London to stope great gaps and that Sir Tho. hath soe much to pay when he comes to towne that she dread the consequence of it. I am sure this letter hath made Sir John's heart very heavy for several reasons and his journey I doubt but melancholy. He told me he always takes his last leave when he leaves that place, never expecting to come againe'.[24]

Chicheley's daughter, Mrs Fountaine, also wrote to Richard Legh about her worries for her father and for Wimpole:

> Wimpole looks sweetly, and the old gentleman and I had a deal of discourse about people that might and would not live there; they ought to be beaten [...] my father says he will go every summer for as long as he can. My brother John thinks (my father says) there is nothing to be done without 3 or 4 thousand pd. in his pocket, and therefore would be going to the Straights again to get it for 2 or 3 years'.[25]

In 1686, with reported even temper and patience in the face of adversity, Chicheley completed the sale of Wimpole to Sir John Cutler (c.1608—93). Cutler's son-in-law, Charles Bodville Robartes, 2nd Earl of Radnor (1660—1723), whose alterations to the hall and gardens are as poorly documented as Chicheley's work, is at least known to have treated the Legh family with kindness and consideration.[26]

Abbreviations and conventions

BAL	British Architectural Library
BL	British Library
Bod.	Bodleian Library
BRO	Bedfordshire County Record Office
CCA	Canadian Centre for Architecture
CL	*Country Life*
CUL	Cambridge University Library
CRO	Cambridgeshire County Record Office
EH	English Heritage
HMC	Historical Manuscripts Commission
HRO	Hertfordshire County Record Office
NT	National Trust
ODNB	*Oxford Dictionary of National Biography*
OS	Ordnance Survey
RA	The Royal Archive
RCHME	The Royal Commission on the Historical Monuments of England
SAL	The Society of Antiquaries of London
SM	Sir John Soane's Museum.
SRO	Staffordshire Record Office
UN	University of Nottingham
V&A	Victoria and Albert Museum
VCH	Victoria County History
WRO	Warwickshire County Record Office
WSRO	Wiltshire & Swindon Record Office
cat.	Catalogue
ed./eds.	Editor(s)
exh.	Exhibition
fig.	Figure
fo./fos.	Folio(s)
ill.	Illustration
lit.	Literature
Ms(s)	Manuscript(s)
pl.	Plate
r.	Recto
repr.	Reproduced
v.	Verso
vol.	Volume

On her death in 1976 Mrs Elsie Bambridge (1896—1976) left Wimpole and its contents, together with nearly 3,000 acres of park- and farmland, to the National Trust. Those drawings in the catalogue marked 'National Trust' are part of the National Trust's Bambridge Collection and remain at Wimpole.

Dimensions are given in millimetres and, for larger items such as oil paintings, centimetres, the vertical axis first. Cross-references to the drawings are given in round brackets, e.g. (*No.1*). A cautionary note about scales: those given on eighteenth-century drawings do not always obviously conform to one of the traditional fractional scales—i.e.: $^1/_8$ in., $^1/_4$ in., $^1/_2$ in. etc., to 1ft. Where this is the case, rather than mislead by attempting to shoe-horn the drawing into the closest but almost certainly incorrect category, or offer a very complicated formulation, I have simply indicated that a scale is given. Maya Hambly shows that before the late-eighteenth-century, when fractional divisions were introduced, decimal sub-division of imperial units into twenty-five, thirty, thirty-five, forty, fifty or sixty parts was common.[27] The history of paper watermarking is similarly complicated and its literature a specialist one.[28] Watermarks are described very simply in the following catalogue entries. The spelling of transcribed words has generally not been modernised, and both case, whether upper or lower, and superscript reflect the original.

opposite: No.95, Dessert plate decorated with a view of the Upper Lake at Wimpole, showing the Gothic Folly and Chinese Bridge, 1773—4

The Catalogue

1   (i to v) Benjamin Hare (active 1630—52).
Map of the Wimpole Estate, 1638

Cambridge Record Office R77/1
Inscr.: In a cartouche (top-left sheet): 'A DESCRIPTION of the Mannour of Wimple in the Countie of Cambridge, being part of the possessions of the right Worshipfull Tho: Chicheley Esquire Anno. Dom: 1638 Perfourmed by Ben. Hare sen. surveyour'. A decorative compass appears on the sheet at top-right.
Pen and ink on vellum, sheets of various sizes (376 x 562mm, 379 x 587mm, 374 x 578mm, 580 x 711mm and 570 x 732mm). The map was originally made up of a mosaic of six sheets, pasted together and arranged as two rows of three. The north-western sheet (ie. bottom left) is now missing.
A highly legible infra-red photographic copy made in 1948 is at BM Maps 6.c.55.
NB: The map is unconventionally orientated, with east at the top. The former Great North Road, built by the Romans as Ermine Street, bounds the western side of the estate and is, therefore, shown running along the bottom edge of Hare's map.
Exh.: County Hall, Cambridge (1978), cat.42.
Lit. & repr.: VCH (1973); RCHME (1968), detail showing the moated manor house, pl.121 (left), and fig. on p.239, showing Hare's map superimposed on an OS base; Souden (1991), (detail, ill. on p.6); Bendall (1992); Pattison & Garrow (1998), (details) figs.2, 6a & 18, reissued as Pattison & Barker (2003), figs.3 & 18.

This spectacular survey was commissioned by Sir Thomas Chicheley only two years before building work started on his new house. The 'High Parke' and 'Low Parke' (separated by what John Phibbs has suggested may have been an avenue of walnut trees), and the hedged fields around the manor house and tenants' cottages, clearly show that the processes of emparkment and enclosure, that were to be finalised with the landscaping works of the 1760s undertaken by Lancelot 'Capability' Brown (1716—83), were well under way by 1638.[29] Hare's map is essentially backward-looking and records in exacting detail the appearance of the estate as it must have been for much of the later Middle Ages. It reveals in a striking way the degree to which the shape and line of the medieval field and road systems, and the pattern of tree planting, influenced not only the landscaping work that Charles Bridgeman (d.1738) undertook in the 1720s (*Nos.29–39*) but also that of subsequent overlays.

In the eighteenth century it was suggested that the ridge and furrow at Wimpole might be smoothed out for aesthetic reasons—and in areas of dense planting, such as Bridgeman's so-called 'grid' of lime trees, this appears to have been done. Despite this threat, and the localised blurring of such features in more recent years, the plough pattern left by medieval strip farming practice is generally very well-preserved. Recent detailed topographical survey of the park at Wimpole provides a very accurate reference against which to study the details shown on Hare's map: the individual strips, marked with the name of the tenant who held and tilled them; their arrangement into blocks or furlongs; their headlands; and the dispersed hamlets of Thresham End, Bennall End, and what may be the 'Green End' referred to in earlier documents, which were swept away as part of Chicheley's landscape improvements.

Smaller groups of houses are also shown at Brick End and Little End and relict roads, tracks and house-platforms can still be read on the ground by the keen-eyed walker. The remnant corrugations of these ancient strips and their headlands leap into strong relief when low, winter light plays across the park, and the shades of Wimpole's ploughmen and their teams can be imagined toiling across the sward. As Angus Wainwright has shown, the names recorded on the cultivation strips can be cross-referenced to Hearth Tax returns and parish records and provide us with an indicator of relative wealth—John Baines, for example, held sixty-nine strips while others held only one.[30] Some parishioners had none at all. Chicheley's clean sweep established a new field pattern and the building of a series of new farmhouses. He provided £20 per annum in compensation for the loss of the displaced cottagers' common rights, a responsibility that was exercised for the next 300 years; in the early nineteenth century, 'Chicheley's Compensation Money' was distributed by the rector in the form of coal to the parish's aged poor.[31]

To the north-west of the church lay the four-gabled and moated 'Mannour' and gatehouse, described by John Layer in early versions of his intended history as the 'old faire house'. All trace of Wimpole's medieval manor house and its encircling moat was erased with the building of the new house. On the rising ground to the north-west Hare shows the post-mill on whose mound an ice-house was to be built in the eighteenth century (*No.66*). The two tributaries of the river Cam that run across the Wimpole estate, the Holden Dene to the north, and the river Rhee, with its low-lying pasture, to the south, are also recorded here. Fish-ponds were to be dug along the course of the Holden Dene in the late seventeenth century, and their banks were serpentised by 'Capability' Brown in the 1760s. The drawing, made immediately before the landscape architect's improvements (*No.82*), shows a remarkably similar pattern of fields to those recorded on Hare's survey, each with enduring names such as 'Avenells Piece', 'Bushie Avenells' and 'Great Avenells'.

Benjamin Hare was involved in the contemporary fen drainage scheme orchestrated by Francis Russell, 4th Earl of Bedford (bap. 1587—1641), and was active as a surveyor and map-maker in the counties of Cambridgeshire and Hertfordshire. In 1637 he made a map of Stonea, and in 1652 mapped Thorney for the 5th Earl of Bedford. It seems likely that Chicheley, though not himself an Adventurer until after the Restoration, came into contact with Benjamin Hare through Bedford's offices, indeed some of Bedford's land appears on the Wimpole map.[32] Sarah Bendall suggests that a map of this sort, in addition to being an accurate tool for estate management—for it must surely relate to a lost terrier—would have been a prominently displayed status symbol.[33]

2   Jean Tijou (active 1688—1712).
Design for a Gate Screen, 1693

Victoria & Albert Museum, E.2296 - 1909
Inscr.: 'J. Tijou. In. et del:', 'P. Vanderbanck. Sculp:'
Engraving (245 x 365mm)
Lit. & repr.: Harris (1960), fig.10; Jackson-Stops (1971), pp.182–3, fig.8; *idem* (1979:2), p.659.

This design closely matches the screen that is shown in the middle ground of Johannes Kip's (1653—1722) engraved view (*No.3*), and was published in 1693 as plate 5 of *A Newe Booke of Drawings Invented and Desined by John Tijou*. The book's full title proclaims that 'the most part' of the illustrated 'Gates, Frontispeices [sic], Balconies, Staircases, Pannells &c.' had been 'wrought at the Royall Building of Hampton Court', but that others had been made for 'Severall persons of Qualityes Houses of this Kingdome'; presumably Radnor and Wimpole were amongst them.

Daniel Defoe (1661?—1731) described Wimpole as being 'formerly built at a vast expence, by the late Earl of *Radnor*; adorn'd with all the Natural Beauties of Situation; and to which was added all the most exquisite Contrivances which the best Heads cou'd Invent to make it artificially as well as naturally pleasant'.[34] It seems likely, as has been suggested by Gervase Jackson-Stops, that the involvement of members of the Office of Works is implied—that is of the Royal gardeners George London (d.1714) and Henry Wise (1653—1738), the architect William Talman (1650—1719), and the French master blacksmith Jean Tijou. An émigré, Tijou may have come to England in the company of Antonio Verrio (1639—1707), Louis Laguerre (1663—1721)—Tijou's future son-in-law—and other continental European artists and craftsmen who were later employed at Hampton Court. Laguerre was to design the engraved frontispiece to Tijou's book.

Jackson-Stops has shown that Tijou's *Newe Book* designs contain elements unashamedly derived from earlier French engravings. The side gates and ironwork piers of the 'Wimpole' screen are directly copied from an engraving of *c.*1640 by the Parisian designer Jean de Mortin. The Wimpole design offers alternative treatments for the finials to each of the four piers. In

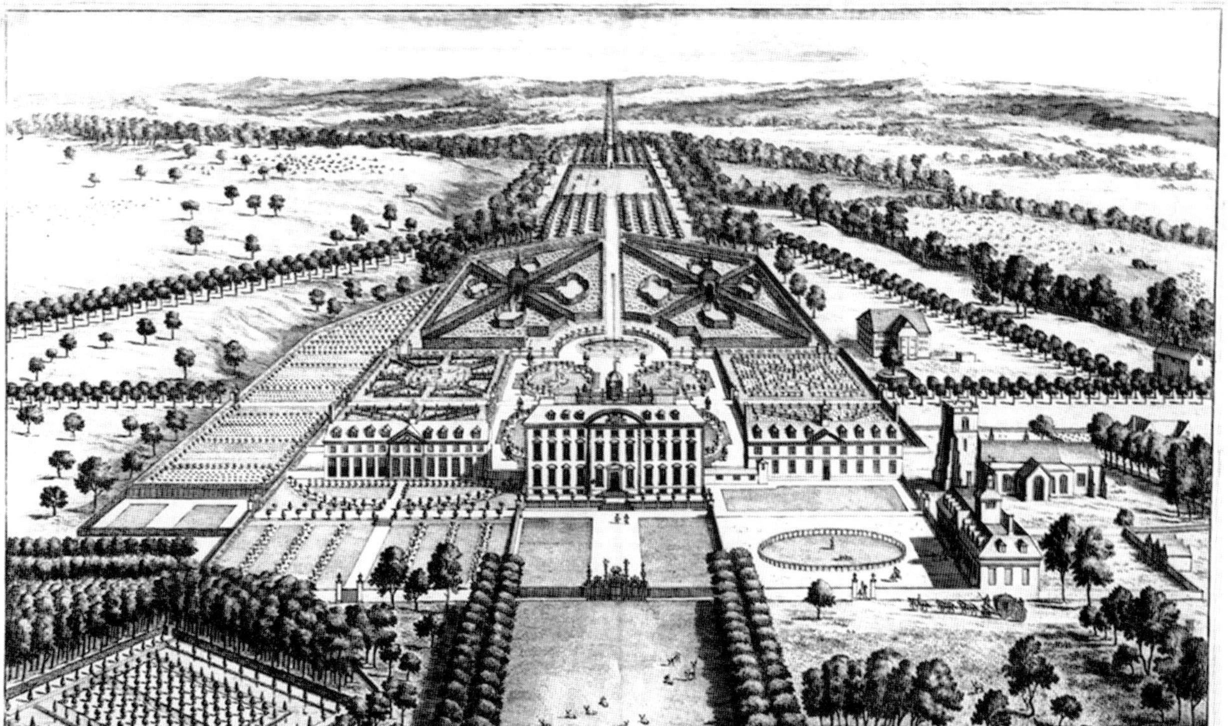

1 *(detail)* 2
3
5 *(detail)*

15 The Catalogue

turn, Batty Langley (1696—1751) plagiarised Tijou's design in his 1740 publication: *The City and Country Builder's and Workman's Treasury of Designs: or, the art of drawing, and working the ornamental parts of architecture*. The central and right-hand sections of the screen are illustrated in an engraving (plate clxxxiv) by Thomas Langley.

What appears to have been Tijou's screen was re-sited during Charles Bridgeman's landscape improvements of the 1720s before being finally swept away with the changes made by the subsequent generation. Bridgeman's heroically scaled South Avenue was both considerably wider than its predecessor and its northernmost trees were planted further to the south. This had two effects: it enabled the creation of a grander forecourt to the house, and of long views into the water gardens to the south-west and south-east, and beyond, via a diagonal vista, to the spire of Whaddon church. The extended central forecourt was contained by a curving railing screen at whose centre Bridgeman indicates a gate, '44' 6"' wide (*No.37*). It seems likely that this was Tijou's gatescreen re-used. John Cossen (fl.1713—23), Edward Harley's agent at Wimpole, reported in September 1723: 'The Greater part of the Iron Gates and Ornaments are fixed in their proper places in ye Great Court'.[35] It must have been this arrangement that Sir Matthew Decker (1679—1749), visiting in 1728, described as the 'Bassecour with handsome iron gates'.[36]

3   Johannes Kip (1653—1722).
    View of Wimpole Hall, Cambridgeshire, 1707

National Trust WIM/D/589
Inscr.: 'L. Knyff Delin. J. Kip Sculp. Wimple in the County of Cambridge the Seat of ye R^t. Honble Charles Bodville Lord Robartes Baron of Truro Viscount Bodmyn & Earl of Radnor L^d. L^t. & Custos Rotulorum of ye County of Cornwall'
Engraving (345 x 485mm)
Lit. & repr.: Hussey (1927:1), fig.15; Jackson-Stops (1979:1), p.52; *idem* (1979:2), pp.658-61, fig.1; Harris & Jackson-Stops (1984), pp.72-3; Souden (1991), p.9; Jackson-Stops (1992), p.41-2, pl.17.

After a lost drawing by Leonard Knyff (1650—1721), this bird's-eye view was engraved by his business partner Johannes Kip for their 1707 'survey' of country houses, *Britannia Illustrata, or Views of Several of the Queens Palaces also of the Principal Seats of the Nobility and Gentry of Great Britain*, which was sold by the publisher and bookseller David Mortier. The engraving also appeared in Joseph Smith's two-volume edition of 1715, and as plate 32 in volume 1 of Mortier's five-volume miscellany of the same year: *Nouveau Théâtre de la Grande Bretagne: ou description exacte des palais de la Reine, et des maisons les plus considerables des Seigneurs & des Gentilhommes de la Grande Bretagne*. Knyff surveyed and drew views of eighty estates over a ten-year period with those for Brittania Illustrata made between 1699 and c.1703. In some cases the prospects were commissioned and in others he and Kip solicited interest in the hope that an owner would subscribe to the projected publication.

This image has been reproduced in almost every account of Wimpole, but it is vital to an understanding of the evolution of the house, gardens, and surrounding landscape. In the absence of any seventeenth-century architectural drawings for Wimpole, Kip's engraved view is our only visual key to the cumulative improvements made by successive owners of the estate: Sir Thomas Chicheley, Sir John Cutler, and the 2nd Earl of Radnor. In all but one respect it appears to be an accurate record.

As Henry Flitcroft's (1697—1769) survey drawings of c.1742 (*Nos.46 & 49*) clearly demonstrate, the eleven-bay house shown at the centre of this engraving can never have existed. Rather it must illustrate how Radnor, the then owner, intended to modernise and extend the principal elevation; his arms are shown within the tympanum of the segmental pediment. Chicheley's house survived intact as the central block of an enlarged composition until Flitcroft's remodelling campaign. Is it possible that this was, as the Merly sale catalogue suggests, a design by Wren? Stylistically, at least, this seems plausible

In 1701, recommending places that Sir John Percival might like to visit during his planned tour of East Anglia, the antiquary Peter Le Neve (1661—1729) advised: 'Turn off on the right hand to go to wimple [*sic*], cross the country if you have a mind to see the fine gardens lately made by the Rt. Hon. the Earl of Radnor, I am told worth riding twenty miles out of the way to see'.[37] In 1710, only three years after the publication of Kip's view, Radnor was forced to sell the Wimpole estate, for his aspirations had far outstripped his resources. Writing from Paris three years later, Russell Robartes congratulated Robert Harley, 1st Earl of Oxford and Mortimer (1661—1724) on his son's marriage and thereby inheritance of Wimpole: 'since my Lord Radnor managed his affairs so ill as to dispose of so fine an estate from his family as Wimpole, after having laid out at least 20,000 L there, I most heartily rejoice that it is now in your Lordship's family'.[38]

Subsequent survey drawings substantiate much of the detail shown in Kip's engraving. Flitcroft's 1748 survey of the church (*No.57*) shows the form of the surviving medieval structure just as depicted here. John Soane's (1753—1837) assistants David Laing (1774—1856) and Guibert included in their detailed survey drawings of 1790 (*Nos.103, 104 & 107*) the orangery to the west of the Hall, and the service block to the east—both perhaps the work of William Talman (1650—1719)—recording them almost exactly as shown by Kip. Record drawings made by Thomas West in 1805 (*No.200*) similarly corroborate Kip's representation of the stable block which lay to the south of the church. Charles Bridgeman's surveys and landscaping proposals of the 1720s, together with later planimetric evidence, written documentation, and park surveys and field archaeology undertaken in recent years, demonstrate that the garden and park features illustrated in Kip's view existed largely as shown.

4   Jan Goeree (1670—1731), after Johannes Kip.
    View of Wimpole Hall, Cambridgeshire, 1707

National Trust WIM/D/586
Inscr.: 'WIMPLE in the County of CAMBRIDGE', at top right 'Pag. 116c'
Engraving (plate size 130 x 165mm)

This smaller and inevitably cruder version of Kip's view, engraved by the Dutchman Jan Goeree, was included in James Beeverell's ambitious eight-volume compendium *Les Delices de la Grand' Bretagne, et de l'Irlande, où sont exactement décrites les antiquitez, les provinces, les villes [...] la religion, les mœurs des habitans* [etc.]', published in Leyden in 1707 by Pieter Van der Aa. The view of Wimpole appears as part of plate LXI (345 x 420mm), p. 872 (114) in the fifth volume with the accompanying caption: 'Wimple in the County of Cambridge, ou Wimple dans le Comté de Cambridge, Maison de Campagne de très-honorable, Lord Robartes, Baron de Truro, Vicomte Bodmyn & Comte de Radnor, Lord Lieutenant, & Custos Rotulorum du Comté de Cornouaille'. Amongst the many categories that Beeverell included in his survey were 'les principales Maisons de Campagne & autres beaux Edifices des Familles Illustres, avec leur Armoires, &c.'.

5   Johannes Kip (1653—1722), plate altered.
    View of Wimpole Hall, Cambridgeshire, 1730

National Trust WIM/D/471
Inscr.: 'WIMPLE, in the County of CAMBRIDGE, formerly the Seat with a large Estate there of Sr. JOHN CUTLER Bart. who devised the same by his last will to his daughter Elizabeth COUNTESS OF RADNOR and after her decease without Children, to Edmund Boulter Senr. of the City of LONDON Esquire who for want of the same being intailed in his family unhappily gave it to the Right Hon.ble Charles Bodville Robert Earl of Radnor Husband to the aforesaid Countess; the said Earl sold the same to the most noble John Holles Duke of Newcastle, from whom it descended to ye Right Hon.ble Edward Harley Earl of Oxford & Mortimer, and his Countess the Lady Henrietta Cavendish Holles Harley, the said Duke's Daughter. This Plate is with great respect dedicated Anno Dom 1730 to John Boulter of Gawthorp Hall and

Harwood [sic] in the county of York Esq.r and to his Brother Edmund Boulter Jun.r of Hasely Court, in the County of Oxford, and Harwood aforesaid Esquire the two last heirs male of their name & family by their obliged and most obedient humble servant Joseph Smith near Exeter Exchange in the Strand'.
Engraving (370 x 500mm)

Kip's 1707 plate was reworked in 1730. Radnor's arms, whose ghost can be seen in the crudely stippled grass in the foreground, were replaced with a row of smaller armorials (left to right) belonging to: Sir John Cutler; Charles Bodville Robartes, 2nd Earl of Radnor; Boulter, for John and Edmund; and Edward Harley, 2nd Earl of Oxford (1689—1741).[39] The gloss below the engraved view only partly explains the circumstances of Wimpole's complicated history of ownership and the reason for the plate's dedication to the Boulter brothers, John and Edmund Junior, the nephews of Edmund Boulter (c.1630—1709).[40] In 1689, without his consent, Sir John Cutler's daughter Elizabeth, by his second wife Alicia (d.1685), married the 2nd Earl of Radnor. Mistrustful of the son-in-law he found himself with, Cutler appointed his nephew Edmund Boulter as his sole executor and residuary legatee. While 'it was widely reported that Cutler had left his estates in Yorkshire, Cambridgeshire and elsewhere, worth about £6,000 p.a., and half his personal estate, worth £60,000, to his daughter, the Countess of Radnor', failure of issue would see the lands remaindered on Boulter.[41] Cutler's dubious reputation as a financier, who 'specialised in lending money to impoverished landowners on the security of their estates'[42] and his disapproval of Radnor—who fully expected Boulter, then aged sixty-four and unmarried, to predecease his wife—are satirised in Alexander Pope's third 'Moral Essay':

> Cutler saw tenants break, and houses fall;
> For very want he could not build a wall
> His only daughter in a stranger's power;
> For very want he could not pay a dower.

When, in January 1696, Elizabeth died without issue exchanges between the Earl of Radnor and Edmund Boulter became increasingly litigious. Wimpole, where Radnor was already resident, was at least secure, for on his deathbed in 1693 Cutler had seen fit to forgive Elizabeth and the Cambridgeshire estate was settled on her. Cutler's wider estate, however, would now devolve on Boulter. Radnor exhibited a bill in Chancery and threatened to sue. In February 1699 he petitioned the House of Commons, for Boulter, who had conveniently been returned the previous year as MP for Boston, was protected by parliamentary privilege. Boulter set out his counter arguments in a printed bill, *The Case of Edmond Boulter, Esq; in Answer to the Petition of the Earl of Radnor*. In this Boulter asked that he might be allowed to settle amicably so as to avoid 'a Troublesome and Chargeable Suit in *Chancery*'. Boulter explained that while he had borne the cost of Cutler's 'Funeral Expenses, Debts and Law-Charges'—the funeral supposedly cost a staggering £7,666—his adversary had in fact not only received a moiety, or part share of the estate, but had also 'enjoyed the Profits of Lands with his Countess, since her Father's Death, amounting to about £14,000'. A settlement was reached out of court.

Boulter inherited the estates at Gawthorpe and Harewood in Yorkshire which Cutler had bought in 1657 from one of his major creditors, the 2nd Lord Strafford, who was then facing bankruptcy. Boulter in turn settled them on his nephew John, one of the dedicatees of this engraved plate and one of his four beneficiaries. A legacy of the Boulters' association with the Wimpole estate which has all but been forgotten, is that the parishioners there had the right to elect one poor man to the almshouses in St. Clement's parish, Oxford, in accordance with the will of Edmund Boulter. Almost opposite the 'Hospital for ye Poor and Sick' on St. Clement's Street, Oxford—founded by the Rev. William Stone in 1700 and now known as Stone's Court—can be found Boulter Street.

Drawings by James Gibbs (1682—1754) for Wimpole Hall

The connection between the architect James Gibbs (1682—1754) and the Harley family predates his involvement at Wimpole. It was partly to the influence of Robert Harley, 1st Earl of Oxford, that Gibbs owed his appointment in 1713 to one of the two surveyorships to the Commission for Building Fifty New Churches in London. He thereby also won the important opportunity to design the church of St. Mary-le-Strand (1714—7), and it was to the 1st Earl of Oxford that Gibbs looked for patronage when, in September of the same year, he first conceived the idea of publishing 'a book of architecture'.

The 1st Earl was at the time Lord High Treasurer and wielded enormous political power, but he was shortly to suffer a great reverse. In July 1714, only five days before she died, Queen Anne dismissed him from office, and twelve months later he was impeached and arrested, before being incarcerated in the Tower of London for a period of two years. With a Hanoverian king on the throne and a Whig rather than Tory government in power, Oxford's release brought neither political favour nor financial preferment. It was his son, Edward Harley, who was to be James Gibbs's sponsor thereafter.

In August 1713, on the eve of his father's troubles, a brilliant match was made: Edward Harley married Henrietta Cavendish Holles (1694—1755) in the Drawing Room in the mid-seventeenth-century house at Wimpole. She had inherited Wimpole, together with Welbeck Abbey, Nottinghamshire, and a substantial London estate, from her father, John Holles, 1st Duke of Newcastle, of the second creation (1662—1711), one of the wealthiest men in England. Newcastle's legacy, however, was acrimoniously disputed and was only settled by an Act of Parliament in 1716.

It seems likely that from the outset Harley chose to focus his energies and resources on Wimpole rather than Welbeck because it was nearer to London and to the universities—whose book trades fed his bibliomania—but uncertainty about the Newcastle inheritance must have delayed plans for possible architectural and landscape improvements. In the event, Henrietta received a much reduced share of the family fortunes, her cousin, Thomas Pelham-Holles (1693—1768), 1st Duke of Newcastle (of the third creation), inheriting the greater part. News of this resolution, and Henrietta's reconciliation with her dying mother, nonetheless prompted Humfrey Wanley (1672—1726), the Harleys' library-keeper, to celebrate by consuming, so he claimed, a gallon of brandy and punch mixed with twelve lemons and snake root.[43]

The earliest reference to Gibbs working for Edward Harley dates from November 1714, when the architect wrote to him at Wimpole: 'Your house goes one very forward, and I wish I had ane answear about these locks, what sorts and sises you would please to have'. This is almost certainly a reference to Edward Harley's London townhouse at No.34 Dover Street rather than to Wimpole.[44] At Harley's death, the Dover Street house contained a staggering 150 presses filled with manuscripts and books; Gibbs no doubt had helped to adapt the building to accommodate these collections.

It has been presumed that two drawings dated February 1713—some months before Harley's marriage—and traditionally said to be by Gibbs, show a preliminary proposal to annexe a vast library wing to Wimpole (*Nos.6 & 7*). This suggestion is questioned here, but the housing of the constantly burgeoning Harleian Library, begun by Robert Harley and continued by his son, was certainly a major factor in driving Edward Harley's building activities. Of necessity, the various parts of the library—which at the 2nd Earl of Oxford's death comprised 50,000 printed books, 8,000 volumes of manuscripts,

41,000 prints and 350 pamphlets—occupied different locations at different times. With the 1st Earl of Oxford's imprisonment and uncertain future the safe housing of the library and search for new premises became a pressing concern. It is largely in the correspondence and diaries of Edward Harley's circle of literary friends, notably those of Wanley and the poet Alexander Pope (1688—1744), that we find clues to the progress of Gibbs's work at Wimpole.

In February 1715 we find Gibbs acting as a forwarding agent for Edward Harley, sending pictures and sculpture to Wimpole from London: 'I saw all your picturs safly pack'd up this morning but ye 4 large ones, the boxes are all pritty strong and cloase so that I belive they are under no danger, I sent them with a Carte this affternoon to the vine Inn in Bishop Gait street where Mr Cutrel to morrow morning will see them put in the Cart for wimple. I have sent Mr Curtel [sic] your little Homers head in Ivory'.[45] The bulk of the Harleys' printed books was similarly sent to Wimpole, and by 1716 they appear to have been installed in the first of what was to be a series of interconnected rooms designed by Gibbs in which the function and trappings of *biblion* and *mouseion* were combined; the written word living cheek by jowl with works of art, antiquities and curiosities. Harley wrote to Wanley 'You will be wanted at Wimpole, now the room for my books is finished, to put them up and catalogue'.[46]

By September there were more than 12,000 volumes in the house. The catalogue that Wanley produced, with the books press-marked I.A.1 to XXVII.O.32, implies that there were twenty seven presses of up to fifteen shelves, but it is difficult to establish where these were housed. As David Souden has observed, 'so many changes have been wrought in the built fabric of Wimpole since Gibbs worked there that it is not always easy to identify the chronology of the rooms'.[47] But in a letter to his master, Wanley gives us a tantalising glimpse of the character of Gibbs's first library room at Wimpole, explaining that: 'The Green Strings your Lordship sent down, are putt up, & the Room looks with an uncommon & grand Air; the rest are put up in the lesser Room, where Five more are still Wanted. For, One came without a Tassel. One Skrew broke in Trial; for I bad the Workman try each, whether it would bear any weight, after it was put up; as thinking it better that he should break a Skrew or two, than I (or any other) break our Necks'.[48] Wanley explained that some of the 'strings' needed to be twenty three inches long 'as your Lordship very well remembers, the Joyners work there, comes down as low, almost as the Window. The sooner they are sent down, the better; that the Room may look Uniform'.[49]

There was pressure for space in London too, for in August 1717 the 1st Earl of Oxford's manuscripts were moved to his son's townhouse, causing Edward Harley to write to Wanley with barely veiled exasperation about the arrangement: 'There can be no room in the House in Dover Street be allowed for the Library. The Garden House is the only room that can be spared, and if that will not do I cannot help it'.[50]

In the summer of the following year, Dr Covel (1638—1722), the Master of Christ's College, Cambridge, whose own books were eventually purchased for the Harleian Library, wrote, somewhat fawningly: 'No man shall be more ready or industrious to assist or promote your most noble and magnificent design of building and furnishing a Vatican at Wimpole than my poor self'.[51] Only quoted in part, this has often been interpreted as evidence that Harley was then building a great palace at Wimpole; but by 'design' Covel is surely referring to Harley's intention to build, and the Vatican parallel is presumably to the papal library rather than its buildings; a library of books, that would outvie 'the great Ptolemy himself', rather than bricks and mortar.

Nonetheless, building works had clearly started, for in June 1719 Wanley was able to write: 'Within a few weeks I hope to be at Wympole, where his Lordship hath lately built Five large Rooms for a Library, which I hope to fill this Somer, with as choice a parcel of Books as any in England'.[52] A week later he notes: 'Yesterday morning early, my Noble Lady & my Lord sett out for Wympole, (as 'tis said) to see how their Workmen in or about the Chapel, Library, Stair-case, Garden, &c. go on; and are expected up soon. As to the Library there, the books are all in heaps upon the Ground, & some Waggons Loads are here to be sent down & added to them, so that the great Work of putting all in Order, will not begin suddenly; nor [...] can I now [...] tell when the Library will be open'd'.[53]

Gibbs extended westward the north and south piles of Chicheley's house, and linked the new ranges with a cross-wing. Three inter-linked cabinet rooms were formed within this wing, and, with two others—perhaps the present South Drawing Room and Red Room, in the south and north ranges respectively—they made up the sequence of 'Five large Rooms' dedicated to Harley's books and antiquities.

A receipt of July 1719 for various design drawings shows that the library was not the only concern at this time—architectural work was planned on a broad front:[54]

A drawing of a Cabinet	03. 03. 0
Drawings for two fine urnes	06. 06. 0
Three urnes of the Strand Church	03. 03. 0
Several dores for ye Liberary	03. 03. 0
Several drawings for ye Chapple	10. 10. 0
Four drawings for summer houses	06. 06. 0
Three drawings for urnes	03. 03. 0

The challenge of accommodating the fruits of the Harleys' bibliomania, however, must have continued to dominate Gibbs's brief. The new additions proved inadequate in scale, and Dr William Stratford (1672—1729), Edward Harley's former tutor at Oxford and a Canon at Christ Church, commiserated with him in August 1719: 'I am sorry to hear your new library was so calculated so much short of your stock of books as not to be able to hold half of them [...] you will be forced to have recourse at last to what I once suggested of turning your greenhouse into a library'.[55]

In May 1721 further payments were made to Gibbs:[56]

For a plan and upright of a house	5: 5: 0
For several drawings for a monument and inlarging ye drawght for ye model	21: 0: 0
For the moddell neatly done in pear tree and the figure done in beard [sic] earth	40: 0: 0
For two plans and uprights for stables proposed to be built att Wimpol	3: 3: 0
For two fronts for Wimpol	8: 8: 0
For two summer houses with the Roofe done in large	3: 3: 0
Two urnes in large	1: 1: 0
For a drawing for ye altar of ye Chapple	1: 1: 0
For two Fronts for Wimpl more carefully drawn than the first	10: 10: 0
For a Bridge and obelisque	1: 10: 0
For ane other drawing for ye Altar of ye Chaple	1: 1: 0
For two new drawing [sic] for ye monument carefully done to be adjoynd to ye Contracts and drwing [sic] ym up	10: 10: 0

The new stables that Gibbs clearly proposed can never have been built, for Thomas West's 1805 survey drawing (*No.200*) records a building strikingly like that shown in Kip's view. The existing stables must have been repaired and refurbished instead. John Cossen records that a new floor was laid in 'the Greatest Corn Chamber over the Stables', and he documents the agonisingly slow progress of the repainting of the stable clock: first we hear of Newman the Painter who 'primed the Dial

Board on each side the Cupulo over the Stables', and subsequently that 'M[r]. Warren the Painter has made a beginning of the Figures to y[e] Finger Board to the Stable Clock'.[57]

Neither designs for a bridge nor an obelisk at Wimpole have as yet been identified. The bridge may have been intended to replace the Arrington Bridge, where the Old North Road crossed the River Rhee, or alternatively have been associated with Charles Bridgeman's projected south avenue which also marched across the river. A monumental obelisk would have been an entirely appropriate ornament given the scale of Bridgeman's landscape improvements, and had it been erected it would—following the Ripon obelisk (1702) and that of Vanbrugh's Marlborough Monument at Castle Howard (1714)—have been one of the earliest examples in Britain.[58] A number of generic obelisk designs were included in Gibbs's 1728 *A Book of Architecture*, while another, topped by a flaming urn and carrying Oxford's arms and the cypher HO, can be found at the centre of a medal struck in Edward Harley's memory (*No.44*).

Harley also commissioned Gibbs to design a number of monuments: to the Cavendish family at Bolsover, to his wife's father the 1st Duke of Newcastle, and to his friend the poet Matthew Prior (1664—1721). The drawings and a clay model listed in the 1721 account refer to the Newcastle Monument in Westminster Abbey, carved by Francis Bird (1667—1731) and completed in 1723.

In 1728 Sir Matthew Decker, a then director of the East India Company and an expert on the economics of trade, recorded a visit to Wimpole, in an 'Account of a journey into East Anglia' made between 21 June and 12 July:[59]

> The house is mostly rebuilt within, and added greatly to by the present Earl. The library on the left hand coming in the house, is wonderfull magnificent; the first room consists only of cases and cabinets, full of rare old and modern manuscripts. Then 3 rooms of which the last is the largest, all full of books, in great order placed, finely bound, and the choicest in their kind. Besides this there are two other little rooms, one of which is call'd my Lord's Study; these lay not in that neat order, and seem not to be of that value, many of the pamphlets of the past times. The great Library besides the bookes is adorned with many anticq bustoes of great value, and other curiositys of immages, and other things more fitt to be admired by virtuosos than by us.

A Frenchman, identified as Jacques Fougereau, visiting in the same year includes a sketch plan of the house and its garden setting (*No.42*) in his diary, but this shows no sign of the great library to the north of the orangery. Neither does it show Gibbs's additions to the west side of Chicheley's house which must have long been complete and which would have met the eastern end of the orangery, here shown free-standing.[60]

The final phase of building at Wimpole appears to have been completed by 1730, the date on a lead hopper-head on the west face of the library wing. A letter from Pope to Oxford, it is thought written in June of that year, imagines the poet welcoming his patron on the steps of Wimpole and walking with him through the house, and its evidence suggests that the ante-library may have served as the last of a sequence of museum rooms or *studioli* that heralded the vast double-cube room built to the north of the orangery:

> I will fancy I am standing on the Stone-Steps at the Great door to receive you, & that I have just been Setting the bells a-ringing in your parish church & I am impatient to follow you to the New-roof'd Library & see what fine lodgings the Ancients are to have. I salute the Little Gods & antiquities in my way in the Anti room wishing them joy of the New Temples they are to be Inshrined in.[61]

In October of that year, Alexander Pope flattered Oxford that his library was where 'I look upon all good papers to have a sure retreat, safe from all Present & Future Curlls. I rejoice at the finishing of your New Room, the Palace of learning. I wish my Head had as good right to be with the Authors there, as my Heart has to be with the Master'.[62] In the following month Harley replied: 'I am very busie about my new Room, there I hope to spend some days with you, and there I hope to be free from the impertinence […] of this world'.[63]

Amongst the following drawings are unexecuted proposals for the re-facing of Chicheley's house, designs for the great staircase, for the ceilings of the library and ante-library, for the chapel, and for various garden ornaments.

A manuscript memoir, thought to have been written by James Gibbs, very briefly lists the architect's works, and it records that: 'The Earl of Oxford employed him to build his handsom Chaple near Cavendish Sq., and his fine Library and Chaple at Wimpol in Cambridgeshire, being the seat of his Lordship at that time'.[64] George Vertue (1684—1756) gives a slightly fuller summary of Gibbs's work there: 'At Wimpole in Cambridgeshire whilst he lived in it many years 20 at least—he there made great & noble additions, to the house a fine Elegant chappel he built which was adornd with the pencil of S[r]. James Thornhill our English History painter of greatest Fame. To this house he added another wing several lofty[r] Rooms for his book & Library there at first, & a grand room after the designs of James Gibbs architect'.[65]

6 **Unidentified draughtsman. Design for a Library annexed to a seven-bay house, 1713**

Sir John Soane's Museum, SM vol.111/33
Inscr.: 'Feb. 4th 1712/13 MDCCXIII 103
Pen and ink with grey wash (357 x 598mm)
Lit. & repr.: *The Wren Society* (1935), pl.xxxviii, as a line drawing copy by A T Bolton; Harris (1985), pp.198–203, fig.8; Parry (1986), pp.36–55, fig.8.

This drawing and the following variant (*No.7*) are included in the catalogue because successive historians have argued that they represent a preliminary proposal for the remodelling of Wimpole for Edward, Lord Harley. The scheme, frequently attributed to James Gibbs, is said to provide a monumentally scaled library room at the right-hand—and perhaps east—end of the existing house, to which it is connected by a neck containing an elliptical stair. In 1935 the then Curator of Sir John Soane's Museum, Arthur T. Bolton, made line versions of these two drawings and published them in *The Wren Society*, 1935 (vol.XII), together with a group of others identified—because one of them bears Newcastle's motto and arms—as being for an unexecuted house for John Holles, 1st Duke of Newcastle-upon-Tyne, of the second creation. Bolton suggested that the Newcastle drawings were by Sir Christopher Wren (1632—1723), possibly assisted by the young James Gibbs.

In *The Wren Society* volume for 1940 (vol.XVII), the attribution of the Newcastle drawings was revised to William Talman, (with the 'Wimpole' plans remaining as Gibbs's) and, on the strength of correspondence with Holles, it was suggested that they were devised for the rebuilding of Welbeck Abbey, where Talman was engaged in 1703. Sir Howard Colvin explains that Newcastle dismissed Talman from the Welbeck job because he 'demanded such stiff terms'. It was suggested too that others in the Newcastle group, of *c*.1712–3, may be by Sir John Vanbrugh (1664—1726) and were perhaps commissioned by Newcastle's nephew, Thomas Pelham-Holles, for the rebuilding of Haughton, Nottinghamshire. He was made 1st Duke of Newcastle-upon-Tyne (of the third creation), and later, -under-Lyne (a misspelling of Lyme that was consciously perpetuated), for his part in putting down the 1715 Jacobite rebellion, and he

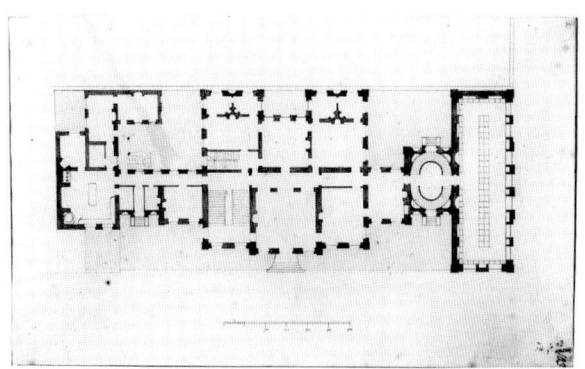

inherited the greater part of Newcastle's fortune. He bought Vanbrugh's Chargate, Surrey, renaming it Claremont, and in 1718 commissioned Vanbrugh to alter the interior of Nottingham Castle.

Pelham-Holles's uncle, the earlier 1st Duke of Newcastle, acquired Wimpole in 1710 but died in a riding accident the following year. Because he cannot, therefore, have commissioned the two plans under consideration here (one of which is dated February 1713), Newcastle's daughter, Henrietta Cavendish Holles, and her husband, Edward, Lord Harley, as he was then known, have naturally been considered prime candidates, for as we have seen they married at Wimpole in August 1713. The vast scale of the cross-wing shown in these drawings, and what can probably be interpreted as book presses at the centre of the room and around three of its sides, has helped cement the idea that they show a Harleian project. If so, and given that the drawings were made nearly eighteen months before Robert Harley was dismissed from office, might they not be a proposal for the housing of the 1st Earl of Oxford's library? They do not, however, tally with the layout of his seat at Brampton Bryan, Herefordshire. Terry Friedman, John Harris, Eric Parry and David Souden have all repeated Bolton's suggestion that the two plans are for Wimpole and by James Gibbs.[66]

There are also problems, however, with this identification. Firstly the house shown at the centre of the two plans, although also of seven bays, bears only a very passing resemblance to the plan of Sir Thomas Chicheley's house as recorded by Henry Flitcroft (*Nos.49 & 50*). The two parallel ranges in the supposedly Gibbsian plans are separated by a narrow enfilade running through the centre of the house, rather than by the broader space shown in Flitcroft's survey, that was to have

Wimpole Architectural Drawings   20

accommodated the principal and secondary stairs. None of the major, structural walls of Chicheley's house correspond with those shown in these drawings, nor are their outer envelopes of the same proportions. To have altered the mid-seventeenth century house at Wimpole to accord with either one of these two plans would have necessitated its demolition and wholesale rebuilding. Bolton noted that a wall, marked in red on the plan, runs along the back of the house and he argued that it 'evidently relates to a particular site', and 'excludes any development of the back elevation'. While a wall, screening a service corridor, did link the eastern side of Chicheley's house with the return wall of the service block, Flitcroft's basement survey (*No.50*) shows it to have been in a different position and of a different length. Moreover it did not extend along the entire length of the garden façade.

Let us assume, for argument's sake, that the two variant drawings are orientated conventionally. This would mean that the seven-bay library was intended to have east-facing windows, as was the case with the double-cube library that Gibbs eventually built at Wimpole. Its proposed siting, however, at the east end of the house is distinctly odd if the reuse of existing fabric was ever a consideration. The plans would imply the wasteful demolition of the then existing service wing, and the awkward placement of kitchens and other service rooms at the west end of the house. This would have reversed the previous arrangement at Wimpole in which the working end of the house, the relatively recently built stables, and associated roadways, were all sited to the east. A new service wing to the west would also have encroached upon the east end of the impressive thirteen-bay orangery that had presumably only been built some twenty years earlier. Turning the drawings through 180° places the library more happily at the west end and the new service block at the east. But the relative positions of the library and existing orangery then become even less reconcilable.

Could the 'library' be alternatively identified as an orangery and its 'bookcases', which appear to run across the front of embrasures, apsidal niches and windows - though levels in this and the following drawing are ambiguously expressed - indicate the positions of staging for the display of plants? Could the hollow piers between the windows of 'east' and 'south' elevations have carried heated flues? But why with a handsome Talmanic orangery only relatively recently erected would the building of another similar structure be contemplated? Such a reading, and particularly at this date, seems unlikely and Gordon Higgott has pointed out to me that the dimensions of the lines of boxes in the centre of the room and along the side and back walls are similar to the plan divisions of library shelving designed by Wren for the library at Trinity College, Cambridge in 1686.

If not for Wimpole, for what other purpose might the plans have been made? Are they, as the presence of the wall to the rear of the building might suggest, plans for an unidentified grand aristocratic town house, an *hôtel particulier*, squeezed on to a tight urban plot; or for an institutional library? Their authorship too remains a mystery.

7   **Unidentified draughtsman, possibly James Gibbs**
    Variant design for a library annexed to a seven-bay
    house, *c.1713*
    Sir John Soane's Museum, SM vol.111/26
    Pen and ink with grey and pink washes (400 x 1050mm)
    Scale: 1in: 6ft
    Lit. & repr.: The Wren Society (1935), pl.xxxviii, as a line drawing by A T Bolton.

This drawing, which has had its scale bar cut off at the bottom, is a modified version of the previous plan, with the rear pile of the central block extended laterally. It appears to have been drawn by a different draughtsman than *No.6*. A long, open area,

some 16ft wide between the back of the house and the existing wall, is created here by repositioning the small rooms that make up the symmetrical apartments. The principal stair is turned through 90° and made accessible from the entrance hall via a columnar screen—a feature reminiscent of a design attributed to William Talman for Kiveton Park, Yorkshire. The plan of the stair in the linking pavilion is altered to a single semicircle.

8   **Proposal for the remodelling of the north(?) and south**
    fronts, *c.1721*
    National Trust WIM/D/472
    Pen and ink, with grey wash (417 x 543mm)
    Scale: 1in: 10ft
    Lit. & repr.: Friedman (1984), pp.114 & 115, bottom halves of pls.111 & 112.

Amongst the drawings for which Gibbs received payment on 17 May 1721 were: 'two fronts for Wimpol [*sic*] £8.8.0', and 'two Fronts for Wimpol more carefully drawn than the first £10.10.0.'. These were clearly his alternative proposals for the remodelling of the entrance (or south) and garden (or north) fronts of Chicheley's house, and the addition of two-storied flanking wings of five bays each to east and west. Two of the 'fronts', or perhaps alternatives for the same one, are presented together in this drawing—the proposal for what may be the north elevation placed at the top of the sheet—while the other two were drawn on separate sheets (*Nos.9 & 10*).

Gibbs's proposals for the south front were fairly conservative and his intention was clearly that much of the fabric of the earlier house should be preserved. The projecting, single bay 'towers' to either end of Chicheley's house were to be retained and extended upwards to form a full attic storey. The triangular pediments to the first-floor windows were to be removed and the windows heightened. The central, projecting bay was to be scraped back to the plane of the main build, and the existing 'mannerist' doorway, window and gabled aedicule replaced by a Doric porch, a pedimented window carrying reclining sculptural figures, and above that a pedimented cartouche displaying Oxford's supporters and coat-of-arms. Alternative proposals for the wings are shown, with and without the attic storey of the central block, which lends the drawing a curious, unbalanced appearance comparable to the bizarre effect of the several decorative alternatives often offered in furniture pattern books. A balustrade carrying urns serves to unify the old and proposed work and to mask the lower part of the hipped roof. The improvements, the recasting of the central lantern, and the truncation of the chimney-stacks would together have had the effect of reducing the old-fashioned verticality of the house.

Top half: This, perhaps a proposal for the north front, is uncharacteristically austere, the only ornament being the mask and flanking cornucopia above the central, segmentally headed window on the first floor. It may, alternatively, be for a more radical refacing of the south front along the lines later effected by Henry Flitcroft.

9   **Proposal for the remodelling of the south, or entrance**
    front. Elevation with part plan, *c.1721*
    Sir John Soane's Museum, SM vol.111/17
    Inscr.: 'Wimpole', and annotated in pencil: 'Guibert'
    Pen and ink with grey wash. Pencil additions (425 x 832mm)
    Scale given
    Lit. & repr.: The Wren Society (1940), bottom half of pl.XVI; Hussey (1967:1), fig.9; Friedman (1984), p.114, top half of pl.111.

This alternative proposal for the remodelling of the south front is similar to *No.8*, above, and is perhaps the first of the 'more carefully drawn' schemes. Here the flanking five-bay wings are shown at their final height. The carved armorial at parapet level is replaced by a lower, triangular pediment, and the roof-line

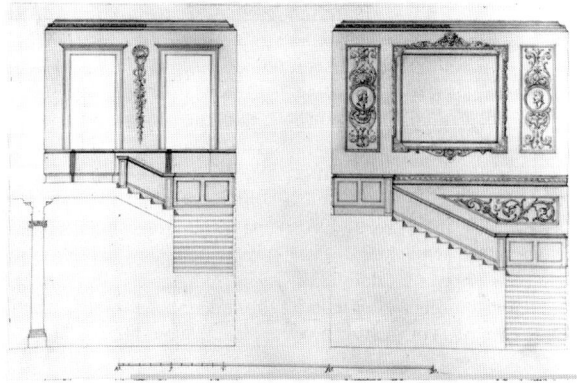

parapet of the central block is shown solid to differentiate it from the balustrades proposed for the lower wings. The sculpture at first-floor level is gone, and the parapet urns are of a more commanding size. Gibbs here proposes that the memory, at least, of the central tower which had served as the frontispiece to the mid-seventeenth-century house should be preserved—as a shallow feature expressed by quoins.

The first-floor windows in the central block retain the triangular pediments that Flitcroft's survey shows us were a feature of Chicheley's house; the chimney stacks are drawn in greater detail; and the central lantern and its cupola are of fleeter form. The pencil additions, seemingly made some seventy years later by Guibert, a mysterious Frenchman in John Soane's office (see *Nos.103–7*), show the recessed central five bays brought forward to the line of the flanking towers, recording what Flitcroft had done in his remodelling of 1742, and a proposed addition to the east of the chapel (far right) of a matching two-storey range with an arcade at ground level—perhaps an undeveloped idea to remodel the eastern service block.

10   Proposal for the remodelling of the north front. Elevation and part plan, *c*.1721

Sir John Soane's Museum, SM vol.111/18
Inscr.: 'North Front'
Pen and ink with grey wash (425 x 743mm)
Scale given
Lit. & repr.: *The Wren Society* (1940), top half of pl.XVI; Friedman (1984), p.115, top half of pl.112.

In surprising contrast to the scale of the entrance front, Gibbs here proposes the use of a giant Corinthian order, placing an engaged temple portico at the centre of the garden façade. Terry Friedman relates this to Gibbs's work at Cannons House, Middlesex. In other details the drawing reveals itself to be the pair to *No.9*, above.

11 & 12   Internal elevations for the Great Staircase, *c*.1719

Ashmolean Museum, Western Art, Gibbs II. 55 a & b
Pen and ink with grey wash (237 x 365mm, & 241 x 382mm)
Scale given

These two drawings for the rebuilding and decoration of the Great Stairs are not mentioned in Gibbs's receipt of March 1719, but a letter from Humfrey Wanley of June that year shows that Edward Harley and his wife visited the site in the expectation of seeing how their workmen were progressing with the 'Stair-case'. As might be expected, the alterations to the stairs must have been amongst the earliest works undertaken by Gibbs at Wimpole.

These two sheets provide, from left to right, elevations of the south, west, east, and north walls of the staircase hall. Gibbs inserted his new staircase in the space previously occupied by the main stair in Sir Thomas Chicheley's house. The drawings provide no detail of the upper part of the ceiling beyond the relatively modest cornice that Gibbs suggests. The architect may have decided that the old-fashioned plasterwork—bold garlands of fruit, flowers and laurel leaves—in the high-coved ceiling at the upper register served his purpose well enough. Certainly the seventeenth-century decoration survives today at this upper level. It seems unlikely that Gibbs inserted a flat ceiling above his new staircase, and the evidence of Henry Flitcroft's 'before' and 'after' plans for 'the Attick Story' suggest that Gibbs left the void of the staircase hall open to the attic level.

The scheme proposed in these drawings is recognisably for the staircase at Wimpole and includes all the essential elements of the staircase as finally constructed. Gibbs's proposals,

Wimpole Architectural Drawings   22

however, show only a small upper landing, serving a door in the north corner of the west wall. The upper landing as built, and as recorded on Flitcroft's survey drawing of the first, or 'One Pair of Stairs' floor, extends across the full width of the hall, allowing access via a centrally placed doorway to the cross-gallery that lay immediately to the west. In plan, Flitcroft also shows a large, single window, lighting the stair, in the east wall rather than Gibbs's framed plaster panel. The window was presumably a survival from Chicheley's house and it was only with John Soane's construction of a service stair on the other side of this wall that the window was finally blocked.

The decorative wall panels, containing plasterwork trophies and medallions of Roman philosophers and orators, were probably undertaken by the stuccador Giovanni Bagutti (1681—after 1730) who not only did similar work at Orleans House, Twickenham but also worked with Gibbs on the University Senate House, Cambridge in 1725—6. In February 1731 John Cossen, Harley's agent for the Wimpole estate, reported that: 'The Italians follows [*sic*] there business very well they are at work in the Little Room wch they hope to finish in 3 weeks time. The Cornice of the great Room is yet to do and the whole they say will be done before East^r'.[67] By 'the Italians', Cossen presumably means Bagutti and his compatriot Giuseppe Artari (1697—1769); James Gibbs describes the pair in his *Book of Architecture* as 'the best frett workers that ever came to England'. The spirit, at least, of the plasterwork suggested in these drawings was realised on the staircase at Wimpole, although the ornate *rinceau* work in the lower register was not included.

On his visit to Wimpole, made sometime between 1735 and 1740, Jeremiah Milles (1714—84) noted that 'The stair-case is adorn'd with very large pieces representing Buffalo, Bear and Staghunting'.[68]

13 Plan and section for a square, coved ceiling, *c*.1720—30

Ashmolean Museum, Western Art, Gibbs II. 7 b
Pen and ink (322 x 239mm)

This design coincides very closely with the form, proportions and detailing of the ceiling of Gibbs's ante-library at Wimpole, which, together with a western extension by John Soane, is now known as the Book Room. In particular the shape and arrangement of the plasterwork panels both in the cove and on the flat of the ceiling correspond to those at Wimpole. The form and pattern of the cove is also strikingly similar to that designed by Gibbs for the Bowling-Green House for Down Hall, Essex.

It is not clear when the ante-library was built within the easternmost two bays of the orangery. Dr Stratford's comment, of August 1719, that Edward Harley might 'be forced to have recourse at last to what I once suggested of turning your greenhouse into a library', suggests that if this work was not part of the first phase of the building operation, the room must have been completed by the time the double-cube library was roofed in 1730, and may have been so several years before. The evidence of a sketch plan made by a French visitor in 1728 (*No.42*), which shows the orangery still detached from the body of the house, is at odds with the dating evidence.

14 Design for the Library ceiling, *c*.1720—30

Ashmolean Museum, Western Art, Gibbs II 52
Pen and ink with grey wash over black chalk (353 x 353mm)

This muscular design, with its central paterae of swirling acanthus leaf decoration, corresponds exactly with the ceiling in the great library room at Wimpole, which, at 50ft 6in long by 23ft 3in wide, is almost a double cube. The plasterwork is attributed to Isaac Mansfield (*fl.* before 1697—1739) who, like Bagutti, worked with Gibbs at the Senate House in Cambridge, but who is more usually associated with the architect Nicholas Hawksmoor (1661—1736). The detail of the decoration, for which alternative patterns are provided (some incorporating human faces, others shells), is given in only one half of the drawing. One end of the drawing is missing. The library ceiling at Wimpole bears a strong family resemblance to that designed by James Gibbs—gratis in his capacity as a governor—for the Great Hall of St. Bartholomew's Hospital, Smithfield, London, the greater part of which was rebuilt between 1730 and 1752.

15 Design for doors and library shelving, *c*.1719—30

Bodleian Library, Gough Maps 46, 271
Pen and ink with grey wash (205 x 352mm)
Scale given
Lit. & repr.: Adshead (2002), pp.191–206, fig.5.

Gibbs was paid '£3 3s' for 'Several dores for the Liberary' on 24 July 1719. This drawing perhaps corresponds with that payment, though in 1719 the focus was on the creation of a series of library rooms within the new westward extension. The language of this drawing is reminiscent of that of the great library completed in *c*.1730. But if it does relate to an earlier, lost interior, it reveals that, from the outset, round-headed arches were an important ingredient in Gibbs's proposals. The three arches together extend to nearly 27ft, wider than both Gibbs's new cross-wing that contained Edward Harley's three cabinet rooms and the later great library. This may suggest that, rather than being a triple arcade, the drawing offers a series of alternative designs for doors flanked by shelves. The alternative decorative treatments offered in the margins, spandrels and 'mask' keystones of each arch, appear to confirm this.

Drawings by James Gibbs (1682—1754) and Sir James Thornhill (1676—1734) for the chapel at Wimpole

As has been noted earlier, the first record of payment to James Gibbs for work associated with Wimpole is a receipt dated 24 July 1719. The various items include: 'Several drawings for ye Chapple 10: 10: 0'; 'For a drawing for ye altar of ye Chapple 1: 1: 0'; and 'For ane other drawing for ye Altar of ye Chaple 1: 1: 0'.[69] The private chapel was designed to occupy the greater part of the new south-east wing, located, perversely it might seem, a matter of yards from Wimpole's parish church. It has been suggested that, in commissioning this work, Edward Harley sought to rival the splendour of Cannons House, Edgware, Middlesex, which James Brydges (1673—1744), Viscount Wilton and Earl of Carnarvon, later 1st Duke of Chandos, began to aggrandise in 1713. It is said that he lavished some £200,000 on the remodelling, decoration and furnishing of Cannons, the scale of this patronage drawing satire. Despite the poet's—too strong—denial, contemporaries recognised the 'Timon's Villa' of Alexander Pope's *Of false taste; an epistle to Richard Earl of Burlington* (1731) as Cannons:

> At Timon's Villa let us pass a Day,
> Where all cry out, 'what Sums are thrown away!

Gibbs was employed there in 1716 and, amongst other works, designed the chapel.[70] Brydges's princely pretensions extended to having his own choir, a musical director in John Christopher Pepusch (1666/7—1752), and, at least for a two-year period, a composer in residence in none other than Georg Friedrich Händel (1685—1759). Gibbs was dismissed from the work in 1719. It was presumably with Edward Harley's encouragement that he recycled elements of the Cannons design at Wimpole. Cannons was demolished in 1747, but Gibbs's drawings show that the two chapels were of a very similar size. Both were of five bays, were aisleless, the architecture of their walls was treated similarly, and both had family pews, or galleries, supported by columnar screens at their west ends. The two chapels also owe a debt to the body of Gibbs's architecturally more complicated church, St. Mary-le-Strand (1713). The low vaulted ceilings of all three buildings, coffered and decorated with rosettes, look in part to the precedent of Inigo Jones's Queen's Chapel at St. James's Palace (1623—7).

Eighteen months after Harley had paid Gibbs for his preliminary designs, Sir James Thornhill was brought on board; it seems that Edward Harley wanted an overlay of coloured, fictive architecture. The Duke of Chandos was also the patron of the church of St. Lawrence, Whitchurch (Little Stanmore), whose walls Louis Laguerre filled, after 1715, with an alternating pattern of monochrome paintings depicting the Evangelists and Cardinal Virtues, rendered as fictive reliefs and statues.

Sir James Thornhill's decoration of the chapel at All Souls College, Oxford, of *c*.1715 may also have been an inspiration to Harley. His work there included an altarpiece painting of the *Resurrection of Archbishop Chichele*, the co-founder of the college with King Henry VI, and, coincidentally, the one-time owner of the Manor of Wimpole; fictive urns with bas-reliefs of the two sacraments recognised in Protestant liturgy; feigned coffering on the ceiling; and, on the north wall, the Four Doctors of the Church.

On 16 March 1721, the poet Matthew Prior wrote breathlessly to Edward Harley to report that John Wotton, James Gibbs and Charles Bridgeman were about to set out from London to Wimpole, adding that 'they expect Sir James to be of the same opinion'.[71] Two days later, and clearly regretting not being part of the expedition, he wrote again: 'Sir James, I presume, has rather been speculating in the chapel he is to paint, than praying in the neighbouring church'.[72] This may imply that the carcass of the room had already been built.

Thornhill was then at the apogee of his career: in 1718 he had been appointed History-Painter-in-Ordinary to the King, succeeding his master Thomas Highmore (1660—1720); in April 1720 he was made Serjeant-Painter to the Office of Works; and two months later he became the first British artist to be knighted. But these were Pyrrhic triumphs. In his first foray to Britain in 1708, Giovanni Pellegrini (1675—1741) heralded a new, less rigid approach to painted decoration than the Baroque illusionism offered by Thornhill. More importantly perhaps, William Kent (1685—1748) returned from Italy in 1719 and, despite his indifference as a history painter, was determinedly promoted by the Earl of Burlington at Thornhill's expense. In March 1722 the King's History-Painter suffered the ignominy of losing to the newcomer the commission to paint the Cupola Room in Kensington Palace.

Thornhill would already have known those in Edward Harley's circle of artists and literati. Like them, he was a member of the Artists' Club of St. Luke—the club named in honour of the patron saint of painters—which George Vertue thought 'one of the Tip top Clubbs of all, for men of the highest Character in Arts & Gentlemen Lovers of Art'.[73] In 1718, the year he served as Steward, Thornhill hosted the annual St. Luke's feast for the club's members at his house in Covent Garden, and the invitation card he drew for the occasion survives.[74] It was an exclusive club which in 1727 boasted a membership of just twenty-eight. With the exception of Thomas Tudway, all Edward Harley's 'virtuosi' were members, and appear in Sir James Thornhill's sketch for a group portrait *The Connoisseurs & Sir James Thornhill* of *c*.1719.

On 25 March 1721, Prior wrote again to Edward Harley, exclaiming: 'I hear Sir James has made a ballet; it is fine to have an universal genius.'[75] There are three manuscript versions of a ballad, entitled 'A Hue and Cry after Four of the King's Liege Subjects, who were Lately suppos'd to be seen at Roystone in Hartfordshire', written, it seems, after the virtuosi's expedition to Wimpole, but a case for ascribing its authorship to Charles Bridgeman has also been made.[76] A draft version of the ballad has a pencil sketch on the verso of the second sheet which appears to be a preliminary outline for the *Adoration of the Magi* (*No.18*).[77] Perhaps Thornhill and Bridgeman penned rival accounts. In the ballad Thornhill's name has been latinised to 'Monte Spinosa':

> The one they call'd MONTE SPINOSA I think
> A Brownish Complection, a lover of drink
> A drawer of Devils they say was his trade
> My Landlord drew worse in his House, I'm afraid.

On 16 April 1721, only a month after Thornhill had visited to 'speculate in the chapel', Dr William Stratford asked Harley: 'Your lordship forgot one thing [...] which you can tell me, whether your noble chapel at Wimpole is likely to be finished this summer'.[78] Perhaps that had been the (over-optimistic) intention, because surviving scores for a celebratory 'Te Deum et Jubilate For ye Solemnity, & Consecration of Ye Right Honourable Edward Lord Harleys Chapell at Wimpole [...] Compos'd wth instrumental music, by Tho: Tudway B.M and Master of ye Music, in his lordships Chappell, together wth the Ev'ning Service, of Magnificat & Nunc Dimitties and likewise Anthems Suited to that Occasion' are dated 31 August 1721.[79] Thornhill was to draw a pencil portrait of Tudway, seated at a harpsichord; he was to make similar drawings of fellow members of the Artists' Club of St Luke.[80] Tudway harboured ambitions to become the 2nd Earl of Oxford's music master at Wimpole, as Händel had been to the Duke of Chandos at Cannons House, but his death in 1726 dashed this hope.

The regular reports sent to Edward Harley, from John Cossens at Wimpole, give only fragmentary clues to the progress of work on the chapel. In January 1722 he wrote: 'The Painters seem concern'd at their dissaopment of Lodging here and since so small an Obligation could not be granted em they believed S[r]. James Thornhill would oblige the people here in y[e] same manner or to that purpose'. In July Cossens reported: 'Go on wth the far End of the Chapel wth that work y[s] to be painted upon', and in April he expressed uncertainty about what to 'do about Kelly's coming up this week', 'S[r]. James will want attendence if Kelly go', finally suggesting 'it best that Kelly stay to attend S[r]. James and come the next week with the goods pack up for London'. A few days later he reports: 'S[r]. James Thornhill is very well and M[r]. Pilgrim of Trinity College y[e] Greek Professor preach'd and din'd wth S[r] James this day'. Not until August 1724 do we learn that scaffolding is erected, presumably to allow the walls and ceiling to be decorated: 'I rec[d]. your Lordship's Lre. [letter] concerning y[e] scaffold and sent S[r] James Thornhill's note y[e] next morning to M[r] Pridmore and y[e] Scaffold is near finished'.[81]

It seems hardly fair to lay the blame at Thornhill's door for the apparently slow progress of the work. It seems unlikely that he could have made a start before the decoration of the cupola of St. Paul's Cathedral was finished, in late summer 1721; he was also engaged with the rebuilding of his own house in Dorset; and in 1722 not only did he take on the burden of being the Member of Parliament for Weymouth and Melcombe Regis but he suffered the crushing blow of the Kensington Palace decision.

Tudway's composition had been premature. According to George Vertue's witness, the completion of the chapel was to take another three years: 'The Chapple finely painted by S[r]. James Thornhill. A large Altar piece. Representing the Virgin sitting with the child Jesus on her lap & the Kings of the East presenting Mirh & Franckinsense. finish'd Sep. 27. 1724'.[82] This corresponds with the *trompe l'œil* incised lettering: '1724', 'IAC: THORNHILL EQ[s]: FACIEBAT' that Thornhill painted on the gallery door-case.

The work had not been entirely straightforward. Thornhill's expertise came at a notoriously high price, and Edward Harley, in an uncharacteristically prudent moment, asked Dr Stratford if he could establish how much the work at the Chapel of All Souls, Oxford had cost the College. Stratford explained that, although it was not directly comparable, 'for the painting over the altar, Thornhill had £250' and that 'the roses [on the ceiling canvas], and for new painting the figures on the walls, and the two vases, Thornhill had £260 10s'.[83] George Vertue records that Thornhill's work cost a total of £1,350.[84] 'Five [drawings] for lord Harley's Chapel at Wimple by Thornhill' were sold as Lot 41 in the sale of George Vertue's books and prints in March 1757.[85] The Earl of Hardwicke added a note to Tudway's bound scores: 'This Book was bought at the Sale of the late Earl of Oxford's Library. Note the Chapel at Wimpole never was consecrated but probably this music was compos'd in order to such a solemnity. H'.

Following his visit in 1728, Jacques Fougereau wrote admiringly of the chapel interior: 'La Chapelle est ce qu'il y a de plus beau. Elle est toute pointe par Le Chevalier Thornhill, qui y a représenté l'adoration des Rois et les anciens peres de L'Eglise. La voute est en roses feintes et dorée; Il n'y a Rien de plus propre la peinture à l'huile est le meilleur. Les teintes n'en sont pas Sages et Sentent L'Enharmonie'.[86]

Visiting Wimpole in July 1735, Jeremiah Milles, the budding young antiquary, described both the ante-chapel and the chapel:

In ye room next to this on [the Entrance Hall] ye right hand over ye chimney is St John preaching in ye wilderness by Sr James Thornhill & round about ye are ye pictures of AB: Laud Bp Sprat, Smaldridge, & Gastrell, & Dr Stratford, on each side of ye door as you go into ye chappel is a head in profile of white marble modern, & ye salutation by Sr James Thornhill. ye chappel wch is next to this is a most beautifull room; it is painted all over in chiaro oscuro by Sr Ja: Thornhill on ye left hand are ye statues of ye four Drs of ye church in ye same. ye picture of ye altar piece represents ye offering of ye wise men, and under it another with our Saviour & Nicodemus both by Sr James: ye roof is painted to represent compartments.[87]

A futher religious picture by Sir James Thornhill, *The Last Supper*, was sold in March 1742 during the posthumous five day sale of the Earl of Oxford's collection.

16 James Gibbs. Plan and sections showing internal elevations for the east, south and west walls of the chapel, c.1719

Sir John Soane's Museum, SM vol.111/19
Inscr.: In addition to the title 'Wimpole', and the labelling of the elevations – 'East End', 'South Side', and 'West End'—the dimensions '53/60 foot' and '20 foot' are given. The annotations are not in Gibbs's hand.
Black chalk, pen and ink with grey and pink wash (460 x 720mm)
Scale given
Lit. & repr.: The Wren Society (1935), pl.XXXV; Friedman (1984), pl.57; Allen (1985), fig.2.

The architecture of this preliminary design is shown in the round rather than in the *trompe l'œil* of the executed scheme. Nor at this stage is there any suggestion of the Adoration scene that James Thornhill was to provide for the east wall, although the arch-headed frame shown above the reredos was presumably intended to house some sort of painted altarpiece. It seems too that Gibbs intended to light the chapel from windows in both the south and north walls. Before Flitcroft added a 'sham' wing at the north-east corner of the house, it would have been possible for light to have entered the chapel from the north.

Terry Friedman likens the wall treatment (a panelled lower register supporting paired Ionic pilasters), and the coffered ceiling, decorated with rosettes, to the similar elements in Gibbs's 1713 church St. Mary-le-Strand, London—a commission that, as we have seen, was secured partly through the 1st Earl of Oxford's influence. Friedman also compares the west elevation of this drawing—in particular the Doric columns supporting the family pew and the pedimented door connecting with the ante-chapel beyond—to that of Gibbs's design for James Brydges's chapel at Cannons House, Middlesex.

17   James Gibbs and Sir James Thornhill. Design for the north wall of the Chapel, showing the Fathers of the Church, c.1721

Cecil Higgins Art Gallery, P. 120
Inscr.: The position of the family pew or gallery, at the west end, is shown in section and marked 'Gallery floor'; the door beneath it indicated; while the plinths to the trompe l'œil statues carry, (from left to right) the names of the four Latin Fathers of the Church: SS. Gregorius, Augustinus, Ambrosius and Hieronimus.
Brown ink with grey wash (256 x 465mm)
Scale given
Lit. & repr.: Allen (1985), pp.204–11, fig.7; Joll (2002), p.261.
Exh.: Cecil Higgins Museum, Bedford (1959), p.28, pl.I

Friedman suggests that this, and the following drawings (Nos.19–22) may be of shared authorship—the product of the combined pens of Gibbs and Thornhill, one precise and the other wonderfully free. The characteristics of the scale-bar, however, are unlike those drawn by Gibbs and Richard Hewlings has suggested to me that these drawings may be wholly Thornhill's work. The crouching figure peering out from behind the curtain in the westernmost niche is presumably Thornhill's self-portrait. In the executed scheme, this humorous touch was replaced by a painted urn with a bas-relief of the Resurrection. It has been noted above that Thornhill had previously painted the Four Doctors of the Church on the north wall of the chapel of All Souls College, Oxford. Brian Allen has shown that both series almost certainly derive from the sketch studies that Thornhill made in 1711 of the statues of the patron saints of Tournai, by François Girardon (1628—1715), in Tournai Cathedral, in the Spanish (later Austrian) Netherlands, now Belgium.

The architectural framework provided for Thornhill's painted scheme is recognisably that of Gibbs's earlier proposal (No.16). Both drawings have a rhythm of shell-headed niches (rather than windows) and paired pilasters which support 'plough-share' vaults that run, with the quadrant cove, into the ceiling flat; and a lower register or plinth, modelled with the alternating pattern of niches and piers. Despite the structural similarities, this scheme is considerably more exuberant than the earlier one. The plinth has a channelled surface, and the Ionic order is swapped for the more feminine and ornamental Corinthian. In each pier, and in the bays between, Thornhill offers his client alternative decorative solutions for the swags beneath the statuary plinths; the floral drops between the pilasters; the decoration in the head of each arch; and the spandrels between the arches (crossed olive branches, winged female herms, and an incense burner billowing smoke on a scroll-legged stand).

Friedman observes that Thornhill's involvement transformed Gibbs's 'sedate Protestant room into a glorious, colourful reminder of the Venetian Baroque'. It is ironic, perhaps, that Gibbs was the Roman Catholic, though an undemonstrative one, and Thornhill the Protestant who probably only secured the commission to paint the Cupola of St. Paul's in the face of stiff competition from Italian and French artists because of the prevailing attitude, which found voice in Archbishop Tenison's insistence, that 'the painter employed be

18

a Protestant; and secondly that he be an Englishman'.[88] Thornhill had previously painted fictive statues, on almost identical socles, in shell-headed niches in the Sabine Room at Chatsworth in 1706. This and the other two drawings now in the collection of the Cecil Higgins Art Gallery and Museum were acquired from P & D Colnaghi Ltd. in September 1956.

18   Sir James Thornhill. Sketch for 'The Adoration of the Magi', 1721

British Library, Lansdowne MS. 846, fo. 166v.
Black chalk (181 x 225mm)

This slight pencil sketch is on the verso of the second sheet of a draft of the ballad 'A Hue & cry after 4 of ye Kings Liege Subjects who were lately supposed to be seen at Royston in Cambs' (see above). It appears to be Sir James Thornhill's preliminary idea for the composition of the canvas painting depicting The Adoration of the Magi that he was to paint for the east end of the chapel.

19   Sir James Thornhill. Preliminary design for the east wall of the Chapel—The Adoration of the Magi, 1721

Tate Britain, T088522
Pen and ink over black chalk and grey wash (220 x 175mm)

This and the following drawing are almost indistinguishable from Nos.21 & 23 and were acquired by the Tate as part of the Oppé Collection in 1996.

20   Sir James Thornhill. Alternative preliminary design for the east wall of the Chapel—The Adoration of the Magi, 1721

Tate Britain, T08521
Pen and ink over black chalk and grey wash (221 x 175mm)

Wimpole Architectural Drawings   26

21 Sir James Thornhill. Design for the east wall of the Chapel—The Adoration of the Magi, 1721

Cecil Higgins Art Gallery, P.112
Inscr.: On verso: 'Sr. James Thornhill'
Brown ink with grey wash (222 x 172mm)
Lit. & repr.: Allen (1985), pp.204–11, fig.12; Joll (2002), p.261.
Exh.: Agnews', London (1962), p.10, no.5; Reading Museum and Art Gallery (1965), no.52; Castle Museum, Norwich (1965), no.54.

Two further, almost indistinguishable, versions exist of this and the following drawing—in the Tate (*Nos.19 & 20*) and in a private collection in Holland (see Courtauld Institute, Witt Collection, No.2160). The number of drawings for Thornhill's proposed treatment of the east wall, therefore, totals six. Brian Allen reproduces the Tate versions, then in the Denys Oppé collection.

Here the Adoration scene, painted on canvas rather than on the plaster of the remainder of the chapel, is set above a plain panelled lower register and framed by a coffered basket arch supported on Corinthian columns. Ruinous ancient architecture serves as the backdrop to the figure group, whose composition is similar to that of the realised painting. Above the draped altar-table—an unusual arrangement for a Protestant chapel at this period—the dove of the Holy Ghost rises in a triangle symbolic of the Holy Trinity.

22 Sir James Thornhill. Alternative design for the east wall of the Chapel—The Adoration of the Magi, 1721

Cecil Higgins Art Gallery, P.113
Pen and ink with grey wash (222 x 172mm)
Lit. & repr.: 'J.L.C.' (1962), p.1018; Allen (1985), pp.204–11, fig.12; Joll (2002), p.261.
Exh.: Agnews', London (1962), p.10, no.5; Reading Museum and Art Gallery (1965), no.52; Castle Museum, Norwich (1965), no.54.

In this alternative design, Thornhill establishes the Serliana or tripartite arch that he was to use as the architectural framework of the realised scheme. Brian Allen notes that the combination of Venetian arch, its garniture of Baroque decoration, and association with a painted and coffered vault, recalls Inigo Jones's Queen's Chapel at St. James's Palace. The composition of the figures, their positions reversed, is less like the executed canvas than that indicated in the previous drawing.

In the lower register Thornhill offers the channelled rustication that he shows in his drawing for the north wall. The drops of fruit and flowers, and naked and winged female terms (presumably intended as seraphim) that provide a somewhat louche frame for the reredos (which contains the letters of Christ's name instead of the triangle of *No.21*, with the dove of the Holy Ghost rising above, instead of inside, it) are also in concert with the drawing for the north elevation (*No.17*). Jeremiah Milles noted, some fourteen years later, that another devotional painting by Thornhill had been hung beneath the Adoration: 'ye picture of ye altar piece represents ye offering of ye wise men, and under it another with our Saviour & Nicodemus both by Sr James'.[89]

23 Sir James Thornhill. Study for The Resurrection, *c*.1721

British Museum, 1865-6-1-1339
Pen and ink with brown wash over black chalk (160 x 122mm)
Lit. & repr.: Allen (1985), pp.204–11, fig.9.

This is a study for the fictive urn with its bas-relief of the Resurrection painted in the westernmost bay of the north wall, where in his design (*No.17*) Thornhill shows himself peeping from behind a curtain.

Drawings by James Gibbs for the garden at Wimpole

24 Drawing for an octagonal garden pavilion, elevation and plan, *c*.1719

National Trust WIM/D/465
Pen and ink with grey wash (438 x 265mm)
Scale: 1 in: 3ft
Lit. & repr.: Croft-Murray (1962), 273b; Jackson-Stops (1979:2), pp.658–61, fig.9; *idem*., (1992), p.43, no.19.

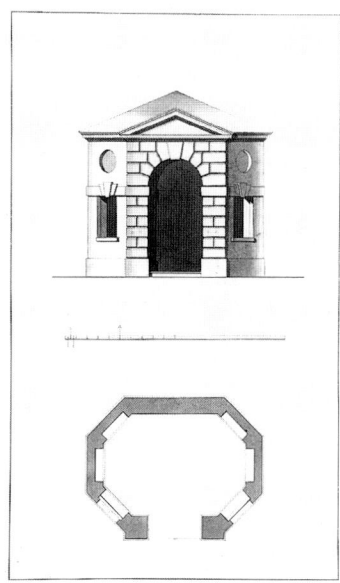

On 24 July 1719 Gibbs was paid for 'Four drawings for summer houses 06. 06. 0', and, on 17 May 1721, for 'Two summer houses with the Roofe in large 03. 03. 0'. This drawing may be one of the former. None of Bridgeman's drawings of the gardens record the building which Sir John Clerk of Penicuik (1684—1755) in 1727 described, reservedly, as 'a neat summerhouse painted by Sir James Thornhill a man of great invention rather than correct design'[90]; and which Sir Matthew Decker wrote of more favourably in the following year: 'At the end, a Bowling green, with a fine summer house in one of the corners. This, inside, as also the Chappel in the house, are painted, and the best that I ever saw done by Sir James Thornhill'.[91]

It is not clear why both accounts mention only one building for in 1728 Jacques Fougereau notes that the garden 'est terminé par un grand boulingrin, avec deux pavillons peints et fort propres en dedans, qui bornent la terrasse de bout'.[92] The diarist's accompanying sketch plan (*No.42*) clearly shows a rectangular, hipped-roofed pavilion on either side of an octagonal bowling green. This is exactly the arrangement recorded in Robert Greening's proposals for a walled garden (*Nos 78 & 79*) of *c*.1752. Sadly the mysterious 'Mr S', perhaps the poet William Shenstone (1714—63), recommended in his 'Hints [...] about Alterations in the Garden' that the summer houses 'shd. be pulled down'.[93]

The buildings described in the above accounts and drawings are undoubtedly pavilions designed by Gibbs. A number of examples, both generic and specific, of garden pavilions and summer houses of various plan forms—square, octagonal, and circular—and roof configurations, often domed, were illustrated in his *Book of Architecture*; and a number of these were associated, as at Down Hall, Essex and Gubbins, Hertfordshire, with bowling greens. This octagonal example, whose canted windows would have afforded views of the bowling green to the south, is presumably a preliminary proposal.

An alternative reading of this drawing might be entertained; that it is a later proposal by Henry Flitcroft. Not only is the scale-bar more like those employed by Flitcroft, but the shading of the pavilion roof—fading from ridgeline down, as was John Webb's practice, and Vincenzo Scamozzi's before him—is similar in style to that used in the architect's drawings of the Hall and church at Wimpole.

25, 26 & 27 Three designs for stone urns, *c*.1719/20

Bodleian Library, Gough Maps 46 - 266, 267 & 268
Pen and ink with grey wash (370 x 170mm; 380 x 203mm; and 420 x 230mm)
Lit. & repr.: Colvin (1952) pl.8; Gunnis (1968), p.83.

All three designs were subsequently engraved by Edward Kirkhall for Gibbs's *A Book of Architecture* (1728), p.xxv, Plate CXXXVIII (*No.28*). The second of these designs, illustrated at the centre of Kirkhall's engraving and indebted to the vase designs of Jean Berain I (1640—1711), corresponds to the pair of large, hexagonal urns now at the far east and west corners of the south railings screen at Wimpole—'two Vases well executed in Portland Stone according to the middle Draught'. The third drawing is inscribed: 'This design for a Vase is by Mr.

Gibbs & executed by Mr. Carpenter set up at Wimpole'. Carpenter is the anglicised name adopted by Andries Carpentière (b.167?—1737). In July 1719 Gibbs was paid for: 'Drawings for two fine urnes 06.06.0'; 'Three drawings for urnes 03.03.0'; and in May 1721, for 'Two urnes in large 01.10.0'. Friedman notes that in turn 'Carpenter received £85.10.0 between 6th November 1719 and 16th January 1720 for carving 12 vases and 24 baskets'.

28 Edward Kirkhall (b.*c*.1695), after James Gibbs. Engraving of three stone urns, 1728

Inscr.: 'Jacobo Gibbs Architecto'; E. Kirkhall sculp.'; and 'p.138'
Engraving (245 x 355mm)
Published as Plate CXXXVIII, p.xxv, in James Gibbs's *A BOOK OF ARCHITECTURE, Containing Designs of Buildings And Ornaments* (London, 1728).

In September 1713 James Gibbs first had 'a mind to publish a book of architecture' and explained to Robert Harley, 1st Earl of Oxford, 'this is my design, which I think to go about this summer if your Lordship will encourage me by accepting the dedication, and being at the expense of the plates'. The project was abandoned, however, until the mid-1720s when, with the help of Henry Hulsberg (d.1729), John Harris, Edward Kirkhall, and George Vertue, Gibbs began to assemble engraved plates that would illustrate his work.

Surprisingly perhaps, Gibbs's 1728 publication was not dedicated to the new Earl of Oxford, Edward Harley, but instead to the Whig soldier John Campbell, 2nd Duke of Argyll and Greenwich (1678—1743), who in 1715 had been responsible for the defeat of Gibbs's friend and early patron John Erskine, 11th Earl of Mar (1675—1732) and his insurgent Jacobite army. This was presumably an expedient decision. Not only had Argyll commissioned Gibbs to rebuild Sudbrook House, Petersham, Surrey (1715—9) but he had in 1727 appointed him to the lucrative post of Architect of the Ordnance. Eileen Harris notes that, with this enormously influential volume, Gibbs became the first British architect to publish a book dedicated to his own designs.[94] She explains further that the publication was in response to the deliberate exclusion, by Colen Campbell (1676—1729), of any of Gibbs's buildings from the third and last volume of *Vitruvius Brittanicus* (1725). Gibbs had the satisfaction of employing Hulsberg, who had been Campbell's principal engraver.

Harley's patronage and influence is represented in the book by the following engravings: the monuments to the Duke of Newcastle and Matthew Prior in Westminster Abbey and

that to the Cavendish family at Bolsover, Derbyshire; the Oxford chapel in Marylebone; the Senate House complex at Cambridge; and the house and garden buildings at Down Hall, Essex. The engraving of the urns is the only example of the work he undertook at Wimpole. Not only were the Earl and Countess of Oxford, and their daughter Margaret Cavendish-Harley subscribers, but so too were Gibbs's friends and fellow collaborators at Wimpole, the virtuosi Charles Bridgeman, Michael Dahl, Michael Rysbrack, Sir James Thornhill, and George Vertue.

The gloss to Plate CXXXVIII reads: 'These Designs for Vases, done for the Right Honourable the Earl of *Oxford*. There are two Vases well executed in Portland Stone according to the middle Draught, which are set up on two large Peers on each side of the principal Walk in the Gardens at *Wimpole* in *Cambridgeshire*'. This presumably means the gardens on the north side of the house. Charles Bridgeman's drawings (*Nos.38 & 39*) show large piers flanking the southern entrance to the Bowling Green approach. The only record to have come to light of the minor building works that the Duke of Newcastle undertook during his brief ownership of the Wimpole estate includes an estimate for 'The Building of two brick walls Of [*sic*] each side of the Bowling Green Being 800 foot long each Wall and that wall on the left hand side facing The House is to be 8 foot high above Ground'.[95] It was perhaps on these walls that Gibbs's urns were placed. They now sit at the south-east and south-west corners or the south railing screen.

Drawings by Charles Bridgeman (d.1738) for the park at Wimpole

As we have seen, a group of virtuosi—'four things like men, that look'd something wild'—set out from London on an expedition to Wimpole in March 1721. The landscape gardener Charles Bridgeman was one of them and, according to the evidence of its closing couplet, 'Surrounded with Pickax, wth Maddox, and Spade/The Ballad is ended, in Wheelbarrow made', he (his name latinised to Ponshomo), rather than Sir James Thornhill, would appear to be the author of the comic ballad that marked the occasion.[96] Wimpole was already familiar to Bridgeman, for not only does Humfrey Wanley's diary record that he had visited the Wimpole library in February of the previous year, but there is some evidence to suggest that his father, 'Mr. Bridgeman Senior', was already Edward Harley's head gardener and living on the Wimpole estate.[97] Although not elected to the Artists' Club of St. Luke until 1726, Bridgeman would have been familiar with the various members of Edward Harley's artistic and literary circle.

Bridgeman, whose mentors had been the Royal Gardeners George London and Henry Wise, was himself to become Royal Gardener to George II and Queen Caroline in 1728, and is of pivotal significance in the history of the English landscape garden. His work straddles the divide between the formality of the previous age and the 'natural style' of the succeeding one, and was admired by such influential critics as Alexander Pope and Horace Walpole (1717—97).[98] His was a difficult challenge, for, as Peter Willis notes in his pioneering monograph on Charles Bridgeman, early attempts at landscape gardening were often 'as artificial in their irregularity as the formal layouts had been in their regularity'.[99]

Walpole understood that Bridgeman's style of landscape gardening was a transitional one and forgave him any latent regularities in his work, noting that: 'Though he still adhered much to strait walks with high clipped hedges, they were only his great lines; the rest he diversified by wilderness, and with loose groves of oak, though still with surrounding hedges'.[100] Famously, Walpole accords Bridgeman the 'capital stroke' of the invention of the 'Ha! Ha!' which made possible a novel relationship between garden and the wider landscape, and enabled Lancelot 'Capability' Brown's generation to 'call in the country' as Pope had advised.[101]

From the outset Bridgeman imposed 'his great lines' on Wimpole's agricultural landscape. What appear to be his early proposals for the place are uncompromisingly symmetrical, running somewhat counter to Walpole's claim that the gardener 'disdained to make every division tally to its opposite'.[102] However, it should be remembered that although Bridgeman, like Pope, was able to rise above the divide of politics and religion, both making friends of and working with Whigs, Tories, Protestants and Catholics alike, he was at Wimpole and under Harley's patronage amongst Stuart sympathisers and Tories for whom anachronistic, baroque extravagance continued to hold appeal.

On the occasion of the March expedition, Matthew Prior correctly supposed 'friend Bridgeman's devotion has consisted chiefly in contriving how the diagonal may take Waddon [sic] Steeple exactly in the middle'.[103] The specificity of this supposition suggests that the idea of using the church as the focus of one of the 'great lines' had been discussed before. Prior's remark refers to the diagonal vista which Bridgeman created from the front of the house to the steeple of Whaddon church, some three-and-a-half miles to the south-south-east. This, and an intended balancing vista to the south-south-west—replacing a more acute avenue of what are thought to have been closely planted horse-chestnuts surviving from Radnor's landscape—were to act as foils to Bridgeman's *coup de maître*: a colossal, double avenue of elms, some ninety yards wide, which was to extend south from the house for no less than two-and-a-half miles, crossing first the Cambridge Road and then the River Rhee.[104] Each side of the avenue comprised two rows of trees set fifty feet apart, with the same interval between trees in the rows. The resulting pattern was not a true quincunx, but had the appearance of one when viewed from the side. It was further proposed that at the crossing with the river an octagonal basin should be built and enclosed with a circus of trees.[105]

These plans must have been formulated rapidly, for only three weeks after the whirlwind expedition news of their scale and scope had reached Dr Stratford: 'Tudway indeed did give me a noble idea of the vast alterations that are projected at Wimpole. I could not but admire them, though at the same time I begged leave to bestow one tear upon the loss of my beloved grove, and the old trees of the old Avenue'.[106] The 'grove' that Stratford refers to was perhaps the grouping of trees in and around the water gardens shown, in an immature state, in the bottom left-hand corner of Kip's engraving (*No.3*), for Bridgeman's preliminary proposals for a vast, geometrically planned 'Parade' to the south of the house took no account of its position, while Thomas Chicheley's avenue too would have been swept away. Clearly Harley took notice of his former tutor's advice for only four days later the Oxford don wrote again: 'I am mightily pleased to hear that my sweet grove and the old avenue have got a reprieve. I hope it will be for my life'.[107]

The landscaping work is likely to have begun in the summer of 1721, for in October of that year the following 'strange account from Wimpole' was related: 'Lord Harley having order'd a Visto from his fine House there to the North Road of about three miles in length with a Bason in the middle, the workmen as they were digging up the ground for this latter, dug up the Bones of fourteen Human Corpses most of them having large Nails drove through their skulls'. It was suggested, improbably, that the victims may have been 'Murther'd in a House in the neighbourhood'.[108] This sensationalist report refers to the digging of Bridgeman's great octagonal basin. John Cossen played an active part in the developments, particularly where matters of water supply and drainage were concerned, and he supplied his master with regular reports on progress and on comparative projects that were being undertaken on other estates. In April 1722 he wrote:

> Yesterday I went to see the Bason and Canal at ye Duke of Norfolk's and found ye Bason design'd to be 250 ft. square (whch is little more than $1/3$ of ye bignes of the Bason at Wimpole) in good forwardness: and somewhat more than an Entrance upon ye Canal designd to be in length feet 1650 and 100ft broad. The whole length 1900 feet. I perceive they are yet undetermined how the Bason and Canal must be supply'd wth. Water whether by Land flood [...] Wch I believe will prove difficult to effect I cannot see: But when the whole is completed it will be very Grand. The Canal at Welbeck is 1000. Do. at New[..]sie about 450[109]

The planting of Wimpole's great avenue had also clearly been started in 1721, for in August 1722 Cossen reported: 'A great many of the trees planted in the Avenue the last season between the River and the Park are already dead and more are going off'.[110] Additional planting was also being undertaken, probably with the benefit of advice from Bridgeman, in areas of the estate for which we do not have his designs. In March 1723 Cossen explained that: 'Mr. Cole has planted the Ground on ye South and North sides of the Upper Fish Ponds wth White Lymes and Oak Plants of a considerable size, and on ye morrow begins to support em wth stakes to defend and keep em from being blown down. He also purposes to plant wth a same sort of trees part of a hill in ye lower ground between the Ponds and give over for this season'.[111] This was the plantation that linked and partly screened the Earl of Radnor's fishponds, shown in Bridgeman's survey drawing of the wider estate (*No.30*).

Cossen appears too to have overseen the practical realisation of some of the landscaping ideas that must have been in the air at this time. In February 1724 he explained to his master:

> I have very exactly trac'd the Line from the Hall Door thro' the Park towards Arrington Church and cut an Opening of 6 Yards in the Hedge where it crosses the Park Pail but makes no improvement to ye View from ye Hall Door without the cutting down 2 Walnut trees where ye Line intersect that Walk, also 2 or 3 of the young trees in the Wither-end of the Lime Walk wch when grown to have Large Tops will hinder in part the seeing of ye Church also that Line carry over the place where the Deer is foddered wch your Lordship may chuse to be removed at pleasure and ye cutting down the Walnut trees will very little injure the Beauty of that Walk.[112]

Like Dr Stratford, Alexander Pope must surely have helped to shape Bridgeman's evolving plans for Wimpole, and Edward Harley clearly valued his advice. But he appears to have visited only towards the completion of the landscaping works. In September 1724 Harley wrote to the poet: 'I do not know any letter has given me so much pleasure and satisfaction because you tell me you are resolved to see this place [Wimpole] this year. I shall not move from hence above these three Weeks'.[113] Pope, Bridgeman and Lord Bathurst were at this time collaborating on the design of the gardens at Marble Hill, Twickenham for Henrietta Howard. Pope and Bridgeman may have first met in 1709. Delayed for various reasons from visiting Lord Oxford at Wimpole, Pope writes: 'I am heartily disappointed, and so is another man, of the Virtuoso-Class as well as I; (and in My notions, of the higher kind of class, since Gardening is more Antique & nearer God's own Work, than Poetry) I mean Bridgeman, whom I had tempted to accompany me to you'.[114]

His visit was delayed for a further year, and in September 1725 Pope wrote a mock facetious letter to Oxford scolding him for not, in turn, having visited him at Twickenham; he describes Wimpole as 'the place to which I'm to leap, at an hours warning, from any other part of the land, the Neplus-ultra of this year, & in a word the next Sign of my Zodiack. Some Phaëton must drive me quite out of my regular course; if I see any place before I see Wimpole, be it winter or summer, or spring, or autumn'.[115] Teasing Oxford too about the child he and his wife were then hoping to have, Pope writes; 'Make Wimpole as good as you will, improve it as much as you can, you can't make so good a thing as your Father made before. I leave you to explain this Riddle'.

Harley's accounts show that payments of almost £3,000 were made to Bridgeman and confirm the evidence of the correspondence discussed above that the landscaping works were undertaken, broadly, between 1721 and 1726:[116]

	£
1721	221
1722	400
1723	470
1724	1,474
1725	280
1726	126
Total	£2,971

In April 1726 Oxford explained to Pope: 'I am extreamly busie at this place but I will not tell you what I am doing nor of my designs till you come to the place and see it with your own eyes and you shall have power to alter and I am sure that will be amending, anything I shall think of [...]. The very sudden death of old mr. Bridgeman has obliged me to stay longer than I thought to do'.[117] The reference to old Mr. Bridgeman probably does mean that Oxford is describing late developments at Wimpole, but he may well also have been referring to work undertaken at Down Hall, Essex, the house that he had helped Matthew Prior to acquire in 1719 and which reverted to his ownership on Prior's death in September 1721. Although the plans that Gibbs drew up for the rebuilding of Down Hall were never executed, Harley does appear subsequently to have undertaken landscaping works there with help from Bridgeman and Gibbs. Indeed the payments to Bridgeman listed above may relate to his work both at Wimpole and Down Hall.[118] Bridgeman also benefitted from Harley's patronage in London where he provided a layout for Cavendish Square, which lay at the heart of the earl's Marylebone estate. In 1725 the gardener took a lease of a house on the estate, in Henrietta Street, where his friend James Gibbs lived.[119]

No record has survived to show where the trees that were planted at Wimpole came from, but it is possible that they were supplied by the great nursery at Brompton Park, in Kensington which had been established by George London in 1681, and with which Bridgeman had connections, perhaps first working there for London and Wise as an apprentice.

29 Charles Bridgeman. Survey of the Park at Wimpole with outline proposals, *c.*1721

Bodleian Library, MS Gough Drawings a4 fo.35
Inscr.: Verso, 'Wimpole'
Pencil (1040 x 743mm)
Scale: 1in: 198 ft, ie. 3 chains
Watermark: with † IHS and I VILLEDARY beneath, and coat-of-arms with 4 LVG beneath
Repr.: Willis (2002), pl.228.

Bridgeman's survey records in outline the landscape that Radnor had created between 1689 and 1710 and confirms the extraordinary accuracy of Knyff and Kip's bird's-eye view. While the spiral of six fish-ponds to the south-east of the house must have been dug after the publication of *Britannia Illustrata*, all else tallies in an astonishing way: the buildings added by Radnor (the orangery, service wing and stables); the avenues extending into the landscape, the walled, garden enclosures; the planting; and the polygonal fish ponds to the north-east, and water garden to the south-west.

But Bridgeman's plan also reveals that, from the outset, the gardener had grand designs. At the bottom of the plan, below the diagonal line that marks the line of Rushbrooke Way—a medieval road that served as the southern boundary of the park—Bridgeman has drawn the lines of a great avenue. This was to be three times (ninety yards) wider than Chicheley's (ninety foot wide) avenue, which is shown immediately to the north. A second intervention, alluded to by Matthew Prior, is the 100 foot-wide vista cut through Radnor's planting, which would allow a view from the front of the house to the distant tower of Whaddon church to the south-south-east. This drawing appears to have been made in preparation for *No.30*.

30 Charles Bridgeman. Survey of the Park at Wimpole with outline proposals and planting indicated, *c.*1721

Bodleian Library, MS Gough Drawings a4 fo.69
Pen and ink with pencil and wash (647 x 333mm)
Scale: 1in: 396 ft, ie. 6 chains
Watermark: Coat-of-arms with 4 LV GERREVINK beneath, and letter V
Repr.: Jackson-Stops (1979:2), pp.658–61, fig.3; Phibbs (1980), p.18; Willis (2002), pl.75.

This drawing is essentially much the same as a4 fo.35 but Bridgeman has added dots to indicate avenue trees and solid blocks of planting, and hachures to indicate the rising ground to the north and west and the quarry to the south-west. The circle of trees on Johnson's hill—the future site of the Gothic folly—which terminated Radnor's northern avenue, and

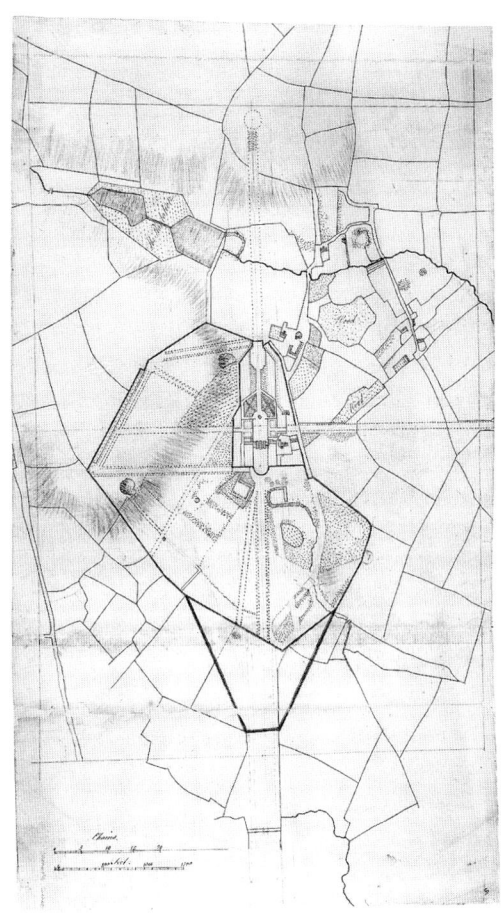
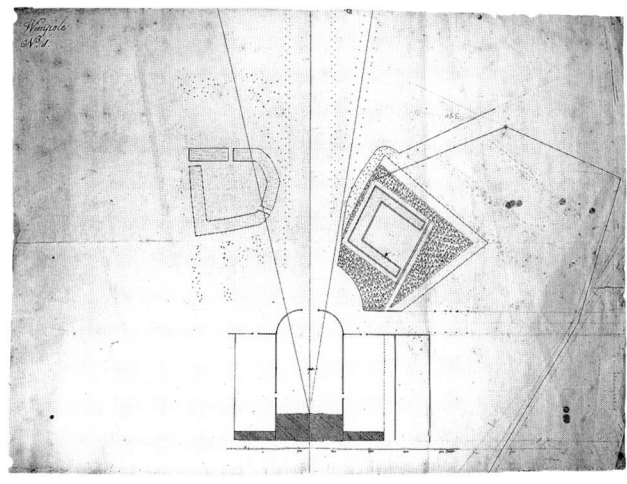
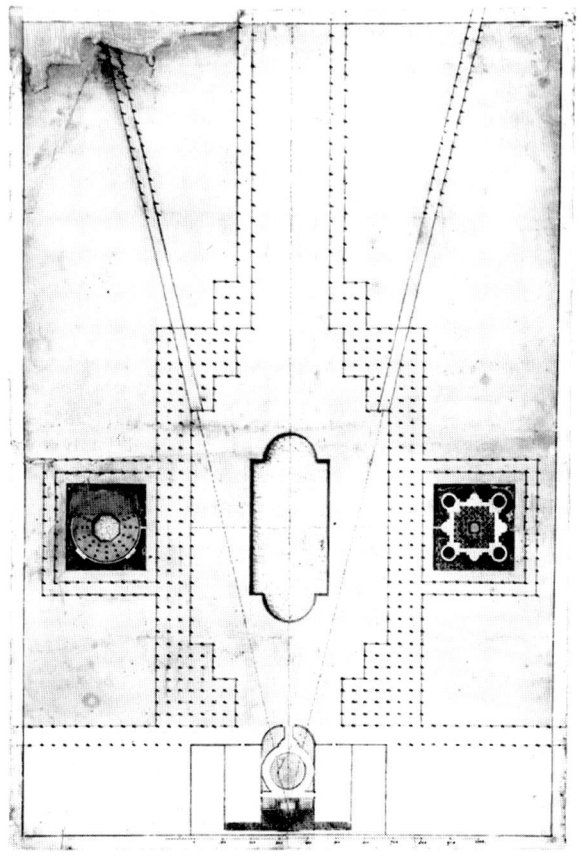
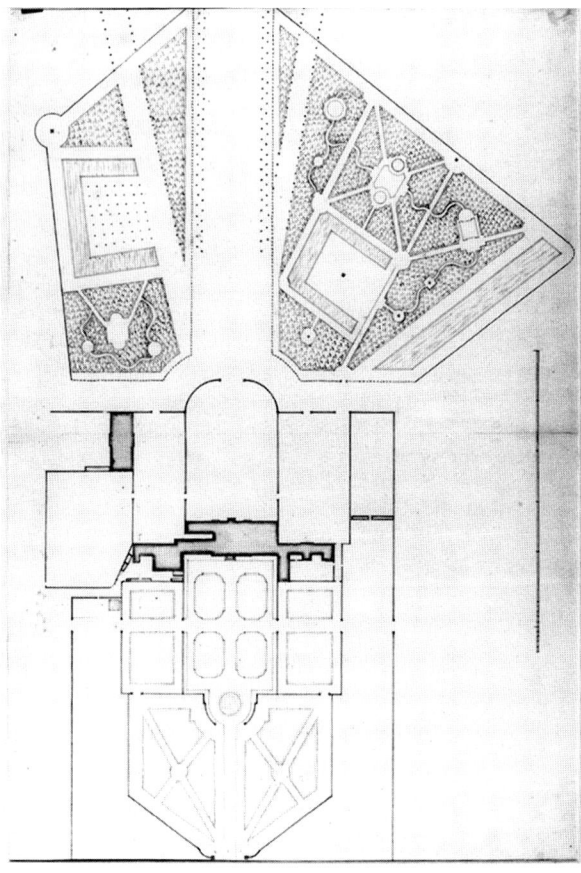

Wimpole Architectural Drawings

possibly planted in fir, is also shown. Woods are marked, as is the plantation between Radnor's two polygonal fishponds. The boundaries of the gardens around the hall and those of the park are emphasised with a heavy line. Curiously, the church is shown in elevation.

31 Charles Bridgeman. Part survey of, and part proposal for, the park to the south of Wimpole, *c*.1721

Bodleian Library, MS Gough Drawings a4 fo.30
Inscr.: In top left corner 'Wimpole No.1'
Pen and ink with pencil (711 x 536mm)
Scale: 1in: 60ft
Watermark: Coat-of-arms with 4 WR beneath, and letters IV
Repr.: Willis (2002), pl.230a.

The drawing shows at a larger scale the land to the south of the forecourt. To the left, or east, are shown four of the spiral of fish ponds across which the vista to Whaddon was to be cut. To the right, or west, of Chicheley's main avenue (shown here at a little over 100 feet between the double rows of trees) is Chicheley's south-south-west avenue which, touching only tangentially the grove of trees around the water gardens, lay at a more acute angle to the central avenue than did the vista to Whaddon. Bridgeman appears here to be suggesting that a polygonal bastion might be thrown out into the park to the south-west, beyond the water garden—reminiscent of Bridgeman's placement of the Rotundo at the western edge of the gardens at Stowe two or three years previously.

32 Charles Bridgeman. Survey drawing of the Park to the south, west and north of the house, *c*.1720

National Trust WIM/D/502
Pen and ink with pencil (335 x 420mm)
Scale not given
Watermark: 'LVG', 'PRO PATRIA' with a lion and Brittania within a palisaded enclosure and a bell beneath
Lit. & repr.: Willis (1993), p.261, fig.103 (a).

Peter Willis included this in his 1993 essay 'Charles Bridgeman and the English Landscape Garden: New Documents and Attributions' but, doubtful about its authorship, excluded it from the second edition (2002) of his monograph on Bridgeman. It does nonetheless appear to relate to *Nos.29 & 30*. This is a fairly roughly inked survey plan of the pre-Bridgemanic landscape, in part drawn over pencil set-up lines, but which appears to include several proposed features. Phibbs argues that the double lime avenue, shown here striking westwards from the south-west corner of the garden boundary, and running up to meet the southern end of the diagonal fir avenue, was one of Bridgeman's contributions.[120] However, the avenue is here plotted in ink, and the slight irregularity of the trees perhaps suggests that it is a record rather than proposal.

More certainly new elements, and here finding their first tentative expression, are the triangular-shaped and regimented planting of lollipop-headed trees, drawn in pencil, to the north-west of the house (which was to become Bridgeman's 'grid' of lime and horse-chestnut), and the great south avenue, here indicated by the faux quincunx pattern of planting, pencilled in between ruled tramlines. The vista to Whaddon church is also shown and the westernmost of the spiral of fish ponds to the south-east of the house, that lay along the path of the *clairvoyée*, is removed. From the outset Bridgeman clearly decided that Chicheley's south avenue should be replaced with an even grander one. Bridgeman also records in pencil the position of the ring-shaped earthwork to the east of the northern end of the Fir Avenue—this was to serve as the focus of a diagonal avenue which he subsequently proposed. The drawing is clearly unfinished.

33 Charles Bridgeman. Design for the South Avenue and Parade, *c*.1721

Bodleian Library, MS Gough Drawings a4 fo.31
Inscr.: 'Wimpole No.3', 'Scale of Feet', and:
'Number of Trees in this Plantation
From the further end, to the Circle around
   the Great Octangular Bason   358
Round the said Circle   98
From the Circle to the Great Parade
Next the House   456
Round the Said Parade   804
                                 1716'
Pen and ink with pencil (2,140 x 470mm)
Scale: 1in: 165ft ie. 2½ chains
Watermark: Coat-of-arms and letters IV
Lit. & repr.: Jackson-Stops (1979:2), pp.658–61, fig.5; Phibbs (1980), p.16.; Willis (2002), detail pl.233.

Bridgeman here proposes a great parade to the south of the entrance forecourt, surrounded by a planting of trees five rows deep, and at its centre a vast rectilinear basin with semicircular ends. The position of the fish ponds and water garden that would necessarily have been destroyed had this grandiose scheme been realised is shown very faintly. Bridgeman resolves here the unsatisfactory problem of the angle of Chicheley's avenue to the south-south-west. The ghost of its line remains but a new avenue, properly balancing the avenue to Whaddon, is indicated. Phibbs explains that while Chicheley's avenue—which he suggests might have been of horse-chestnut—was almost entirely felled, its replacement was never planted.

The colossal avenue, *c*.4,000 yards long with a central vista ninety yards wide, was, as we have seen, bounded by double, staggered rows of lime trees fifty feet apart. Humphry Repton describes the south avenue in somewhat equivocal terms in his 1801 Red Book: 'a great line of an avenue which was on too vast a scale to be destroyed by the new system and therefore it remains as a specimen of former Magnificence'. A later visitor, Mary Berry (1763—1852) the diarist, was more explicitly critical; in her *Journal* for November 1801 she described driving 'in the jaunting car down the avenue, two miles and a half long. Never was there such an unnecessary avenue; it ends in nothing, not even in a gateway [...]. The trees [...] are none of them good, though planted in the days of Lord Oxford, and half way down is a round piece of water (five acres), which can only be perceived from the garrets of the house as the ground rises between. It is no longer used as the approach to the house'.[121]

34 Charles Bridgeman. Design for the 'Grand Parade' at Wimpole Hall, *c*.1721

National Trust WIM/D/463
Pen and ink with wash (750 x 520mm)
Scale: 1in: 100ft
Lit. & repr.: Jackson-Stops (1979:2), pp.659–60; idem. (1992), pp.42–3. cat.18; Willis (1993), pp.247–64, fig.102(a); Willis (2002), pl.232.

This, and the following, nearly identical but badly torn, drawing *No.35* proposes a 'Grand Parade' to the south of the house. Here the inner and outer edge of the surrounding phalanx of trees is shown stepped, and to either side Bridgeman proposes bosquets—square enclosures of geometric planting.

35 Charles Bridgeman. Design for the 'Grand Parade' at Wimpole Hall, *c*.1721

National Trust WIM/D/561
Pen and ink with wash (755 x 520mm)
Scale: 1in: 100ft
Lit. & repr.: Willis (1993), pp.247–64, fig.102(b); Willis (2002), pl.231.

36 Charles Bridgeman. Revised proposals for the gardens to the south of the Hall, *c.*1721—4

National Trust WIM/D/551
Pen and ink with pencil (560 x 535mm)
Scale given
Lit. & repr.: Willis (1993), pp.247–64, fig.103(c)—NB. the caption incorrectly gives it as 103(b).

Bridgeman must have devised this scheme in the face of criticism of his initial proposal for a 'grand parade' to the south of the house. As has been noted, in April 1721 Dr William Stratford wrote to Harley explaining that while he 'could not but admire' Bridgeman's proposals for the grand parade, he would regret the loss of his 'beloved grove and the old trees of the old avenue'. Chicheley's avenue did not get a reprieve, but Stratford's love of the groves surrounding the water garden to the south-west of the house ensured that the plans were rethought.

This scheme preserved the moated water garden and proposed the remodelling of the spiral of ponds on the other side of the avenue to create a balancing, three-sided canal. John Cossens reported to Harley that a boat sent from Welbeck for the fish ponds at Wimpole was damaged in transit as a result of the waggoner's carelessness; a new boat 'for ye service of the Fish Pond to be made of Oak fitted up completely flat-bottom and to carry 4 or 5 men' was subsequently made.[122] The fish ponds were to be surrounded by woodland cut through by *allées* and sinuous paths leading to facetted cabinets some of which were clearly intended to contain garden buildings and statuary. The diagonal vistas, edged with avenue trees, were to be cut through the woodland. The avenue to the south-south-west is shown along the alignment established by Chicheley.

Note that the house and flanking wings are indicated in the same, simple block form as in previous plans—it clearly uses the same base as *No.31*. The bastion possibly suggested in the latter is in the revised proposal moved to the east side of the avenue—a detail reminiscent of the gardens at Stowe, Buckinghamshire.

37 Charles Bridgeman. Block plan survey of Wimpole Hall, and ancillary buildings, *c.*1721

National Trust WIM/D/552
Inscr.: 'The General Plan', with dimensions marked.
Pen and ink (450 x 575mm)
Scale given
Repr.: Willis (2002), pl.229b.

With the initial proposals for a grand parade discarded, a more detailed survey was needed of the house and the area to north and south. This survey drawing records the external dimensions of the house—taking account of Gibbs's alterations—the church, stables, ancillary service and garden buildings and the various walled enclosures that surrounded the house.

38 Charles Bridgeman. Survey of the gardens to the north of the house, *c.*1721

British Library, Add. MS 36278 M1
Pen and ink (600 x 515mm)
Scale given
Lit. & repr.: Willis (1993), pp.247–64, fig.103(b)—NB. the caption incorrectly gives it as 103(c); Willis (2002), pl.230b.

This drawing records in detail Radnor's arrangement of the gardens—left unaltered by Bridgeman—immediately to the north of the house. The plan confirms the evidence of Kip's view. Steps from the house led into a central walled area containing four parterre beds with a circular fountain basin at the northern end. To either side are further walled enclosures—in Kip these are also shown as containing geometric parterres. A transverse path running across all three enclosures is aligned on Radnor's east and west avenues.

Still further to the north are symmetrically arranged gardens whose edges and cross paths, we know from Kip's view, centred on a pair of gazebos and were defined by high, clipped hedges.

39 Charles Bridgeman. Survey and final proposals for the gardens to the south of the house, *c.*1721—5

National Trust WIM/D/464
Pen and ink (850 x 630mm)
Scale given
Lit & repr.: Willis (2002), pp.436–7, pl.229a.

This drawing combines the survey information of the buildings and parterre garden provided in *Nos.37 & 38* with the revised proposal for the gardens to the south of the hall, the great avenue and its two subsidiary vistas, show in *No.36*. It appears, therefore, to be Bridgeman's final proposal.

Topographical paintings of the park at Wimpole by John Wootton (1682—1764) (40–1)

James Gibbs was probably responsible for introducing John Wootton to Edward Harley in 1714.[123] The artist was to paint some forty pictures for him, patronage that proved important in helping establish Wootton's reputation as a painter of sporting subjects and landscapes. Wootton became a vital member of Harley's circle and in 1717 the Steward of the Artists' Club of St. Luke.[124] He is identified as the third character in the comic ballad 'A Hue and Cry' (1719):

> The third was Outlandish I'm sure by his name
> A spinner of Battells, of Fire, & Flame
> BURGINION[125] they call'd him; whenever he spoke
> The fire came out of his mouth in a Joke

In Sir James Thornhill's sketch *The Connoisseurs and Sir James Thornhill*, probably made in the same year, Wootton is shown standing second from right; the accompanying note—explaining how each sitter would be identified by what attribute—simply reads 'horse or dog'.[126]

Wootton painted a number of portraits of the Earl and Countess of Oxford's thoroughbred horses which, as Arline Meyer explains, he enriched with identifying devices such as attendants, race-cups and racing achievements.[127] Examples of this type include: *Bonny Black* (1715), *The Countess of Oxford's Dun Mare with Thomas Thornton, Groom* (1715), *Leeds* (*c.*1720), and the *Bloody-Shouldered Arabian* (1724). More exotic are the animal paintings Wootton made of a *Wolf* and an *Antelope* in 1720, supposedly from Harley's menagerie.[128] But Wootton was more than just an animalist. In 1728 George Vertue lauded him as being 'well esteemd for his skill in Landskip painting amongst the professors of Art & in great Vogue & favor with many persons of y[e] greatest quality'.[129]

Two landscape paintings, showing Lady Harley hunting in the park at Wimpole on her favourite horse, the dun Arabian mare, are of topographical interest and the pictures are therefore included in this catalogue. Artistic licence has been taken with the scenery, but we have George Vertue's witness that they depict the Harleys' Cambridgeshire estate. In his 1747 catalogue of the pictures at Welbeck Abbey, Vertue describes the hawking scene as a 'Prospect taken from Wimpole Park'.

The two paintings of Lady Harley hawking at Wimpole and hunting the hare on Orwell Hill are described by William

Cavendish-Bentinck, the 6th Duke of Portland as being in the House Library (formerly known as the Music Room) at Welbeck Abbey:

> The pictures in this room are all portraits of members of the Harley family. The most interesting are perhaps those of Robert Harley in his robes as Lord High Treasurer, and of his daughter-in-law Henrietta, Countess of Oxford, in an olive-green riding habit, both signed by Kneller; of the little heiress, Lady Margaret Harley, who married the 2nd Duke of Portland, painted as a shepherdess by Michael Dahl; and two great landscapes by Wootton, showing Lady Oxford hawking at Wimpole and hunting the hare on Orwell hill in its vicinity.[130]

A third, smaller painting, *Lady Henrietta Harley out Hunting with Harriers* (*c*.1716) (Private Collection) is related to the two Welbeck canvases. The Countess's horse and pose derive from the hawking picture (*No.40*) while her riding habit is similar to that in the hare hunting scene (*No.41*). For these reasons the picture has been exhibited and catalogued as a view of the Wimpole estate from the high ground to the north.[131] It is difficult, however, to relate either the arrangement of the house and its ancillary offices—in the middle distance—or the outlying estate buildings with what is known of Wimpole at this date. That said, no candidate other than Wimpole suggests itself. With its progression of riders and attendant figures, and with the house in the background, this picture is reminiscent of Wootton's later painting of *Stag Hunting at Badminton*. Both Wootton and Bridgeman worked for the 3rd Duke of Beaufort in 1733/4. Resident from the late 1720s at 23 Cavendish Square, Wootton was a close neighbour of Bridgeman's.

40 **Lady Henrietta Harley Hawking in Wimpole Park, 1716**

Private collection
Oil on canvas (215 x 304cm)
Lit. & repr.: Goulding (1936, p.114); Meyer (1985), pp.212–9, fig.12.

A bill dated 10 November 1716 gives: 'A Large Landskip wth figures a Hawking 53: 15: 00'. George Vertue's 1747 catalogue, p.1, no.2 lists: 'A large Hawking piece, the Prospect taken from Wimpole Park'. Henrietta Lady Harley is shown in scarlet and gold habit, accompanied by a falconer and a clergyman, perhaps the Harleys' chaplain Timothy Thomas. In the middle distance, to the left of Lady Harley's horse, the spire of what must be Arrington church can be seen. The topography illustrated—the lie of the land and the position of the church—is remarkably similar to that shown in the Hon. Henry Reginald Yorke's watercolour of 1836 (No.227). This high ground with its commanding views was the site chosen for James 'Athenian' Stuart's prospect building or 'Hill House', and offered one of the five view points that Humphry Repton identified on 'Capability' Brown's circuit drive: 'The first is that towards the village of Arrington with its pleasing little spire' (Humphry Repton, Red Book for Wimpole).

41 **Hunting the Hare on Orwell Hill, 1716**

Private collection
Oil on canvas (210 x 295cm)
Lit. & repr.: Goulding (1936), p.113; Sparrow (1922), p.112; *VCH* (2002), opposite. p.282.

Wotton's bill of 10 November 1716 reads: 'A Landskip of ye same size wth figures a Hunting 53: 15: 00'. In George Vertue's 1747 catalogue, p.1, No.3, it is described as 'A Large Hunting Piece, the Prospect taken from Orwell Hill near Wimpole by Wootton'. Henrietta Lady Harley is shown in a green and silver habit.

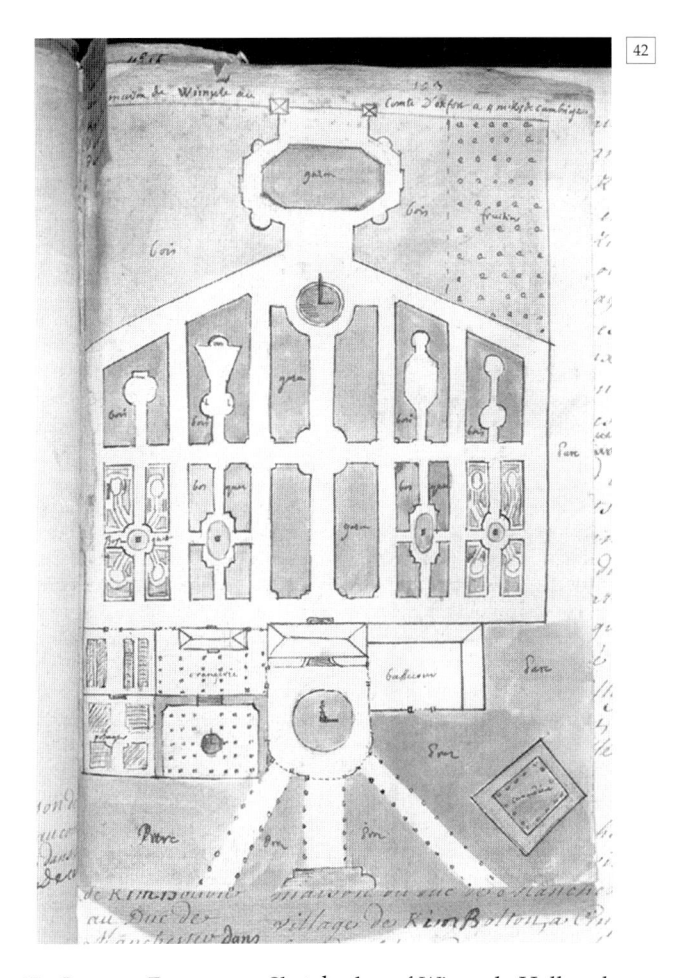

42 **Jacques Fougereau. Sketch plan of Wimpole Hall and gardens, 1728**

Victoria and Albert Museum Library, 86NN2 (MSL/1912/1255) fo.102
Pen and ink with watercolour (287 x 200mm)

This sketch plan of the house, ancillary buildings and gardens was made by the French author of a manuscript 'Voiage D'Angleterre, D'Hollande et de Flandre. Fait L'année 1728'. It provides a valuable, if suspect, record of the transformations that the Earl of Oxford was then making to the house and gardens. Gibbs's garden pavilions, with their hipped roofs, are shown to either side of the bowling green. Curiously there is no sign here that the building of the great Library extension to the north of the late-seventeenth-century orangery—still detached from the house—had begun.

The labelling of the *bassecour* clarifies that this was the courtyard associated with the service block and stables, separated from the principal forecourt, or grand court. We learn from John Cossen that the wall between the two was built in October 1722: 'The wall on the East side the great court [...] Brick were carryd up the last week but Thomas Juxson is yet so ill that he cannot come to lay on the capping altho' the Stone Work is made ready'.[132]

A sketch and engravings by George Vertue (1684—1756)

George Vertue's election in 1717 as a Fellow of the Society of Antiquaries of London, and, perhaps as importantly, his appointment to the post of engraver to the Society, brought him into contact with a small group of aristocrats and intellectuals who were to provide him with patronage. Amongst them was Edward Harley's father, Robert Harley the 1st Earl of Oxford, for whom Vertue undertook genealogical research. Edward Harley 'inherited' Vertue, just as he had his father's library-keeper Humfrey Wanley. Vertue was to become devoted to Edward Harley and in a draft of his autobiography wrote of his demise in melodramatic terms: 'The death of this great and Noble Collector of arts and encourager was an unhappy loss to the public but to Mr. Vertue most fatal indeed [...] from this loss and time of death Vertue may date his great decline of friends and interest'.

The engraved portrait illustrated below (No.45), with its various ancillary images has an elegiac quality, while the very rare pendant medal at the centre of the sale catalogue of Oxford's collections (No.44) bears a Latin inscription on its edge whose translation reads: 'This ticket was executed by George Vertue as a memorial of the benevolence and long friendship of the most noble Lord, the Earl of Oxford'.

The sketch of the south front of Wimpole was included in one of Vertue's many notebooks whose disjointed observations on English Art were distilled and used by Horace Walpole as the foundation of his *Anecdotes of Painting in England* (1762—71).

43 George Vertue. Sketches of the south or entrance façade of Wimpole Hall and the font in St. Andrew's parish church, 1733

British Library, Add.MS 22, 042, fo.31 (formerly 29), George Vertue's Memoranda 1730—4, November 1733
Inscr.: 'greenhouse', 'Wimpole', 'Chappel', and 'a font in Wimpole church'
Pen and ink (page, 157 x 95mm)
Lit. & repr.: 'Vertue Note Books V', *Walpole Society*, vol.XXVI (1938), p.108; Lees-Milne (1962), p.218; Baggs (2004), p.158, fig.8.

These rapid sketches are accompanied by the brief note: '3 Nov. set out to Wimpole to wait on the Earl of Oxford—at his request rturnd to Lond. the 13 November'. This is a far from accurate representation of the building as it must have appeared in 1733. We know from Henry Flitcroft's survey drawings that the central block of Chicheley's house survived in its mid-seventeenth-century form until the architect remodelled it in the 1740s. Yet Vertue does not appear, even, to have indicated the positions of the three projecting 'towers' which punctuated the south elevation. Rather than being a topographical record, the sketch appears to be an interpretation of James Gibbs's, only partially realised, proposals for the house. Confusingly, Vertue suggests here a central lantern and tall weather vane more akin to that on Chicheley's house than to the lower and simpler structure proposed by Gibbs.

Most oddly, Vertue shows the central block as being of five rather than seven bays. The flanking blocks, which are of five bays, are shown here with an attic storey whose balustrades follow the line of that to the central block—an unexecuted idea which is shown as an alternative in all Gibbs's elevational proposals (No.8). Vertue indicates the orangery, or 'greenhouse', and chapel ends of the house. Part of the late-seventeenth-century service block to the east is also shown.

44 George Vertue. Engraved frontispiece to the 1742 Sale Catalogue of the Collections of Edward Harley, 2nd Earl of Oxford, 1742

Collection Tim Knox and Todd Longstaff-Gowan

Inscr.: 'COLL. HARLEYANA 1741'; and with pendant monograms, composed of the initials of the peer's name and title, Edward Harley, Earl of Oxford, under earl's coronets; together with other inscriptions in Latin and Greek; all inside the plate. Lettered below: *Virtue in.*
Engraving (240 x 190mm)
Lit. & repr.: Wright (1962), pp.158–74, pl.D, facing p.169; Harris (1985), p.199, pl.2; Adshead (2002), pp.191–206, fig.2.

This engraving served as the frontispiece to the 1742 sale 'CATALOGUE OF THE COLLECTION OF THE Right Honourable Edward Earl of Oxford DECEASED'.

The frontispiece includes a library interior, hidden largely behind the central, pendant medal and the works of art massed in the foreground. The medal helps to obscure what appears to be an uncomfortable juncture of two walls, proportioned, articulated and shelved in quite different ways. It may be a conflation of two real interiors, the libraries at Wimpole and Oxford's London town house in Dover Street (see Adshead, *art.cit.infra.*, for the arguments in favour of this interpretation).

The pendant medal, an engraved version of one struck as a memorial for Lord Oxford, contains elements that allude to his interests in architecture, landscape gardening, and book collecting. Oxford's heraldic supporters, the angel, stag, and lion, stand before an obelisk and flaming urn that symbolise his tomb and the idea of immortality.

45 George Vertue. Engraved portrait of Edward Harley, 2nd Earl of Oxford, together with a vignette of the interior of the Library at Wimpole, 1746

The Society of Antiquaries of London, Harley collection vol.1, 196H Frontispiece
Inscr.: On a banderole hanging from the engraved picture frame: 'The Rt. Honble. EDWARD Earl of OXFORD and Earl MORTIMER &c. Obt. 1741'; 'M Dahl p.' and 'G Vertue f. 1746'. In a medallion at top right: 'S.M./ PRENOBILIS DNI. DNI./ EDVARDI HARLEY/ COMITIS OXONIAE ET MORTIMER/ ARTIVM ET SCIENTIARVM/ PATRONI MUNIFICENTISSIMI./ LIBRORUM/ MANUSCRIPT ET IMPRESS:/ IN PATRIAE COMMODVM ET/ HONOREM DESIGNATORVM/ COLLECTORIS INDEFESSI/ ET VERE MAGNIFICT./ OB. ÆT. LII. DIE XVI/ IVNIT MDCCXLVI'
Engraving (287 x 184mm) by George Vertue of a portrait by Michael Dahl, surrounded by ornaments and scenes of his own devising.
Lit. & repr.: Wright (1962), pp.158–74, pl.A, facing p.168; Saunders (1997), pp.27–32, fig.29; Adshead (2002), pp.191–206, fig.1.

In 1746 George Vertue engraved what was to be the last of his various renderings of portraits of Edward Harley, 2nd Earl of Oxford. The engraving, after a half-length of 1720 by the Swedish *émigré* artist Michael Dahl (1656—1743), shows Oxford seated on a high-backed chair at a table with a medal of Queen Anne in his left hand, five coins scattered on the table-top before him, and his right arm resting on a tome in a Harleian binding.

The engraving under consideration here combines Vertue's portrait after Dahl with elements borrowed from his frontispiece to the 1742 Sale Catalogue (No.44). These borrowings include the obverse of the medal at top left (the inscribed reverse is at top right); the Roman sarcophagus, or cist, at bottom left; canopic and other jars; urns and elaborately wrought vases; busts; scrolls and piles of books. Many of these objects are identifiable from the descriptions in the sale catalogue.

Positioned immediately below the portrait and framed by exuberant *rocaille* ornament is a diminutive perspective view of a large rectangular room. *Prima facie*, this is quite unlike the present library at Wimpole; however, various adaptations have been made to the room since its completion. The fireplace (and possibly a different chimney-piece) was originally positioned at the north end of the room in the place of the polygonal bay window, while the fenestration was limited to five windows in the east wall. With these successive changes taken into account, Vertue's vignette may be plausibly compared to James Gibbs's double-cube library at Wimpole.

The changes in fenestration and the position of the

37 The Catalogue

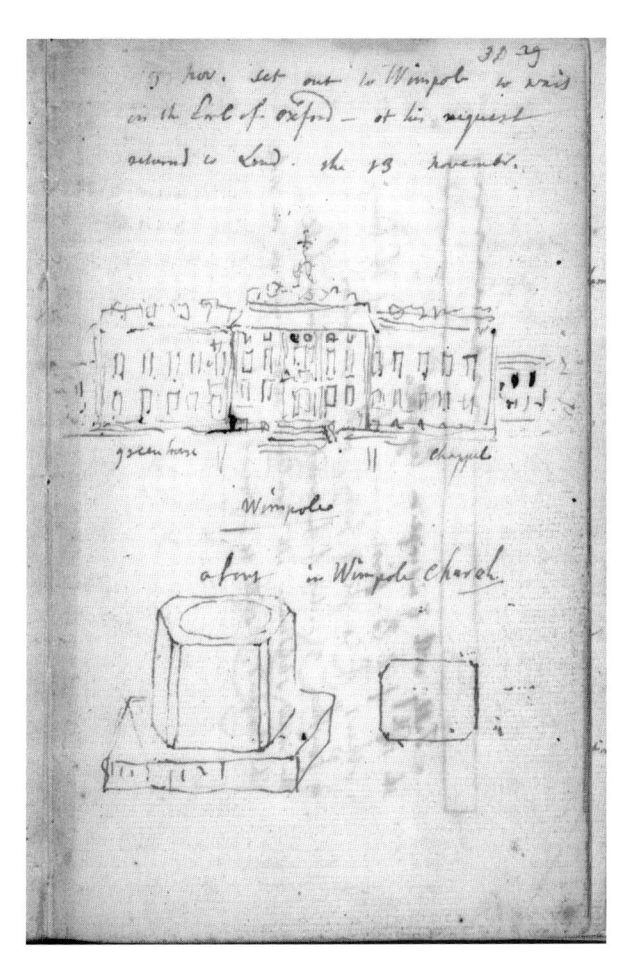

chimney-piece are relatively straightforward matters to explain; other discrepancies between the engraved view and the carcass of the room are less easy to account for. The shallow relief arches above cornice level that divide the room longitudinally into five bays, and which relate to the rhythm of windows and book-presses, are absent from the engraving. The engraving also appears to show a barrel-vaulted ceiling which is at odds with the way the Wimpole library is ceiled. However, the considerable depth of the cove might conceivably—in half-remembrance—have been confused with a barrel-vault form. There is no evidence in Vertue's notebooks that he ever visited Wimpole after it had been bought by Lord Chancellor Hardwicke (for a more extended discussion of these issues, see Adshead, *art.cit.infra*).

A series of busts, presumably writers and philosophers, appear above the book presses at cornice level, while at the north end a globe and armillary sphere flank what appears to be a statue of Hercules. The vignette is completed with a scattering of library furniture and peopled by a standing, begowned scholar and a seated writer, possibly Humfrey Wanley, Lord Oxford's librarian, propping up his head with his hand.

The engraving was subsequently published in Arthur Collins's *Historical collections of the noble families of Cavendish, Holles, Vere, Harley and Ogle, with the lives of the most remarkable persons* [...] *The lives of the Earls of Oxford* [etc.] (1752), facing p.212.

Drawings by Henry Flitcroft (1697—1769) for Wimpole

The architect Henry Flitcroft, or 'Burlington Harry', worked almost exclusively in the Burlingtonian neo-Palladian style for members of the Whig establishment. For Philip Yorke, Baron Hardwicke (1690—1764), created Lord Chancellor in 1737, Flitcroft must have seemed an ideal choice. By refashioning the mid-seventeenth century house at Wimpole in the grand but austere neo-Palladian manner, Hardwicke could signal to his contemporaries and peer group that his family had arrived, socially and politically.

The first payments to Flitcroft's workmen, made by Hardwicke's steward, Devereaux Serjeant, date from December 1742.[133] The architect's survey and proposal drawings were presumably made earlier that year. Flitcroft was at the time Clerk of Works at the palaces of Whitehall, Westminster and St. James's, and it appears that at Wimpole, as elsewhere in his already established country house practice, he made full use of the craftsmen from the government building agency, the Office of Works. In the accounts they are referred to variously as 'the London Tradesmen' and 'the Town Workmen', although some preliminary work was shared with the estate's craftsmen, as was the case with the local carpenter William Ratford who, amongst other duties, seems to have overseen the making of bricks.

One of the great values of Flitcroft's meticulous survey drawings for Wimpole is that they provide detailed plans of Sir Thomas Chicheley's apparently little altered house and, Vertue's rough sketch aside (*No.43*), the only known elevation of its principal front. Flitcroft refaced the south front of Wimpole, placing at its centre, beneath a triangular pediment, an amalgam of neo-Palladian elements, and he modernised the garden façade by adding a characteristic canted bay. The work to the south front must have been a major engineering exercise, but with his origins as a carpenter, and experience as an architect, Flitcroft took pains to provide a very precise 'Explanation of the Severall Works that will be Necessary to make the proposed Alterations at Wimple'.[134] This was presumably intended for his client's reassurance rather than for the instruction of the various trades. With the final balance of payments listed in January 1746, the remodelling of the Hall appears to have taken just three years.

The 'Explanation' and accounts conjure up a bustling scene: Portland stone was carried from Cambridge and lead brought from London, while, on the estate, earth was dug for the burning of bricks, and 'Great Ladders' materialised. Will Dickinson was paid 'in part to Making bricks' and Thomas Blow for '30 bundles of Oak lath for slating of Great House'. The recasting of the south and north fronts necessitated altering the roof, and the old house, sandwiched between James Gibbs's recent additions, was thoroughly overhauled. The carpenter was required to supply a new truss roof to the attic storey, and 'a Balustrade and new Cupola'.

The scale of these works had an impact on the interiors of the house, and the opportunity was taken to renew joinery and replace floors. In addition, the secondary staircase was replaced and a ground floor gallery created by throwing together James Gibbs's suite of three cabinet rooms at the west end of the house. The 'Explanation' of the 'Carpenter's Work' gives a good indication of the nature of these improvements:

> To Shore up the Severall Floors, while the Alterations are making, and Front is rebuilding, to make all the naked Flooring, Quarter'd Partitioning, according to the Plans, to make a new Back Staircase, in which to employ, as much of the old, as will come in, to Prepare Sound Lintalling, and Bond Timber, to make all Centering, to Trimmers' Doors, and Arches, to make a new Clean Deal or wainscot Floor, in the Gallery, and a second best Floor, in the upper Gallery, and to make good all the Timber Work, and to furr Do. to the Floor, and relay all the Boarding to the severall Floors.

Flitcroft employed some of the finest craftsmen of the time to provide the decorative finishes to Wimpole's improved carcass. The accounts reveal several successive payments to 'Mr. Allkins, Carver' or 'Sefferin Alken, Carver' and 'Mr. Artari Italian Plasterer' or 'Joseph Artari for Stucco Work'. Giuseppe Artari was an Italian-speaking Swiss *stuccatore* who worked regularly in partnership with Giovanni Bagutti, whom Daniel Defoe described as 'the finest artist in these particular works now in England', until *c*.1730, and in combination with other decorative plasterers such as Francesco Vassalli (*fl*.1724—63) at other times.[135]

Artari worked regularly for James Gibbs, usually with Bagutti—for example at Orleans House, Twickenham, Middlesex (1720); the Senate House, Cambridge (1722—30); at Houghton Hall, Norfolk (1726); and at the Radcliffe Camera, Oxford (1744). It seems probable that both men had worked at Wimpole in the 1720s during James Gibbs's rebuilding campaign for the 2nd Earl of Oxford. Geoffrey Beard explains that the carver Sefferin Alken (*fl*.1744—82) was held in high regard 'by architects of great ability and connection', and not only worked for Flitcroft but also for Sir William Chambers and Robert Adam. Chambers referred to him in 1772 as one of 'her late Royal Highnesses workmen'.[136]

The plasterer's work was to include the following:

> To make an Ionick Cornice, round the Hall, Vestibule and Gallery, and finish the sides of the Hall, and Vestible in Stucco, to make new Ceilings to all the Front Rooms, and the three Garden Rooms, and Corinthian Cornices to the three Garden Rooms, to make an Ionick Cornice, a new Ceiling, and Stucco the sides of the Chamber Gallery, and make new Ceilings, to the Rooms, next the Court, and to all the Attick Rooms, and

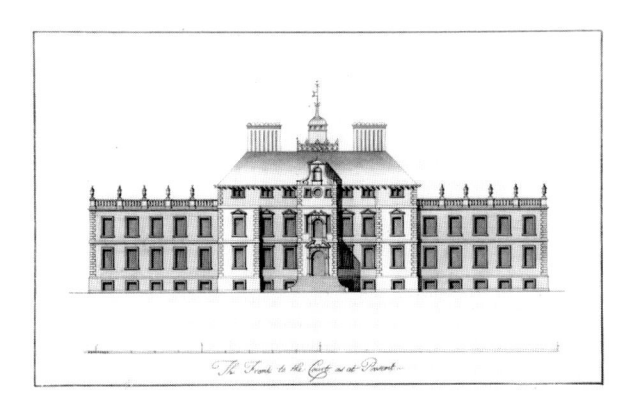

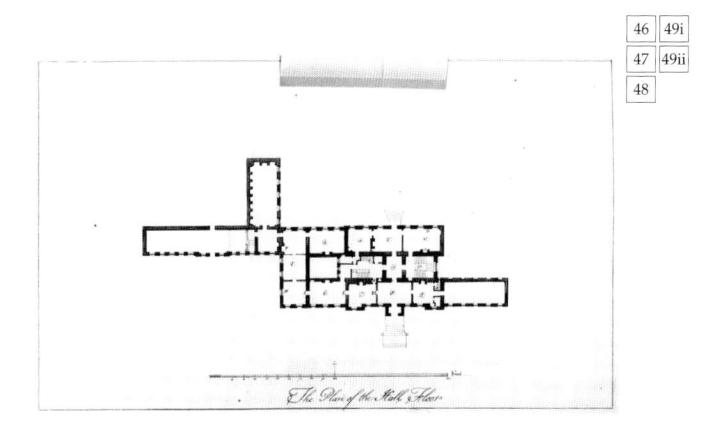

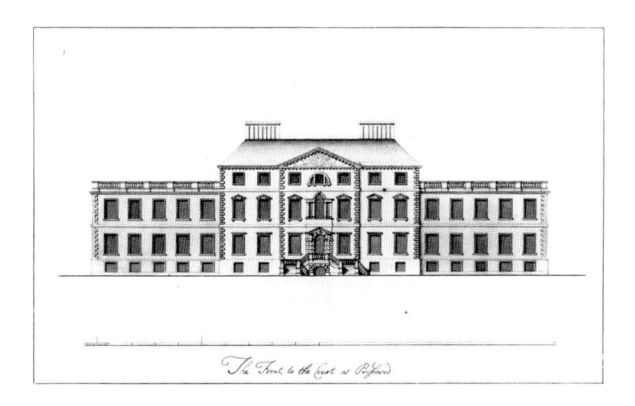

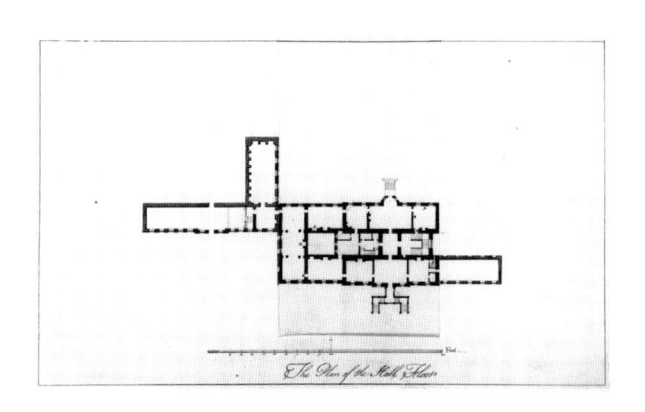

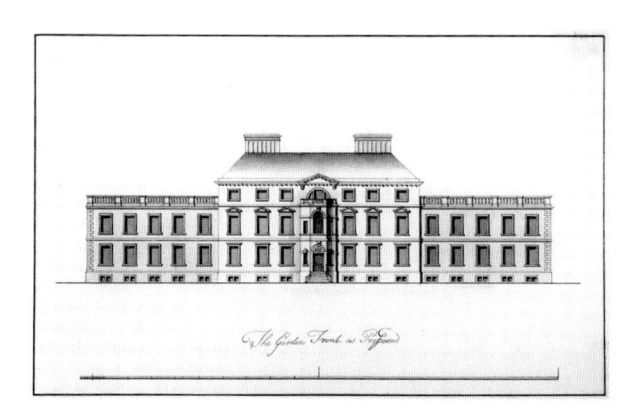

to Plaister the Timber Partitions on both sides, and Render the Walls, and make good the Plaistering in the lower Story, and Whitewash all the Ceilings &c.

The carver was expected 'to Carve the Capitalls to the Collumns, and Pilasters, and Trusses to Door Cases, and to Carve five Ornamented Chimny tops. Carveing the Mouldings, of the three Garden Rooms'. The 'fine Marble Chimny Pieces, one for the Gallery, the other for the Salon' were to be supplied by the mason, John Devall who was presumably related to the various Devalls employed by the Office of Works.[137]

The finishing of the interiors must have taken a few years longer for on 20 August 1749 Baron Hardwicke's daughter-in-law, Jemima Marchioness Grey (1722—97) wrote: 'This summer has finished the Gallery which really is a charming room'.[138]

By that date Flitcroft had already begun work on the remodelling of the church, with the help of his assistant Kenton Couse (1721—90), then a writing clerk in the Board of Works office in Scotland Yard. Payments to Flitcroft continue throughout the 1750s, as do references to his ongoing work at Wimpole. In 1752 Flitcroft had to write to the Baron expressing his disappointment and surprise 'at Mr. Devall's conduct' and promised to 'send to some other mason' about 'doing the copeing': Devall by name and perhaps devil by nature.[139] The same letter refers to the making of 'canvas coverings for the Hot Houses', and it is conceivable that Flitcroft worked alongside the landscape gardener Robert Greening (d.1758), providing designs for building structures such as the hot-houses shown in Greening's kitchen garden plan (*No.79*), and the thatched ice-house which has been attributed to him (*No.66*). Flitcroft and Greening had worked together for Prince

William Augustus, Duke of Cumberland (1721—65) at Great Lodge, Windsor Great Park, where amongst other works Flitcroft designed a thirty-two-bay hothouse with a three-bay pedimented centre. In 1749 the Duke wrote to Lord Chancellor Hardwicke about his 'several new improvements' there.[140]

The main architectural changes made to Wimpole in the 1750s included the addition of a bow window to the north end of the library, and the building of a corresponding laundry wing on the east side of the house. There is evidence that the gentleman architect Sanderson Miller (1716—80) provided the inspiration, at least, for the remodelling of the library. The Rev. William Cole writes: 'Mr Miller of Edge Hill in Warwickshire, calling upon me this morning, Apr. 10 1760 told me, that he was the occasion of altering the Library at Wimpole, by removing the large Chimney Piece & making a Bow Window into the park & that the Arms put up in the windows was also thro' his means'.[141]

In December 1752 Robert Greening had given the head gardener, Mr Moses, instructions to 'Take away the Grass & Earth next the House & in the North Front as wide as the Library Extends', and to 'Take away the large Elms at the end of the Library, as soon as the Ground is prepared'.[142] In March 1754 the Earl of Hardwicke asked his agent, John Bird, to 'Send me word next week how far the Stone-masons are advanced in their work at the Bow-Window, & when they will have finished'.[143] The canted bay is one of the defining features of Henry Flitcroft's work, and this, combined with the fact that the carving and plasterwork details—pilasters, lions' masks and garlands of flowers—that flank the opening at the north end of the Library are identical to those in the bay of the Saloon, points to Flitcroft's executive hand.

In July 1755 John Bird reported: 'My Lord the Repairs to the Kitchin and the Rom over it is don all but whitt washing and the wainscoting of the Audit Room is allmost don but not the painting of it and your Lordship Dressing Room is don all but painting the outside of the dore and M[r]. Flitcroft was at Wimpole on Monday last and ordered the dore to be painted on the outside and now it is finished'.[144]

The evidence of Flitcroft's design for a spillway between the middle and lower lakes suggests that he continued to be involved at Wimpole almost until his death in 1769. Payments made to Flitcroft and Lancelot Brown in the late 1750s, recorded in the bank book of Philip Yorke, Viscount Royston (1720—90), later 2nd Earl of Hardwicke, relate to their respective works at Wrest Park, Bedfordshire. In addition to working at Wrest, it appears that in 1759 Flitcroft also undertook modernising works at Tyttenhanger, Hertfordshire, for Hardwicke's second son, the Rt. Hon Charles Yorke (1722—70), and his first wife Catherine Freman (1736/7—59).[145]

46 Survey drawing of the south, or entrance, façade, c.1742

National Trust WIM/D/469
Inscr.: 'The Front to the Court as at Present'
Pen and ink with grey wash (215 x 345mm)
Scale given
Lit. & repr.: Hussey (1967:1), pp.1400–4, fig.6; RCHME (1968), pl.133 (top); Jackson-Stops (1979:1), p.8; Souden (1991), p.7; Baggs (2004), p.158, fig.9.

The five-bay wings that flank the central block in this drawing are James Gibbs's additions of the 1720s. Purposefully plain, they defer to the earlier house and reflect its proportions and detailing. The wings are both of two storeys on a basement plinth, with a regularised pattern of fenestration and have roof-top balustrades ornamented with urns.

The real interest of this survey drawing, however, is that the seven-bay house shown at its centre is the only visual record to have survived of the 'extraordinary curious neat house' that John Layer had described Sir Thomas Chicheley as

building in c.1640, almost exactly a century earlier.

To the modern eye, the central 'tower' and the lower projections at either end of the house give the elevation an antiquated appearance, distantly echoing similar features in Jacobean country house architecture, indeed Jeremiah Milles visiting sometime between 1735 and 1740 noted of it: 'The house does not appear to be very modern on ye outside'. Yet Chicheley's Wimpole, while lacking the sophisticated badge of an applied temple front or classical orders, and perhaps unfashionable by the time the cloud of the interregnum had passed, is deserving of closer analysis.

The architectural components of the central tower in particular might lead one to suppose that Chicheley's house was a curious, transitional hybrid that fits happily into the stylistic pigeon-hole of 'Artisan Mannerism', devised by Sir John Summerson and alternatively named 'Subordinate' by John Harris.[146] The broken pediments of its entrance doorway and first floor window (triangular above segmental), together with the shaped gable at eaves level, might be said to typify the Netherlandish-inspired mannerism which it has been argued was favoured by London craftsmen and merchants in the early seventeenth century. Chicheley was of course a merchant and a leading light of the Grocers' Company.

Strikingly similar to the crowning element in the exuberant entrance façade of Swakeleys, Middlesex (1638), Chicheley's gable does, at least, appear to conform to the 'Amsterdam gable' type identified by H.J. Louw in which 'a classical aedicule is flanked by two large scrolls' and 'subdivided into various separate units by means of vertical and horizontal elements'.[147] But an alternative thesis suggests that Chicheley's house bears the hallmarks of Jonesian and more direct Italian influence.

Giles Worsley has made a case for the emergence in the 1630s of another strain of English Classicism—Serlian rather than Palladian—under the influence, and in some cases direct guidance, of Inigo Jones (1573—1652).[148] In his mature, and particularly domestic, work Jones augmented his knowledge of Palladian and Scamozzian architecture with a study of the designs of Sebastiano Serlio (1475—1554). Serlio's seven volumes of L'Architettura (the last, and in this context most important, of which was published posthumously) were of immense influence in northern Europe and for Jones, and particularly his Netherlandish contemporaries, they offered models for handsome but not overly grand, astylar houses (appropriate for use beyond courtly circles), and a particularly rich repertory of door and window types.

Worsley counts among the defining characteristics of this new style compact, three-storey country houses on raised basements, of double-pile plan, with hipped roofs supported by modillion brackets; windows placed on a regular grid and pedimented on the *piano nobile* and supplemented by Serliana and *œil-de-bœuf* windows; and ground and first floors of equal height separated by plat bands.

Every one of these elements is present in the south façade of Chicheley's house. The central first-floor window with broken pediment has narrow slip windows to either side, and while not a conventional Venetian window in the Burlingtonian manner, it is nonetheless a tripartite Serliana. The bull's-eye window at the attic level, beneath the shaped gable and sandwiched between a pair of small rectangular windows, has echoes of Nicholas Stone's remodelled north front of Kirby Hall, Northamptonshire (1638—40) and, at a pinch, might be seen as a paraphrase of the upper register of Jones's design for the west front of St Paul's Cathedral (c.1633—4).

Desirous of seeing classical architecture flourish in Britain, Jones provided guidance both to Nicholas Stone (1587—1647) and to Isaac de Caus in their respective rebuilding of Goldsmiths' Hall, London (1635—8) and the south front of

Wilton House, Wiltshire (*c.*1636). Following the Civil War, he gave further advice at Wilton, to his protégé John Webb, and possibly to Sir Roger Pratt at Coleshill. Worsley further speculates whether Peter Mills (*c.*1600—70) might have benefited from Jones's help in the early stages of planning at Thorpe Hall, Cambridgeshire (1654) before Jones's death in 1652. Why might not Chicheley, whom it has been suggested may have been his own architect, have similarly benefited from Jones's advice, or at least been influenced by the clutch of Jonesian astylar houses that were built in the 1630s? Peter Mills has also been suggested as a possible guiding hand, but might Nicholas Stone (for stylistic and political reasons) be a more likely possibility? Compounding on the Oxford Articles, it was into Goldsmiths' Hall that Chicheley paid his fines.

47   Proposal for remodelling the south façade, *c.*1742

National Trust WIM/D/470
Inscr.: 'The Front to the Court as Proposed'
Pen and ink with grey wash (344 x 209mm)
Scale given
Lit. & repr.: Hussey (1967:1), pp.1400–4, fig.7; Jackson-Stops (1979:1), p.8; Parry (1986), pp.36–55, fig.22.

In the remodelling of Wimpole's principal front, Flitcroft's brief must have been to excise all vestiges of the architecturally arcane and unfashionable: the central tower and flanking two-storey projections and the roof-top lantern would be swept away, while the vertical emphasis provided by the deep roof and tall chimney stacks would also be lessened. Pulling the face of the house forward to the plane of the flanking projections, Flitcroft added a pedimented three-bay centre, raised the attic storey (thereby reducing the apparent depth of the roof to the ridge), almost halved the height of the chimney stacks, and in addition removed the urns from the parapet balustrade of Gibbs's wings.

At the centre of the composition Flitcroft proposed a 'tower' of neo-Palladian elements. At basement level a balustraded stair, supported by a low, powerfully voussoired arch—a *cryptoporticus* that recalls William Kent's garden grotto and cascade designs—leads to a heavily rusticated doorcase of smooth bossed columns and an open pediment supported by giant diglyphs. Inigo Jones's interest in Mannerist gateways of the Doric and Tuscan orders is echoed here. Flitcroft, whom Colvin describes as a 'careful student' of Inigo Jones, drew out the illustrative plates for Kent's publication *The Designs of Inigo Jones* (1727). In *c.*1748 Flitcroft almost exactly repeated his Wimpole doorcase design, but with a broader opening, as the entrance façade for the boat house he designed for the Duke of Cumberland's Great Meadow Pond in Windsor Great Park.[149]

Above Wimpole's new entrance, Flitcroft places a Serlian, or Venetian, window, and above that a Diocletian, or therm, window. This composition is associated with Burlingtonian Palladianism because of the single but influential occasion on which Richard Boyle, 3rd Earl of Burlington (1694—1753) employed it in the refacing of old Chiswick House (*c.*1723). This formula is thought, in spirit at least, to derive from Andrea Palladio's (1508—80) reconstruction drawings of the Baths of Caracalla, Rome, in which he showed open pediments of a therm character above serliana.

In his 'Scheme of the Works propos'd at Wimpole', Flitcroft explains that the bricklayer (a Mr White) would 'take down the Court Front to the level of the Ground and rebuild it, in a solid, and Workmanlike manner, with the Cross Walls, according to the Plan'. The mason (Mr Devall) would provide a 'Dorick Portico, and Bow window over it, with the Balustrade all of Portland Stone'.[150]

48   Proposal for the remodelling of the north, or garden, façade, *c.*1742

National Trust WIM/D/468
Inscr.: 'The Garden Front as Proposed'
Pen and ink with grey wash (335 x 225mm)
Scale given

If Flitcroft made a survey drawing of the then existing north elevation, it has not survived. He here repeats the formula of a tower of neo-Palladian elements—Diocletian window over Venetian window over entrance door—but imposes it on and above a canted bay added to the centre of the house. It sits beneath a small, open pediment at eaves level, enriched with dentils and supported on brackets.

The classical canted bay was used by Nicholas Hawksmoor at Panton Hall, Lincolnshire (*c.*1720) and was an idea taken up by architects such as William Kent and Roger Morris (1695—1749). Its use—for example in the recasting of the garden façade of Carlton House, Pall Mall, for Frederick Prince of Wales (*c.*1733), and in an unrealised library addition (*c.*1748) to the Duke of Cumberland's Great Lodge in Windsor Great Park—was to become a particular feature of Henry Flitcroft's work.

In *c.*1750 the 3rd Earl Fitzwilliam commissioned Flitcroft to remodel his rambling, asymmetrically fronted Northamptonshire seat, Milton House; and in the refacing of its elongated south front, the architect placed a tower of Palladian elements at its centre and canted bays to either side. The component parts can all be recognised in his earlier work at Wimpole. The first Earl of Hardwicke's improvements may have spurred on his eldest son to employ Flitcroft at Wrest Park, Bedfordshire, where in 1760 he created a new dining room with a canted bay.

At Wimpole, Flitcroft also appears to have added the five-bay wing—or at least its façade—to the east, or left, of the central block. Prior to this, the northern face of the chapel would have been visible over the garden wall that linked the house and service wing, giving the garden façade of the house a decidedly unbalanced appearance. The addition may have been an afterthought for, other than as a sketchy, pencil emendation (*No.*49), it does not appear on the architect's plans. Flitcroft's written explanation, however, confirms that the work was undertaken at this time. The bricklayer was 'To Build the Sham Front in the Garden with Butresses to D', while the mason was to provide '10 frames for Blank Windows in the Sham Front'. Kenton Couse, Flitcroft's assistant, was later to finish this block and to build within it a new, neo-classical dining room (*No.*96).

49   Survey plan of the ground floor, with flap, *c.*1742

National Trust WIM/D/466
Inscr.: 'The Plan of the Hall Floor'
Pen and ink with pencil additions (367 x 220mm)
Scale given
Lit. & repr.: Hussey (1967:1), pp.1400–4, fig.8; RCHME (1968), pl.133 (middle).

Flitcroft employed a paper flap or slide in this and in the following plans of the house: with the flap raised, his survey of the mid-seventeenth-century house and James Gibbs's additions are revealed, and with the flap lowered, his proposals advocated. The rooms in the survey drawings are each marked with a circled number, while other features are indicated by a letter. Although Flitcroft's specification for the modernising of Wimpole survives, the key to the numbers and letters given here is unfortunately lost.

The principal differences between the ground-floor plan as then existing and as proposed are as follows. The projecting one-bay tower, or frontispiece, of the south front was to be removed and the entire elevation refaced. The outer bays of the recessed five-bay central portion of the original were to be pulled forward to the line of the existing one-bay towers to east and west. The central three bays were to form a pedimented break front. The steps to the earlier house were replaced by a *perron* stair. The *enfilade* that ran east-west through the centre of the south range was to be shifted further to the south and, with the adjustment of door-cases and the creation of a new opening between Gibbs's western wing and the earlier house, a similar *enfilade* was proposed for the north range. The present, symmetrical saloon at the centre of the north range of the house was created by pushing the eastern wall of the room marked '2' one bay further to the east and by engaging the half-octagon canted bay to the north. New garden steps were provided. The secondary stair, rising in the space to the left, or west, of the inner hall, '11', was remodelled and a third staircase provided. James Gibbs's relatively recently built series of three cabinet rooms in the north-south block at the west end of the house (its central room marked '5') was opened up to form a continuous gallery—the lines of the previous partition walls being replaced by columnar screens—and a fireplace added at the centre of the east wall. Flitcroft's 'Explanation' of the works reveals that 'a new clean Deal or wainscot floor', a 'fine marble chimney piece', and four 'Ionick Collumns and four Pillasters with Entablatures over them' were provided for the new gallery.

Faint pencil additions mark the future position of John Soane's Yellow Drawing Room.

50 Survey plan of the basement floor, with flap, c.1742

National Trust WIM/D/525
Inscr.: 'The Plan of the Lower Offices'
Pen and ink with pencil additions (235 x 380mm)
Scale given

Flitcroft here confines his alterations to the oldest, central part of the house: the service stair at the west end is reordered, and a spur corridor to serve rooms '3' and '4' in the south range created. The base survey data was used again for *No.53*, to which the details of drainage were added. Gibbs's lost box pews and the axially placed octagonal pulpit in the chapel are washed in yellow.

Because no plans by James Gibbs survive for the house, Flitcroft's surveys are particularly useful. This drawing gives us the plan of the late-seventeenth-century service block to the east, and its associated walled courtyard to the north-east, and that of the service buildings attached to the rear of the orangery at the west end of the house. Bridgeman, who was interested in the relative positions of the buildings and the spaces between them, furnishes us with block plans only (*Nos.37 & 39*).

51 Survey plan of the first floor, with flap, *c*. 1742

National Trust WIM/D/467
Inscr.: 'The Plan of the One Pair of Stairs Floor'
Pen and ink with pencil additions (368 x 222mm)
Scale given

Again, it is essentially only the area of the secondary staircase at the west end of the mid-seventeenth-century house that Flitcroft proposes to alter here. The plan shows how the central cross-gallery was to terminate in the new canted bay of the garden façade.

52 Survey plan of, and proposed alterations to, the attic floor, with flap, *c*.1742.

National Trust WIM/D/526
Inscr.: 'The Plan of the Attick Story'
Pen and ink with pencil additions (240 x 370 mm)
Scale given
Watermark: IV

Proposed alterations are again confined to the secondary stair. The repositioning of the stairwell allowed Flitcroft to create an open lobby above the centre of the cross-gallery.

Drawings by Henry Flitcroft for the park

53 Drawing showing the layout of water pipes and drains, 1749

Sir John Soane's Museum, 6/1/18
Inscr.: 'The Earl of Hardwicke', entitled 'A Plan of the Water Pipes and Dreins at Wimpole, with the House, Offices, Church etc. 1749', and the names of the drains marked: 'Drain from Fountains emptys into Ladys Pond'; two 'Drain[s] from the House' which discharge into 'The Principall Drain'
Pen and green and pink inks (440 x 636mm). The blue pigment that in this and the following drawing presumably once indicated the presence of water—in cisterns and pipes—is now green.

This drawing extends beyond the house (whose basement plan is incorporated) to include the reservoir (A) to the north-east, the remodelled church and the late-seventeenth-century stable block, whose internal layout is only otherwise known from Thomas West's survey of 1805 (*No.200*). At the far left of the drawing a drain marked 'Drain from Fountains emptys into Lady's Pond' detours around the west end of the orangery from what must have been the circular basin at the centre of the parterre gardens to the north of the house (and off the edge of the plan), shown in Kip's view, in Bridgeman's survey drawings, and, still surviving in 1747, in William Stukeley's sketchy view (*No.75*).

54 Drawing showing the layout of water pipes and drains, 1749

Sir John Soane's Museum, 6/1/19
Inscr.: 'The Earl of Hardwicke', 'Plan of the Ground Floor of the House at Wimpole'
Pen and green and pink inks (463 x 649mm)

This drawing is identical to *No.53*, other than for identifying letters and labels.

55 A survey plan showing part of the water reservoir in the east park and the mechanisms for allowing water into and out of it, 1749

Sir John Soane's Museum, 6/1/20
Inscr.: 'Scetch of the Water &c. in the East Part of the Prk'; 'The Earl of Hardwicke', with the following key:
  A. The Drain from the Ponds
  B. A Well ^{F}6.0 Diameter, ^{F}4.8 Deep, such receives the Water from the Drein A the Water in which stands levell, with the Water, in the Piece of Water M
  C. A Bason ^{F}10.Diam^r. with a Stone Cylinder, which Plays from the Drein, or Waste of the Piece of Water, and runns of in the Drein D in which there is a Stop to keep up the Water, to fill the said Bason C to its proper levell
  NB. There are Plugs & Pipes to let out the Water both of B & C which discharges the Water, into the Drein D.
    And another Plug to keep the Water from coming back, out of the Pond M into B &c.
  D. A Bason ^{F}10.0 Diam^r. into which the Sluice G lets the Water, off the
  E. Pond
  F. The Drein thro' which the Water passes
  G.
  H. The wooden sluice, much out of order
  I. Drein from the Bason E to the Well I
  J. A Well ^{F}8.0 Diam^r. from which the Water passes away in the Drein K
  Q. [Question]: Why should there be any thing more than the Drein A the Well or Cesspool B arches over, leaving an Opening to be covered with a Flags to come at the Plugs
  C. Taken away and the Drein made good
  E. Taken away and the Drein made good to I & I either covered, or left open, with an Upright Fence.
Pen and ink with green (originally blue) and yellow washes (345 x 457mm)

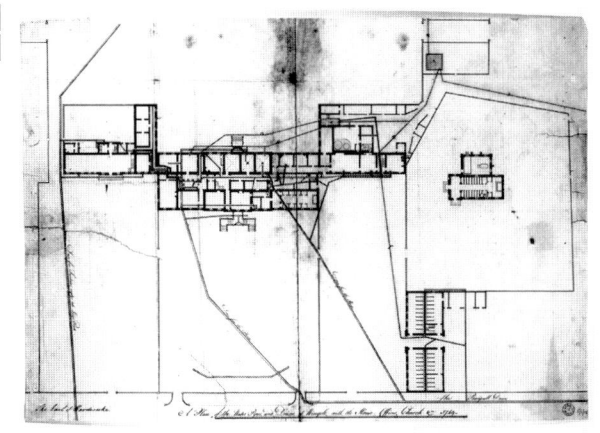

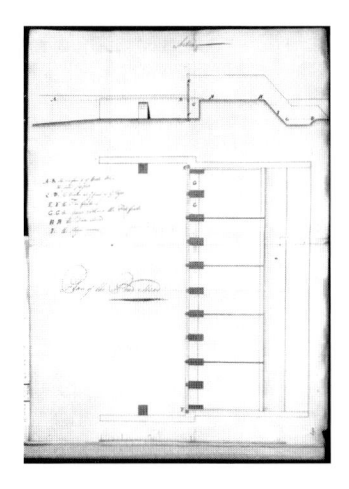

56 Drawing for a Spillway, *c.* 1767

British Library, Add. MS 35,679 fos.436 & 437
Inscr.: Fo.436 recto: 'Drawing of the Head of the pond in Avenal's Mead'. The drawing: 'Plan of the Pond Head' and 'Section', with various parts lettered. The lettered key reads:
  'A:B the Surface of the Water when the pond is full
  C:D the Water at the Slope
  E.F the Fish Grates
  G.G the Spaces without the Fish Grate
  H.H the Dam Head
  F. the Slope'
Pen and ink with grey wash (323 x 440mm)
Scale given
Watermark: Coronet, fleur-de-lis and LVG

This is described at fo.436 as 'Drawing of the Head of the Pond in Avenal's Mead'. It was over this spillway, between the middle and lower lakes, that the Chinese bridge was placed. Hitherto it has been assumed that Brown designed the bridge at Wimpole, but it must surely be assigned to Flitcroft on the strength of this drawing. In 1748 Flitcroft designed a not dissimilar structure—a water step or floodgate—as an integral part of a bridge for Hurst Lake (now Obelisk Pond) in Windsor Great Park, and, sometime before 1754, a wooden, hump-back Chinese bridge on Great Meadow Pond. Mary Delany (1700—88) refers to this in her diary for June 1757 as the 'piece of water and bridge so much talked of—and more cannot be said than it deserves', before describing it in the following terms: 'the bridge, which is made of timber, is only one arch, 164 feet wide from abutment to abutment; the workmanship is most curious, and any piece of wood that is decayed may be taken out and repaired without weakening the rest. Carriages of all sorts go over it every day, but it is desperately steep, and we walked over it'.[151] According to Lady Amabel Polwarth's Frog Service views (*Nos.92 & 95*) the Chinese bridge at Wimpole was originally of a steeper form—much like the Great Meadow Pond bridge.

Drawings by Henry Flitcroft for St. Andrew's Church

Flitcroft's commission in 1747 to rebuild the parish church of St. Andrew followed on from his remodelling of the Hall. What he produced was essentially an aisleless brick preaching box, with the relict Chicheley chapel attached to the north, perhaps the neo-Palladian estate church *par excellence*. The project is remarkably well documented, for not only does a complete set of eight, immaculately finished, contract drawings survive, but they are supported by a detailed description of the 'manner in which it is proposed to be Built, Finished and Furnished', and by itemised building accounts.[152] In the same year Flitcroft was appointed Master Mason and Deputy Surveyor of the King's Works, in succession to William Kent.

Flitcroft's church, particularly the west elevation, is certainly an accomplished if understated essay in neo-Palladianism and together with the grander, somewhat Gibbsian, St Giles-in-the-Fields (1731—4), London, for whose building he also contracted, it is his only surviving church commission. St Olave's (1738), his church in Southwark, is demolished; while his design of the same year for an Anglican church for Savannah, Georgia, USA, was not executed.

The rebuilding of St. Andrew's, Wimpole, appears to have taken about eighteen months. On February 20 1748 Flitcroft sent Lord Hardwicke 'plans, Elevations & Sections for your Church at Wimpole, consistent with Keeping up the Chichley Chapell', and a month later his detailed proposals followed.[153] The Wimpole parish records tell us that the 'Old Parish Church was [...] begun to be pulled down' on 25 March 1748, and that 'it was for the first time made use of for Divine Service on the 27th of August', 1749.[154] This met the terms of the agreement that 'the Whole Work [would be] finished before Midsumer Day 1749'.

The demolition work must in fact have begun somewhat later for the order of vestry for obtaining a faculty was not signed—by minister, church wardens and parishioners—until 28 March when it was recorded that 'the Parish Church of wimple is greatly out of Repairs' and that Lord Hardwicke had signalled his willingness to rebuild it at his own expense.[155] Flitcroft was to be paid £1,000 on completion. The 'Repairing and Clearing Chichley Chapple and moving the Bells and Hanging one' came to an additional £58 10s, but this was more than covered by the value of the lead remaining after the demolition of the medieval church. Kenton Couse, Flitcroft's assistant and his only known pupil, appears to have assisted Flitcroft in the supervision of the works at Wimpole. As we have seen, he was to continue to work at Wimpole after his master's death (*No.98*).

In a letter of October 1752 the antiquary William Stukeley, who was a friend of Flitcroft's, congratulated the Lord Chancellor on 'rebuilding your parochial church at Wimpole, a thing more beneficial to the commonwealth, & to mankind', adding 'I was extremely delighted with the sight & it afforded me an agreeable fund of meditation all the way home'.[156]

With the exception of the survey of the old church, the drawings, in pen, ink and grey wash, are all numbered (1 to 7), drawn to a common scale, on similarly sized, watermarked paper, and, perhaps for contractual reasons, are all flamboyantly signed 'H. Flitcroft'.

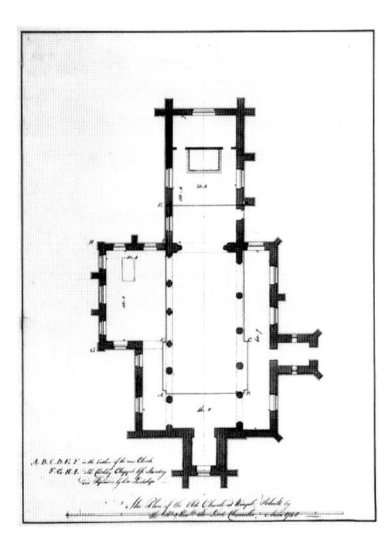

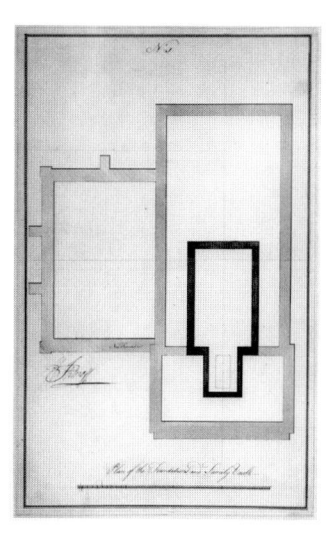

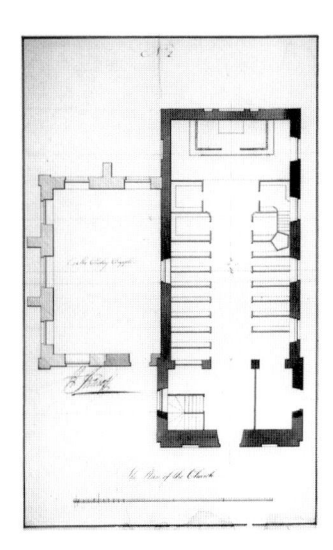

57 **Survey of the medieval church with the outline of the new church superimposed, 1748**

National Trust WIM/D/527
Inscr.: 'The Plan of the Old Church at Wimpole, Rebuilt by/the R^t. Honble. the Lord Chancellor. Anno 1748'; the key reads: 'A.B.C.D.E.F. is the Outline of the new Church/F.G.H.I. The Chichley Chapple left Standing and Repaired by his Lordship'
Pen and ink with grey wash (470 x 355mm)
Scale: 1 in: 10 ft
Watermark: Crown, Fleur-de-lis, I V G

Flitcroft's brief was to retain the Chicheley chapel, which contained the table tomb of Sir Thomas and Lady Dorothy Chicheley, whose position Flitcroft indicates, while demolishing the rest of the church 'levell with the Ground, & Lower, if the walls will easily come down'. The east end of the chancel, the south aisle and porch, three bays of the north aisle, the west end of the nave and the west tower were all taken down.

58 **Plan showing the foundations of the new church and the proposed position of the Family Vault: No.1**

National Trust WIM/D/522
Inscr.: 'No.1', 'Plan of the Foundation and Family Vault', and 'New Foundation'
Pen and ink with grey wash (465 x 290mm)

The new vault, shown beneath the western half of the church, was to be '20 feet long, 10 feet wide, and 7 feet high', and 'a proper Way to come at the Same' was to be provided, 'with Stone Cirb, and Covering under the Pavement, and to pave the said Vault with Brick on Edge'.

59 **Plan for the new Church: No.2**

National Trust WIM/D/523
Inscr.: 'No.2', 'The Plan of the Church'; 'Chichley Chapple', and the length and breadth of the nave, '48ft' and '24ft', indicated. Flap: 'My Lord's Gallery'
Pen and ink with grey wash (460 x 295mm)

The drawing includes a paper flap over the west end which shows the plan of the first-floor gallery. This served as the family pew, and for comfort's sake 'a Portland Stone Chimney piece, & Slab' were included in the south-west corner. The timber partition wall below the gallery, which created two lobbies, presumably allowed for the separate use of the west and south doors of the church—one by the family and its guests and the other by the parishioners.

Above the pews on the south side of the nave, Flitcroft proposed to build 'a Pentagon Pulpit, the Floor of which to be as high, as the top of the Pewing, with Steps up to D^o'. This plan also shows the position of the new door to the Chicheley chapel, which until the nineteenth century was to remain walled-off from the nave of the church.

A copy of this drawing, submitted for the purpose of obtaining a faculty, can be found in the Ely Diocesan Records (*No.65*).

60 **Elevation for the west front: No.3**

National Trust WIM/D/460
Inscr.: 'No.3', 'The West Front'
Pen and ink with grey wash (440 x 272mm)

This simple but pleasing elevation was built, and survives, exactly as proposed here. With its symmetrically arranged round-headed niches, it has something of the character of the central part of Lord Burlington's 'communication' or Link (*c*.1733) between Chiswick Villa and Old Chiswick House. The 'Stone Doorcases, and the West Window the Cornice all round, & two Pediments, the Window Cills & Cills to Nieches', also 'the Steps' were to be made 'of Portland Stone'.

Flitcroft contracted to 'Frame the Turrett and Dress it according to The Design with Strong Seasoned Yellow Deal' and to 'put up a Ball & Fane, which is to be Guilt'.

61 **Elevation for the south side: No.4**

National Trust WIM/D/524
Inscr.: 'No.4', 'The South Side'
Pen and ink with grey wash (273 x 440mm)

The western bay of the church, containing the family gallery, was also built in stone, but the body of the church, lit by four round-headed windows in the south wall, was constructed in brick. Brick earth was dug and fired locally according to Flitcroft's instruction. It seems, however, that the red brick we see today was to have been disguised. Elizabeth Anson (1725—60), Baron Hardwicke's eldest daughter, explains in a letter of June 1749 that Flitcroft had given her advice on the painting of brick to imitate stone, adding that the church at Wimpole was to be similarly treated.[157]

The windows were to be glazed 'with the best Crown Glass, in strong lead'. Michael Archer has suggested that Mr Minns, Flitcroft's glazier, responsible for the repair of the glass in the Chicheley Chapel, is likely to have been Richard Minns, Master Glazier to the Board of Works from 1744—61. A Minns senior and junior had been paid for glazing work done during the remodelling of the Hall.[158] The roof was to be covered with Westmorland slates, partly recycled from those already at Wimpole.

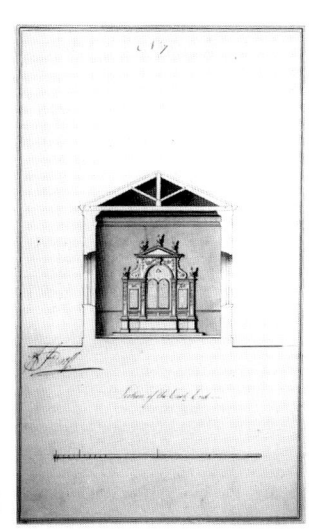

62 Elevation for the east end: No.5

National Trust WIM/D/554
Inscr.: 'No.5', 'The East End', signed 'Henry Flitcroft'
Pen and ink (440 x 275mm)
Watermark: Fleur-de-lis over LVC

Flitcroft provided interest and modelling to the east wall with a blind Venetian window. This was opened up in 1834—5 to allow for the insertion of a panel of stained glass, moved from the window above the south door (*No.229*).

63 Section south/north through the nave and north chapel (dotted), showing the gallery at the west end: No.6

National Trust WIM/D/461
Inscr.: 'No.6', and 'Section of the West End'
Pen and ink with grey wash (438 x 270mm)

The squat Tuscan columns supporting the 'Lord's Gallery' and its Ionic order were replaced in the late nineteenth century by piers capped with stiff-leaved Gothic ornament whose 'elephantiasis' left Nikolaus Pevsner 'bewildered'.[159]

Flitcroft contracted to 'make the Collumns, and Pillasters and Architrave over The Pillars, the Galery Front, with Balisters, and to Wainscot round the Walls of the Galery, to the bottom of the Windows, with good Yellow Deal'. The seventeenth-century roof of the Chicheley chapel, which Flitcroft shored-up, can be seen in section on the right-hand side of the drawing.

64 Section north/south through the chancel showing the reredos at the east end: No.7

National Trust WIM/D/462
Inscr.: 'No.7', and 'Section of the East End'
Pen and ink with grey wash (440 x 272mm)

Flitcroft agreed 'To make an Altar Piece of Deal, to be carved and painted, with the Commandments'. The altar piece, itemised separately, cost £57, of which the joiner's work accounted for £16, while that of the carver and painter amounted to £26 and £15 respectively. Although the architectural framework to Flitcroft's reredos is elaborate, with its simple Decalogue, flanked by the Lord's Prayer and Creed, it is severely orthodox in comparison to the one designed by Gibbs for the house Chapel, and its only nod to imagery is the Trinitarian triangle hovering above its centre.

65 Copy plan of the new church at Wimpole, with flap, 1748

Cambridge University Library, Ely Diocesan Records – EDR D3/1a/68 (D3/69/68)
Pen & ink with grey wash (441 x 291mm)

This is a copy of plan No.2, submitted to the Bishop of Ely on 28 March 1748 for the purpose of obtaining a faculty to take down and rebuild the church. The Bishop granted permission on 22 April.

Drawings for an Ice-House at Wimpole

66 Henry Flitcroft (attrib.). Plan and section for a thatched ice-house, *c*.1750

British Library, Add. MS 36278 M.3
Inscr.: The drawing is dimensioned and the 'arch' of the dome and the 'rafter' and 'thatch' over it are labelled in the section. The water-damaged, and in part illegible, key on the right reads:
'B
diam^r of ye doom	14-0
Ribs	8-0
diam^r of Outer Circle	21-0
diam^r of Iner Circle on the top of the Planking	12-0

K a pear in the Middle to Support the beam of the flore the Joysts to be Planked with Inch ½ oak Pland bored full of Large holes to Let out the weeping of the Ice upon which is to be laid faggots to keep the Ice Clear from it and straw over the out-side & at […] fill'd
L a Sink Stone to which the Pavement must be Inclined which Is to take of the weeping of the Ice'
A: B the Surface of the ground from whence it is to be sloped up with earth width […] To the Thatch drain made 9^{ln} wide'
At bottom left:
'[…] Plate
6 by 4
Small Circle Scantlings […]
At CC'
Pen and ink, with pencil (480 x 375mm)
Watermark: IV
Lit.: Beaman & Roaf (1990), p.217; Jackson-Stops (1992), p.45.

Neither the designer nor the date of the construction of this ice-house is documented but Gervase Jackson-Stops tentatively attributed the drawing to Henry Flitcroft; it most probably dates from the landscaping works of Robert Greening in the early 1750s. Although a small number of ice-houses were built in the seventeenth century, principally for the gardens of the royal palaces, the majority of the 3,000 or so examples known in the British Isles date from the mid-eighteenth (when an ice-house would certainly still have been considered a costly luxury) and the late nineteenth centuries. Philip Yorke, and Jemima, Marchioness Grey had an ice-house—supposedly dating to 1673—on their estate at Wrest Park, Bedfordshire, and it was perhaps this which inspired the Lord Chancellor to have one at Wimpole.

Greening's *c*.1752 proposals for the garden and park at Wimpole (*No.77*) show what appears to be a small igloo-like structure within a ring of trees at the northern end of the fir walk. The legend 'Ice House' marks the same feature on Robert Withers's estate survey (*No.220*) of 1815. A circular mound survives in the park at this spot (grid reference NG TL 33175126), at the northern end of what is now known as the 'One and a Half Avenue'. Benjamin Hare's map of 1638 (*No.1*) reveals that a post-mill had previously occupied this site. The RCHME's (1968) Inventory description suggested that the mound might originally have been a small motte, but this interpretation has now been discounted.

Having first commented on the parlous condition of the nearby Hill House, the Rev. James Plumptre (1711—1832) noted, in his manuscript *A Journal of a Tour to the Source of the River Cam made in July 1800*, that the ice-house at Wimpole was in a poor state: 'We took our way along the fir walk to the Ice-house which is likewise beginning to fall to decay. It is sheltered by a small grove of Chestnuts which are excellent trees for forming a thick shade'.[160] Five years later the artist John Claude Nattes (1765–1822) was to make a spirited sketch of the building (*No.224*).

The ice-house shown in this drawing conforms to a fairly standard arrangement: an entrance and passageway leading to a chamber, drained below and vaulted over, and protected from the heat of the sun by an insulated roof. The earliest known ice-houses were usually thatched but the use of this material is not a reliable indicator of age: the insulating advantages, relative cheapness and picturesque quality of thatch clearly continued to appeal in both the eighteenth and nineteenth centuries, despite the increasing prevalence of brick-domed ice-houses.

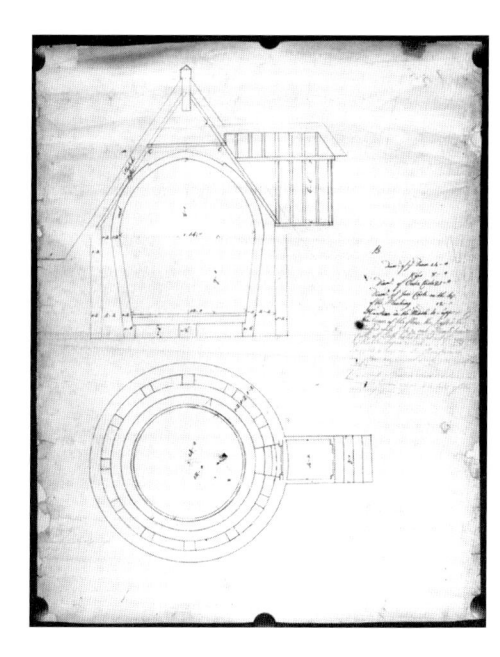

The Wimpole design was intended to exploit a gently sloping site, with the floor level of the entrance passage shown on the right of the drawing higher than the ground level to the left. This was partly achieved by 'sloping up' the earth to the thatch on one side. The site was presumably chosen because its elevation and the underlying chalk offered the possibility of good drainage, and because it was part way between the fish ponds or lakes, from which the ice would have been taken, and the house (some 500 yards to the south-east), to which ice for desserts or for the chilling of wine—or indeed cold-preserved meat and fish—might be taken. An ice-house of this size, the chamber fourteen feet in diameter at its widest point, would probably have contained several tonnes of ice.

A new ice-house was eventually constructed at Wimpole between 1825 and 1829. Perhaps John Soane, who designed a number of ice-houses for other clients, advocated its replacement. On 24 December 1825 the gardener James Dale was paid £3 5s 10d 'for digging out foundations for new Snow House'. In 1828 an estimate was submitted for:

> contracts, to brick an Ice Well, or House, of the dimentions [sic] as under; 20 feet long x 12 feet wide in the clear - the depth to be 11 feet, and from the top of this 11 feet High, of wall, an arch of the thickness of nine inches. Brick work is to be thrown or made. The under Side of the center of such arch is to be 6 feet above the top of the 11 feet high side and end walls, with an oval or circular hole of a size to admit of ice or snow, of which the well may be filled with and a Door or wicket in the East end of the well for the purpose of obtaining the ice or snow for use.[161]

In February 1829 Thomas French submitted a bill for £10 'for taking down the brickwork of Old Icehouse, & Cleaning & Stacking up the brickes', and in November 1829 the bricklayer J. French was paid £45 2s by way of an advance for 'the new Icehouse'.[162]

Designs for, and views of, the Gothic Folly at Wimpole

As a text-book exemplar of the architecture of the Gothic Revival, the sham ruins at Wimpole appear in almost every book on the English landscape garden. The ruins occupy a commanding position on Johnson's Hill in the north park at Wimpole, where they serve both as a general eye-catcher glimpsed across the estate and as the focal point to the carefully contrived axial *clairvoyée* which leads the eye northwards to the heart of Lancelot 'Capability' Brown's naturalistic parkland. Although the folly was conceived in 1749, building work did not start until *c*.1768, the delay resulting in the involvement of two generations of patrons and architects.

The Wimpole folly is one of a small family of similar, picturesque structures which the gentleman architect Sanderson Miller (1717—80) designed for a circle of friends and connoisseurs of the 'Gothick'. Most celebrated amongst these was the gothic castle he designed in 1747 for Sir Thomas Lyttleton's Park at Hagley, Worcestershire, which Horace Walpole declared 'bore the true rust of the Barons' wars'.[163] Hardwicke so admired the building that he resolved to have a similar ornament for the park at Wimpole. His interest was immediately relayed to the architect:

> You great genius's [sic] in Architecture must expect to be importuned by your friends, of which I am going to give you a Proof. My Lord Chancellour told me, in a conversation I had with him lately, that he wanted to see the Plan of my Castle, having a mind to Build one at Wimple himself. Upon further Enquiry I found it would be better for him not to Copy mine, but have one upon something like the same Idea, but differing in many respects, particularly in this, that he wants no House or even room in it, but mearly the Walls and Semblence of an Old Castle to make an object from his House. At most he only desires to have a staircase carried up one of the Towers, and a leaded gallery half round it to stand in, and view the Prospect. It will have a fine Wood of Firrs for a backing behind it and will stand on an Eminence at a proper distance from his House. I ventured to promise that you should draw one for his Lordship that would be fitt for his Purpose, because I thought it would be agreable to you to do him this pleasure, and because I am sure nobody else can do it so well […] With regard to the Dimensions of my Ld. Chancellor's Castle, you are not confined, but may make it of just what Height & Breadth you think fitt. He desired me to make his Compliments to you, and to say he would take it as a great Favour if you would sketch it out for him as soon as you conveniently can.[164]

A month later Lyttleton wrote again: 'My Ld. Chancellour desires me to Return you his thanks for the Castle. He seems mighty well satisfied with it, but says he shall Deferr the Building it till next year, and consider it upon the spot when he goes to Wimple this summer'. In March the following year Hardwicke wrote to thank Miller for his 'kind attention' explaining that there was no urgency in the matter, adding:

> 'As the building of this Castle requires no great haste, I think there will be no great harm if it remains in the air a few months longer. Therefore there will be no occasion to send Hitchcox to Wimple yet; but, when your other occasions shall call you to this Town, I shall take it as a particular favour if you will be at the trouble of seeing you here, by which means the whole may be more fully understood'.[165]

Remarkably, four drawings, almost certainly by Miller, survive at Wimpole (*Nos.*68 to 71). Visits to Wimpole are recorded in both of Miller's surviving diaries, for the years 1749—50 and 1756—7, and the brief entries help to clarify the sequence of events at this early stage of planning and design. During a three-day visit in September 1750, Miller made various notes: 'Survey'd Ground for the Castle & rode in the Pk 3h'; in the evening 'Looking over plans of the Castle &c.'; and 'Came f^{m} Wimple at 7 after sketching out the Castle'.

Miller subsequently described his visit to Charles Lyttleton, the Dean of Exeter, observing: 'His Lordship, by dint of good sense has done every thing which suits the character of the place. I find about half the plan I sent him will fit the place very well, and if it is well executed it will be a great improvement'.[166] The idea that the folly might be called Chicheley Castle was made by Elizabeth Yorke, but this conceit—worthy of Horace Walpole for the Chicheleys' moated manor house bore little resemblance to Miller's battlemented tower—did not stick.

For more than fifteen years no further progress was made, until the improving energies of Philip Yorke, 2nd Earl of Hardwicke, and his wife Jemima, Marchioness Grey, came to bear on Wimpole in the later 1760s. The idea of the hill-top ruins was resurrected as part of 'Capability' Brown's orchestration of the northward extension of the park. Brown appears to have assumed responsibility for the construction of the folly, with expert help from the Cambridge joiner, architect, antiquary and pioneering scholar of gothic, James Essex (1722—84). On 30 October 1767 Lady Amabel Yorke, the eldest daughter of the house, wrote:

> I ought in justice to afford as much paper to the great Mr Brown, who has been two days here surveying his Improvements, [which] as yet furnish no great matter for Description, nor the Tower neither, tho' that our architect Mr Essex promises will make a figure next year. The Ground and the Water will go on shortly I doubt.[167]

In 1772 Jemima complained to her daughter:

> The Tower is better for being raised, but the additions Mr. Brown has quite changed from our plan, though he undertook to follow it and said he liked it. That is, he has 'Unpicturesqued' it by making it a mere continuous solid object, instead of a Broken one. The wall—which is still going on—is continued entire at the bottom from the whole Tower to the Broken one, and is to be fractured only in the upper half of the Gateway, which is, I believe, to resemble our design. However as it makes altogether a greater object it won't do ill, and the upper part of wall, if well done, may yet be sufficiently varied.[168]

Brown and Essex may or may not have 'unpicturesqued' the folly, but there are certainly substantive differences between Miller's original sketches, which are presumably what the marchioness refers to by 'our plan', and the finished building as depicted in Hardwicke's celebratory engraving (*No.*72). Despite the involvement of the scholarly James Essex, Miller's original proposal was, as Jackson-Stops has noted, perhaps more 'believable as the ruin of a medieval castle, with proper overhanging machicolations, cracked masonry rather than smooth ashlar, an absence of string courses and fewer windows and arrow-loops'.[169]

Essex's knowledge of medieval architecture was essentially of ecclesiastical rather than castellar gothic. But the final proportions of the Wimpole tower give it a more elegant character than its somewhat squat counterpart at Hagley. The Hagley tower had benefited associationally and materially from the robbing and re-use of window tracery from the nearby site of Halesowen Abbey, and a few earlier fragments were similarly incorporated into the new building at Wimpole. A carved stone mitred head, possibly fourteenth century in date, was set above the north door of the middle tower, together with a fake medieval tablet inscribed with dog-latin: 'STRIKEIVS ABBA. CROYLANDIE AD 946 FVNDATOR ACADEMIARVM CANTABRIGIE ET STANDFORDIE'.[170]

Despite Marchioness Grey's initial reservations about the tower, her daughter, Lady Amabel Polwarth, chose it as a subject for two of the topographical drawings of the Wimpole landscape that she sent to Josiah Wedgwood for inclusion in the great 944-piece dinner and dessert service made in 1773—4 for Catherine the Great, Empress of Russia (*see No.85 and Nos.92–6*).

The folly also found favour with other members of the family. On 7 September 1774 Agneta Yorke wrote to Jemima: 'The ruins have a noble effect from every part where they meet the eye; and are of such a magnitude and so well executed that tho' I saw them begun and finished yet I can scarce persuade myself that they are artificial'.[171] The dazzling white of the clunch—some perhaps freshly dug, some re-used and perhaps redressed—must, however, have remained an uncomfortable distraction in the landscape for several years, although by 6 August 1785 Mary Yorke was able to write reassuringly to Jemima: 'The ruin is beautiful and will grow every year more so, as the ivy comes about it. The colour of the stone, however, already begins to mellow'.[172]

William Hawkes has established that Miller, who had remained on intimate terms with the Yorkes, visited Wimpole one last time in July—August 1775, presumably to see the completed sham ruins that had been his brainchild twenty six years earlier. Apart from the damning verdict of the Hon. John Byng (1743—1813), later 5th Viscount Torrington—he thought them 'foolish, fantastic, mock ruins, unlike every thing they wou'd wish to represent'—other contemporary visitors generally admired the Folly.[173] In 1800 the Rev. James Plumptre noted: 'The tint of this building is very much mellowed by time, and the ruin has a very good and natural effect. I have nowhere seen so good an imitation'.[174] Humphry Repton suggested that the folly might be adapted to house one of the estate labourers.

The 2nd Earl of Hardwicke and his wife shared a delight in gardens and garden buildings and the erection of the folly should be seen within the context of their wider aspiration to improve the landscape at Wimpole and to furnish it with interesting and appropriate buildings. The folly, though dominant because of its axial placement, was intended to complement the Prospect House or Hill House designed by James 'Athenian' Stuart (*Nos.86–9*). Hardwicke saw the two buildings as a didactic 'contrast between ancient and modern times'. An almost identical contrast was provided in the park at Hagley by Sanderson Miller's gothic castle and Stuart's Greek Revival temple which was based on the Theseion in Athens.

Drawing by Henry Flitcroft (here attrib.) for a Gothic Eyecatcher

67 Elevation and plan for a gothic eyecatcher, *c.1749*

National Trust WIM/D/450
Pen and ink, with grey wash (407 x 320mm)
Scale given
Watermark: Fleur-de-lis in crowned cartouche above IVG
Lit. & repr.: Adshead (1998), pp.76–84, fig.8.
Exh.: Fitzwilliam Museum, Cambridge (1984), p.36, cat. no.70.

It is not clear how this drawing, for a somewhat rectilinear and only very slightly ruinous eye-catcher, with octagonal corner turrets, crenellated parapet and a large window to the central, projecting bay, fits into the story of Wimpole's Gothic folly.

Thomas Cocke has suggested that it may be by James Essex, who appears to have assisted 'Capability' Brown in the construction of the folly. Does it, however, have the spirit and scholarly plausibility that characterise Essex's work? If indeed it does date from the late 1760s or early 1770s, 'Capability' Brown might be considered a more likely author, for the drawing is not unlike his relatively pedestrian designs for garden buildings and lodges.

The drawing is, however, more strikingly like those produced by Henry Flitcroft for the rebuilding of the church at Wimpole in 1748—a matter of months before the Lord Chancellor's sudden enthusiasm for Sanderson Miller's tower at Hagley. The meticulous, hard-lined draughtsmanship, distinctive grey wash and shading, together with the characteristics of the scale bar suggest that Flitcroft, an otherwise dyed-in-the-wool neo-Palladian, might be its author. The wove paper and watermark are identical to those of Flitcroft's survey drawing of the medieval church (*No.57*).

Is it possible that this scheme for a Gothic stage flat is a precursor to Miller's scheme for a castellated folly, and that the idea of an ornamental ruin suggested itself when the greater part of the parish church was demolished, and quantities of time-worn clunch and dressed and carved stone became available? Certainly we know that Miller was to have had the use of the stone from the 'Old Church in the Parish'. By the mid-eighteenth century, ecclesiastical fragments mined from ruined abbeys and abandoned churches were often incorporated in garden and park buildings and were valued for their romantic effect.

The building of mock-ruinous churches was somewhat rarer, but precedents and parallels can be found in the gothic façades and screens built at Shotover, Oxfordshire, for James Tyrrel; at Fawley Court, Buckinghamshire, for John Freeman before 1732; and at Shobdon, Hereford, where major elements from the demolished Norman church were recycled to create the hill-top arches. Having seen Miller's powerful, castellated folly at Hagley, Hardwicke may have decided that he could do better than erect this awkward Carpenters' Gothic proposal.

Drawings by Sanderson Miller (1717—80) for the Gothic Folly

68 Elevation drawing A, *c*.1749—51

National Trust WIM/D/452
Inscr.: 'A' in red ink at the top, and in pencil at the bottom
Pen and sepia ink with pencil (205 x 325mm)
Watermark: illegible
Lit. & repr.: Adshead (1998), fig.2.
Exh.: Sir John Soane's Museum, London (1999), pp.19–20, cat. no.5.

The sham ruins as built are V-shaped in plan—each of the points of the 'V' terminating in a tower—an idea that Miller seems to have established from the outset. This drawing appears to be a suggestion for the south-west facing side. The shattered tower at left, with its interior surface and floor joist sockets exposed, corresponds with similar features shown at far left in Miller's perspective (*No.71*).

These inked drawings and their carefully pencilled backdrops of trees have a specificity that distinguishes them from most of the doodles that can be found on the backs of Miller's letters, but they share something of the character of his sketches for the ruinous towers at Edge Hill and Hagley.[175]

69 Elevation drawing B, *c*.1749—51

National Trust WIM/D/453
Inscr.: 'b' in pencil
Pen and sepia ink with pencil (170 x 240mm)
Lit. & repr.: Adshead (1998), fig.3.

This drawing shows a section of curtain walling, containing an archway and three gothic windows with trefoil-headed lights. This corresponds to the inner wall that Miller shows in his perspective drawing (*No.71*) behind the *enceinte*—presumably he intended the additional illusion of there being a hall or chapel within the defensive bounds of the castle. The idea of this secondary 'scenic drop' was perpetuated in the scheme of the late 1760s.

70 Elevation drawing C, *c*.1749—51

National Trust WIM/D/454
Inscr.: 'C' in red ink
Pen and sepia ink with pencil (214 x 352mm)
Lit. & repr.: Adshead (1998), fig.4.
Exh.: Sir John Soane's Museum, London (1999), pp.19–20, cat.no.6.

This third elevation appears to show part of the curtain wall, engaged with towers at either end with a gateway flanked by arrow loops partway along its length. The drawing might otherwise be an alternative to 'B'. The pencil additions include three armorial shields above the gateway—elements that were to be incorporated in the south-west side of the folly's curtain wall.

71 Perspective drawing for the folly at Wimpole, c.1749—51

National Trust WIM/D/455
Pen and sepia ink with grey wash over pencil (190 x 275mm)
Lit. & repr.: Dickins & Stanton (1910), pl. facing p.272; Dixon Hunt & Willis (1975), pl.31, p.29; Jackson-Stops (1979:1), p.45; Souden (1991),p.45; Adshead (1998), fig.5.
Exh.: Colnaghi, London (1987), p.60, cat. 332; Jackson-Stops (1992), pp.86–7, cat.59; Sir John Soane's Museum, London (1999), pp.19–20, cat.4.

Although their final interpretation would be different, all the essential ingredients of Wimpole's sham ruins are embodied in this drawing—the general form of the ruin's central tower, the artfully slighted curtain wall which links it to the two smaller bastions to the north-east and north-west, and the use of large, traceried windows.

This is an accomplished perspective drawing rendered convincingly in light and shade, and clearly made for the purpose of presentation. The pencil set-up lines, showing the station and vanishing points, are clearly visible, while the geometry of the hidden base of each tower has been indicated with dotted lines. Although different in type to the elevation drawings, the similarity between the structure of the fir trees in this perspective rendering and those sketched in drawing 'b' suggest that they are by the same hand. Miller was taught perspective drawing by Sir Roger Newdigate (1719—1806), in exchange for a lesson on gothic arches, and when occasion demanded he was capable of producing competent drawings.

Just as in the built version, where a wall pierced by a large traceried window (as if lighting a chapel or great hall) lies within the encircling curtain, Miller here draws a wall, inside the castle, which contains the remnants of three windows. In front of this, the castle wall is interrupted by the remains of another structure, square in plan, that was perhaps supposed to be a gatehouse or porter's lodge. A slight pencil sketch in perspective of an arch within a section of walling appears at the bottom right of the sheet.

72 Anonymous. View of the Gothic Tower at Wimpole, 1777

National Trust WIM/D/559
Inscr.: 'GOTHIC TOWER at WIMPLE'. The accompanying four-stanza verse of twelve rhyming couplets, by Daniel Wray (1701—83) reads as follows:

When Henry stemmed Iernes stormy Flood,
And bon'd to Britains yoke her savage brood;
When by true courage and false zeal impell'd
Richard encamp'd on salems palmy field
On Towers like these Earl, Baron, Vavasor,
Hung high their Banners, floating in the air.
Free, hardy, proud, they brav'd their feudal Lord
And try'd their rights by ordeal of the Sword,
Now full board with Christmas plenty crown'd
Now ravag'd and opprefs'd the country round.
Yet Freedoms cause once rais'd the civil broil,
And Magna Charta clos'd the glorious toil.
Spruce modern Villas different Scenes afford;
The Patriot Baronet, the courtier Lord,
Gently amus'd, now waste the Summers day
In Book-room, Print-room, or in Ferme Ornée
While Wit, Champain, and Pines and Poetry,
Virtu and Ice the genial Feast supply.
But hence the Poor are cherish'd, artists fed,
And Vanity relieves in Bountys stead.
Oh might our age in happy concert join
The manly Virtues of the Norman Line,
With the true Science and just Taste which raise
High in each useful Art these Modern Days

Engraving (405 x 610mm)
Lit. & repr.: Jackson-Stops (1979:2), pp.658–61, fig.12; Cocke (1984), cat.68, p.60; Adshead (1998), fig.1; Menuge & Cooper (2001), fig.4.
Exh.: Fitzwilliam Museum, Cambridge (1984); 'An English Arcadia 1600—1990' (1992), pp.86–89, cat.60; Sir John Soane's Museum, London (1999), fig.5, p.11, and pp.19–20, cat. 7.

This engraved view shows the completed folly on the brow of Johnson's Hill in the north park. Framed by trees, the folly is backed by a stand of New England pines, and set off by a crescent-shaped ditch filled with water whose size and effect has been exaggerated. The accompanying verse, its meaning opaque in parts and which Jackson-Stops describes as a 'mixture of high romanticism and playful cynicism', was first published in *The Annual Register [...] for the year 1775*.[176] It serves as a mock-elegy for a glorious medieval past in which a chivalrous, provincial nobility struggled for political liberty—an interpretation that sat happily with Whig ideology and with eighteenth-century notions of associationism.

William Hawkes records that a John Jeffreys wrote to Sanderson Miller in November 1777, explaining: 'I have a Print to show you, which will give you pleasure. It is of the ruin at Wimpole done from your old Plan, and finely engraved by Stewart, with a copy of verses under the print written by my brother, Mr. Wray'; Hardwicke sent Sanderson Miller a copy the following month. Miller made his last visit to Wimpole in 1775, and was no doubt delighted to see the ruins finally realised.[177]

On 18 February 1778, Hardwicke sent a copy of the engraving to William Legge, 2nd Earl of Dartmouth (1731—1801), then Lord Privy Seal, with the accompanying note:

In return for the marks of affection from you, I beg leave to send your Lordship the print of a Gothic Chateau—a ruin, which I have erected at Wimpole. Perhaps the views may strike you as no bad contrast between ancient and modern times. They are by a friend, I furnished the hint. I am, as a companion to this antique, engraving a modern italian loggia, which I have set up at Wimpole, under the auspices of Mr. Stewart. It shall be sent to your Lordship when finished.[178]

A reduced copy, entitled 'GOTHIC FOLLY at WIMPLE', and without the verse, was published by Fielding and Walker in March 1781—presumably as a pendant to the engraving of James 'Athenian' Stuart's Hill House (*No.90*). The names of neither artist nor engraver are known. It seems plausible, however, that the Hill House view, engraved by Daniel Lerpinière, is after a lost drawing by Stuart. Might the architect also have drawn, and Lerpinière engraved, the view of the folly—Jeffrey's witness that it was 'finely engraved by Stewart' perhaps means after Stuart's preparatory drawing?

Wray's verse had a second public airing when it was published in *The Gentleman's Magazine* in 1779.[179] Wray's biographer, George Hardinge, who also reproduces it, noted 'when Mr. Wray wrote the following Inscription I have not ascertained. Short as it is, it makes me lament that so lively a vein has been so negligent of its treasures'. Wray's joke to Miller that he might discover in the poem 'pieces of older and better versifyers' perhaps suggests that this classical scholar, who Hardinge says was 'very fond of quoting Latin verses from classical authors', and who contributed to the Yorke brothers' pseudonymous and fictitious correspondence of the Peloponnesian War, Athenian Letters (London, 1741—3), recycled various lines from ancient poetry, but it has too something of the flavour of Alexander Pope's *Essay on Man*.

73 Anonymous. View of the Gothic Tower at Wimpole, 1781

Author's Collection
Inscr.: 'GOTHIC TOWER at WIMPLE'
Engraving (185 x 220mm)

This smaller version was engraved for inclusion in *The Westminster Magazine* for 1781. The engraving was folded to fit within the magazine's small format. But for a more animatedly clouded sky, this view is essentially the same as the larger version.

Topographical drawings by William Stukeley (1687—1765)

These two spirited ink sketches, made by the celebrated antiquary William Stukeley, record the axial views—to the north and south of the house—that could be had from the windows of the first floor gallery. The circumstances of Stukeley's visit to Wimpole on 8 October 1747 are not recorded, but a diary entry for 8 September reads: 'I paid a visit to Lord Chancellor at Wimpole. His lordship has built a good deal of it, and repaired the rest, and rendered it a compleat and noble seat. A fine chapel painted by Sir James Thornhill. The park is grand. I admired the parterras, or flower garden'.[180] Wimpole was not new to Stukeley, however, for in the Earl of Oxford's day he had consulted the great Bibliotheca Wimpoleana, and its library-keeper Humfrey Wanley, on the subject of ancient English dress.

Stukeley and Lord Hardwicke appear to have been well acquainted. Hardwicke at one time offered the clergyman the living of St. Mary's, Stamford. For his part, Stukeley dedicated the first volume of his *Palaeographia Britannica or Discourses on Antiquities in Britain* (1743—52) to the Lord Chancellor. This comprised an account of the extraordinary cave discovered beneath the market square in Royston in 1742, and triggered off what was to be an ill-tempered and long-running dispute with the Rev. Charles Parkin of Oxborough, Norfolk, about its origins and purpose. Stukeley's second offering on the subject, his 1746 defence against 'the Calumny of Mr. Parkin', was also addressed to Lord Hardwicke. In 1749 Stukeley printed a sheet of verses 'called a philosophical hymn on Christmas day, inscribed to Lady Hardwick [*sic*]'. And a surviving letter from Stukeley to the Chancellor, written in a familiar vein, includes congratulations on the rebuilding of the parish church at Wimpole.[181]

Stukeley's interests were astonishingly eclectic. In addition to his record of ancient and medieval sites and objects are drawings of country seats and prospects of their parks; parterres, cascades and grottoes seem particularly to have appealed to him—these two drawings of Wimpole are of that ilk.

74 Sketch of the Great Avenue to the south of the house, 1747

Bodleian Library, MS Top. Gen d14 fo. 48 recto
Inscr.: 'View of the grand avenue, Wimpole hall. oct.8. 1747'
Pen & ink over pencil set-up lines (133 x 183mm)
Lit. & repr.: Phibbs (1980), p.20.

The trees shown here in Charles Bridgeman's avenue would have been twenty-five years old when Stukeley visited Wimpole. The courtyard, in the foreground, appears to be separated from the landscape beyond by a ha-ha, interrupted and gated in two places to east and west of the central axis. This arrangement has been attributed to the landscape gardener Robert Greening on the evidence of his plans for Wimpole (*Nos.77 & 78*) and the topographical view (*No.80*) attributed to him. Stukeley's drawing, however, predates Greening's involvement at Wimpole by some five years.

Either Greening's authorship of these features must be called into question, or, as may be suggested by other evidence, the date of Greening's initial involvement at Wimpole may be earlier than previously thought. The curving railing screen shown in Bridgeman's drawings projecting southwards into the park, and whose central opening perhaps accommodated Tijou's relocated screen, may never have been realised, or may have been dismantled before 1747. The large trees shown here on the far right-hand side form part of the grove associated with the water garden which Dr Stratford had pleaded should be retained by Bridgeman.

75 Sketch of the parterre garden to the north of the house, 1747

Bodleian Library, MS Top. Gen d14 fo. 47 verso
Inscr.: 'View of the parterre garden Wimpole hall. oct.8. 1747'
Pen and ink over pencil set-up lines (130 x 205mm)
Lit. & repr.: Phibbs (1980), p.20; Laird (1999), p.117, fig.65.

This shows, if in skeletal form, the surviving elements of the formal gardens—the parterres, the central, circular fountain basin, and the axial vista to the north flanked by piers—established by Lord Radnor. Stukeley struggles to render in perspective the arrangement of the twelve plats that are recorded in the 1728 sketch plan made by Jacques Fongereau (*No.42*). Both drawings show that the walls, recorded in Bridgeman's plan, that divided the north gardens into three compartments had been removed. The planting to the north of the fountain has changed dramatically in the forty years since the engraving of Kip's view; Mark Laird suggests that these groves of trees were made up of limes and fir under-planted with laburnum. Despite the bosky character of these groves it should have been possible to see them from Stukeley's station point; he does not record them, however.

The Catalogue

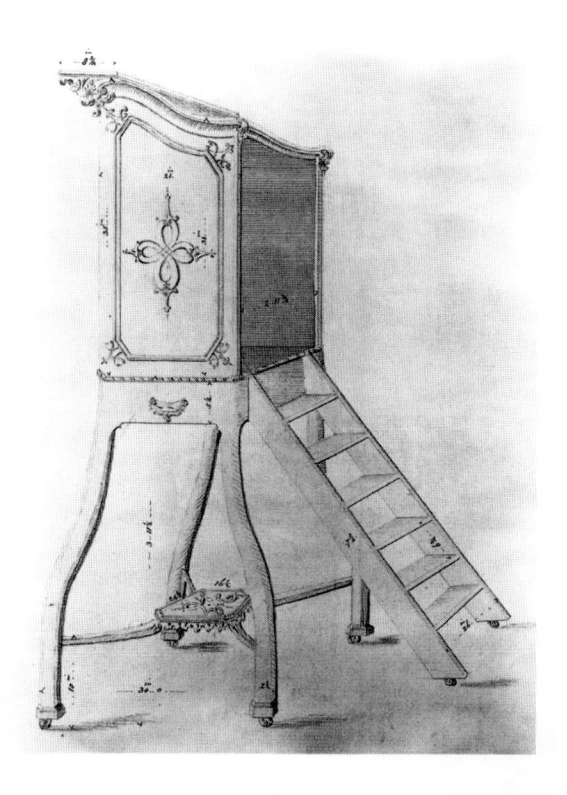

Furniture design by Henry Keene (1726—76)

76 Design for a set of Library Steps, c.1750

Victoria & Albert Museum, E.919-1921
Inscr.: 'Library Steps, at L^d. Hardwickes at Wimple. Wain^s.' [ie. wainscot]; various measurements given
Pen and ink (229 x 178mm)
Lit. & repr.: Ward-Jackson (1984), cat.189; Collard (1990), pp.34–38, fig.1.

This design for an elegant set of library steps of pulpit form corresponds almost exactly to the library steps that survive at Wimpole. Frances Collard notes that the practical requirements of steps, platform and book-rest are here ingeniously combined to produce an attractive piece of furniture. She suggests that Keene's expertise in designing Gothic Revival furniture may in part be attributable to his exposure to Gothic forms during his thirty-year-long surveyorship of Westminster Abbey and to his various collaborations with Sanderson Miller. Keene designed Gothic furniture for the Gothic folly at Hagley and perhaps the intention had been that he would provide similar pieces for the Wimpole folly.

Collard further speculates that Keene may have prepared this design for inclusion in the first edition of Thomas Chippendale's *The Gentleman and Cabinet-Maker's Director* (1754), but, for whatever reason, it was instead made use of for Wimpole.

Drawings by Robert Greening (d.1758) for the Gardens and Park at Wimpole (77–80)

Robert Greening was, with his brothers Thomas (c.1710—57) and John (c.1715—70), one of three gardening sons born to Thomas Greening (1684—1757).[182] The elder Thomas Greening owned a nursery at Brentford, Middlesex. This was a strategic location that enabled him to supply plants and trees to the gardens of the royal residences, great houses and villas that decorated the Thames between Chiswick and Windsor. As a nurseryman he was equally well-placed and qualified to provide advice to the owners of those gardens.

Some confusion remains about the roles of the respective family members, and this is particularly true of Thomas senior and junior. The elder Thomas worked for the 1st Duke of Newcastle at Claremont, Surrey, his son John becoming the duke's head gardener and steward in 1751. In the same year John was elevated to the position of gardener to King George II at Hampton Court. In 1738 either Thomas senior (then fifty four) or junior (twenty eight) was appointed gardener to George II at Richmond, and in 1754—it is more likely to have been Thomas junior—assumed responsibility for Kensington Gardens and St. James's Park. Robert, for his part, served as head gardener to Princess Augusta at Kew.

The Greenings became Lancelot 'Capability' Brown's foremost rivals in the gardening world—in addition to discharging their royal responsibilities, they provided designs, horticultural advice, and presumably trees, to a number of landowners. David Jacques argues that with the deaths of Thomas senior and junior in 1757 and Robert's in the following year, the way was left clear for Brown to achieve pre-eminence in his field.[183] Royal preferment was only to come to Brown—later than many thought was his due—when he succeeded John, the last surviving gardening Greening, as Master Gardener at Hampton Court in 1764.

Robert Greening's first documented involvement at Wimpole is dated September 1752, and this is consequently the date that has been given to the three plans and one topographical drawing attributed to him. It has been argued that, during the first ten years at Wimpole, Baron Hardwicke quite naturally concentrated his efforts on the house, modernising it externally and remodelling its interiors to suit his family's needs, and that only thereafter did he turn his attention to the gardens and wider landscape. But a letter written by the Duke of Newcastle from Wimpole suggests that by September 1751 landscaping works of some sort were already in train there:

> I rode out all yesterday morning, & was greatly surprised to see a charming fine agreable place & Park. There are very pretty Hills, wood enough, & almost all well disposed, a pretty <u>little</u> Gravel Road almost all round it. & upon the whole a delightful comforatable thing. There is one thing wanting, but that I hope will be in time, the laying the park down well, & roling, & getting a fine sward. Ld Chancelor has done a vast deal, & well. It is a most convenient comforatable House; with Rooms enough, & all well fitted up, some extreamly so; It <u>would</u> hold a great family, & very agreeably.[184]

It is even possible that Newcastle may have recommended the Greening family to Hardwicke. The Lord Chancellor would, however, have already been aware of their work for in 1749 the Duke of Cumberland wrote to him describing 'my several new improvements' at Cumberland Lodge, Windsor Great Park; both Henry Flitcroft and the Greenings undertook work for

Wimpole Architectural Drawings

him there in the 1740s.[185]

Robert Greening's principal role at Wimpole was to sweep away the then unfashionable formality of the Earl of Radnor's late-seventeenth-century gardens, whose broad outline had survived Charles Bridgeman's wider landscape interventions of the 1720s. As we have seen, the appearance of the garden parterres and central fountain that Greening banished is recorded both in the plan sketch made by Jacques Fongereau in 1728 and in a topographical sketch made by William Stukeley in 1747 (*Nos.42 & 75*). Greening laid the area to lawn, and edged it with island beds of laurel and other shrubs. He retained the central vista northwards to Johnson's Hill—the intended site of Sanderson Miller's castellated folly—but planted up other views, such as that eastwards to the great medieval barn shown in Kip's engraving (*No.3*). Greening's proposals appear to have followed closely the advice contained in an anonymous memorandum of October 1752 entitled 'Hints from Mr S. about alterations in the Garden':

> To take away the Parterre, & the old Shrubbery or Wilderness work beyond it, & to turn all that part of the Garden into a Lawn, with a piece of Gravel extending from the Grass Margin before the House to the Corners of the Wings.
> To raise the Ground a little gently on the left Side, so as to give the Lawn some appearance of a Vally, with proper Drains to carry off the water.
> On the Rise on the left-side to make a Screen of Wood to hide the wall of the Barn; & in [...] to give a ground appearance of Rising on the Side, to begin with Low Shrubs, Laurrels [...] &c., & so rise gradually with Cyprus, New England Pines & afterwards [...] trees to conceal the Barn; and to bring that Screen forward so as to take of sight of the wall of Pear Trees; which may—a little distance from the [...] side to the Kitchen Garden Dorr, &c.
> To plant nothing in the middle of the Lawn; but only sides some Shrubbs as Laurels, Laurestinas, & Syringas may be admitted, but Evergreens & Grass.[186]

Jackson-Stops has suggested that 'Mr S' may have been the poet and gardener William Shenstone (1714—63).[187] But the fact that Shenstone and Sanderson Miller, then advising Hardwicke, were bitter rivals may cast doubt on this possibility. Robert Greening's 'Instructions for Mr Bird' of the previous month, September 1752, had described in detail the various tasks that were to be undertaken in order to effect the proposed improvements at Wimpole.[188] Greening explains to John Bird, Hardwicke's agent, how a new fosse or ha-ha should best be formed, and how to dispose of the surplus earth. These instructions, and those for the training of vines against a trellis that was to be set against a hot wall in the new kitchen garden, suggest that designs had been produced and agreed upon, and that construction work was already underway. Greening's first involvement at Wimpole may, therefore, be a little earlier than 1752:

> Level a Row of Stakes on the Slope of the Fosse (parrallell [sic] to those in the bottom) ten feet from the bottom, & levell them in the same manner as those on the Top of the Fosse were, these Stakes will enable You to make the Slope of the Fosse regular on the bottom part & then finish the Top of the Slope by Eye (rounding) which will prevent a great deal of Trouble & Expence, as the Top need not be brought to a True Level.
> Continue to Carry away the Earth which is thrown out of the Fosse and as soon as you can conveniently take down the Elms in the row that are mark'd, & cast all the best Earth into the Garden as it will save carrying away & be of use in the Garden.

On the entrance, or south, side of the house, the new fosse was to follow the line of the east-west boundary with the park which in Kip's view (*No.3*) is shown partly as a wall and, where it crosses the avenue, partly as railings (with Tijou's gate-screen at its centre). As we have seen, in the 1720s Charles Bridgeman (*Nos.36, 37 & 39*) proposed that the gate-screen should be moved further to the south and linked to the existing masonry to east and west with quadrant walls. The fosse that Greening describes in his plans and memoranda did away with this arrangement. The iron gates that were introduced at the south-east and south-west corners of the main forecourt, and which framed the new *clairvoyée* of Bridgeman's great south avenue, were to be the only visual barriers to an uninterrupted view of the park to the south. Greening's instructions of September 1752 appear to advise on how these changes on the south side of the house might be made:

> Get Tiles & one of the bricklayers in the Country to finish the coping of the Wall till it is Intersected by the Court Wall, from where the Stone Coping is to be finished to the Iron Gate.
> When the Wall of the Stable Yard is taken down the new Gate for the enterance is to be put near to the Stable & the pavement widened for the Coaches.
> There are three rows of Trees between the Fosse & Green House, the middle row are limes which are to come down as soon as You can conveniantly, take them away.[189]

Further on in the document he adds: 'My Lord will Order the remainder of the Walls to be thrown down when we shall be able to see more Exactly what will be necessary to be done'. The plans, it seems, were not entirely fixed. As has been noted, the existence of William Stukeley's 'View of the grand avenue, Wimpole hall. oct.8. 1747' (*No.74*), dated four or five years before the start of Greening's work at Wimpole, must, however, cast doubt both on the date and authorship of these rearrangments.

The remainder of Greening's initial set of 'instructions' calls for the preparation of plant material for relocation to the new kitchen garden. He also touches on tree planting in the park:

> Let the Espalier for the Kitchen Garden be gettting ready this Winter to be set up in Feb.y there must be an oak post of four Inches Square between each Tree five feet above ground, & the Spaces between are to be filled up with Stakes of one & half Inch or two Inches diameter & finish'd at Top by a rail made of pantile lath plain'd, to which every post & every Stake is to be pail'd.
> [...] Get Tan as soon as possible for the shifting the Pine apple plants.
> Build a Shed against the North East Side of the Great Barn, for the Peat to be laid in, which may be done by putting in two or three Strong posts to bear a Wall plate to Carry the rafter, then this Shed will be ever ready to receive the peat which Should be got in, in a dry Season other ways the Expence of Carriage & the loss in the peat will be great.
> My Lord agrees to have the New England Pines planted on the Side of the Hill lately taken into the Park where I mentioned.
> Get about Twenty loads of Such Earth I shew'd for the Pines.
> Level with Some of the Spare Earth among the large Elms in the front of the House & Cover their roots to Encourage their Growth.
> Make a lattice to Tye the Vines against to put up before the Hot Wall.[190]

A month later, Greening sent a further set of detailed

'directions' to Mr Moses, Baron Hardwicke's head gardener.[191] Greening's 'instructions' to Mr Bird required the organisation of large-scale labouring works, the 'directions' for Mr Moses describe more specific gardening activities, albeit many of a hard-landscaping nature. They list in detail the works required to remove all vestiges of the formal gardens to the south and west of the orangery, referred to in other eighteenth-century documents as the 'Green house', and for the salvaging of plants for future use. His insistence that no trace of the foundations of unwanted walls should be left near the surface, lest they show up later as summer parch-marks, is particularly interesting. Clearly this phenomenon is not the discovery of the modern-day archaeologist:

> Get 2 Turfing Irons, 2 Rasers, 4 Lines, 6 Iron teeth Rakes, and 20 Wheelbarrows, Mean While take up all the Shrubs, and all the different sorts of flowers, & also all the box Edging, in tht part of the Garden in the front of the Green house, & lay them in Earth carefully in the Nursery (that is in the Slip of Kitchen Ground on the back of the Grove) observe to keep each different Sort of Shrub by themselves, that when you are planting, one may fetch the Sort that is wanting, without being obliged to pull up other Sorts to come at what is wanting, which is often the Case.
>
> Take up the Turf before the Greenhouse & Cart the Earth that came out of the Fosse, which lays against the Chesnut Trees, to fill up the hollow part between the Fosse & the foot of the House in the front of the Greenhouse, & be very carefull to ram this very well as it is lay'd, & don't raise it above three or four Inchs at a Time, & Cart over it to settle it.
>
> Dig & Carefully pick the Couch Grass, horse Radish, & other weeds from that part of this Ground that was Kitchen Garden, so that the weeds may not grow through the Turf, for if this is neglected it will be difficult to get this ground clean after it is layd with Turf.
>
> Cut down & carry away Immediately the Row of Limes that are between the Row of Horse Chestnuts & the Row of Elms on the West Side of the Garden.
>
> Get the foundations of the Walls dug out at least eighteen Inches deep, below the Surface of the Ground, else in the Summer the Grass will burn & Shew where each wall was, also get all the brick rubbish into heaps, near where the Serpentine Gravel Walk is to be & dig all the rich Earth out of the borders & preserve it in heaps for Finishing, & take great care to mix the walk part & the border parts well together, else when it comes to be all Grass it won't be all alike, but the border parts will be greener as they will be richer than the others. Then Ram these places very well else they will Settle Hollow & require to be work'd over again, which will be a double Charge.
>
> When the Ground before the Greenhouses is leveled agreable to these directions, it is to be Turfed with the Turf that comes off the Turf from the fountain Garden in the North Front, Make the Grass to begin from the West Corner of the Mansion house, to leave a space of Gravel before the Greenhouse so wide as the Mansion house projects forwarder than the Greenhouse.
>
> Make the old part of the Kitchen Garden on the East Side of Grove, where the Spring is, into a Nursery for the Preservation of all the Shrubs, & flowers, which lay in Earth & Observe to mix the Earth well into their Roots, & keep each sort of Shrub & each sort of flower in Seperate Parcels that there may be no difficulty to find what may be wanting.
>
> Get Several Hatchets & bill sharpened against RG comes again to Wimpole, that he may see the trees under cut, that want.
> (order'd nothing to be done by way of Undercutting the Trees till I am there. Nov[r]. 1752).

The great works appear to have been finished in August 1753 when, with evident relief, John Bird reported to his master: 'My Lord this afternoon I paid the laboureres that worked in the gardens the sum of £10.11.1 ½ and glad I am of this Joyfull day that they have don: sometimes when they want it [...] & Littel place to sow with grass seed next the new Foss and then I think finishd. My Lord this day Saturday it began to Rain [...] a fine soft Rain. I hope that it will help wash away the flies of the plants and make the plants thrive'.[192]

By September 1753 the changes that Robert Greening had brought about in the gardens at Wimpole were sufficiently dramatic and complete for Jemima, Marchioness Grey to describe them in the following way to her friend Mary Talbot:

> I have found here quite a New Place, my lord having now completed his Gardens, & nothing ever made greater change or a more different scene. Instead of straight Gravel walks with Borders & Cross plots surrounded by walls, & views into the Park through Iron Gates, there is now a large green Lawn behind the House, bounded by Clumps of Trees & flowering shrubs, a broad serpentine walk through them, & inclosed with a Sunk Fence that lets the Park quite into the Garden. The Views of the Park are, a Hill that rises in an easy slope directly from the Ha! Ha! with some scattered Trees upon it, & the deer feeding under them; some little Groves of tall Old Elmes in the flatter part of the ground that seem to join the Garden; or the Wider Opening of a very fine & extended Avenue that leads to the House. And I am particularly fond of a long green walk of Arched Trees that is enliven'd by all these different views gilded by Sunshine, & has been exceedingly pleasant to saunter in these hot mornings, for my only Objection to the Modern Improvements of Gardening is their not encouraging Shade enough or Privacy. All this you may imagine forms a very agreable scene & to make it more Picturesque, there is at this Minute a Flock of Sheep feeding upon the lawn under my windows, tended by a Shepherd Boy who does not indeed Pipe, nor is his voice so musical as a Pipe, but sings all day, or employs himself to erecting lime-twigs to catch the poor harmless Birds, however the Birds are luckily too wise to go near them.[193]

A new garden required a new management régime and in January 1754 an 'Agreement for keeping the Gardens' was drawn up between John Bird and Mick Moses.[194] Moses agreed to 'keep the Lord Hardwick's Gardens at Wimple, together with the Hot-house and Green-house and all the Plants therein, as the Great Court Yard before the House, and also the three Orchards now enjoy'd with the Mansion-houses' in good order, and to 'gather and look after the Fruit'. He was also responsible for keeping 'all manner of Utensils and Working Tools for this use of the said Gardens, Hot-house, and Orchards, in good Repair; and also the Bell Glasses and other Glasses', and for ensuring that 'all the locks belonging to the Kitchen Garden' and 'all the other locks about the Garden' were 'kept clean and in order'.

The gardener was to 'find all manner of Plants and Seeds for the Garden (Except Pine-Apple Plants when wanting) and be at his charge of finding Men to Cart Dung, Mould, and other things'. For his part of the contract, Lord Hardwicke was to provide 'Tanners Bark for the Hot-house', and 'new Tubbs for His Green-house where they are wanting, and also new Barrows where wanting'. Moses was to be paid £170 per annum, allowed 'to keep a Horse to roll the Gardens and Court

55 The Catalogue

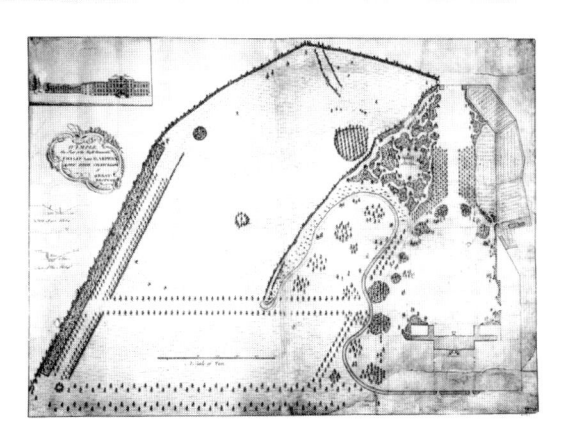

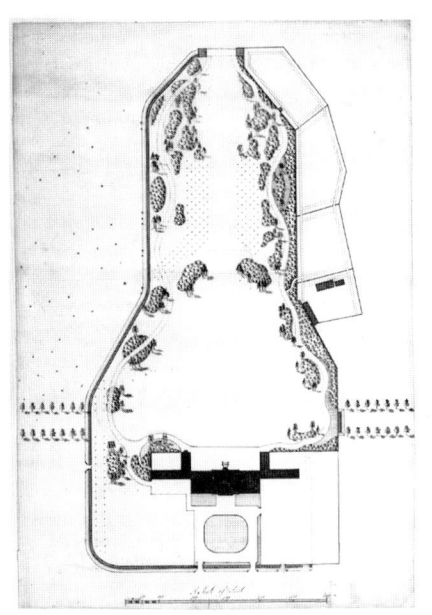

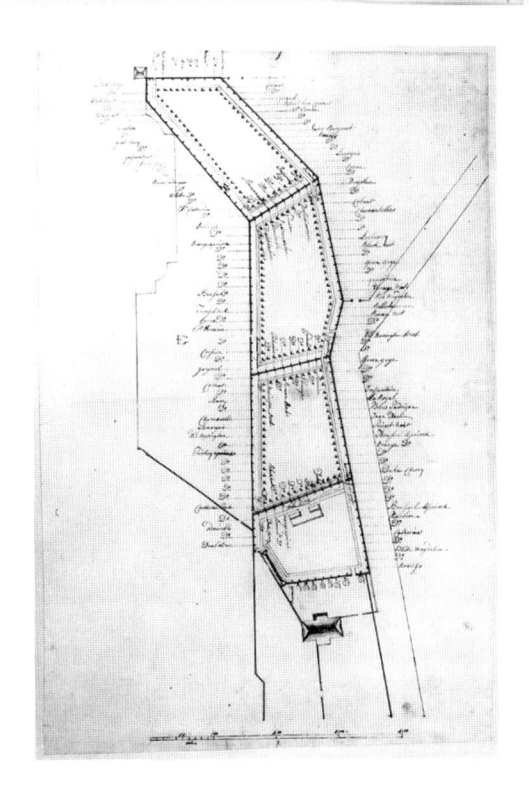

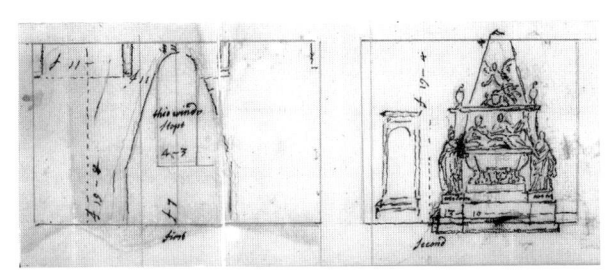

Yard', to have 'such of the Walnuts which shall grow in the Park, as shall be over and above what shall be used in His Lordship's Family', and the use for the gardens of 'all the Dung, that shall be made in his Stables, and about the Mansion-house'.[195]

Greening continued to give advice—perhaps until his death in 1758—and further planting was clearly envisaged. In March 1754, Hardwicke answered a query from Bird: 'As to the Spot in the new Park-ground, which Greening thinks best to make a Nursery, I have no objection to it, provided you think that it is open enough to the sun & air'.[196] Later that month Bird was instructed to 'let the Pales of the Clump, which was taken away, be used for the new Nursery, as far as they will go'.[197] In later correspondence John Bird reports on how the 'Plantations in the Clumps' and the trees in the new nursery were fairing, and on one occasion enclosed Moses's 'account of the Pine apples and the other fruit'. In the spring of 1757 we learn too from Bird about the care of specific trees, perhaps those that (by then the Earl of) Hardwicke planned to plant as a stand behind the Gothick folly: 'I have told Moses abought the Scotch Firs and he sais that He understands the mater of them varey well and will Take all the care of them as he can he sais that thay must not be planted yet—he has taken care of them that they may be a littel revived by fore they be planted and the weather a little better'.[198]

77 Robert Greening. Proposal for the gardens and park to the north and west of the house, c.1752

National Trust WIM/D/459
Inscr.: Within a rococo cartouche, 'Wimple the Seat of the Right Honourable Philip Lord Hardwick [*sic*] Lord High Chancellor of Great Brittain'. Two, dimensioned, marginal drawings marked: 'Section of an Ahha!' and 'Section of the Ahha!'.
Pen and ink (680 x 950mm)
Scale given
Lit & repr.: Jackson-Stops (1979:2), p.661, fig.11; Jacques (1983), pp.69–70, pl.27; Jackson-Stops (1992), pp.44–5, cat. & pl.20; Laird (1999), p.115, pl.63.

The complicated proposals set out in this drawing appear to have been undertaken only in part. While the clearing of the parterres to the north of the house and the thinning of the surrounding planting to form clumps was effected, there is no evidence that the area to the north-west with its sinuous island-beds arranged around an oriental kiosk or pavilion was created. In the late 1740s 'Robert Greening and Company' had planted up Smith's Lawn at Cumberland Lodge, Windsor Great Park in a similar way. The contrived irregularity of the Wimpole scheme, particularly the proposed layout to the north-west is reminiscent of the Rococo garden designs published by Batty Langley (1696—1751).

The Lord Chancellor would have had access to expert advice on chinoiserie from a number of possible sources: Sanderson Miller was probably responsible for supervising the construction of a number of Chinese buildings in the 1740s and 1750s on the estate of Frederick North, later 2nd Earl of Guilford (1732—92), at Wroxton Park, Oxfordshire; while the Lord Chancellor's son-in-law, George, Lord Anson (1697—1762)—who had travelled to China—had built a Chinese house on his brother's estate at Shugborough, Staffordshire, in 1748. Anson could have advised on the authenticity of any proposed Chinese building. Jemima, Marchioness Grey, the Lord Chancellor's daughter-in-law had also visited, and described in her journal the Chinese pavilions at Studley Royal, Stowe, Wroxton and Shugborough. Philip Yorke and Jemima Marchioness Grey built a Chinese pavilion at Wrest Park in 1761, three years before they were to inherit the Wimpole estate, but in the absence of any further documentation about the Wimpole pavilion, it may be assumed that Greening's design was never built.

At the top left of the drawing is a small vignette of Wimpole Hall, viewed from the south-west—an uncomfortable perspective, naïvely assembled from elevations of the main block and the late-seventeenth-century orangery. The south front of the main block is shown as re-faced by Henry Flitcroft, and James Gibbs's gallery extension is shown connecting with the orangery—its easternmost two bays adapted to take the windows of Gibbs's library ante-room.

The newly built ice-house, perhaps to designs by Henry Flitcroft (*No.66*), may be the igloo-like structure shown in the circular clump of trees at top-left, the northern end of the 'Fir Walk'.

78 Robert Greening. Proposal for the gardens to the north of the house, c.1752

National Trust WIM/D/456
Inscr.: 'A Scale of Feet'
Pen and ink (620 x 425mm)
Scale given
Lit & repr.: Souden (1991), p.82; Laird (1999), p.116, pl.64.

The scope of the scheme described in this drawing is less ambitious than that in *No.77*, and is confined to the area to the north of the house. The shape and boundaries of the new garden were to be defined by the bones of the earlier arrangement shown in Kip's engraved view (*No.3*). Here it is proposed that the ha-ha should run from the base-court at the front of the house along the western boundary of the garden to meet the westernmost of James Gibbs's pair of garden pavilions—shown as square structures on this and on Greening's other two plans.

As in the previous drawing, a circuit path winds through clumps that we know were to be evergreen shrubs and syringas, interspersed with honeysuckle and roses.

79 Robert Greening. Proposal for a walled kitchen garden to the north-west of the house, c.1752

National Trust WIM/D/457
Inscr.: The names of the different species of wall fruit are given.
Pen and ink (535 x 360mm)
Scale given
Lit. & repr.: Pattison & Garrow (1998), fig.9.

This smaller-scaled drawing provides detailed planting proposals for the walled kitchen garden. The unconventional plan form of this enclosure, elongated and 'cranked', was generated by the eastern shoulder of the earlier formal gardens, and the line of a track which formed its eastern boundary. The great medieval, hipped-roof barn with its opposed porches (unusual in barns before c.1750), illustrated in Kip's view, is recorded here at the southern end of the new kitchen garden; while the easternmost of James Gibbs's pair of garden pavilions is shown at its northern end. Running south from the pavilion can be seen the scalloped and checked western edge of the bosky planting that flanked the bowling green and whose shape is recorded in Jacques Fougereau's 1728 sketch (*No.42*). In his wider proposals for the gardens to the north of the house (*Nos.77 & 78*), Greening made use of this existing tree planting, but loosened and thinned it.

The walled garden is divided into five 'slips' by cross walls running at a variety of angles, that provide a series of short, valuable south-facing walls against which particularly tender plants could be grown. But different species of fruit trees, more than 200 plants in all, are indicated against the inner faces of all the walls—apricots, cherries, figs, greengages, and peaches. The exception is the second slip from the south. Here against the northern wall, which is drawn at twice the thickness to the other cross-wall, the legend reads 'All Vines'. This thicker wall presumably contained a system of heating flues and must be the one that Greening refers to in his instructions of September 1752: 'Make a lattice to Tye the Vines against to put up before the

Hot Wall'.[199] The Greening family had similarly built heated walls in the gardens at Claremont, Surrey where they were referred to as 'fire' walls.

The instruction in the same document 'Get Tan as soon as possible for the shifting of the Pine apple plants' is intriguing. These valuable fruits may previously have been grown in what appear to be lean-to glasshouses shown to the south-west of the house in Kip's view. Perhaps they were destined for the building that is shown in this drawing immediately to the south of the vine wall. Might it be possible that Flitcroft designed this building in partnership with Greening? When the two men worked together in Great Windsor Park Flitcroft designed, c.1748, a hothouse range for Cumberland Lodge.

Greening's kitchen garden may have lasted less than twenty years and been swept away as part of Brown's landscaping works—certainly there is no sign of its walls on an anonymous estate survey drawing of the early 1770s (No.97). The lines of the garden's boundary and cross-walls can be seen from the air and on the ground when conditions are favourable. These slight garden earthworks were recorded by the RCHME in 1997 and 1998 (see below).

80 (Attrib.) Robert Greening. View of the South Avenue at Wimpole, c.1752

National Trust WIM/D/458
Pen and ink with wash (265 x 415mm)
Lit. & repr.: Jackson-Stops (1979:2), p.661, fig.10.

In this drawing Whaddon church, the intended focus of Charles Bridgeman's *clairvoyée*, has been given a false emphasis and exaggerated elevation as have the Royston Downs which rise behind it and here serve as a dramatic backdrop to the main vista.

The avenue trees are shown in somewhat fuller form than in Stukeley's sketch which had been made five years earlier.

81 Peter Scheemakers (1691—1781). Sketch design for a monument to Philip Yorke, 1st Earl of Hardwicke, 1764

Staffordshire County Record Office, D615P(S)/1/6/86
Inscr.: 'first', 'second', 'this window stopt', the flanking statues labelled 'wisdom' and 'justice', and dimensions marked.
Pen and ink over pencil (88 x 279mm)
Lit. & repr.: Roscoe (1987), pp.181–2, figs.9 & 10; Roscoe (1999), pp.243–4, cat.92, fig.79; Soros (2006), p.393, fig.9–8.

The parish church of St. Andrew contains three monuments carved by the Flemish sculptor Peter Scheemakers. The earliest of these—the 1761 monument to Catherine (Freman), the first wife of the Hon. Charles Yorke—was designed by James 'Athenian' Stuart. Three years later Philip Yorke, 2nd Earl of Hardwicke—disregarding his father's instruction that he should be buried 'privately and without pomp'—asked the architect and sculptor to collaborate again on a monument to the Lord Chancellor, Philip Yorke, 1st Earl of Hardwicke. Ingrid Roscoe notes that Stuart sent a 'slight sketch' for the monument to his friend and patron Thomas Anson. The present drawing, in Scheemakers's hand, with figures marked Wisdom and Justice flanking a sarcophagus carrying reclining effigies, may be it.

Three months later, on 4 September 1764, Stuart wrote again to Anson with a detailed description of the final composition: the flanking figures had been replaced with statues of Minerva 'the Eloquent', carrying a caduceus, and Pudicitia, the matronal Virtue, holding a 'Stem of Lilies'. In 1777 the antiquarian William Cole (1714—82) described the monuments to the Lord Chancellor and Charles Yorke—in whose design Stuart does not appear to have been involved—as 'awkward large Monumental Pyramids against the South Wall'.[200]

The drawing appears to offer alternative placements for the monument: the 'first' against the south wall of the chapel—so blocking the window that communicated with the nave—and the 'second', apparently, against the west. The former position was chosen, where, corroborating Cole's witness, it is recorded in a survey drawing made by John Soane's outdoor clerk Henry Provis (No.210). The monument was later moved to the east wall.

Stuart may also have collaborated with Peter Scheemakers—or perhaps his son Thomas Scheemakers (1740—1808)—on the statuary which ornamented the Hill House at Wimpole (No.87).[201]

Lancelot 'Capability' Brown's (1716—83) improvements to the Park at Wimpole

Philip Yorke, when Viscount Royston, and Jemima, Marchioness Grey first employed Lancelot 'Capability' Brown in 1758.[202] He was asked to make a series of improvements to the gardens of Wrest Park, Bedfordshire. The strongly architectural character of the Great Garden (1706—40) there, with its intersecting *allées* and rides, symmetrically arranged to either side of the Long Water—a canal terminated by a Baroque pavilion designed by Thomas Archer (?1668—1743)—must have severely limited Brown's opportunity to effect radical change. Certainly his modifications to the landscape, undertaken between 1758 and 1760 and commemorated by a column in the north-east quadrant, were relatively conservative; he serpentised the canals that enclosed the Great Garden on three sides, and opened up views to the pleasure grounds.

In 1764 Philip Yorke succeeded his father as the 2nd Earl of Hardwicke and inherited the family seat at Wimpole. Brown was also elevated in that year to the position, which he held until his death in 1783, of Master Gardener at Hampton Court. Three years later the young couple called upon Brown to advise them on a vastly more ambitious plan, for their new estate, that would considerably extend Wimpole's park to the north, taking in fields and pastureland that had changed little since the time of Benjamin Hare's seventeenth-century survey. In September 1767, a weary but dazzled Marchioness Grey wrote to Catherine Talbot:

> "Break off, Break off, we tread Enchanted Ground"—is almost literally true with me at present. Mr. Brown has been leading me such a Fairy Circle & his Magic Wand has raised such landscapes to the Eye—not visionary for they were all there but his Touch has brought them out with the same Effect as a Painter's Pencil upon Canvass that after having hobbled over rough Ground to Points I had never seen before, for two Hours I return half Tired, & half Foot sore, & must really break off, it being just Dinner-time & post time.[203]

The following month her eldest daughter, more ready it seems to reserve judgement, wrote to Miss Talbot: 'I ought in justice to afford as much paper to the great Mr. Brown, who has been two days here surveying his Improvements, as yet furnish no great matter for Description, nor the Tower neither, tho' that our architect Mr. Essex promises will make a figure next year. The Ground and the Water will go on but shortly I doubt'.[204]

This is the first indication that the 2nd Earl planned to resuscitate his late father's plans to build an eye-catcher on the brow of Johnson's Hill (Nos.68 to 71).

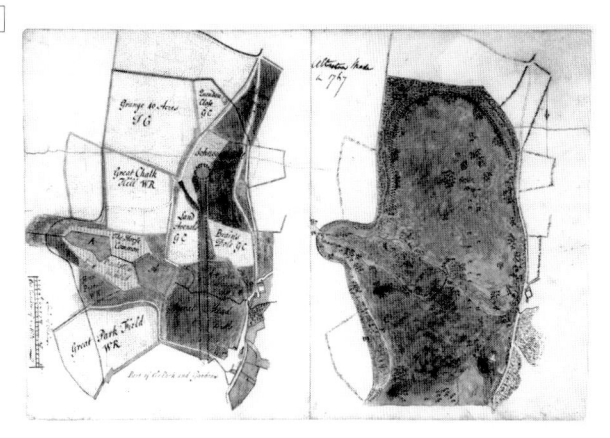

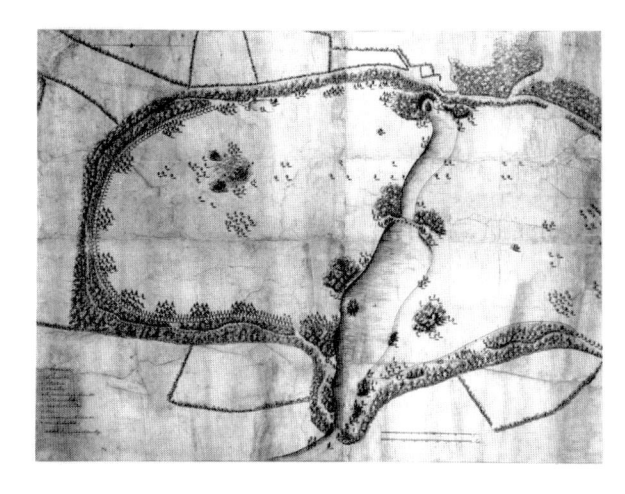

Having made a first payment of £300 to Brown on 18 December, Yorke prevailed upon the gardener, with a letter penned on Christmas Eve, to set out a clear, costed programme of work that could be followed over a number of years: 'I hope you will have Leisure in the Holy-days to make out the Minute for our Proceedings at Wimple; specifying more particularly the Plan of Operations for next Year & with the Expence thereof, & marking out […], the Works of the 2 succeeding years, when/viz: in 1779 the Whole Plan is to be completed […] absurd to look so far forward, but however the […] of the whole may be of […] in every Event'.[205]

Clearly works were under way in the autumn and early winter of 1767. The evidence of the family's correspondence is supported by that of a marginal annotation—'Alteration Made in 1767'—on a pair of coloured drawings that show the park to the north of the fosse, or sunk fence, 'before' and 'after' Brown's improvements (*No.82*). It has been assumed that this pair of drawings is a *post facto* record drawing, but it seems equally plausible that it formed a part of Brown's initial presentation to his client. The larger drawing (*No.83*), monochrome and more obviously a product of Brown's office, may be a development of his proposals.[206] Neither of the drawings tallies in every respect with the landscape as we know it to have been re-ordered, and this suggests that they were probably both made at a fairly early stage in the commission.

Brown's explanatory note on the larger drawing, 'N.B. The Pricked Lines are according to the Present Plan', and the pricked holes themselves, show that he used an existing survey plan as the basis for his initial proposals. By pouncing, or dusting, coloured powder through a line of perforations, he would have been able to transfer the key lines and features of the original to his new drawing. The smaller 'presentation' drawings suggest that Brown may have made use of one of Charles Bridgeman's survey drawings; in its key essentials the 'before' plan corresponds closely with the information given in (*Nos.29 & 30*).

At Wimpole, Brown made use of all the landscape devices that characterise his approach. He threw into one a great expanse of land that had previously been divided into fields by hedges and ditches, and crossed by tracks and roadways of medieval origin. He formed a single, serpentine lake from the two polygonal fish ponds that the 2nd Earl of Radnor had made along the course of the Holden Dene, and dug an additional, lower lake to the east, twisting its two ends away from the viewer to create the illusion that it was a broad, sinuous river.

With the exception of a few individual specimens, the trees of the north avenue, that had stretched from James Gibbs's garden pavilions at the north end of the bowling green to a circus of trees on Johnson's Hill (*No.30*), were swept away, and, with disregard for the principles of picturesque planning, an eye-catcher, marked on the plan as the 'Intended Building', was erected to terminate the *clairvoyée*. Around the open parkland that Brown had created he looped a perimeter carriage drive. Henry Flitcroft appears to have returned to Wimpole, only some two years before his death, to provide a hump-backed Chinese bridge over the spillway between the two new lakes—of a type he had designed for Great Windsor Park—straddling a weir and with a set of fish-gates.

Hardwicke's polite 'improvements' meant a very different future for his tenants, whose family names are recorded on the plan. Their houses were razed and the fields they had tilled and used for pasture were flooded, following a pattern that Oliver Goldsmith (?1730—74) deplores in his poem *The Deserted Village*:

[…] The man of wealth and pride,
Takes up a space that many poor supplied;
Space for his lake, his park's extended bounds
Space for his horses, equipage, and hounds[207]

Brown's Account Book records a series of payments from Lord Hardwicke from December 1767 to July 1772 (total £3,330) and these correspond, with only minor differences, with those given in the Earl of Hardwicke's Bank Book in the Hertfordshire Record Office (total £3,412 10s), and the complementary ledgers at Hoare's Bank (total £3,662).[208] A further insight is provided by the ledger for Wood and Ingram's Northamptonshire nursery for the period 1748—84. This shows that in October and November 1769, Lord Hardwicke ordered 6,300 trees at a cost of £175 13s 4d.[209] The trees included elms, limes, chestnut, planes, beech, ash and pines. Planes were a particular leitmotif of Brown's planting schemes, and at Wimpole a group of the trees announces the presence of the causeway, bridge and spillway between the upper and lower lakes. Brown's plan shows clumps of pines ranged along the park side of the perimeter drive, not recorded on later maps. Lord Hardwicke's name is given against the order, but it is not clear whether he or Brown would have paid for the trees. Brown patronised the Huntingdon nursery himself in February 1770, ordering 160 elm trees for the planting of his own estate at Fenstanton.[210]

On 21 October 1770, three years into Brown's 'Plan of Operation', Lady Amabel Yorke wrote to her mother from Tyttenhanger: 'I daresay your ladyship will make Wimple as fine a place as the situation will allow of, I am sure what I saw executed of the plan which you have formed, convinces me of the beauty of the whole; it is a great operation and I suppose will take some time before it is finished'.[211] While in October of the followng year Agneta Yorke wrote to the marchioness: 'the description your Ladyship gives of Wimple convinces me how much your taste and Mr. Browne's [sic] capability have improved that place. I shall hope by Lady Bell's assistance to have a perfect idea of the alterations'.[212]

With his various works Brown had completed the naturalisation of the landscape at Wimpole, begun by Robert Greening, a change of fashion that Alexander Pope neatly encapsulated in the following distich in *Of false taste; an epistle to Richard Earl of Burlington*:

> Tir'd of the Scene Parterres and Fountains yield,
> He finds at last he better likes a Field.

In 1781 the new lakes were the scene of a 'most melancholy accident'. Robert Plumptre, the President of Queen's College, Cambridge and the then rector at Wimpole wrote to Lord Hardwicke explaining that the seventeen year old 'Son of my B[r]. Harry Newcome who has been us'd to spend the Whitsuntide holidays with us, was yesterday by going in the new Water that M[r]. Brown made in the meadow, drowned. It is imagined that by diving with too much force at his going off, he stuck in the mud, and could not disengage himself'.[213]

82 Anonymous. 'Before' and 'after' plans of the North Park, after 1767

National Trust WIM/D/451
Inscr.: 'Explanations', and the following, in two columns:
'The Lefthand Plan is a Representation of the Grounds &c. as they were before Mr. Brown's Alterations were begun, with the Addition of the Line only, which denotes the Outward Boundary of the intended Alterations.
The deeper-green narrow Lines are Hedges dividing the General Fields
The Green Plats are Pasture Ground
The Plats pricked with red, Arable Land
The dark-coloured Plats A and *A* two Ponds of Water. The Black Line connecting them, and continued each way from them, the Water-course, of which the Current is from A towards *A*.
The White Linear Spaces thro' the Grounds, are the New Roads
The Double Capitals, after the Name of the Grounds, are the Initial Letters of the Tenants Names in whose Occupation the Grounds now are, Zach. Moul, Wm. Ratford, Tim. Cole, or Geo. Conderage
S is the Place of the Summer Houses at the North End of the Pleasure Garden, near which on the Right Hand are Z Moul's Farm House, The Carthorse Stable, a Dovehouse, a Fishpond & an Assemblage of Buildings which are, The Cart Shed, the Carpenter's Work Shop, Tenant Moul's Cowhouse & Barn, & Storehouse for Plow & Cart Timber, &c.'.
'The Right-hand Plan is according to Mr. Brown's Drawing (Colouring excepted) in which [here a coloured line] is the Outline of the Alterations.
The Dark Part AA is the intended Water.
B, about the Middle of it, a Sham Bridge.
C, at the Lefthand End, a real Wooden Bridge. In this Water are two Islands, one about the Middle of the Wider Part, and the other near the Right-hand End.
D, the New Tower, at Johnson's Hill.
E, the New Plantation to the Water
F, on the Right-hand Side of this Plantation, a sunk Fence to enclose ditto.
G, In the Middle of This Plantation, near the letter R, a Seat. Thro' the Middle of this Plantation is a Serpentine Way Down to the Water.
H, The Plantation against the intended Park Pale.
From I, round towards the North & then the East is a Ride between a double Row of Trees with Clumps planted at Intervals'.
Beneath, in another hand is noted: 'abt. 160 Acres near mile round, above 2 miles & halfe'.
Pen and ink with wash (353 x 544mm)

83 Lancelot Brown. Design for the lakes and the northern extension of the Park, *c*.1767

National Trust WIM/D/448
Inscr.: Bottom left, under the title 'References':
'A. The Intended Waters
A Sham Bridge
A Wooden Bridge
The Intended Building on Johnson's Hill
New Plantation to the Water
A Sunke Fence to Inclose Ditto
A Seat
New Plantation against the Intended Park
A Ride on the outside of Ditto
N.B. The Pricked Lines are according to the Present Plan'.
Pen and ink with wash (965 x 1298mm)
Scale: 1in: 100ft. The scale is given both in feet and chains.
Lit & repr: Stroud (1950), p.134, with a detail on p.135; Stroud (1979), p.758, fig.3; Jacques (1983), p.80, pl.32; Jackson-Stops (1992), cat.58, p.85; Williamson (1995),

pl.33, p.82.
Exh.: *English Landscape Gardening of the Eighteenth and early Nineteenth Centuries*, 1951, The Arts Council of Great Britain, cat.33; *An English Arcadia 1600—1990* (1992), cat.58, pp.85—86.

84   Mary Wray (*c.*1740—1803). View of the South Avenue, 1769

Bedfordshire Record Office, L 33/140
Inscr.: 'M.W. 1769'
Pen and ink with wash (240 x 380mm)
Lit.: Adshead (1996), p.35.

Mary Wray is known for her silhouette portraiture rather than as a topographical artist. She and her husband, the antiquary Daniel Wray (1701—83), author of the doggerel verse below the celebratory engraving of the Gothic Folly (*No.72*), were close friends of Philip Yorke, 2nd Earl of Hardwicke and his wife Jemima, Marchioness Grey. Daniel Wray contributed to the Yorke brothers' *Athenian Letters*, and served as Hardwicke's deputy Teller of the Exchequer. Mary Wray appears to have been an occasional drawing companion of the Hardwickes' eldest daughter Lady Amabel Yorke. This drawing is similar in composition to (*No.85*), a sketch attributed to Amabel, and could, conceivably, have been drawn on the same occasion. Of one of her topographical views of the north park, lakes and folly at Wimpole Amabel wrote, both half-apologetically and a little archly, to her mother 'I can only say in its Favour, that it is more like than M^{rs}. Wray's Drawing'.

85   (attrib.) Lady Amabel Polwarth (1751—1833). View of the South Avenue at Wimpole, and the *clairvoyée* to Whaddon church

Bedfordshire Record Office, L 33/141
Pen and ink (265 x 355mm)
Lit. & repr.: Adshead (1996), p.35, fig.5.

This view is drawn from a position slightly to the south of Mary Wray's prospect, so allowing a glimpse of the tower of Whaddon church along Charles Bridgeman's diagonal *clairvoyée*. It is possible that the two views may have been drawn on the same occasion in 1769; Amabel de Grey, as she then was, would have been eighteen. Another sketch in the same hand, and almost certainly of a section of the serpentised canal system at Wrest Park in Bedfordshire, survives in the Bedfordshire Record Office. Amabel's topographical views only otherwise survive as etchings or as images on the dessert service made by Wedgwood for Catherine the Great, the Empress of Russia, the so-called 'green frog' service.

Drawings by James 'Athenian' Stuart (1713—88) for, and engraved views of, the Hill House

At some point in the late 1760s or early 1770s a prospect house, which commanded views of the Royston Downs and the village of Arrington, was built on high ground to the west of the hall. Its architect was James 'Athenian' Stuart, who in 1761 and 1764 had designed two neo-classical monuments for the Yorke family in collaboration with the sculptor Peter Scheemakers (*No.81*). Previously thought to have been designed in 1775, the idea of the 'Hill House' may have been conceived as early as 1766. In January of that year, Stuart wrote to Hardwicke: 'I have bestowed some thoughts on your Lordships building, before I proceed I shall be glad to know the length & breadth proposed for the Room above Stairs & the Porticos below, 60 in length & 15 in breadth will make a fine passeggio—for the Portico—a noble walk in all weathers, & a noble object from all the country in view of it'.[214] This would place the building more happily in association with the landscaping works undertaken by Lancelot 'Capability' Brown between 1767 and 1772, a campaign that also saw the construction of the Gothic folly.

Indeed it seems likely that the buildings were conceived to complement each other, providing a didactic 'contrast between ancient and modern times'. They might have been inspired by the contrasting classical temple (1758), designed by Stuart, and Gothic folly (1747/8), designed by Sanderson Miller, set up by George Lyttleton in the park at Hagley, Worcestershire, which Hardwicke and his wife visited in 1763. The two buildings are illustrated in a single engraved view published by Smith and Vivares in 1759.

The building's elevated position brought its troubles. In January 1782 Hardwicke's steward Richard Barton reported that 'a violent wind' had torn some of the lead from the roof, and in December 1785 he recommended that 'The painting of the Park Building wants renewing very much, the knots appearing thro' and the Wood becomes liable to Damage. Nothing can be done in these things till Spring gives us Hopes of a Succession of fine Days'.[215] The building suffered attack from critics as well as the elements. In the diary of his 1790 'Tour in the Midlands', the Hon. John Byng described the structure as 'an ugly summer-house building'.[216] It was similarly castigated by Brayley and Britton in *The Beauties of England and Wales* as: 'a heavy and ungraceful building [...] whose weight has caused the foundation to give way'.[217]

A fuller account of the building, showing how rapidly it had fallen into decay, was made by the Rev. James Plumptre in July 1800[218]:

> the Pavillion [*sic*] itself was a scene of desolation and ruin. It has been built about 25 years and cost about £1,500 building. When finished it was one of the most elegant buildings I ever remember. The Tea room was simple and elegant; the little room on the side was a rare specimen of painting, of Etruscan figures in colours. It was done by Stewart and cost £700. What the inside is now, we did not see, but we could discern from the outside, that the blinds were falling to pieces. The pillars which supported the Center [*sic*], were rotting away, and the building supported by rough props. A railing of posts & wire, which formerly extended all round it, and kept off the cattle, was removed and the pavement and steps torn up, and the place made a shelter for deer & sheep, whose dung sadly soiled the place. The stucco which covered the outside, and gave it the appearance of stone, was every where falling off. I brought away a piece of it. It is

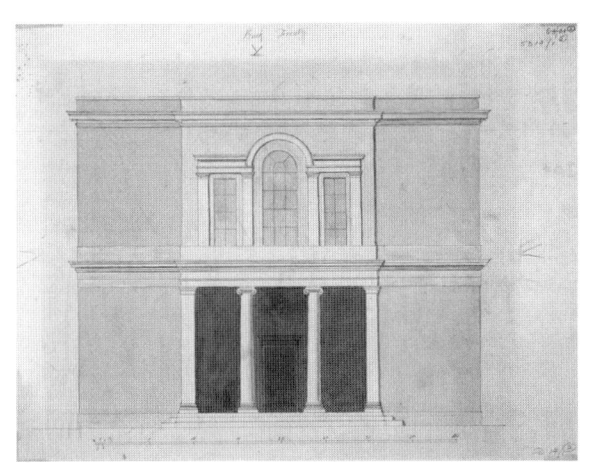

The PARK BUILDING at Wimple, Cambridge Shire, the Seat of the EARL of HARDWICKE.

At secura quies, et nescia fallere Vita   Mugitusq. boum, mollesq. sub arbore somni
Dives opum variarum, at latis otia fundis   Non absunt.

Published 1 March 1781 by Fielding & Walker, Paternoster Row

61   The Catalogue

almost as hard as stone, and seems to have been made in pieces about 12 inches by 8 and $^3/_8$ of an inch thick, and stuck on with some kind of cement.

Bank books show that between 1774 and 1777 'Jas. Stuart' received payments totalling £293.[219] According to Plumptre, the final cost of the park building was in the order of £1,500. The building last appears on an 1815 estate survey plan by Robert Withers (see *No.220*), but it must have survived for much of the remainder of the nineteenth century, for in his 1914 typescript essay *Wimpole As I Knew It*, the Rev. A.C. Yorke, then sixty-two, wrote: 'On the hill to the west of the mansion stood the "Hill House", a Georgian pleasure house for tea and spadille. It was of brick and stucco, with interior fittings of wood painted to look like green marble. From its upper floor could be viewed a lovely prospect of wood and tilth to the Royston Hills'.[220] A rectangular depression, some thirty feet square, created by the robbing of its foundation stones, now marks the site of the building.

86 James 'Athenian' Stuart. Elevation for the south front of the Hill House; after 1766, before 1774

Royal Institute of British Architects Library, Drawings Collection SD 62/7 (1)
Inscr.: 'South Front'; various calculations in the margin
Pen and grey wash (235 x 300mm)
Lit. & repr.: Harris (1979), p.75, pl.21a; Adshead (2000), pp.150–63, fig.4.; Soros (2006), p.347, fig.7-46.

With the exception of the form of the central Venetian window, the detailing of the window surrounds and the line of the roof behind the cornice parapet, this drawing accords with the building shown in Lerpinière's engraving (*No.90*).

87 James 'Athenian' Stuart. South-north section of the Hill House, looking west; after 1766, before 1774

Royal Institute of British Architects Library, Drawings Collection SD 62/7 (2)
Inscr.: 'Section thro' both fronts'. Various dimensions given, and the note – 'the Room 20 feet Square/15 high', and the labels 'Roof' and 'Pannel'.
Pen and grey wash (235 x 270mm)
Scale: '4$^1/_2$ feet to an Inch'
Lit. & repr.: Harris (1979), p.75, pl.21b; Adshead (2000), pp.150–63, fig.4.; Soros (2006), p.347, fig.7-47.

Read in conjunction with Thomas West's part survey of the building (*No.204*), the section reveals how the interior spaces worked. Behind the entrance portico lay a narrow stone hall aligned east-west. At either end, opposed doorcases served symmetrically planned and modestly sized spaces (each some ten feet by twelve feet). The room to the east contained a fireplace and probably served as a small kitchen. The double-height space to the west housed a dog-leg stair which led to the upper floor. The rear third of the ground floor took the form of a loggia, open to the north, with statuary niches at either side.

In addition to the figure in classical drapery that Stuart shows standing on a plinth within the western niche, he suggests placing a bust flanked by urns over the door leading to the staircase, while on the first floor proposes a framed *tondo* above the doorcase—perhaps a portrait medallion or allegorical relief. We know that statuary, perhaps supplied by Peter Scheemakers or his son Thomas, was incorporated in the finished building. On 30 June 1788 Lord Hardwicke's steward, Thomas Daintry, reported 'that the two statues set up opposite each other within the Piazza, of the Hill Building at Wimple [had been] thrown down [...] & demolished', explaining that 'Richard Newell a Labourer of Wimple a person dis-ordered in his mind' was thought to be responsible for the 'rash act'.[221]

On the first floor a banqueting room, twenty feet square and lit by the Venetian window, occupied the deepest, central portion of the building which oversailed the Ionic portico to the south and the open loggia to the north. Warmth was provided by a fireplace whose flue rose, according to this drawing, behind the parapet wall. To the east, was a small private chamber which may have been the little room painted with 'Etruscan figures' described by Plumptre in 1800. Stuart was responsible for the earliest 'Etruscan'-painted room in the country—at Spencer House, London and, more pertinently, painted the ceiling of the drawing room at Hagley for Lord Lyttleton.

88 James 'Athenian' Stuart, Elevation for the South front of the Hill House; after 1766, before 1774

Royal Institute of British Architects Library, Drawings Collection SD 17/1 (1)
Inscr.: 'South Front', 'Scale of 2$^1/_2$ Inches to 10 feet', with various measurements given
Pen with ochre, brown and grey wash (312 x 414mm)
Scale: 2$^1/_2$ in: 10ft
Watermark: IV

This elevation is more carefully drawn than No.86 and incorporates a number of developments. Firstly, the intercolumniation of the portico is regularised from the diastyle, araeostyle, diastyle rhythm of the sketchier drawing. Secondly, the form of the Serliana on the upper floor is changed, reflecting the new intercolumniation below and revealing more clearly its relationship to the tripartite windows, employing the Greek Ionic order, that Stuart designed in c.1756—8 for Simon, 1st Earl Harcourt's house at Nuneham Park, Oxfordshire. These derived from the architect's survey, reproduced in *The Antiquities of Athens*, of the Roman Ionic screen at the reservoir of the Aqueduct of the Emperor Hadrian in Athens, whose central arch springs from the architrave—cutting through the frieze and cornice—rather than the upper surface of the cornice, as is more common in the Venetian window type adopted by English neo-Palladians. Thirdly, triangular pediments are shown over the first floor windows.

In the shadow of the portico can be seen the central doorcase to the building's spine wall and placed above it a rectangular sculptural relief framed by egg and dart decoration, rather than the tondo of Lerpinière's engraving (*No.90*). The scale shows the building to have been some forty-six feet long.

89 James 'Athenian' Stuart, Elevation for the North front of the Hill House; after 1766, before 1774

Royal Institute of British Architects Library, Drawings Collection SD 17/1 (2)
Inscr.: 'Back Front'
Pen with ochre, brown, blue and grey wash (310 x 409mm)
Scale: 2$^1/_2$ in: 10ft
Watermark: fleur-de-lis in cartouche over LVG

This drawing reveals that the loggia on north elevation was articulated by an Ionic screen, in antis, of the same width as the portico on the south, with a corresponding, but simpler Serliana, with a yellow brick relieving arch, above. The position of this window, though it emphasises the idea of commanding prospects in two directions, begs the question of how the chimneypiece and associated flue, shown in the sectional drawing (*No.87*), could be accommodated.

90 Engraving by Daniel Lerpinière (1745—85), after (?) James 'Athenian' Stuart, 1778

British Library, K. Top vol.8 pl.83A
Inscr.: 'The PARK BUILDING at Wimple, Cambridge Shire, the Seat of the EARL of HARDWICKE', 'At secura quies, et nescia fallere Vita/ Dives opum variarum, at latis otia fundis/ Mugitusq. boum, mollesq. sub arbore somni/ Non absunt', 'Stuart Architect', and 'Lerpinière sculp, 1778'
Engraving (402 x 570mm)
Lit. & repr.: Stroud (1979), p.759, pl.6; Jackson-Stops, (1992), pp.88–89, cat.61; Adshead (2000), pp.150–63, fig.3; Bristol (2000), p.51, fig.10; Soros (2006), p.318, fig.7-4.

The Rev. James Plumptre refers to this engraving, and to a smaller version published in 1781: 'There is a large print of this, which I believe is only a private plate in the family. From this a small one was done for the *Westminster Magazine* for Feb.' Stuart is credited here as 'architect', but it is not clear whether he was also the author of the lost drawing from which Lerpinière made his engraving. The smaller version, published in *The Westminster Magazine* for February 1781, opposite p. 64, bears the same title and Latin verse but does not include the names Stuart and Lerpinière; it is, however, additionally inscribed, 'Publish'd 1 March 1781 by Fielding & Walker, Pa^{r}noster Row' (*No.91*). A short accompanying account, entitled 'The Park buildings at Wimple, Cambridgeshire, the seat of the Earl of Hardwicke', notes the successive ownership of Wimpole, and concludes: 'a great deal has been done both to the Mansion, the Park, and the Gardens, by the present Earl. The Taste of Messieurs Browne and Stuart show themselves to great advantage at this place'.

The Latin text below the view is excerpted from a passage in Virgil's poem *The Georgics* (Book II, lines 467-71), which in the Rev. Joseph Warton's contemporary translation is rendered as follows:

Yet calm content, secure from guilty cares,
Yet home-felt pleasure, peace, and rest are theirs,
Leisure and ease, in groves, and cooling vales,
The lowing oxen, and the bleating sheep,
And under branching trees delicious sleep![222]

In the engraving the words mugitusque and mollesque are abbreviated and line 469, 'Speluncae, vivique lacus; et frigida Tempe', or 'Grottoes, and bubbling brooks, and darksome dales', inappropriate to the dry, hilltop setting at Wimpole, is omitted. Hardwicke was an accomplished classicist and would have taken pleasure in this association with the dream landscapes of the ancient poets.

In February 1778 when Hardwicke sent his friend William Legge, 2nd Earl of Dartmouth, a copy of the engraving of the gothic folly he wrote: 'I am, as a companion to this antique, engraving a modern Italian loggia, which I have set up at Wimpole, under the auspices of Mr. Stewart [*sic*]'.[223]

91 View of the Hill House, 1781

Author's collection
Inscr.: 'The PARK BUILDING at Wimple, Cambridge Shire, the Seat of the EARL of HARDWICKE.'; 'At secura quies, et nescia fallere Vita Dives opum variarum, at latis otia fundis Mugitusq. boum, mollesq. sub arbore somni Non absunt';
'Publish'd 1 March 1781 by Fielding & Walker, Pa^r.noster Row'
Engraving (210 x 232mm)

This is the smaller version published in *The Westminster Magazine* for February 1781, referred to by Plumptre.

Views of the Park at Wimpole from Wedgwood's 'Frog Service' (92–6)

The extraordinary story of the great 944-piece dinner and dessert service that Josiah Wedgwood (1730—95) and his business partner Thomas Bentley (1730—80) made in 1773—4 for Catherine the Great, Empress of Russia, has been told on a number of occasions.[224] It was an ambitious undertaking, for the service, which was designed for fifty guests, included 1,222 different 'views of Ruins in Great Britain, country seats of the nobility, gardens, landscapes, and other embellishments'.[225] The subject matter of the commission was expressly requested by the empress whose enthusiasms she confided to Voltaire: 'I love English gardens to the point of folly: serpentine lines, gentle slopes, marshes turned into lakes, islands of dry ground, and I deeply despise straight lines. I hate fountains which torture water to make it a course contrary to nature; in a word, my plantomania is dominated by anglomania'.[226]

The assembly of so many views posed a considerable logistical challenge, and Wedgwood sought advice from his friend the artist Samuel Stringer (1750—84) before relaying it to Bentley. The artist 'said it was a very arduous undertaking, & must be a most expensive one if we did tolerable justice to the designs—that there were very few Men in England clever at painting Buildings'. Wedgwood added that Stringer had estimated that if all the views were to be based on newly commissioned drawings from life, the service might take three to four years, and cost as many thousands of pounds, to complete.[227] Wedgwood also intended to ask Lancelot 'Capability' Brown for his help to 'pro'cure us a great number of designs, [and] tell us who had views of their pleasure grounds taken'.[228]

Faced with a prohibitively expensive and impossibly time-consuming task, Wedgwood and Bentley turned their attention to existing engraved sources. The engraved works of Samuel (d.1779) and Nathaniel Buck provided some 250 views, with other smaller groups derived from plates by Richard Godfrey, George Bickham (d.1769), John Boydell (1719—1804), Jean-Baptiste-Claude Chatelain (*c.*1710—71), James Mason (1710—*c.*80), S. Sparrow, François Vivares (1709—80) and William Woollett (1735—85). Views were also taken directly from drawn and painted sources by Stringer and the artists Nicholas Dall (d.1777) and Anthony Devis (1729—1817).

In June 1774, part of the unfinished Frog Service was put on display in Wedgwood's Greek Street showrooms, and the 'Nobility and Gentry' were invited to see it.[229] This was a brilliant marketing exercise whose potential advantages and disadvantages Wedgwood carefully weighed. On the one hand he argued that by bringing 'an immence [*sic*] number of People of Fashion' to the showrooms, the firm might 'complete our notoriety to the whole Island [...] & help us greatly [...] in the sale of our goods', but on the other he was concerned that one influential customer or another might be offended 'by the omission of his seat, when his Neighbours is taken'. Wedgwood needed 150 images to complete the service and by inviting his exhibition visitors to put forward drawings for copying, both problems could be solved at a stroke. The Marchioness Grey took the bait and wrote urgently to her daughter Lady Amabel Polwarth:

> I have been to see Wedgewood's [*sic*] Exhibition of the Service for the Czarina, I want very much to have some of Our Views of your Drawing find a place in it, as it is not quite completed. How can they be got at? Have you any Book that contains them at Wrest or are they in your great Book locked up in London? If so, could you send me the Key—and another Question, should you care to send out any Drawings not framed?

I believe they were all fixed. Those I should wish for are the general View from the Gravel Walk at Wimple which took in the Water, Bridge, & Tower; and The different Views of the Water round the Garden at Wrest; The Small Views at Wimple from the head of the Reed Pond down the Bank to the Other Water—and if you could make it out distinctly, the Piece you took last year of the Window &c at the Ruin; also the Bath & Room at Wrest which you took lately if that too could be finished up. These Smaller Views you have I suppose with you, but if they cannot be taken out or would not be safe to send up & lend out, I by no means Wish to hazard them.[230]

Jemima was not slow to recognize that her daughter's landscape drawings of the family seats at Wimpole and Wrest were ideal for the project, according perfectly with the empress's reported desire to have 'all that could be of Gothic Remains, of Natural Views, & of Improved Scenes and Ornaments in Parks & Gardens which they say are what she wants to collect & Imitate'.[231] Jemima's daughter replied by return of post:

I shall not be displeas'd if Wrest & Wimple make some Figure aux Regions de l'Ourse, as a French Poet would say. And I think they are pretty enough to deserve a good Place, even in a Collection of the prettiest Views in England. Who knows but our Tower may have the inestimable Glory of pleasing her Imperial Majesty, & be mounted upon some Hill at Czarsko Zelo or any other House with a hard Name that you please. Though to say the Truth I rather doubt whether my Drawings of that ancient Ruin are very intelligible, & I cannot finish them better without being upon the Spot.[232]

The dinner and dessert service was designed for the empress's Chesme palace—a small Gothic Revival building of triangular plan designed by the architect Yuri Felten and built between 1774 and 1777—which was conveniently placed part way between the Winter Palace and Tsarskoye Selo. It sat in a marshy area whose croaking frogs inspired its onomatopoetic name Kekerekeksinen, in Finnish, and which Catherine translated as La Grenouillère. Each piece of the service bears a heraldic device containing a spread-eagled frog, painted in

Wimpole Architectural Drawings 64

green enamel. A reference number painted on the back of each piece corresponds to an entry in a descriptive catalogue compiled by Bentley and translated into French for the empress.[233] As many as thirty-three artists, of whom David Rhodes (d.1777) is thought to have served as the directing 'eye', worked on the Frog Service at the Chelsea Decorating Studio.

In addition to the five plates described below, Bentley's catalogue lists '1201 Vue au meme endroit [Wimple]', sadly a long-lost part of the service, and '113 Vue dans les Jardins de Wimple, campagne de Milord Hardwicke', which is illustrated with a vignette comprising a small church with a spired tower and beyond it the upper storey of a house with a roof-top lantern; neither building can be related to any at Wimpole.

92 Dessert plate decorated with a view of the Lower Lake at Wimpole, looking west to the Chinese Bridge, 1773—4

The State Hermitage Museum, St. Petersburg, 9158
Mark: painted view number '1198' in brown enamel
Cream-coloured earthenware (Queen's Ware) painted in purplish-blank and green enamel, after a lost drawing by Lady Amabel Polwarth (1751—1833); diameter 22cm
Bentley catalogue 823: '1198: Vue à Wimple, dans le Comté de Cambridge'.
Lit. & repr.: Raeburn, Voronikhina & Nurnberg (1995), pp.251–2, fig.122; Adshead (1996), pp.31–6, fig.4.

93 Dessert plate decorated with a view of the Gothic Folly at Wimpole, from the south-west, 1773—4

The State Hermitage Museum, St. Petersburg, 9152
Mark: painted view number '1199' in brown enamel
Cream-coloured earthenware (Queen's Ware), painted in purplish-black and green enamel after a lost drawing by Lady Amabel Polwarth; diameter 22cm
Bentley catalogue 824: '1199: Vue d'une Ruine à Wimple'.
Lit. & repr.: Raeburn, Voronikhina & Nurnberg (1995), pp.251–2, fig.123; Adshead (1996), pp.31–6, fig.3.; Adshead (1998), pp.76–84, fig.9.

This view may be based on the drawing Marchioness Grey describes to her daughter as being: 'the Piece you took last year of the Window &c. at the Ruin'.

94 Dessert plate decorated with a view of the Hill House, 1773—4

The State Hermitage Museum, St. Petersburg, 9405
Mark: painted view number '1200' in brown enamel
Cream-coloured earthenware (Queen's Ware), painted in purplish-black and green enamel, after a lost drawing probably by James 'Athenian' Stuart (1713—88); diameter 22cm
Bentley catalogue 825: '1200: Vue d'un pavillon, dans le Parc du Comte de Hardwick, à Wimple'.
Lit. & repr.: Raeburn, Voronikhina & Nurnberg (1995), pp.251–2, fig.124; Young (1995), p.203, cat.G314; Adshead (1996), pp.31–6.

The composition is identical to Lerpinière's very much more accomplished 1778 engraving, suggesting that they were based on a common original drawing, perhaps by James 'Athenian' Stuart. It has been suggested that the building was designed in 1775 (*Nos.86–9*), but the fact that Wedgwood's service was completed and delivered in 1774 argues for an earlier date.

95 Dessert plate decorated with a view of the Upper Lake at Wimpole, showing the Gothic Folly and Chinese Bridge, 1773—4

The State Hermitage Museum, St. Petersburg, 9113
Mark: painted view number '1207' (cat. 832) in brown enamel
Cream-coloured earthenware (Queen's Ware), painted in purplish-black and green enamel, after a lost drawing by Lady Amabel Polwarth; diameter 22cm
Bentley catalogue 832: '1207: Vue dans le Parc du Comte de Hardwick, à Wimple'.
Lit. & repr.: Raeburn, Voronikhina & Nurnberg (1995), pp.251–2, fig.126; Adshead (1996), pp.31–6, fig.2.

This image corresponds with the drawing that Marchioness Grey described as 'the general View from the Gravel Walk at Wimple which took in the Water, Bridge, & Tower'.

96 Dessert plate decorated with a view of the lower lake from the west, 1773—4

The State Hermitage Museum, St. Petersburg, 9130
Mark: painted view number '1208' in brown enamel
Cream-coloured earthenware (Queen's Ware), painting in purplish-black and green enamel, after a lost drawing by Lady Amabel Polwarth; diameter 22cm
Bentley catalogue 833: '1208: Vue dans les Jardins de Wimple'.
Lit. & repr.: Raeburn, Voronikhina & Nurnberg (1995), pp.251–2, fig.127; Adshead (1996), pp.31–6.

This image is probably one of 'The Small Views at Wimple from the head of the Reed Pond down the Bank to the Other Water' that Marchioness Grey requested her daughter should send her. The middle lake at Wimpole, now referred to as the upper lake because the first is dry, was known as the reed pond in the late eighteenth and early nineteenth centuries. This view, taken from the dam above the lower lake, shows the spur of land and planting that screens Henry Flitcroft's spillway (*No.56*) below the Chinese bridge when seen from the southern and eastern shores.

97 (i to iv) Anonymous estate survey, *c*. mid-1770s

National Trust WIM/D/562a to d
Inscr.: All the parcels of land are numbered (1 to 81) on the plan and described in the accompanying 'REFERENCE' table.
Pen and ink: 562a (511 x 911mm); 562b (742 x 880mm); 563c (749 x 863mm); and 563d (706 x 868mm)

This anonymous map, in four sheets, describes the designed landscape at Wimpole from the northern edge of Brown's belts (sheet i) to the point where the southern end of Bridgeman's great South avenue runs into the Great North Road (sheet iv). It postdates Brown's improvements of the late 1760s and the building of the Gothic folly and Stuart's Hill House, and predates William Emes's plan of 1790. Clearly it was made for the purposes of estate managment (the 'REFERENCE' table lists the rental values of each parcel of land) and, because it also lacks 'finish', it may be judged a survey rather than a design proposal. With its several mapping errors, however, it cannot be considered a fine example of the surveyor's art. In September 1774, the 2nd Earl of Hardwicke employed the agricultural improver Nathaniel Kent (1737—1810) to survey his estate at Crudwell in Wiltshire.[234] Might he also have asked him to survey his Cambridgeshire estate? The Wimpole cash books record payments to 'N^l Kent' of £78 on 27 February 1776 and £98 9s 6d on 12 December 1777.[235] Emes must have had access to this survey, and the various erasures—such as the area he was to develop as the Pleasure Grounds and new walled garden—and additions may be his.

Drawing by Kenton Couse (1721—90)

98 Kenton Couse. Laid-out drawing for an apsidal-ended Dining Room, 1778

National Trust WIM/D/449
Inscr.: On the fireplace, or south, wall 'Jan'y 28 1778. Settled that there should be Two Pictures on this Side of Room only', and, similarly recorded on the west wall, 'there should be Two Pictures at this End of Room'
Pen and ink (570 x 490mm)
Scale given
Lit. & repr.: Parry (1986), pp.36–55, fig.23.

This charming neo-classical drawing, creased along the bottom edges of the four 'walls', was clearly devised to enable Couse's clients to gain a three-dimensional impression in miniature of the proposed room, the central ceiling design doubling as a decorative carpet. The folding drawing is now mounted flat.

Kenton Couse first worked at Wimpole as Henry Flitcroft's assistant, and with him rose to relatively high station in the Office of Works; by the time Couse designed this eating room at Wimpole, nine years after Flitcroft's death, he had become secretary to the Board and Clerk Itinerant. According to the evidence of a letter written to Thomas Worsley of Hovingham Hall, Couse was at Wimpole in August 1777.[236]

Couse formed this 'Eating Room' for the 2nd Earl of Hardwicke within the existing north-east block. This range, built sometime between 1742 and 1749 by Henry Flitcroft (*No.48*), and described by him as 'the Sham Front in the Garden', served to balance James Gibbs's work to the west side of the house and appears to have remained an empty shell until 1778. This design, and the evidence of subsequent survey drawings, show the room to have been lit by three windows on the north or garden side of the house, and to have had an apsidal east end. The new room sufficiently impressed Caroline Yorke (1765—1818), later Countess of St. Germans, for her to mention it to her maternal aunt, Lady Beauchamp, of Langley Park, Norfolk, in a letter describing life at Wimpole in 1781: 'Lady Grey, the Marchioness, has just fitted up some new apartments that are beautiful, particularly the new dining-room which is very elegant indeed'.[237]

The estate cash books record a succession of payments to 'Mr. Cowse' some of which may relate to the design and building of the new dining room: 1 December 1775, £597 3s; 16 December 1776, £40 19s 6d; 18 July 1777, £47 9s 6d; 18 December 1778, £291 8s 6d; 24 September 1779, £52 4s; and 23 November 1780, £137; 26 November 1781, £174 10s 6d; 29 November 1782, £43 2s; and 12 December 1788, £679 17s.[238]

The probate inventory made in 1835 after the death of the 3rd Earl of Hardwicke records the contents of Couse's room in the early nineteenth century.[239] The room survived in this form until it was remodelled for the 4th Earl of Hardwicke in *c*.1860.

Couse's involvement at Wimpole continued for a number of years. In 1779 Richard Barton explained that 'The Carpenter in pursuance of Mr. Couses's Directions has taken away the Floor and Wainscot of the House keeper's Room (being very rotten) and brick Drains are made under the Floor to keep it drier in future. The Work of the New Rooms is also going on'; while in April 1781 the architect was asked to examine the Greenhouse, concluding: 'in all my Business I never met with any Building so Dangerous and Ruinous a Condition. I have made Drawings of the Same'.[240]

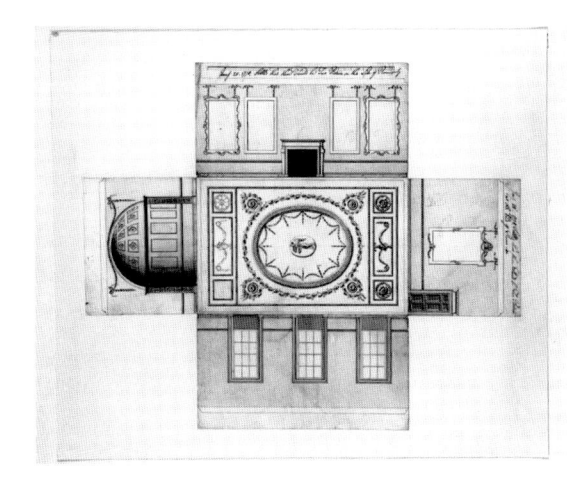

Eighteenth-, nineteenth- and twentieth-century views of St. Andrew's Church, Wimpole

The earliest view of the parish church of St. Andrew appears in Benjamin Hare's survey of the Wimpole estate of 1638 (*No.1*). This stylised representation, which shows a tower at the west end and a simple, pitched roof over the nave and chancel, serves to locate the relative position of the moated house that Thomas Chicheley was to clear away a few years later.

The next earliest surviving representation of the church is found on Kip's engraved view of Wimpole of 1707 (*No.3*). Other than the size of the west tower, which Kip appears to have exaggerated, this image conforms closely with the information provided by Henry Flitcroft's measured survey of 1748 (*No.57*). A pair of rather more detailed late-eighteenth-century views by the Rev. James Plumptre show the church before and after Flitcroft's rebuilding.

99 & 100 Rev. James Plumptre (1770—1832). Sketches of the church before and after the remodelling of 1749, 1779

British Library, Add. MS 58233, fos. 132 & 133
Inscr.: fo.132, 'Wimpole Church before it was taken down to be rebuilt about 1740'; and fo.133, 'Wimpole Church in Cambridgeshire 1779'
Pen and ink with grey wash (60 x 100mm) & (100 x 130mm)

Inscriptions made by the antiquary the Rev. William Cole on the reverse of both drawings explain that they were, 'taken for me March 17, 1779 by Mr. Jas. Plumptre of Queens' College'; and that the, otherwise seemingly anachronistic, 'before' view of the medieval church had been copied 'from a drawing by his Uncle Dr Charles Plumptre, Archdeacon of Ely'. Charles Plumptre (1712—99) had previously been the Rector of Wimpole and Whaddon, and was so at the time of Flitcroft's rebuilding of the church. James Plumptre, a playwright and clergyman, was the second son of Dr Robert Plumptre (1723—88).

The drawing of the church in its medieval incarnation is so uncannily similar to that shown in Kip's engraving—not only in terms of detail but in the viewpoint from which it was taken—that we must wonder if the elder Plumptre used that as the basis for his drawing. It is perhaps odd that in gathering together material for what he referred to as his 'Parochial Antiquities' Cole did not make his own drawing of the building, but W.M. Palmer suggests that there may have been personal or political reasons for this. He writes: 'The only churches of which he left no description are Arrington, Croydon, Little Eversden, Whaddon and Wimpole. It may be only a coincidence, but all these lay within the influence of the Whig Lord Chancellor Hardwicke'.[241] Although in correspondence with Horace Walpole Cole did make explicit his dislike of Lord Hardwicke we know from a surviving account that in July 1777 the antiquary did visit 'the new Church [...] built of Brick, with Stone Coins' with Dr Robert Plumptre, rector of Wimpole and Whaddon (in succession to his brother Charles) and president of Queens' College.[242] It is instructive to compare Plumptre's naïve 'after' drawing with Flitcroft's elevations for the west and south sides of the church (*Nos.60 & 61*); the scale of the bellcote particularly is misrepresented. Oddly, Plumptre has failed to include the church's pitched roof.

101 Samuel Lysons (bap.1763—1819). Pencil sketch of windows in the Chicheley Chapel. Early 19th century

British Library, Add. MS 9461, fo. 78
Pencil (page, 152 x 103mm)

Samuel Lysons, one time lawyer, keeper of the records in the Tower of London, vice-president of both the Society of Antiquaries and the Royal Society, and antiquary professor at the Royal Academy, was the younger brother of the antiquary Daniel Lysons (1762—1834). Samuel Lysons corresponded with the 3rd Earl of Hardwicke in 1806, the year in which *Magna Britannia*, co-authored with Daniel, was published:

> As we propose to begin printing our seond volume, which commences with Cambridgeshire, about the middle of next month, my brother & I intend being in Cambride for about a week in the beginning of the month, in order to make corrections & additions to our MSS, when we shall be happy to have the honour of paying our respects to your Ldship at Wimpole, and to avail ourselves of your obliging offer.[243]

A month later he wrote again hoping to 'take the opportunity of availing ourselves of your obliging promise of permission to inspect such of you Ldship's Deeds as may be necessary for making out the short account we give of the descent of Manorial property'.[244]

Volume two comprised their surveys of Cambridgeshire and Chester. This monumental project foundered with Samuel's death and with only those counties which started with the letter D accounted for.

Pasted into an album of drawings and notes made during his visit to churches and cathedrals throughout the country is a slight pencil sketch of two traceried windows in the Chicheley chapel in St. Andrew's church at Wimpole. Lyson's accompanying note reads:

> Wimpole, in the chicheley Chapel. In the Church South [*sic*] Window near the altar is a very rich window with a figure of K. David & sev. Arms of the Yorke family inserted in a very rich mosaic ground executed by Peckitt of York. In Ld. Hardwicke's Gallery at the west end of the church containing a good number of coats of arms of the York family & their connections on the same kind of rich mosaic ground.

There is no documentary evidence that the celebrated stained glass artist William Peckitt (1731—95) was responsible for this work.

102 James Basire (bap.1730—1802). Engraving of the font in St. Andrew's church, Wimpole, after 'HE', 1792

This engraving, by James Basire, after an original drawing by 'HE', was reproduced in a paper on ancient church fonts published by the antiquary Richard Gough (1735—1809) in *Archaeologia*, vol. X, 1792, p.186, plate XXIV.

A pen and ink copy of the engraving, inscribed 'Wimpole—Archaeol. Vol: 10', and made by the antiquary and Cambridge academic Thomas Kerrich (1748—1828) can be found at BL, Add. MS 6736, fo.65, in a volume of notes and drawings on 'Saxon and Norman Architecture' which includes sections on architectural forms and decoration, pillars, arches, doors, windows and fonts. Kerrich, the Principal Librarian of the University of Cambridge, and President of Magdalene College, inherited James Essex's papers and was similarly interested in preparing an outline history of English architecture. In 1798 Kerrich listed the pictures at Wimpole on behalf of Sir William Musgrave (1735—1800) and his project of compiling lists of painted portraits in order to augment English biographical history.[245]

The Catalogue

Drawings by John Soane (1753—1837) and his office for Wimpole Hall

The circumstances of John Soane's first, providential, meeting with Philip Yorke on 28 January 1779 amongst the ancient Greek temples at Paestum, near Salerno have been related on a number of occasions.[246] Yorke wrote to his uncle, Philip Yorke, 2nd Earl of Hardwicke, a few days later: 'The three temples of Paestum of the old Doric order are magnificent buildings and I was astonished to find how perfect they are. An English architect by name Soane who is an ingenious young man now studying at Rome accompanied us thither and measured the buildings'.[247] While Soane's reaction to the ruins was more cautious—he judged them 'exceedingly rude […] they have all the particulars of the Grecian Doric, but not the elegant taste; they seem all formed with the same materials, of stone formed by petrifaction'—the visit appears to have inspired in both men a life-long interest in primitive classical architecture, and, despite the differences in their personal circumstances, mutual admiration. Soane, the elder by four years, was travelling on a study scholarship from the Royal Academy and was eager to secure the interest of potential future clients, while Yorke, the presumptive heir to the earldom of Hardwicke, was a serious-minded aristocratic Grand Tourist.[248] Three years after his return to England Yorke employed Soane to make various alterations to his house at Hammels, Hertfordshire and to design a number of buildings on the estate. The architect was to enjoy Yorke's patronage, and that of various members of his extended family, both in London and in the country, for more than thirty-five years.

Hammels was to serve as a proving ground, and when in 1790 Philip Yorke did inherit the earldom and the Wimpole estate, Soane was immediately called in to remodel and modernise a house which nine years earlier Caroline Yorke—whilst admiring Kenton Couse's new Dining Room and 'the room below stairs'—had described as being 'most part of it […] furnished in the old style, as for example, Mama's and my apartment are brown wainscots, and the bed-curtains and hangings are crimson damask laced with gold most dreadfully tarnished'.[249]

An ingenious model of Wimpole made by Foster Associates and included in the 1999 exhibition 'John Soane Architect: Master of Space and Light' highlights three areas within Wimpole Hall where Soane made particularly dramatic and inspired interventions, rooms now known as the Plunge Bath, the Yellow Drawing Room, and the Book Room.[250] These exemplify Soane's genius for adapting existing fabric and creating novel planning and spatial solutions. But as the following catalogue entries and illustrations demonstrate, Soane's remodelling was much more extensive, and his distinctive joinery and plasterwork details can be found throughout the house. Not only did the architect reconfigure the internal arrangement of the east service wing, introduce two new staircases into the body of the house, replan the accommodation on the first floor, and create an extraordinary roofscape of no less than seven lanterns which, ranging along the central spine of the house, suffused his new interiors with light, but he designed cottages, model farm buildings and an extraordinary water conduit, or *castello d'acqua*, for the wider estate.

Curiously the Plunge Bath, one of Wimpole's most memorable architectural interiors, does not appear on any of Soane's surviving drawings but its design and construction can be traced through the pages of his Journal. In his Day Book, Soane noted on 1 April 1791: 'took Plan of Situation for Bath'. On 18 October 1792 Soane 'Del^d. a Working drawing for the Bath at Wimpole shewing the Plan & 2 Sect^n. on 1/2 sheet of Cat^r. Paper' and three months later, on 18 January 1793, noted: 'Meyer wrote to Provis, with a sketch for Moldings of Cornice to Bath', and 'Ordered of M^r. Nelson a Portland Stone Chimney piece for Bath Dressing Room as per draw^g. del^d. to him'; a year later, on 5 February 1793, the Journal records: 'Meyer wrote to M^r. Provis and encl^g. a Copy of the Sketch of Bath sent by Provis desiring him to finish it according to his Ideas'.[251] David Souden explains that by the late eighteenth century, in England at least, the idea of the plunge bath, which on country-house estates was usually realised in the form of a free-standing park building, was rather old-fashioned, and that the survival of an indoor bath, particularly in the face of Victorian and Edwardian improvements, is a particular rarity.[252] Indeed Wimpole's extraordinary plunge bath is the only surviving exemplar of the various bath schemes, inspired by ancient Roman forms, that Soane devised. In 1772 Soane gained practical experience with the architect Henry Holland (1745—1806) who, with his father-in-law Lancelot 'Capability' Brown, was then designing Claremont, Surrey (1771—4) for Robert Clive, 1st Baron Clive of Plassey (1725—74). The basement of the house still contains a sunken bath which has resonances of the one that Soane was to fit so ingeniously into an unsatisfactory residual space at Wimpole twenty years later. Whilst in Italy in 1779 the young architect produced a sketch design for a bathhouse, fronted by a colonnade and capped by a saucer dome, which it has been argued may have been intended for the garden of the London townhouse of Thomas Pitt, later 1st Baron Camelford (1737—93).[253] In 1783 he designed a bathroom of somewhat decadent character for the basement of Malvern Hall, Henry Greswold Lewis's Warwickshire house, where an elliptical plunge bath was to be flanked by alcoves, framed by Corinthian columns, one containing a hot bath in the form of an ancient sarcophagus and the other a neo-Classical day-bed.[254] The following year the architect also designed a free standing bathhouse for Miles Sotherton Branthwayte at Taverham Hall, Norfolk. Sadly, none of these schemes were realised, and it is only from a mid-nineteenth century watercolour by Lady Elizabeth Cartwright, *née* von Sandizell (1805—50) that the appearance of Soane's sunken bath at Aynhoe Park, Northamptonshire is known.[255] Brilliantly imaginative though it was, Soane's placement of the plunge bath, and with it more than 2,000 gallons of water, on the north side of the chapel wall, was impractical; Sir James Thornhill's paintings on the wall's southern face have suffered as a consequence and today the bath is shown empty.

Another room at Wimpole, all too little known, that bears Soane's design hallmark, and for which there also appears to be no paper record, is the basement muniment room which contains elegant, but long-damaged, cupboards for the storage of estate and political papers.

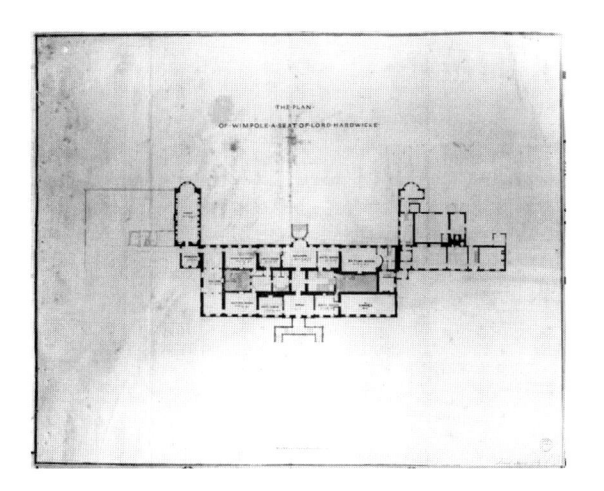

Survey drawings of Wimpole Hall by members of John Soane's office

The drawings produced by John Soane's architectural practice, one of the largest of its time, were necessarily the result of collaboration. In the following catalogue entries, the ascription 'Soane Office' is used where it has not been possible to determine the draughtsman responsible for a particular drawing. In other cases where the hand is recognisable or the evidence of Soane's Day Book is conclusive the author's name is given.[256]

103 Guibert or David Laing (1774—1856). Survey of the ground floor of Wimpole Hall, with a sketch cross-section of the Yellow Drawing Room, c. 1790

Sir John Soane's Museum, 6/1/21
Inscr.: 'Plan of the House at Wimpole', 'The Earl of Hardwicke'. Dimensions and some room names given.
Pen and ink with grey and blue wash and pencil additions. Three sheets pasted together (560 x 1,660mm)
Lit. & repr.: Parry (1986), pp.36–55, fig.29; Woodward (1999), pp.8–13, fig.5; Dean (1999) p.66, fig.4.3, p.67, fig.4.6.

Soane's Journal records that he and Guibert visited Wimpole together on 10 June 1790 and 'took plans', presumably the survey trip that resulted in this series of record drawings.[257] A complementary record in the Earl of Hardwicke's account book for 12 June 1790 reveals that John Ratford, the estate carpenter, spent his time 'In giving Mr. Soam [sic] and his Man the Measures of the House—1½ day'. Guibert's identity remains a mystery, and with both Soane's Day Book and Diary for 1790 missing it seems unlikely that more can be learnt of his involvement at Wimpole.

This carefully annotated survey of the house and the service wing to the east records the layout of the ground floor as Soane's office found it in 1790. The drawing documents the series of changes, such as the insertion of Kenton Couse's Dining Room and the addition of polygonal bays to the northern ends of the Library and Laundry wings, that had been made since Flitcroft's alterations to the house, and it is instructive to compare this drawing with that architect's proposals (*No.49*). It also shows that an inconvenient, central support had been added, presumably for structural reasons, to the columnar screens that Flitcroft had introduced when creating the Gallery from Gibbs's sequence of cabinet rooms.

At the left hand end of the drawing (see separate detail) is a sketch section which suggests how a lantern might emerge between the two parallel roofs of the double pile house. This may be Soane's first sketch idea for the Yellow Drawing Room which was to nestle at the heart of the house.

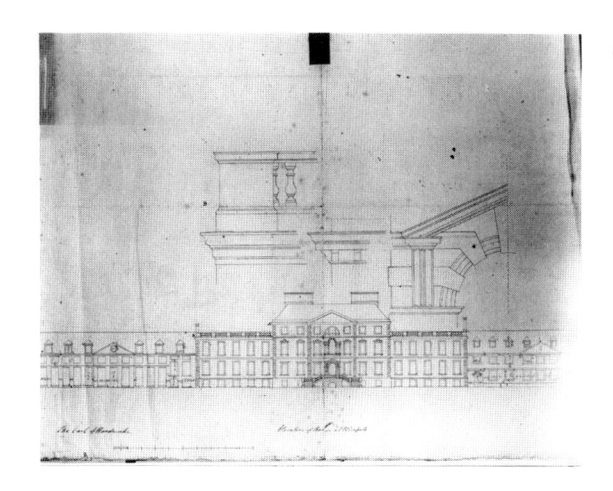

104 David Laing. Survey plan of the ground floor, 1790

Sir John Soane's Museum, 6/1/13
Inscr.: 'The Plan of Wimpole A Seat of Lord Hardwicke', 'David Laing July 5th 1790'. The rooms are labelled and their dimensions given.
Pen and ink with grey and blue wash (450 x 570mm).
Watermark: J WHATMAN and Fleur-de-lis over crest.
Lit. & repr.: RCHME (1968), pl.133 (bottom)

Soane has here already sketched in his proposal to place staircases in the two open lightwells or 'areas' to the east and west of the seventeenth-century house, indicated in blue wash. The form of the bi-exedial, southern end of what was to become the Yellow Drawing Room is also indicated.

105 Guibert. Measured survey drawing of the south elevation of the central, seven-bay block, 1790

Sir John Soane's Museum, 6/1/1
Inscr.: 'The Earl of Hardwicke Elevation of the Centre part of the House at Wimpole', '84' 9" Whole Extent', with dimensions given, and the number of courses of brick marked between each floor. Verso: 'Wimple, Elevation'.
Pen & ink over pencil set-up lines (380 x 480mm)
Scale: 1in: 5 ft. Ruled border
Watermark: I PORTAL and Fleur-de-lis

A dimensioned survey of Flitcroft's refaced central block. Prick-marks in the paper reveal that this drawing must have been copied.

106 Guibert. Dimensioned survey drawing of the western half of the south elevation, 1790

Sir John Soane's Museum, 6/1/2
Inscr.: Dimensions marked
Pen and ink (585 x 350mm)
Scale: 3/16 in: 1ft
Verso: Pen and ink drawing of north façade. Inscr.: 'Wimple Elevation by Guibert'. 'The Earl of Hardwicke', Scale: 1/16 in: 1ft.

107 Guibert. Dimensioned survey of the south elevation, with details of cornice (A), balustrade (B) and the pediment to the entrance door, 1790

Sir John Soane's Museum, 6/1/3
Inscr.: 'The Earl of Hardwicke', 'Elevation of House at Wimpole'. Dimensions of the orangery and east service block are marked. The location of the details are indicated 'A' and 'B'.
Pen and ink (555 x 710mm)
Scale: 1/16 in: 1 ft
Verso: Dimensioned survey drawing of the eastern half of the north elevation.
Inscr.: 'Wimpole, Elevation by Guibert'. Scale: 3/16 in: 1ft.

The laundry block at the east end of the house is recorded here with a flat roof in contrast to the pitch on the balancing library wing.

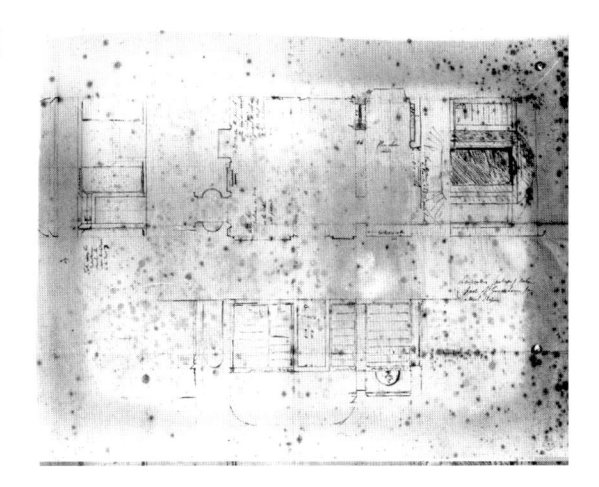

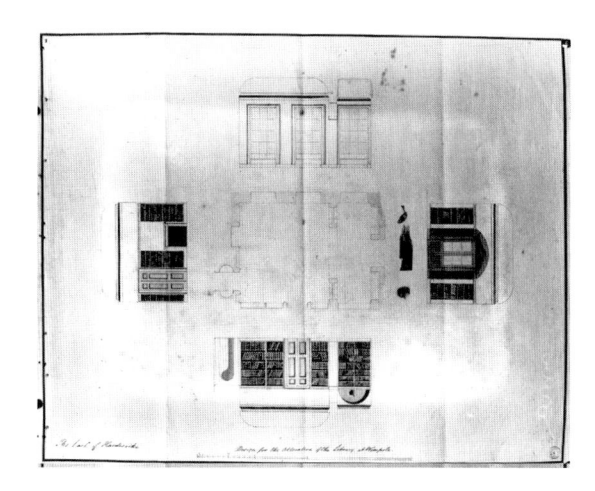

Drawings for the Bookroom

Gillian Darley explains that Soane 'could always find pleasure in books', enjoyed hunting for volumes in bookshops wherever he travelled, and 'when he felt unhappy […] rearranged his shelves or bought more volumes'. She suggests too that Soane 'liked nothing better than to design a library for a favourite client'.[258] The architect's reverence for books perhaps helped to inspire his creation of poetic spaces in which they could be housed and consulted.

In his library interiors elsewhere Soane experimented with a variety of plan forms: square at Albury Park, Surrey (1801—2) and Combe House, Devon (1802—19); semicircular at Mells Park, Somerset (1810—5); columnar-screened at St. Germans, Port Eliot, Cornwall; and bi-exedial at Cricket St. Thomas, Somerset. But, together with those rooms that he designed for himself at Lincoln's Inn Fields and Pitzhanger Manor, the Bookroom at Wimpole must count among the most successful of Soane's many library interiors, perhaps partly because his brief—to extend rather than replace the library and ante-library that James Gibbs had devised—provided him with a catalysing challenge. More often than not the presses designed for those other libraries supported the conventional library garniture of busts and globes, but at Wimpole and in the Library-Dining Room at 13 Lincoln's Inn Fields, vases in the form of classical cinerary urns were substituted. Significantly, bronzed plaster urns were also used in this way in Philip Yorke's library at No.7 (now 63) New Cavendish Street, London. The shelving, designed by Soane, was moved from Yorke's house in Park Street.[259]

At Wimpole Soane's solution was to divide the new space into bays with a series of shallow arches that spring directly from the flanking bookpresses. The full-length windows to the south flood each bay with side-light throwing into relief the plaster *paterae* above the arches, emphasising the sense that each arch, layered one behind another, is a scenic drop on a theatre stage.

In 1967 Christopher Hussey argued that the addition of the Bookroom at Wimpole was probably 'the latest of Soane's alterations to judge from the more developed idiom of its decoration; probably dating after the 3rd Earl's term as Lord Lieutenant of Ireland, 1804—6'.[260] Subsequent accounts of the house have perpetuated his suggestion that the room dates from *c*.1806. The architect's meticulously kept records, however, are silent on this point and the surviving drawings and relevant accounts all date from 1791, when Soane redesigned the shelving in Gibbs's adjoining ante-library and furnished it with a striking new chimneypiece; in December 1791 £21 was charged for the 'Molded Chimney Piece […] enriched wth. Pannels of black Marble'.[261]

A mystery remains, however. The sketch and the worked-up proposal (*Nos.106 & 109*) described below propose the addition of only one bay. Two bays, of unequal width, were in fact annexed from the Orangery, and it seems clear that this must have been the result of two different campaigns of work. In May 1791 John Crace was paid for painting the library, and the accounts specifically itemise '14 large rich Pateras [*sic*] in Ante Library', and 'Bronzing 6 Plaster Vases'.[262] Today the room is enriched with a total of twenty-eight *paterae* and ten plaster vases. At the time of Crace's painting the Ante Library must, therefore, have only been extended by the one bay that is described in Soane's drawings and which would have accommodated the fourteen *paterae* and six vases. The second bay must have been in place by 1809 when the Reptons remodelled the Orangery (*Nos.205 to 209*).

Neither the need for additional shelves for books nor the location of Soane's Book Room were new propositions. In 1772, evidently charged with thinking about these issues, the Rev. Plumptre wrote a remarkably prescient letter to the 2nd Earl of Hardwicke:

> The room above stairs which has books in it would admit of some more, but not a great number […] The late Lord Hardwicke us'd to talk of taking a room out of the Greenhouse for books; but I do not see that can be well effected on account of the different heights of the floors and ceilings of that and the present Anti-library. Your Lordship would probably not chuse to execute what upon the whole appears to me the most promising plan, viz. to convert the Gallery again to its former use, and furnish it with books. I apprehend there may be other objections besides it being a passage room. If there are not, I think it might perhaps be a sufficient answer to that, that it is a passage to no other place than the library, of which it would become a part.[263]

It was Soane who had the ingenuity, twenty years later, to solve the problems of the 'different heights of the floors and ceilings'.

108 John Soane. Sketch plan and elevations for the remodelling of the Bookroom, April 1791

Sir John Soane's Museum, 6/1/9
Inscr.: With various instructions and suggestions. On the plan of Gibbs's ante-library: 'Make the bookcase as deep as the walls will permit', 'NB. make the piers of the windows equal by bringing forward the bookcase on this side, & also the door architraves'. Soane indicates that the floor above the western addition should be raised. On the east wall: 'Take this entablature the same architrave as to door B' [the north door leading to the library proper]. Other comments relate to the hanging of the doors to the west end and a note: 'Carpenters (perhaps) take part of the Greenhouse for a Work Shop'. Verso: 'Wimpole April 1791—Section of Anti-Library with proposed Alterations'.
Pencil and sepia ink (680 x 555mm)

This may be a preliminary sketch for the presentation drawing (*No.111*) or perhaps a working sketch for the clerk who was to oversee the alteration of the room.

109 John Soane. Sketch design for a plaster vase, 1791

Sir John Soane's Museum, Day Book 1791, fo.119
Inscr.: 'Saturday October 1st; Chawner called at Lord Hardwicke's, No.2 Vases are wanting for Library, as per Sketch'; 'Vase' and the dimensions '1: 6' (H) and 11$^{3}/_{4}$' (Diam. at top)
Pen and ink (Detail. Page, 315 x 200mm)

Thomas Chawner (1774—1851) was a pupil in Soane's office from 1788—94. These vases, made in plaster and painted black to simulate the basalte-ware made fashionable by Wedgwood, are decorated with *strigilations*, the cursive ornament commonly found on Roman *sarcophagae* and named after the similarly shaped body scraper, or *strigilis*, used in ancient bathhouses. The conceit here is that these blackened vases, placed in semi-circular niches, that themselves recall the *loculi* of ancient *columbaria*, are *cineraria* for the safe-keeping of funeral ashes. The pair of vases at the northern end of each bay are decorated instead with figurative scenes.

110 John Soane. Detail drawing for the Library doors, 1791

Sir John Soane's Museum, 6/1/8
Inscr.: 'The Earl of Hardwicke, Wimpole', 'Copy Nov. 24 1791'. The positions of the 'Door when shut' and 'Door when open' are shown, and an accompanying explanatory note given: 'NB. as the Doors when open will shew a groove and half the male joint between the moldings and edge of the door the same groove and half the Male joint are be continued around the Top'. Verso: 'Wimpole—Drawing shewing the manner of hanging the Library doors. Nov. 24 1794'.
Pen and ink (575 x 340 mm)
Lit. & repr.: Parry (1986), pp.36–55, fig.38.

Soane's Journal (No.2, fo.141) records that he sent a copy of this drawing to Henry Provis (1760—1830) on 24 November. Provis was Soane's outdoor clerk stationed at Wimpole.

111 Soane Office. Plan and internal elevation for the Bookroom, with flap 1791

Sir John Soane's Museum, 6/1/4
Inscr.: 'The Earl of Hardwicke', 'Design for the Alteration of the Library at Wimpole'. Verso: 'Wimple, section of Ante Library'
Pen and ink with grey and coloured washes (590 x 470mm)
Scale given
Watermark: PORTAL & BRIDGES with crowned fleur-de-lis above CR
Lit. & repr.: Parry (1986), pp.36–55, fig.38.

This appears to be a preliminary scheme for the remodelling of Gibbs's ante-library, showing: the insertion of an elliptical tribune at the entrance from the gallery, the addition of new doors, shelving and a fireplace, and the room's extension to the west by one bay (annexed from the Orangery). An arched recess above the book press on the north elevation contains a cinerary urn.

A paper flap allows alternative views of the west face of the room, with a pedimented doorcase leading to the Orangery beyond flanked by book shelves (up), and a section showing the westernmost arch (down). There is no sign in this scheme of the boldly modelled plaster *paterae* with which Soane was to enrich the arches.

Lady Mary Robinson, Baroness Grantham (1757—1830), was clearly unconvinced by the idiosyncratic form of Soane's shallow segmental arches, which spring from the top of the bookcases, for in September 1792 she wrote to her widowed elder sister Lady Amabel Polwarth, by then Baroness Lucas and Countess de Grey: 'the room enlarged out of the greenhouse is spoiled by being turned into an arch that projects much too far and Lady H. lays all the blame on his lordship'.[264] It has been noted above that the three shallow arches at Wimpole, lit from the south by windows between, have a theatrical effect, as if the planes of successive stage drops; Soane recreated something of this character with the two, even flatter, arches that define the chancel end of St. Peter's Church, Walworth (1822).

Drawings for the Yellow Drawing Room

In December 1790, six months after his initial visit to the house, Soane produced his first substantive proposals for the remodelling of Wimpole Hall. They were intended to solve one of the Yorkes' principal concerns—how, in the body of an old-fashioned house, could a suitably grand room be created for large assemblies, concerts and dancing? Soane proposed an elegant bombé-fronted saloon which was to occupy the entire seven-bay north range of Chicheley's double-pile house. This tri-partite room was to be some eighty feet in length and eighteen feet high at its centre. To enter this light-filled space, with potentially expansive views of the gardens, from the narrow, artificially lit entrance of the Inner Hall, would have been a dramatic experience.

Despite its attractions, the idea was abandoned in favour of an extraordinarily daring proposal that not only determined the future internal planning of much of the first floor, but also included the first executed example—he had suggested its use as early as 1787 for a top-lit gallery at Fonthill Splendens, Wiltshire that William Thomas Beckford (1760—1844) hoped to insert on the second floor of the neo-Palladian house he had inherited from his father—of Soane's use of the canopy dome, an architectural form that was to become one of the quintessential leitmotifs of his style.

Soane's solution was a brilliant piece of lateral thinking. He saw that by exploiting the volume between the two ranges of Wimpole's double-pile plan—essentially a third pile—he could provide a soaring, top-lit space at the very heart of the house. A lantern, rising like a periscope between the two roofs, could bring light flooding down through an oculus to a great domed drawing room below. But rather than disrupt the principal rooms on the central north-south axis—the inner hall, saloon, and, on the floor above, the cross-gallery—Soane realised that he could instead cannibalise a grouping of three lesser rooms that lay immediately to the west. With the dividing walls and ceilings removed Soane would have at his disposal a space of very considerable volume.

In plan the space was T-shaped—the downstroke of the 'T' being formed by one of the anterooms in the north range, which, with its windowed external wall, offered a second source of light. If an analogy is made with church architecture and the downstoke is seen as the nave, and the oculated dome as marking its crossing, then the spaces to east and west might be described as transepts—these Soane proposed should have apsidal ends. This bi-exedial form refines the T-plan to one of a curious 'key-hole' shape.

The ceiling vaults and their decoration were to be no less complex. The 'nave' of the room could be barrel-vaulted and the apses ceiled with semi-domes. But it is the main dome that was a departure for the architect and which so defines the character of the room. When a dome, which must by definition have a circular base, is supported by a structure that is square in plan, the different geometries must be mediated by the insertion of pendentives or squinches. These generate a transitional register, conventionally articulated by architrave, frieze and cornice, but at Wimpole Soane dispensed with this intermediate element, contracting instead the 'academic' parts of his architecture, and in the process pulling the dome down so that it sprang directly from the walls. This necessitated cutting the four supporting arches from the volume of the dome itself. The resulting form is a canopy dome, or sail vault—so described because it is like a sail, when fixed at its four corners and filled by the wind. Rather than rising from pendentives the dome itself becomes a pendentive structure. Sir John Summerson notes that the English language lacks a satisfactory architectural term for this form—Soane preferred the word 'canopy' to 'dome'—but that the French have long described it as a *cul-de-four en pendentif*.[265] Of the Soanian canopy he also writes: 'the architecture seems to fly into space, to be self-poised; it is the Gothic miracle rediscovered at the heart of the Roman tradition'.[266]

Soane's inspiration and model was undoubtedly the extraordinary Chamber of the Court of Common Council, in the City of London's Guildhall, designed by his master, George Dance the Younger (1741—1825) in 1777—9 (demolished 1906), and which may in turn owe a debt to an engraved design by Marie-Joseph Peyre (1730—85). Soane not only adopted its form but also its unusual decorative language. The specification for Dance's canopy dome refers to it as a 'fan shell', because its under-surface is modelled with concave scallops of a shell or umbrella-like form. It has been suggested that this treatment may derive from the scalloped semicircular dome of what is now identified as the Scenic Triclinium of Hadrian's Villa (*c.*118—130AD), near Tivoli, but which in the eighteenth century was thought to be the remains of the Temple of Canopus. It was as such that Giovanni Battista Piranesi (1720—78) engraved it as one of his *Vedute di Roma*. Dance met Piranesi, and Soane claimed to have been given four prints by him.[267]

The scalloped canopy also recalls the idea of the *velarium* or sail that was customarily rigged to fly over Roman amphitheatres, most famously the Colosseum, to provide shade for the spectators. Such canopies, under the changing pressure of the wind, must have strained against their complex of supporting ropes and rings and billowed in concave and convex shapes. The *velarium*, abstracted, is more commonly seen in neo-classical interiors at the centre of ceiling flats—either painted or in shallow plaster relief.

Dance was not alone in translating this type of decoration to three dimensions: Thomas Leverton (1743—1824), whose one-time pupil Thomas Chawner was to render Soane's Yellow Drawing Room designs in perspective, employed the scalloped dome in 1777 in the Etruscan saloon (now entrance hall) at Woodford Hall, Essex; and James Wyatt (1746—1813) adopted it for the apsidal ends of the Painted Room at Heveningham Hall (completed 1788—99), Suffolk, and further hinted at it in the supports to the barrel vault of its entrance hall. Indeed it had a precursor in Soane's own work: an unexecuted design of 1778 for a semicircular summer dining room for Downhill, the county Antrim house of Frederick Augustus Hervey, 4th Earl of Bristol and Bishop of Derry (1730—1803) which was to have had a scalloped ceiling, like the exedra at Hadrian's villa.

Using light to create dramatic effects—whether from overhead lanterns and lay-lights, from concealed sources, filtered through coloured glass, or reflected from mirrors—is a perennial theme in Soane's work. The luminous spaces of ancient ruinous architecture, the precedent of the work of George Dance the Younger, the Royal Academy lecture notes of Thomas Sandby (1721—98), and the theoretical writings of French enlightenment architects, in particular those of Nicolas Le Camus de Mézières (1721—89), were amongst a host of influences that shaped Soane's approach to the handling of light. At Wimpole, however, he was probably not so much in pursuit of Le Camus's light—'*mystérieux ou triste*'—but in the optimal way to light pictures, hung in a room immured at the centre of the house, a challenge he had previously faced at Chillington Hall, Staffordshire, and whose resolution at both houses was to inform Soane's design of Dulwich Picture Gallery (1811—3). The marginal notes to Soane's first presentation drawing (*No.113*) appear to have been intended to reassure Hardwicke of the practicalities of this point.

Soane's architectural experimentation at Wimpole was to fuel his thinking for the series of halls he created at the Bank of England, where re-building work began in May 1792. The Bank Stock Office, the Four Percent Office and the Consols Transfer Office, were all to have oculated canopy domes. The Four Per Cent Office, begun in 1793, was strikingly similar to the Yellow Drawing Room at Wimpole, sharing with it scalloped plasterwork of the Dance-derived fan-shell type.

At Wimpole, in order to allow the parachute-like canopy to be 'anchored' at an even height around the room, Soane also adopted the false, decorated pendentives that Dance had placed between the supporting arches of the Guildhall Council Chamber.

112 Soane Office. Plan and sections for a bombé-fronted Saloon, 1790

National Trust WIM/D/482
Inscr.: In Soane's hand, 'Plan & Section for the Alterations at Wimple, a Seat of the Earl of Hardwicke'; the doors into the 'best Staircase', 'back Staircase', 'Eating Room' and 'Damask drawing room' labelled; and the rooms 'Saloon', and 'Part of the Hall' marked. 'Albion Place, Dec.r 1790'
Pen & ink with grey and yellow wash (390 x 480mm)
Scale given
Lit. & repr.: Parry (1986), pp.36—55, fig.32; Dean (1999), p.67, fig.4.5.

In Chicheley's house the ground-floor rooms of the north range were not disposed symmetrically around the central cross-axis (*No.49*). Flitcroft addressed this awkwardness, creating a central saloon of three bays flanked by two-bay anterooms. In order to form an impressive space of serviceable dimensions, Soane proposed throwing these three rooms together. Entered axially from the Inner Hall, the central space was to have had side lobbies—with lower, segmentally vaulted ceilings—to east and west, communicating respectively with Kenton Couse's 'Eating room' and a 'Damask drawing room'. A pair of fireplaces is shown on the room's south wall to either side of the pedimented entrance.

The most striking part of the scheme is the projecting central bow with five tall windows that would have provided panoramic views of the gardens. This arrangement was an expansion of the tighter bows, each of three windows, that Soane had previously designed, for example, at Letton Hall (1783) and Saxlingham Rectory (1784) in Norfolk, and Tendring Hall (1784) in Suffolk. It was an idea he was to develop further at houses such as Tyringham (1792—1800) in Buckinghamshire and Pell Wall (1822—8), Staffordshire. Soane was also to build a villa—sited with advice from William Emes—with a bombé garden-front for the 3rd Earl of Hardwicke's widowed step-mother, Agneta, the Hon. Mrs Yorke (1740—1820). In June 1793 Agneta complained to her sister-in-law Jemima Marchioness Grey of the slow progress that the workmen were making, joking that 'Mr. Soane is building I think a castle instead of a cottage which I had originally designed and the foundation seems intended to rival that of the largest pyramid'.[268] The upper floor of the villa, Sydney Lodge on the river Hamble, Hampshire, was provided with a covered ironwork balcony. No other drawings survive to show how Soane envisaged carrying the bombé form to the upper stories of Wimpole Hall, or how it was to be expressed in the garden façade.

The bombé front ultimately derives from Louis Le Vau's (1612—70) experiments with rooms of elliptical plan—at Turny and Vaux-le-Vicomte—and their popularisation through French pattern books by authors such as Jacques François Blondel and Charles-Etienne Briseaux. The bombé-fronted *salon d'été* satisfactorily straddled the divide between house and garden, and the form was favoured by other neo-classical architects such as Sir William Chambers (1723—96) and Robert Adam (1728—92) but, as Pierre de la Ruffinière du Prey has demonstrated, British architects' experimentation with it stretches back to William Talman and Sir John Vanbrugh.[269]

113 Soane Office. Plan and section of the Yellow Drawing Room, with key, 1791

Sir John Soane's Museum, 6/1/6
Inscr.: 'The Earl of Hardwicke', 'Plan and Section of the Proposed Drawing Room at

Wimple', and the following key:
'It is proposed to hang the Walls of this Room with Pictures.
D a large Glass to be placed opposite the Chimney C
E a large Glass to be placed here.
The upright skylight will light the back part of the Room in the
most desirable manner for pictures.
By this plan, none of the best Rooms are disturbed the Angular
Chimney & the other irregularitys now existing in the little room
between the damask drawing Room and the Saloon are entirely
removed, & the effect of the Glass E & the light from the upright
Skylight would be pleasing particularly in passing from the Saloon to the
drawing Room; but the strongest reason for my recommending this idea is that
every purpose of convenience & magnificence is attain'd without disturbing
any of the material parts of the Building; & further might be
completed without incommoding the family.
The common Staircase as shewn in the General Plan is in all cases
as convenient & in some more so than the present Staircase
except for Servants coming from the Offices to the Hall door which may
be easily remedied'.
Pen and ink with grey wash (555 x 315mm)
Scale given
Lit. & repr.: Hussey (1967:3), pp.594–7, fig 3; Parry (1986) pp.36–55, fig.31;
Woodward (1999), pp.8–13, fig.3; Dean (1999), p.68, fig.4.7.

With this first proposal for the Yellow Drawing Room, Soane established its unusual key-hole shaped plan and his client's acceptance that it could be carved out of three spaces on the ground floor (the ante-room to the west of Flitcroft's saloon, the secondary staircase, and a room overlooking the west courtyard that contained water closets), together with three corresponding rooms on the floor above.

The form and treatment of the ceilings, however, was to evolve further. Here Soane proposes three types of Roman coffering: octagonal for the barrel vault, square for the apses, and lozenge-shaped for the main dome. It is more common to find coffering of lozenge form used in semi-domes, the *locus classicus* being the remains of Hadrian's Temple of Venus in Rome, but Soane had previously proposed lozenge coffering in his 1788 design for the dome of the Great Room at Chillington Hall, Staffordshire, which has a familial similarity at least to the Wimpole drawing.

In this carefully executed and annotated design, Soane advocated the placement of the principal fireplace (A) in the western apse and a secondary fireplace (C) on the west wall of the barrel-vaulted space, close to the chimney that had served a mid-seventeenth-century corner fireplace, the 'Angular Chimney' of Soane's marginal explanation. Large mirrors, one hung at the southern end of the room, opposite the pair of enlarged widows, and the other opposite fireplace C, were to reflect light—daylight, firelight and candlelight. The lantern and supporting dome illustrated here are broader and squatter than those of the adopted scheme which admits more natural light than this proposal would have done.

Another version of this drawing, dispatched on 3 January 1791, survives at Wimpole (*No.114*).

114 Soane Office. Plan and section of the Yellow Drawing Room, with key, 1791

National Trust WIM/D/481
Inscr.: Key, in Soane's hand, as No.113 above
Pen and ink with grey and blue washes (390 x 480mm)

This drawing is almost identical to (*No.113*), and must be the one Soane records as being sent on 3 January 1791.

115 Soane Office. Dimensioned plan of part of the first floor, with section through the central block, 1791

Sir John Soane's Museum, 6/1/10
Inscr.: 'Plan of the Chamber Floor of Wimple, April 3 1791'. The drawings are dimensioned and related to the following lettered key in Soane's hand:
'A. The Chimney is to be removed and the passage continued to the Chamber D. with a door at E & another door at F (opposite Centre of window) into Dressing Room G
A. The flue of this chy. which gathers towards the door B is for the new Chy

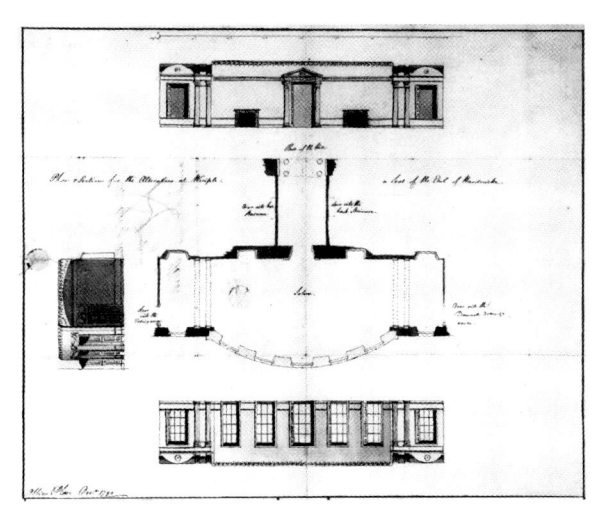

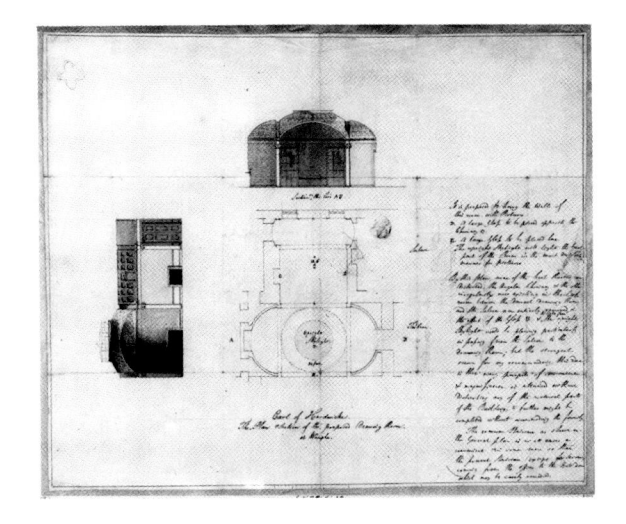

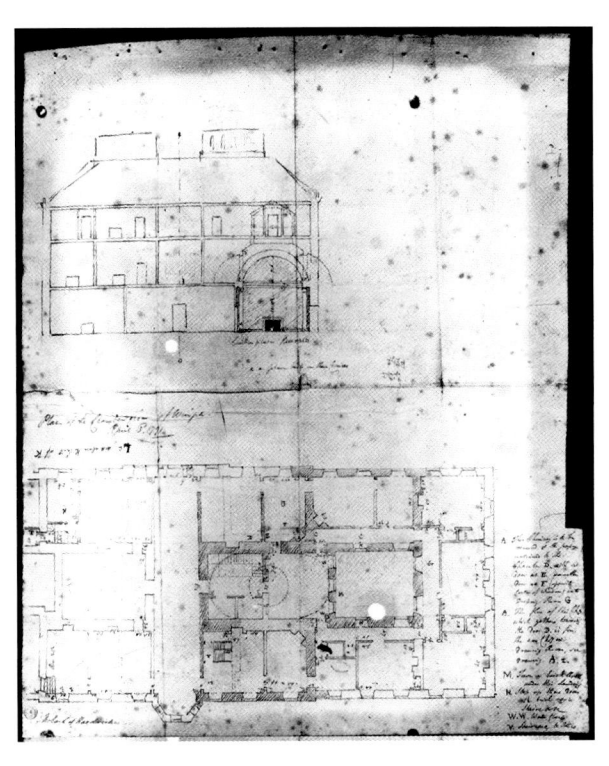

             in Drawing Room, see drawing A.2
- M. Turn a brick Arch under this Landing
- N. Step up these doors 1/2 brick next staircase.

    W.W. Water Closet
- V. Staircase to Attics'

On the section Soane indicates that the Yellow Drawing Room should have 'Corinthian pilasters fluted & cable', and at 'aa. plan busts on these Cornices'.
Verso: 'Wimple April 1791 - Plan of chamber floor'.
Pen and ink with pencil (565 x 680mm)

This sketchy, dimensioned drawing shows Soane exploring and explaining—presumably in answer to hard questions from his client—what effect the insertion of the Yellow Drawing Room would have on considerations of plan and circulation at first-floor level.

    Soane here superimposes the essential outlines of the Yellow Drawing Room on the plan and long-section of the house. The marginal notes take account of the disruption to the circulation at first floor level that the insertion of the Yellow Drawing Room would cause and explore how the corridor running along the north side of the south range might be extended eastwards to allow continued passage from one side of the house to the other. The section shows that the design of the coffered room described three months earlier (*Nos.113 & 114*) had begun to crystallise into something more elegant and etiolated—the highest point of the lantern reaching eaves level, while the segmental arch supporting the dome beneath is of a fuller form.

116 Soane Office. Part plans of the basement and first floors showing the Yellow Drawing Room and the proposed secondary stairs, 1791

Sir John Soane's Museum, 6/1/12
Inscr.: On the right,
'The Earl of Hardwicke, Wimpole, April 1791'; and, on the left,
'Copy Augt. 4 1791'
On the left side:
'Plan of part of the Hall Floor
AB leave an Indent of 9 inches wide at BB and then put the Windows in the Centers of the spaces between AB & BA
CD Observe the floor of these Closets are six steps above the level of the Hall Floor
EF The space between these letters is (I believe 25 feet) take 12 foot for the Staircase and 18 Inches the Wall and then the remainder is to be divided equally between the Water Closet & Maid's Closet'
On plan, in the position of the present jib door from the Red Room to the landing of the secondary staircase: 'do not make this door into the room until directed'
On the right side:
'Plan of the Basement Floor
A The Center of the Window above determines the Center of this door
KK determines the situation of the door L'
Verso: pen & ink sectional sketch, east-west, in Soane's hand, through the north part of the Yellow
Drawing Room. Inscr.: 'Section on the line EF' and marked 'Wimple, April 25 1791'
Pen and ink with grey, pink and yellow washes and pencil additions (565 x 335mm)

The western apse of the Yellow Drawing Room was the only part that could not be accommodated within the envelope of Chicheley's house. The bow would project beyond the lightwell created by James Gibbs's westward extensions to the north and south ranges and linking cross-wing. In order to support the bow Soane added an arcade at basement level, continuing the line of the new wall partition through all floors. Gibbs's lightwell was to be reduced even further to allow the insertion of a handsome Portland stone staircase and—shown here off the first quarter landing—a 'water closet' and 'maid's closet' to replace those that the Yellow Drawing Room scheme would destroy. The cantilevered stair, with its elegant iron balustrade is identical in its details to the east stair at Bentley Priory.[270]

    The string courses and window sills of the south-facing windows of Gibbs's north range can still be seen at high level in the basement corridor between points K and L.

Although the principal fireplace is shown in its final position in this drawing, it was clearly still Soane's intention in April 1791 that the room should have a secondary fireplace.

117 John Soane. East-west section through the Yellow Drawing Room, with plasterwork details, 1791

Sir John Soane's Museum, 6/1/7
Inscr.: 'Wimple, Section of drawing Room', 'The Earl of Hardwicke—Wimpole', with notes against a marginal detail and sketch 'Full size as given to Mr. Papworth, July 12 1791' and 'Plan of fluting'
Pen and inks, black and sepia (650 x 530mm)
Scale given
Verso: section through the barrel vault of the northern part of the room. Scale given.
Lit. & repr.: Parry (1986), pp.36–55, fig.23.

This east-west section through the southern part of the Yellow Drawing Room describes in greater detail the taller, second scheme indicated in *No.115*. Additional height has been provided by inserting crescent-shaped stilting pieces—here with *rinceau* decoration—between the crown of the supporting arches and the uncomfortably angular cove connecting with the base of the lantern drum. The sketches on the left-hand side provide the first indication that Soane would increase the height of the dome even further by introducing Dance's curving and fluted 'fan-shell'.

    The sections of egg and dart and incised mouldings drawn at the top of the sheet perhaps also reveal something of Soane's indebtedness to Dance and his reductive approach to architectural elements such as the entablature. The decoration suggested here for the false pendentives appears to be of winged *genii*, or perhaps *caducei* which Soane used in the equivalent position in the Four Per Cent Office in the Bank of England. The fireplace is shown in its final position at the southern end of the room. The 'Mr. Papworth' referred to is John Papworth (1750—99) who, with his son Thomas (1773—1814) ran one of London's major stucco and plastering firms, frequently contracted by Soane's office.

    During August and September a number of detailed drawings for various elements of the plasterwork were 'delivered to Mr. Papworth' and 'sent to Provis'. These included a 'Capital to Pilaster', a 'Soffite to Arch', 'several sketches of moldings', and drawings 'of the Cornice round the skylight'.

118 Thomas Chawner (1774—1851). Perspective section of the Yellow Drawing Room, 1791

Sir John Soane's Museum, Vol. 68 (formerly Folio XVII), no.10
Inscr.: In pencil, 'Drawing Room at Wimple', 'The Earl of Hardwicke', 'Thos. Chawner. Dec.r 8th 1791'
Pen and watercolour (280 x 455mm)

This extraordinary grisaille rendering, which makes the room appear like the inside of a towering jelly mould, is a one-point perspective whose station point lies behind the fireplace on the south wall, beyond the confines of the room and, like the following renderings, must have been set up in the drawing office from planimetric and elevational information, rather than drawn in the completed interior.

119 Thomas Chawner

Sir John Soane's Museum, P.410, framed with P.408 & P.409
Inscr.: 'THE BANK OF ENGLAND', 'VIEW OF THE VESTIBULE'; 'THE MARQUISS OF ABERCORN', 'THE GREAT HALL AT BENTLEY PRIORY'; and THE EARL OF HARDWICKE', 'THE WITHDRAWING ROOM AT WIMPOLE'
Watercolour with black line-wash, framed with two others, each with accompanying captions (including frame, 412 x 813mm)
Lit. & repr.: Solkin (2001), p.208, fig.182
Exh.: The Royal Academy, London (1792), cat.558; The Courtauld Institute Gallery, London (2001).

Nicholas Savage explains that this watercolour, a triptych of

75 The Catalogue

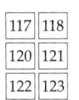

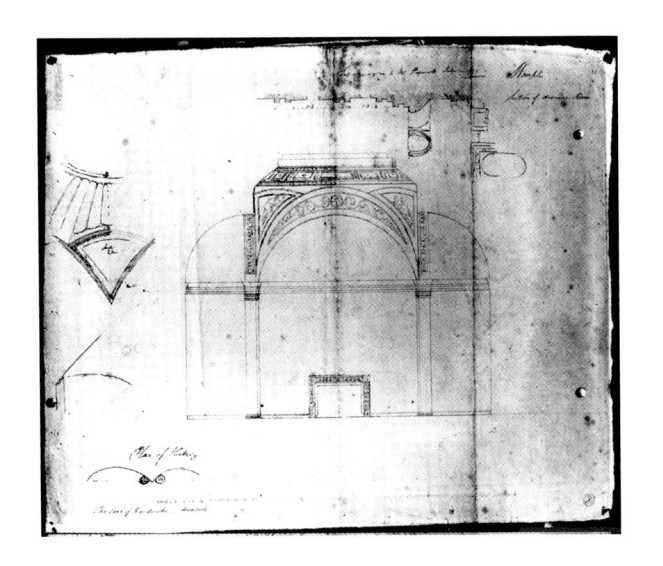

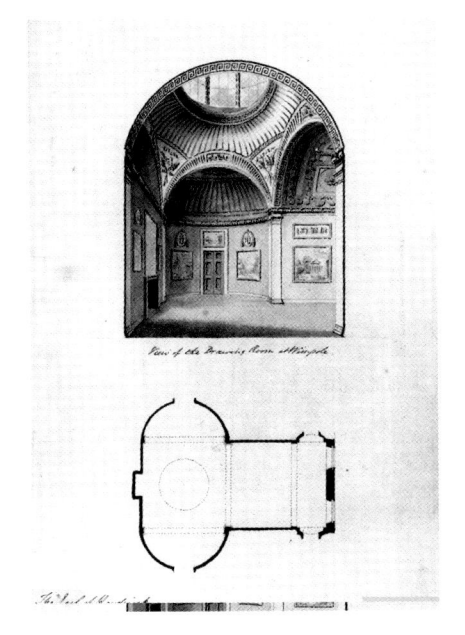

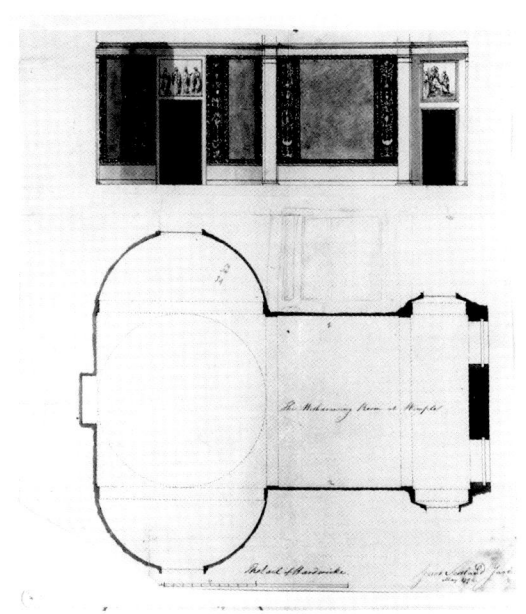

three interiors—the vestibule of the Bank of England, the great hall at Bentley Priory, Middlesex, and the Yellow Drawing Room at Wimpole—which was shown at the Royal Academy in 1792, was probably the earliest composite drawing that the architect exhibited.[271] Beneath the views of the Bank of England and Wimpole are tiny outline plans which enable the viewer to understand the spaces described. The three views survive in their original exhibition frame. The scheme shown appears to predate Lady Hardwicke's decision to have the walls of the drawing room hung in silk. This coloured perspective is taken from the east and shows the walls hung with classical landscapes and grisailles. Presumably it was intended that the two canvases, shown here against the concavity of the room's western 'apse', should be mounted directly on to the curving wall surface.

120   Thomas Chawner. Perspective view, and plan of the Yellow Drawing Room, c.1791

Sir John Soane's Museum, Vol. 60 (formerly Folio V), no.122
Inscr.: 'View of the Drawing Room at Wimpole'. 'The Earl of Hardwicke'
Pen and ink with watercolour (365 x 230mm)
Lit. & repr.: Schumann-Bacia (1991), p.60, fig.45; Souden (1991), p.30; Woodward (1999), pp.8–13, fig.6; Woodward (2000), p.105, fig.6.

This is a version of the watercolour that Chawner produced for the Royal Academy exhibition of 1792 (No.119).

121   Thomas Chawner. Perspective section from the north end of the Yellow Drawing Room looking towards the fireplace, 1791

Sir John Soane's Museum, Vol. 68 (formerly Folio XVII), no.11
Inscr.: In pencil, 'Drawing Room. Dec.r 10th 1791'
Pen and watercolour (280 x 455mm)

All the essential elements of the plaster decoration had clearly been settled by the time this series of perspective renderings was made: the form of the pilasters and the reduced, dentilled entablature, the Greek-meanders that highlight the intrados of the dome and barrel-vault arches, the various patterns of rectangular panels and coffers, the concave fluting to the dome and apses, and the laurel-wreathed *tondo* in the 'pendentives.'

122   Thomas Chawner. Perspective section, east/west, through the Yellow Drawing Room looking towards the fireplace, 1791

Sir John Soane's Museum, Vol. 68 (formerly Folio XVII), no.12
Inscr.: In pencil, 'Dec.r 12th 1791'
Pen and watercolour (280 x 455mm)

This view is similar to *No.121*, but is taken from a point further south, so allowing a fuller view of the 'fan-shell' canopy dome, the lantern and the *exedra* to east and west. The curiosities here are what appear to be billowing clouds above the fluting in the two apses. These two patches of illusionistic sky—glimpsed through the fictive oculus of a semicircular *velarium*—would have echoed the real sky beyond, but not visible through, the windows of the central lantern. In 1791 such decoration would have been the height of advanced fashion. A few years earlier a group of French decorative painters, under the supervision of Jean Jacques Boileau and Louis André Delabrière, had painted several sky ceilings in the state rooms of Carlton House, Pall Mall (1783—5) designed by Henry Holland. Among the English decorative painters who worked at Carlton House were John (1754—1819) and Frederick (1779—1859) Crace, who later proposed further sky ceilings for the Royal Pavilion at Brighton. The Craces not only worked for Soane at Woburn Abbey, Althorp, the Bank of England, and Aynhoe Park, but in 1792 painted the trellised ceiling in the Breakfast Room at Soane's London townhouse at No.12 Lincoln's Inn Fields, and ten years later a similar ceiling at his country house, Pitzhanger Manor, Ealing.

Megan Aldrich notes that John Crace was 'on close terms of friendship with a number of men from Soane's office', counting Messrs. Chawner and Laing—both of whom worked on drawings for Wimpole—among them.[272] An entry in Soane's Journal for 4 May 1792 records: 'Sent per Mr. Crace to Provis a Working drawing of cornice for Winter drawing Room'. To this must be added the compelling evidence of the Earl of Hardwicke's 'Abstract of the Bills and Expenditure for the several Works done at Wimpole in 1791, 1792, 1793 and 1794'.[273] These record that the 'Painter' 'J. Crace' was paid a total of £1,237 18s.10d between 1791 and 1794 — mainly for work in the house, but also at the 'Farm Yard', 'Hothouses', 'Lodges', 'Cottages', and the 'Hardwick Arms'. Crace was also paid for 'Furniture Jappannd'. Wimpole can now confidently be added to the list of commissions where the Craces worked with Soane. Might they have proposed the fictive billowing clouds, that in the executed scheme were to be replaced with additional fluted decoration?

Soane's account book for work undertaken for Lord Hardwicke (1791—4; bills and expenditure for works at Wimpole and Cavendish Square), fo.69 describes Crace's work in greater detail, and gives colours for each space. The grisailles overdoors in the Yellow Drawing Room are thought to be John Crace's work

123   Soane Office. Plan and west elevation for the Yellow Drawing Room, 1792

Sir John Soane's Museum, 6/1/5
Inscr.: 'The Withdrawing Room at Wimpole', 'The Earl of Hardwicke', 'Great Scotland Yard, May 1792'. Verso: Pencil sketches of the proposed wall treatment which suggest that the silk panels should be filled with trophies
Pen and ink with grey and coloured washes (340 x 375mm)
Scale given
Watermark: IV
Lit. & repr.: Parry (1986) pp.36–55, fig.26; Stillman (1988), vol.I, pl.9, opp. p.41; Darley (1999), pl.83.

Elizabeth, Countess of Hardwicke (1763—1858) appears to have been the arbiter on the question of how the Yellow Drawing Room should be decorated and furnished. Her name first appears in Soane's Journal in February 1792 when he records sending her a longitudinal section, another drawing showing the placement of a mirror between the windows, and a long-lost model of the room. The model may have been hinged, as is the surviving model of the *Castello d'acqua*, in order that the interior could be fully understood, for Soane's Wimpole account book A (1791—5) records the cost of 'brass hooks &c. for model of a drawing room'.

On 6 June 1792, a month after this drawing was made, 'Chawner deld. to her Ladyship No. fair drawings of Sections of Drawing Room at Wimpole shewing the Manner of hanging the Silk & ornaments on 1½ sheets of Copy Paper'.[274] The 'ornaments' were perhaps the grisaille overdoors shown in this sectional elevation. The wall panels are shown here in yellow, framed by wide, lateral borders of arabesque or grotesque ornament against a violet ground, the whole edged by a narrower blue border. This striking neo-classical colour scheme was perhaps inspired—directly or indirectly—by the vividly coloured wall painting that had been found on the walls of a Roman house unearthed in the grounds of the Villa Negroni in Rome in June 1777. Soane arrived in Rome the following summer and would certainly have known of the discovery. The Earl Bishop, with whom Soane spent a week journeying to Naples in December 1778, bought the frescoes and, much to the disdain of Philip Yorke, Soane's future patron, who argued that they should have stayed *in situ*, had them cut from the villa walls. Soane later acquired eight of the twelve celebratory engravings—made after watercolours by Anton Raphael

Mengs (1728—79) and Anton Von Maron (1733—1808)—that were published between 1778 and 1802. The strong colours—blacks, reds, yellows and blues—of the frescoes were to influence Soane's palette and his promotion of *all'anticha* schemes.

The fabric currently hanging on the walls of the Yellow Drawing Room is a rayon copy of the late-eighteenth-century Lyons silk, woven for Mrs Bambridge in 1963 to replace a late-nineteenth-century Lincrusta wallpaper. Some pieces of yellow silk with applied arabesque borders on a violet ground, survive at Wimpole; these belong to one of the curved giltwood settees made—it is thought by Charles Smith & Co., 'Upholsterers to Their Majesties'—to fit the shape of the room. Their survival confirms that Soane's intended decoration was realised. Then as now, the rich yellow-gold-coloured fabric shimmers under the light from the lantern and provides a glowing foil for the room's paintings. In September 1792, Lady Mary Grantham wrote to her sister Lady Amabel Polwarth with her impressions of the recently completed yellow drawing room: 'The great room, tho' I should never have built it, far exceeds my expectations. The ceiling is very prettily ornamented, and the upper end is with a skylight. It will altogether be very light'.[275]

Various floor plans and designs for Chimneypieces

124 Soane Office. Perspective view of the Inner and Entrance Halls, *c*.1790

National Trust WIM/D/593
Inscr.: 'View of the Hall at Wimple from the Saloon'
Pen and ink, with blue and grey washes (210 x 195mm)
Watermark: J WHATMAN

This view, looking south from the saloon towards the front door of the house, shows the Ionic columns which Soane added at the threshold between the Inner Hall and the entrance hall. They were carved, without the fluting shown here, by Edward Foxhall. A second pair of columns proposed on the left side of the drawing, to mark the entrance to the great staircase, were not introduced.

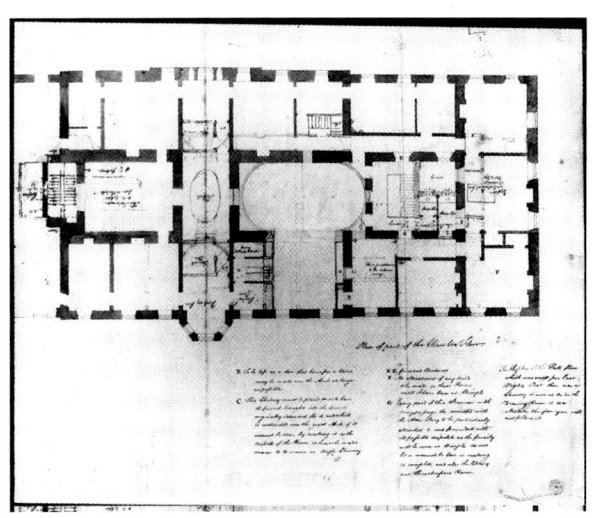

On 22 December 1793, Soane sent to Wimpole a 'View of The Hall in Perspective on $^1/_2$ a sheet of Royal Paper.[276]

125 Thomas Chawner. Plan of the first floor, 1791

Sir John Soane's Museum, 6/1/14
Inscr.: 'Plan of part of the Chamber Floor', 'The Earl of Hardwicke—Wimpole', 'Copy Augt. 5. 1791'. Various instructions are given on the drawing. The lettered rooms and details relate to the following key:

'B   To be left as a door that hereafter a closet may be made over the Arch as large as possible
C   This chimney must be placed so as to have the funnel brought into the funnel originally intended for it and which is contained over the great Arch if it cannot be done by making it in the middle of the Room it must be made nearer to D or even an Angle Chimney
EE Present Windows
F   No alterations of any kind to be made in these Rooms until I have been at Wimple
G   Every part of this Staircase with every passage &c. connected with the Attic Story to be particularly attended to and forwarded with all possible dispatch as the family will be soon at Wimple do not let a moment be lost in making it complete and also the library and Housekeeper's Room In the Plan of the Hall Floor which was sent per last Night's Post there was a chimney drawn at A in the Drawing Room it is a Mistake, therefore you will not follow it'.

Verso: 'Wimple Plan of the Chamber Floor'
Pen and ink with grey, pink and yellow wash. Pencil set-up lines and alterations (505 x 720mm)
Watermark: J WHATMAN and fleur-de-lis with crown

Soane here works up ideas that he had mapped out on an earlier dimensioned survey (*No.115*). The circulation problems caused by the dome and barrel vault of the Yellow Drawing Room could be solved on the first floor by extending the corridor in the south range, and by building a new staircase to the attic bedrooms between the central cross-gallery and the barrel vault of the Yellow Drawing Room. Soane stresses the importance of expediting the work in advance of the Yorkes' return to Wimpole. The bedroom in the north range, whose floor Soane removed to accommodate the barrel vault of the Yellow Drawing Room survives, complete with its north-facing windows, while the new closets to either side were designed to project into this now useless and forgotten space.

A layer of pencil and ink additions introduces the ideas that: the cross-gallery might be sub-divided to create dressing rooms, each with its own closet, to either side of a central, top-lit lobby; an additional, dog-leg stair serving the attic floor might be added in the south range; and that a further staircase could be built immediately to the east of the great staircase.

126 Soane Office. Dimensioned plans for three rooms, c.1791

National Trust WIM/D/499
Inscr.: The names of the three rooms marked, 'Ladies' Dressing Room', 'Gallery' and 'Lord's Bed Room', with dimensions for each. The following key is in Soane's hand.
On the left hand side:
  Width of Grate for Anti [sic] Library 3: 4'
  Ditto for 2d Draw.g Room 3: 5¼'
  For the first room in the Nursery near
  the new wood staircase 3.0 ¼ wide
  Centre Room in nursery 1:6 wide
  Farthest Room near the Chappel (of Nursery) 3.0 wide
  [...] North Room in the Atticks, the North side of the House that was hung with common Blue paper 3. 1 ¾ wide.
On the right hand side:
  Width of Grate for Lord's Bed Room 3.3 ¼
  Do. for My Lady's Dressing Room 3 5 ¾
  D⁰. for Room between Alcove Room and } 3 1 ¼
  New Drawing Room }
Pen and ink (326 x 405mm). The top right hand quarter of the page is missing.
Watermark: CM in oval, and Britannia in crowned cartouche

The 'Ladies' Dressing Room' is the semicircular first floor room which survives at the west end of the south front. The plan of the 'Gallery' shows the central third of Flitcroft's ground floor gallery and suggests that the polished steel grate inserted into Gibbs's earlier chimney piece was one of Soane's additions.

127 Soane Office. Plan of the ground floor, 1791

National Trust WIM/D/474
Inscr.: 'THE EARL OF HARDWICKE. WIMPLE'; 'PLAN OF THE PRINCIPAL FLOOR WITH THE PROPOSED ALTERATIONS'; 'Great Scotland Yard Dec.r 22nd. 1791'; the key 'A. Pedestal for Fire' at bottom left; all rooms are named and their dimensions given.
Pen and ink with grey wash indicating the proposed new work, and blue showing voids and the open lightwells to east and west (525 x 750mm)
Scale given
Watermark: Large fleur-de-lis in crowned cartouche

Soane appears here to be proposing the use of the ante-chapel, to the east of the entrance hall, as a bedroom with apsidal niches in the northern corners of the room, one of which was to contain a 'Pedestal for Fire' or stove. This was a somewhat anachronistic arrangement, for in 1781 the Countess of St. Germans had written to her aunt Lady Beauchamp, describing the changes made to Wimpole during the previous seven years: 'The State Bed, which you may remember stood below stairs, is now moved upstairs into one of the new rooms. The paper with which the walls are covered is common and white to match the bed, and there are two dressing-rooms belonging to it'.[277] Mark Girouard notes that in great houses state apartments often remained on the ground floor until c.1770.[278] The plan also shows Kenton Couse's dining room was to be left intact, although the dressing room to the east is shown here as a service stair. Note too the proposal for the insertion of a columnar screen between the Entrance and Inner Halls (*No.124*).

This, the following two drawings and a perspective—possibly *No.124*—are recorded in the Day Book for 22 December 1791 as: '3 for Plans of designs for Alterations to the Principal, one Pair & Attic Floors of Wimple on 3 sheets of Impl. Paper and 1 view of the Hall in Perspective on ½ a sheet of Royal Paper' giving their authorship to Frederick Meyer (b.1775) and Thomas Chawner.

128 Soane Office. Plan of the first floor, 1791

National Trust WIM/D/473
Inscr.: THE EARL OF HARDWICKE WIMPLE', 'PLAN OF THE ONE PAIR FLOOR'; 'Great Scotland Yard Decr. 22nd. 1791'; all rooms are named and their dimensions given.
Pen and ink with grey and blue washes (525 x 750mm)
Scale given

When raised, a paper flap shows the landing of the Great Stairs and the proposed first floor route (not executed) to the service stair that Soane built to the east, beyond the end wall of the seventeenth-century house. Note the proposed subdivision of the central north-south picture gallery, providing two dressing rooms and two small bedrooms. The Earl and Countess of Hardwicke's apartment at the west end of the house, with its dramatic bow room on the south side is shown here, fully planned.

129 Soane Office. Plan of the attic floor 1791

National Trust WIM/D/557
Inscr.: 'THE EARL OF HARDWICKE WIMPLE'; 'PLAN OF THE ATTIC FLOOR'; 'Great Scotland Yard Decr. 22nd 1791'. Room names indicated.
Pen and ink, with black, grey and blue washes (525 x 750mm)

Soane here suggests blocking the doorways that open from the landing of the great stairs to the bedrooms in the north and south ranges (now known as the Lord Chancellor's bedroom and Mrs Bambridge's bedroom). The landing could instead be opened up to the lobby to the west—replacing Flitcroft's doorcase with a columnar screen. He shows how the lobby could be top-lit and, with doors placed at either end, provide access to broadly symmetrical apartments in the two ranges. These new arrangements were not effected and the division of the former cross-gallery took a different form. The position of the new service stair to the east of the great stair is indicated here. When lowered, the flap shows the skylight above the great stairs.

130 Thomas Chawner. Plan of the west end of the first floor, 1792

National Trust WIM/D/521
Inscr.: 'The Earl of Hardwicke. Plan of part of the One Pair Floor at Wimple'; 'Copy'; 'A. do not make this door until ordered'; G to Scotland Yard, Feby. 4th 1792'.
Pen and ink with pencil annotations and marginalia by Soane (412 x 322mm)
Scale given

The names of the rooms are given, revealing their use or character: 'Lady H. bedchamber', 'Lord H. Dressing Room', 'blue silk room', Pineapple roome', 'the upper part of the Withdrawing Room'.

131 Soane Office. Survey plan of the first and attic floors of the east service wing, 1792

Sir John Soane's Museum, 6/1/15
Inscr.: 'Plans of the Kitchen building at Wimpole', 'The Earl of Hardwicke', 'AA Servants Bed Rooms', 'Store Room for Brewhouse' labelled. The plan of the narrower attic range is inscribed 'Storey in the Roof'. The rooms are all dimensioned.
Verso: In Soane's hand, 'Dec. 1792. Wimple—Plan of Rooms over Kitchen'. Various calculations.
Pen and ink with grey wash (325 x 395mm)

Seven bedrooms were provided on the first floor, four above the kitchen and laundry range and a further three in the attic. The range was served by a stair rising in the seventh bay from the west.

79 The Catalogue

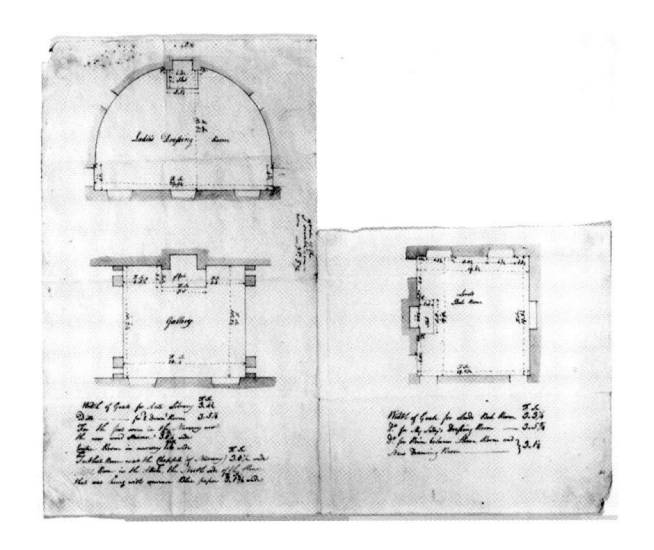

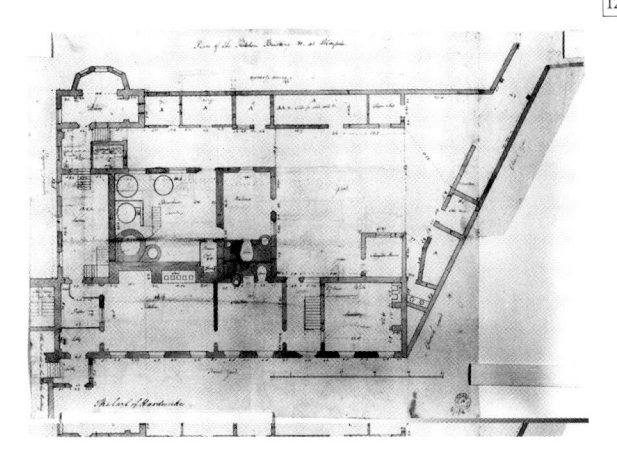

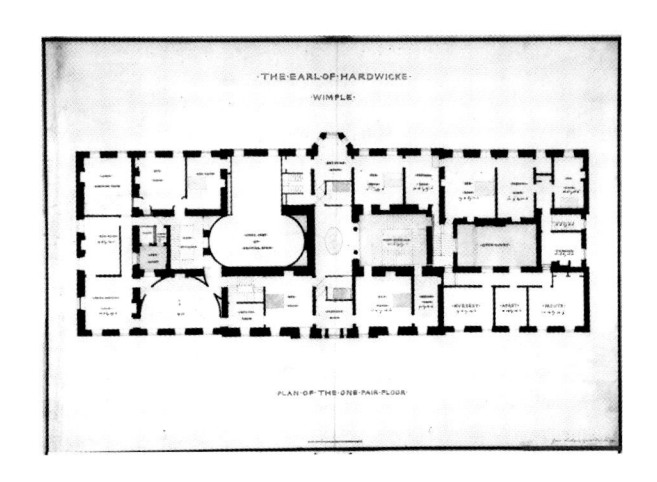

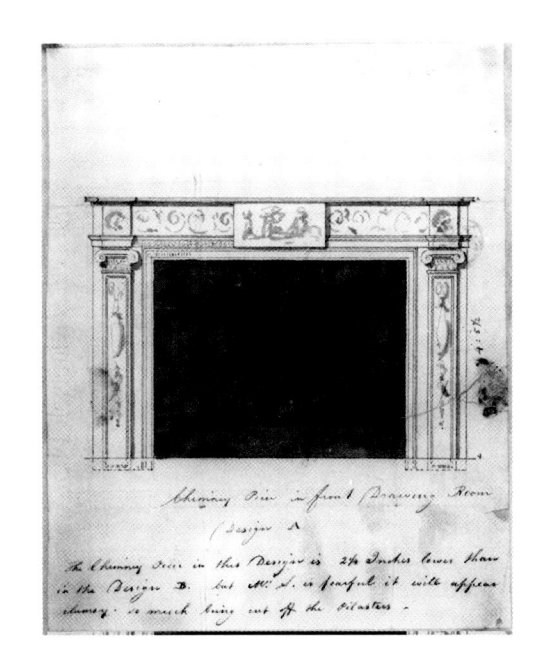

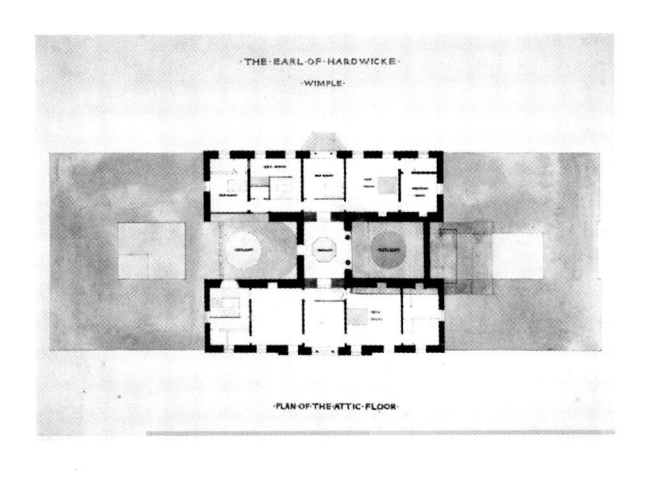

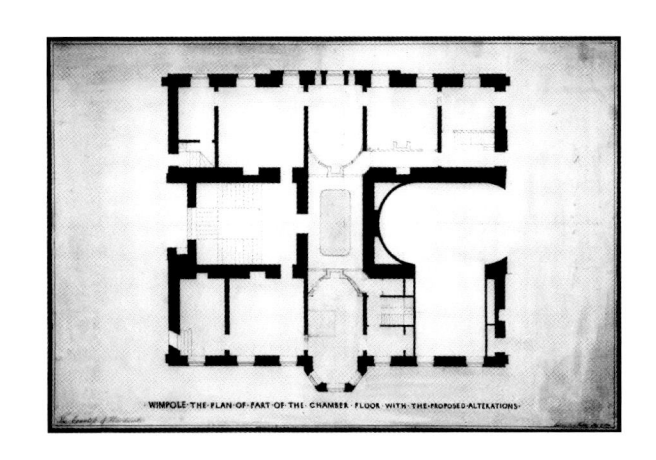

132 Soane Office. Ground floor plan of the service buildings in the east courtyard 1792

Sir John Soane's Museum, 6/1/16
Inscr.: 'Alterations to offices', 'Plan of the Kitchen Building &c. at Wimpole', 'The Earl of Hardwicke'. The rooms labelled and dimensioned. Verso: 'Dec. 1792, Wimpole Plans of Kitchen Offices &c.'
Pen and ink with grey wash (325 x 490mm (top) and 395mm (bottom))
Scale given
Watermark: CM and Brittania in crowned oval

Immediately behind the south range, comprising kitchen, scullery and landing, are shown a large brew-house and wash-house. The wing projecting to the north contained a pastry room, larder, and, in the polygonal bay, a small dairy. In a narrow lean-to range along the northern edge of the courtyard, three additional servants' bedrooms, a shed for wood and coals, and a 'Glazier's Shop' were provided. A similar line of narrow outhouses is shown running along the north west edge of the churchyard and includes a 'shoe house' and an open-ended 'dust hole'—presumably for rubbish.

133 Thomas Jeans, junior. Ground-floor plan showing proposed re-arrangement of the rooms in the east service wing 1793

Sir John Soane's Museum, 6/1/17
Inscr.: 'Plan of Alterations to Offices', 'The Earl of Hardwicke', 'Copy. Great Scotland Yard, Jany. 5th—1793'. The rooms and other spaces are labelled.
Pen and ink with grey wash (340 x 575mm)
Scale given

Soane's proposals involved a re-arrangement of the functions of each room rather than wholesale remodelling. The principal change being to turn the old brew-house into a laundry, with 'Ironing Table, Mangle' and 'Folding Table' indicated, and the old laundry into the brew-house. An additional stair was made on the site of the pastry room, and a new pastry room and a game larder created by sub-dividing the larder in the west range. The dairy was moved to the position of the former servants' bedrooms in the north range and its place taken up by a 'wet larder'. The Day Book for 5 January 1793 records that Frederick Meyer drew the plans for the alteration of the east wing and that they were copied by Thomas Jeans.

134 Soane Office. Designs for two chimneypieces for Lord Hardwicke's house in New Cavendish Street, London, 1794

National Trust WIM/D/483
Inscr.: 'The Earl of Hardwicke, New Cavendish St.', 'Gt. Scotland Yard. Jany. 4. 1794'. The upper fireplace is labelled 'Back Drawing Room' and the lower one 'Chamber'. Dimensions are given.
Pen and ink with grey wash (325 x 265mm)
Scale given

In 1781 Philip Yorke called in John Soane to make alterations to his recently acquired London townhouse, No.7 (now 63) Cavendish Street. Ptolemy Dean describes the work, that, with the help of John Crace, entailed the fitting of library bookcases—designed by Soane and removed from Yorke's house on Park Street—the lining of rooms with silk and the supply of gilded mirrors. A chimneypiece, cut by James Nelson, was supplied in 1793 and, as with this drawing, relates to a second phase of work.[279]

135 Soane Office. Design for a chimneypiece, 1793

National Trust WIM/D/516
Inscr.: 'Chimney Piece in front Drawing Room Design A'; 'The Chimney Piece in this Design is 2 1/4 Inches lower than in the Design B. But M^r. S. is fearful it will appear clumsy so much being cut off the Pilasters'. The height of the chimney piece is given as '4: 5 1/2'''. Addressed on verso to 'The Countess of Hardwicke, Richmond, Surrey'.
Pen and ink with grey wash (227 x 187mm)

This and Design B (No.136) are presumably for a further fireplace for the Earl of Hardwicke's house in New Cavendish Street, London. Might 'Mr. S' have been John Spiller who was paid £75 for two chimney pieces for Wimpole on 4 September 1792?[280]

136 Soane Office. Design for a chimneypiece, 1793

National Trust WIM/D/555
Inscr.: 'Chimney Piece in Front Drawing Room, Design B'; 'G^t. Scotland Yard Oct. 1793'; and 'height of Chimney Piece in its present state'
Pen and ink with grey wash (205 x 263mm)
Scale given

This is a much more detailed, more carefully drawn version of 'Design A'. The chimneypiece is framed by Ionic pilasters which support a frieze of floral swags, carrying a central relief tablet of playing putti. The side elevation of the existing chimneypiece, 5ft. 8in. high, is shown to the right hand side of the drawing. The scheme provides an alternative, 4ft 7^3/$_4$ in. high.

137 Soane Office. Plan of the central block at first floor, 1800

National Trust WIM/D/558
Inscr.: 'WIMPOLE THE PLAN OF PART OF THE CHAMBER FLOOR WITH THE PROPOSED ALTERATIONS'; 'The Countess of Hardwicke'; 'Lincoln Inn Fields, May 7 1800'
Pen and ink with black, grey and yellow washes and pencil emendations (670 x 990mm)

The earlier idea of a columnar screen at the head of the great stair is abandoned here.
   This plan neatly shows how the western apse of the Yellow Drawing Room projected beyond the envelope of Chicheley's house. Soane here returns to solving the practical problems of how the cross-gallery should be subdivided to form a central lobby with dressing rooms at either end and how access could be provided to the western apartment. This is the final form of the dressing rooms, with the design allowing for the provision of a fireplace.

138 Henry Hake Seward (c.1778—1848). Plan for the east end of the first floor, 1800

Sir John Soane's Museum, 6/1/11
Inscr.: 'Wimpole, Plan of part of the Chamber Floor, with the proposed alteration'. 'The Earl of Hardwicke', 'Copy Lincoln's Inn Field June 10th 1800'.
Pen and ink with pencil and grey and pink washes (480 x 510mm)
Scale given
Verso: the outline of a plan in pencil

This shows Soane continuing to experiment with the planning of the north end of the north-south gallery on the first floor. He suggests here the idea of placing a columnar screen in what is now described as the Lord Chancellor's Dressing Room, perhaps to provide a bed alcove. Pencil setting-out lines suggest that a perspective of this room was prepared. The drawing shows too the addition of fireplaces to the apartment above the chapel.

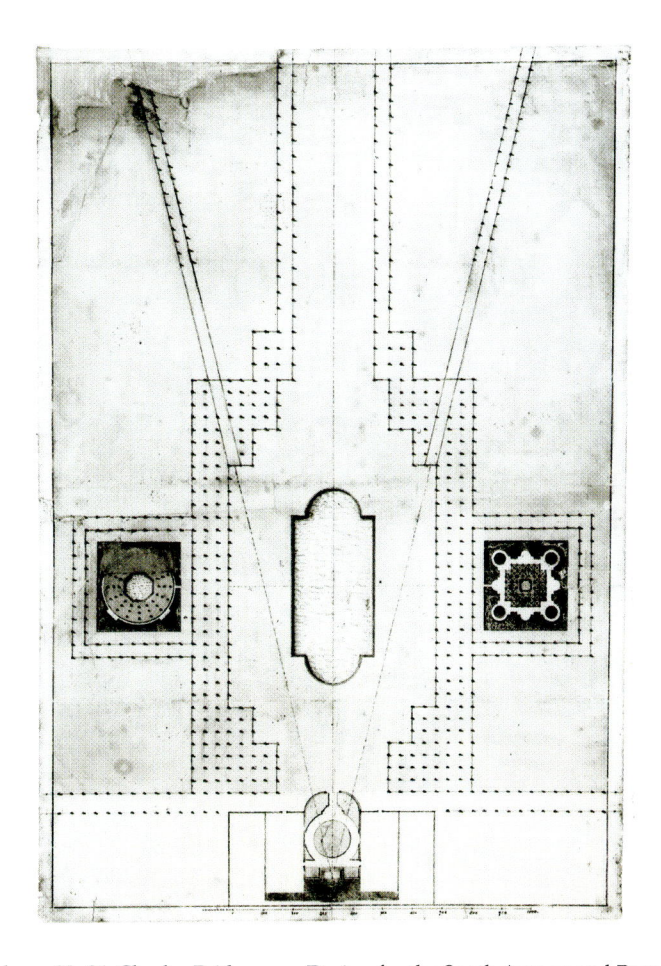

plate 1, above: No.34, Charles Bridgeman. Design for the South Avenue and Parade, *c.*1721
plate 2, below: No.82, Anonymous. 'Before' and 'after' plans of the North Park, after 1767

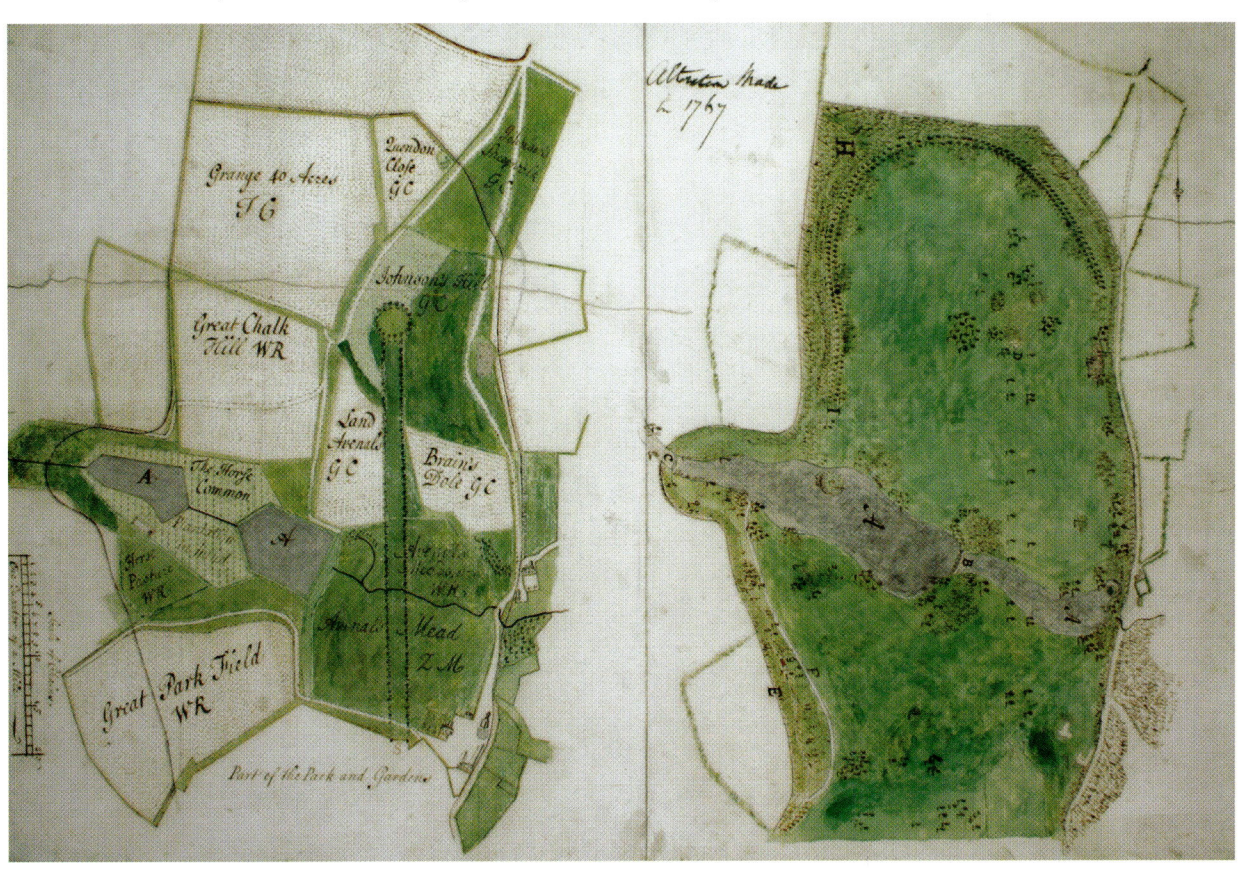

A PLAN
Wimpole
The Right Hon.ble the EARL of
HARDWICKE
with some Alterations
REFERENCE
The House and Offices.
The Church.
Vicarage House & Yard.
Church Yard.
Garden to Vicarage.
Stable Yard.
Approach Roads.
Farm Yard.
The Ruins.
Lands in the Tenants holding.
Back Approach to the House & Parsonage.
Lands for accomodating the Parsonage.
and may be divided as ye dotted lines,
with sunk fences.
The Deer Park.
The Ridings in the Park.
Publick Road by the Parsonage, turned thro' the Village.
Four double Cottages, with a Garden to each Cottage,
may be always clean; in the Centre may be fixed a May Pole.
A Scale of Chains

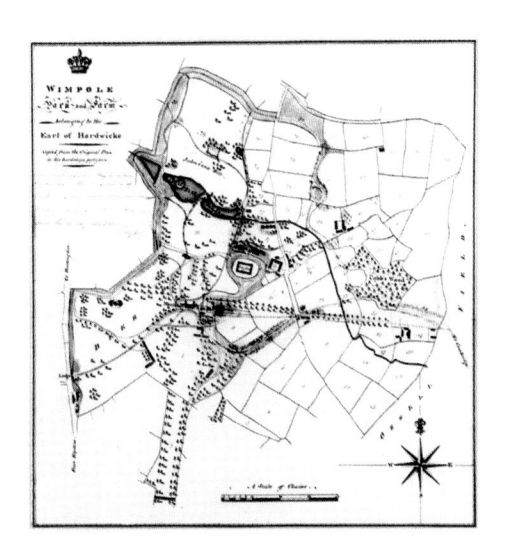

plate 3, opposite: No.139, William Emes. Survey and part proposal for the Park at Wimpole, 1790
plate 4, above left: No.191, Humphry Repton. Map (copy) of the Park at Wimpole, 1801
plate 5, above right: No.193, Humphry Repton. View of the lake-edge with an urn, 1801
plate 6, below: No.192, Humphry Repton. View from the north of the house, with flap, 1801 ('before' above, 'after' below)

III   Colour plates

plate 7, above: No.209, Humphry & John Adey Repton. 'Elevation' of the east end of the Conservatory
plate 8, below: No.226, Joseph Nash the Elder. Perspective view of the Bookroom, looking west into the Conservatory, *c.*1830

Wimpole Architectural Drawings   IV

plate 9, above: No.231, The Hon. Eliot Thomas Yorke, MP, DL. View of the South Avenue at Wimpole
plate 10, below: No.229, The Ven., the Hon. Henry Reginald Yorke. St. Andrew's. Interior view, looking towards the Chancel, 1839

Wimpole Architectural Drawings   VI

plate 11, opposite: No.248, Thomas Allom. Interior perspective of the conservatory, looking east, *c*.1850
plate 12, above: No.235, The Hon. Georgiana Liddell. View of Wimpole Hall from the south-west, after 1843
plate 13, below: No.252, Thomas Allom. West elevation, *c*.1850

plate 14, above: No.265, H.E. Kendall. Plan and elevation for an entrance screen and lodge, *c.*1847
plate 15, below: No.308, William Bruce Ellis Ranken. Watercolour view of the Gallery at Wimpole, 1937

Wimpole Architectural Drawings   VIII

Drawing by William Emes (1729/30—1803) of the Park at Wimpole

William Emes (1729—1803), or Eames, was a professional improver of estates who, while not a known assistant or pupil of Lancelot 'Capability' Brown, worked in an essentially Brownian manner: both men recast earlier landscapes in the distinctive 'natural style' of the day, for a similar clientèle. In 1790, on his succession as the 3rd Earl of Hardwicke and inheritance of Wimpole, Philip Yorke commissioned Emes to improve the great Cambridgeshire estate that Brown had landscaped for his uncle, the 2nd Earl of Hardwicke in the 1760s and early 1770s. There was already established an association between Emes and the Yorke family.

In 1779 Philip Yorke had engaged Emes to improve his own estate at Hammels, Hertfordshire. Emes had been recommended by Yorke's kinsman and namesake Philip Yorke I on whose estate at Erddig, Clywd, he had worked both in an advisory and executive capacity from 1767 to 1789—concerning himself principally with planting and with such projects as the diversion of streams and the creation of waterfalls. Of these, the so-called Cup and Saucer (1774), 'an ingenious and probably novel feature, where the water gathers in a shallow circular stone basin with a cylindrical waterfall at its centre, and then emerges from a tunnel several yards downstream' was perhaps his most impressive engineering accomplishment.[281] Judging from the pattern of other commissions associated with Yorke family members, this may not have been the first occasion on which Philip Yorke, of Erddig, had promoted Emes to his relations: in 1771 Emes worked on the Oakedge estate, Staffordshire for Thomas Anson, brother of Admiral George, Lord Anson (1697—1762), who was married to Elizabeth Yorke, the sister of the 2nd Earl of Hardwicke; and in 1778 he was employed at Belton, Lincolnshire by the 1st Baron Brownlow (1744—1807), whose sister, another Elizabeth, was Philip's own wife.[282]

In November 1779 Philip Yorke wrote to his uncle explaining that he was to meet Mr Emes at Hammels 'concerning whom I wrote to Mr Yorke of Erthig [sic] from Wimple. Our worthy cousin gives him an excellent character & says that on the practice of experience of eight years, he has occasion to hold the best opinion both of his ability & honour, & that next to the great Lancelot Brown he believes him to be the best modern Gardiner'.[283] The earl replied: 'I fancy you will rather see reason to take away [from the landscape] than to add'.[284] Philip Yorke presumably developed a good working relationship with Emes at Hammels, as he had with the architect John Soane whom he also engaged there, and it is little wonder that he sought the help of both men again at Wimpole.

Emes's spectacular plan—uncharacteristic of his other work in that it is coloured—is part survey and part proposal. A careful comparison, however, with Brown's earlier 'before and after' drawing (*No.82*) allows us to gauge what features of Emes's scheme are new departures. Of the unexecuted elements the most ambitious was his plan to create an elongated, serpentine lake stretching eastwards across the South Park from the gardens of The Tiger Inn at Arrington; this was presumably intended to balance Brown's arrangement in the north park. There may have been a practical as well as an aesthetic imperative; Emes was particularly known for his handling of water and its efficient harnessing for estate business—'Mr. Eame excells in the laying out Water'.[285] The digging of the lake would have been a considerable undertaking and would have meant the partial felling of Bridgeman's great avenue.

Emes further proposed siting a hamlet of 'Four double cottages' at the Cambridge end of the east avenue. Arranged as a small circus with a central green at whose 'Center may be fixed a May Pole', the buildings recall Soane's 1784 design for an ideal labourers' community for the Hammels estate, 'Yorke Place', whose five semi-detached cottages faced onto a semicircular green. The placement of a permananent maypole, as there were in London before the Civil War, at the centre of this proposed development may suggest that the Emes or his client had a rose-tinted, idealised view of rural life and that they wished to revive long-lost customs. A letter from Wimpole's rector, Robert Plumptre, makes it clear, however, that the maypole was already part of the estate tradition: 'some of the Pales of the Fence about the Fir trees on Orwell hill are missing, which probably your lordship will think proper to have replac'd. When that is done I should rather apprehen it would be right to take down the maypole'.[286]

139 **William Emes. Survey and part proposal for the Park at Wimpole, 1790**

British Library, Add. MS 36278 G

Inscr.: In a flamboyant cartouche, top left, decorated with spears and banners : 'A Plan of the Park and Demesne lands, &c., at Wimpole, the Seat of the Rght Hon[ble] the Earl of Hardwicke. With some Alterations'. A small oval tablet at the bottom of this reads: 'By William Emes 1790'. The scale at bottom right: 'Scale of Chains'. Buildings and specific features on the plan are numbered. A corresponding key, labelled 'REFERENCE', above the scale, reads as follows:

'N°
1 The House and Offices
2 The Church
3 Vicarage, House & Yard
4 Church Yard
5 Garden to Vicarage
6 New Stables, Wimpole
7 Stable Yard
8 Approach Roads
9 The Belvidere [sic]*
10 Farm Yard
11 Road to [...]
12 The Ruins
13 Cow Pasture contiguous to Farmyard
14 Meadow belonging to the Farm
15 Divided into three Horse Pastures
   or may be let to the Tenant
16 Lands in the Tenant's holding
17 Kitchen Garden the walls 120, by 80 yards long
   comprising Gardeners House, Melon-
   Ground &c. within the Circle.
18 Back Approach to the House and Parsonage
19 Lands for accomadating [sic] the Parsonage
20 and may be divided as p'. dotted lines
21 with sunk fences
22 The Deer Park
23 The Inn Gardens
24 The Pleasure Garden with walks communicating
   with the Kitchen Garden, Farmyard & Rides &c.
25 Rideings [sic] in the Park &c.
26 Publick Road by the Parsonage, turned thro' the Village,
27 Four double Cottages, with a Garden to each Cottage,
   the Area a Circle the windows looking into the Circle
   and the Doors and entrance at the Back, that the Circle
   may be always clean; in the Center may be fixed a May Pole'

Scale: 1-0-15 chains; 1: 3,436
Pen and ink with coloured wash on vellum (840 x 570mm)
Lit. & repr.: Jacques (1983), colour plate VII; Bendall (1992), p.338, cat. WMP79001.

Drawings by John Soane's office for a Hothouse at Wimpole

Various members of Soane's office were involved in the, somewhat protracted, design of a hothouse range built in William Emes's walled garden at Wimpole, between the summer of 1793 and spring of 1794. On 11 August 1792 R. Louch—'an unfortunate young outdoor clerk' who had joined Soane's office in September 1791 only to die in an accident the following year—was paid for spending one day 'Drawing Plan of Hothouse'. A few days later Thomas Chawner was paid for visiting and taking 'plans &c. of the Hothouse &c. at Bentley Priory'. A 'Plan and Section of Pinery at Bentley' is recorded as having been sent to 'Mr. Soane at Wimple', who subsequently drew up 'A Plan Elevation and Section of design for Hothouse With parts at Large on 3 Sheets Of Copy Paper.' In his journal Soane notes: 'NB. They were retd.'. A drawing of October 1792 is signed by Henry Provis. Clearly these preliminary attempts failed to produce what was wanted. With characteristic efficiency, Soane re-cycled one of these rejected schemes for another client, the Duke of Leeds.

Soane is not generally known for having designed horticultural buildings and the half-dozen or so glasshouse schemes that his office produced were chance by-products of his country house practice. Philip Yorke, who as we have seen was one of Soane's first and most constant clients, had previously commissioned Soane to design a hothouse for the walled garden at Hammels. Extraordinarily, following his inheritance of Wimpole, Yorke contemplated moving the Hammels peach house to his new Cambridgeshire estate. In the spring of 1793, Soane records making further charges for visits to 'Hammils [sic.] to take plans of Hothouses &' and to 'Kew to see the Hothouses'. In May 1793, with the benefit of this further round of research, Soane finally produced an acceptable design. Eight sheets of design drawings survive for the Wimpole commission, as do very detailed accounts for its building: the carpenter's 'Measured Bill to the New Hothouse, Shed & Rooms behind the same, Melons' Lights and frames—From Sept. 1792 to Nov. 1793'.[287]

The 'Measured Bill' explains how many feet of timber were 'rough', or 'planed', 'jointed', 'tong'd', 'rebated', 'dovetailed & morticed key'd', 'beaded' or 'rounded', while the painter's bill reveals that the hothouses and melon frames were painted 'four times in oil green'. We know too that the carpentry and joinery work was undertaken by R. Holland for £370 9s 7d, the brickwork and plastering by John Bayley for £526 2s, the painting by John Crace for £77 4s 8d, the iron and other metalwork by J. Mackell for £301 8s, and the glazing work by D.E. Mitchell at a cost of £155 18s 6d. The costs of visiting other hothouses and of producing the various drawings would have been calculated separately. The grand total amounted to some £1,500. The war then raging with revolutionary France was blamed for the 'Extra cost of Fir Timber', which had presumably been hazardously imported from the Baltic.

Soane's solution proposed a fairly standard arrangement: a continuously glazed lean-to structure—though of a monumental thirty-one bays, with a central five-bay show-house—set against the south-facing side of the garden's north wall in the conventional, optimal position. A narrower range of sheds, accommodating stove rooms and bothies, was placed on its other, less valuable, side. Hothouses for the hybrid purpose of growing grape-vines and pineapples were known as 'pinery-vineries'—a popular but relatively short-lived building type, first proposed by Thomas Hitt in 1757, that was superseded in the early nineteenth century with the advent of separate, specialist plant houses.

Soane's drawing and marginal notes reveal how the vines were to be planted outside in a well-drained border, their 'rods' entering the hothouse via arched openings in the brick plinth, just below ground level where they were trained along the underside of the lean-to glass roof. Similarly, the various cross-sections show graphically how the pineapples were to be grown in plant pots thrust into raked forcing pits filled with beds of crushed and fermenting oak bark. Soane describes them as 'tan' beds because the bark, which produced the constant and moist bottom-heat necessary to simulate the tropical conditions required by pineapples, was bought in from tanneries after its fiercest heat had been harnessed in the leather curing process.

Additional, controllable heat was provided in Soane's hothouses by means of a clay flue which is shown in his drawings running, double-banked, against the back wall and around the sides and front of the raked forcing pits. The warm air, which complemented the moist bottom-heat of the tan beds, would have been supplied by stoves housed in the lean-to range on the north side of the wall. Not until the early nineteenth century did piped hot water replace such warm-air driven systems, which derived ultimately from the hypocaust technology of the ancient world.

It is clear from the key to his plan (No.139) that William Emes envisaged there being a gardener's house attached to the walled garden. In Soane's penultimate scheme (No.143) he indicates the outline of a three-bay house with a striking pyramidal roof, but its construction was clearly postponed, for a marginal note reads: 'the Gardener's house when built'. The surviving house at Wimpole, damaged by the same German bomb—jettisoned over the walled garden in November 1941—that destroyed the hothouse, may have been designed by the Wisbech architect-surveyor Thomas West.

140 Soane Office. Elevation, plan and sections for a Hothouse, 1792

Sir John Soane's Museum, 8/3/27
Inscr.: 'The Earl of Hardwicke', 'Great Scotland Yard, Augt. 1792'. The drawings are labelled and dimensioned: 'Elevation of front of Hothouse', 'Section through the Hothouse' and 'Plan of the Hothouse'. A pencil annotation reads: 'A copy of this Drawing Mr. Soane took to the Duke of Leeds—making the whole Extent 100 feet - Aug 11 1792'.
Watermark: IV and fleur-de-lis
Pen and ink with coloured washes and pencil notes (380 x 485mm)

141 Soane Office. Detail drawing showing the arrangement of three tiers of window sashes, 1792

Sir John Soane's Museum, 8/3/24
Inscr.: 'Section of the Sashes & Timbers to the Hothouse, 2 Inches to a Foot'. 'The Earl of Hardwicke, Wimple, Great Scotland Yard 1792'. The drawing is dimensioned and the parts labelled: 'Capping/Upper Sash/Middle Sash/Lower Sash'.
Scale: 2in: 1ft
Watermark: B and fleur-de-lis
Pen and ink with pink wash (380 x 490mm)

Amongst the marginal pencil sketches showing alternative plan forms is an elevation for a central, colonnaded loggia with flanking hothouses.

142 Henry Provis (1760—1830). Plan and cross-section for a Hothouse, 1792

Sir John Soane's Museum, 8/3/26
Inscr.: 'Hot House at Wimpole', 'Oct. 1st 1792, H. Provis'. The passages, flues and central 'Bark bed' are indicated and dimensions given. Verso: 'John Soane Esq., Great Scotland Yard, Whitehall', 'Oct. 1 1790 The Earl of Hardwicke Wimpole. Drawing of Hothouse'.
Pen and ink with grey wash (320 x 400mm)
Scale given

The drawing has been folded, and sealed as a letter. This may either be a scheme for a smaller, 50ft-long hothouse, or for one half (the left-hand end) of a longer range—the threshold of the door at far right is not at ground level and may have been intended to give on to the raised pavement of a central show-house.

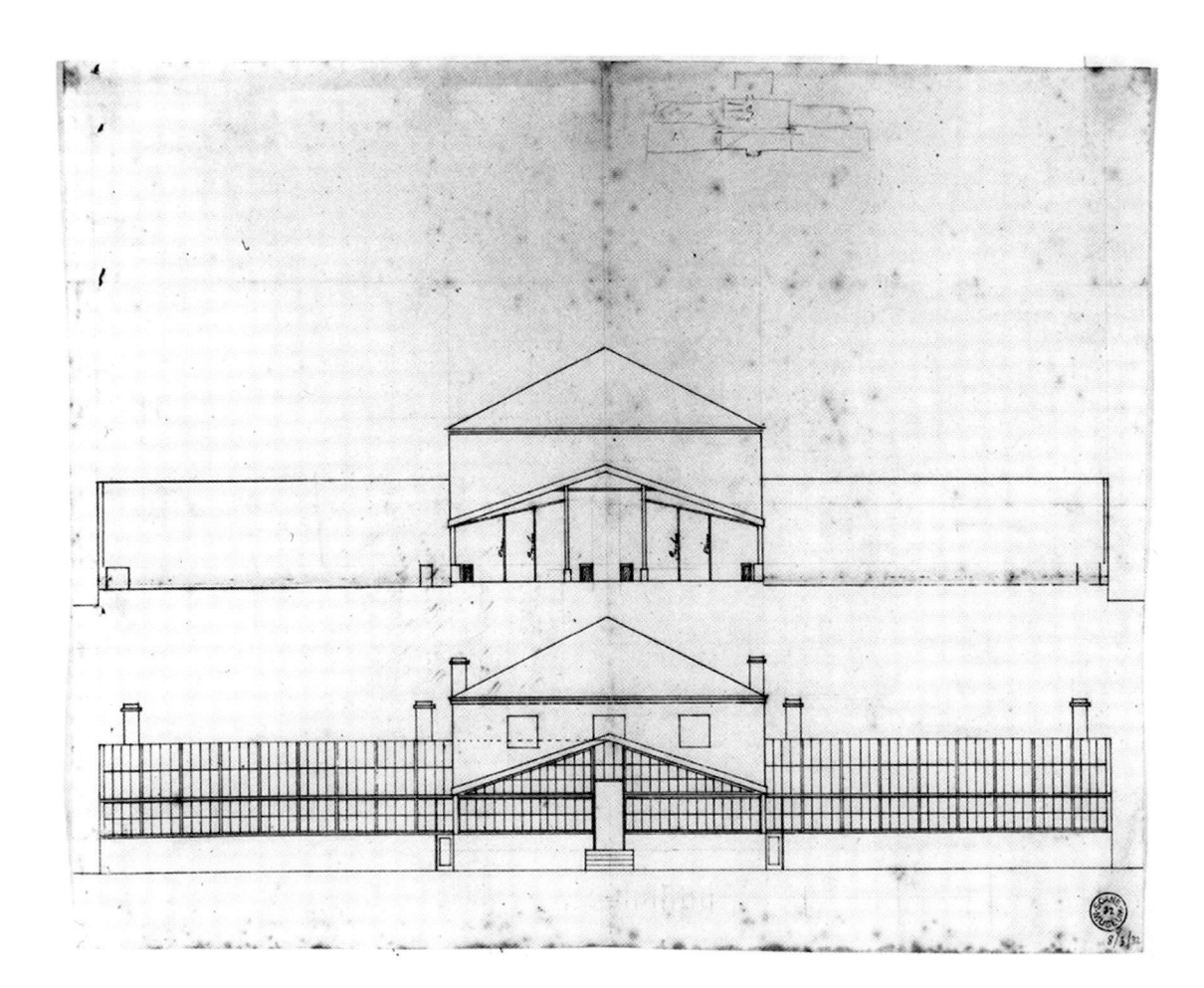

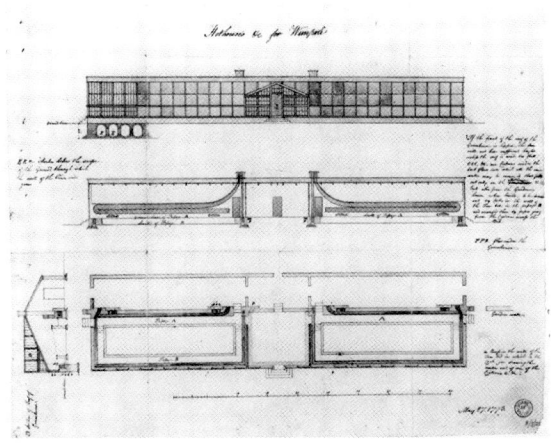

143 Soane Office. Elevation and longitudinal section for a Hothouse, 1793

Sir John Soane's Museum, 8/3/32
Inscr.: 'Vines' and 'Peaches', on the vertical supports of the central showhouse.
Verso: 'April 27 1793 The Earl of Hardwick Plans & Elevations of Vinery &c.'
Watermark: Brittannia and crested GR
Sepia ink (310 x 390mm)

This proposal for ranges of hothouses set to either side of a pyramidally roofed gardener's house, fronted by a central, pedimented show-house, provides for a more grandiose, alternative design. The section reveals that the eight-bay show-house was to have contained slender iron columns around which vines and peaches could have been trained.

144 Soane Office. Elevation, plan and sections for a Greenhouse and Hothouses, 1793

Sir John Soane's Museum, 8/3/25
Inscr.: 'Hothouses &c. For Wimpole'. 'May 27, 1793'. The various parts of the drawings are lettered, and the following marginal notes given: (at left) 'EE Arches below the surface of the Ground through which the roots of the Vines will grow', 'D section of Roof of Greenhouse'; (at right) 'If the front of the roof of the Greenhouse is hipped, the door will not have sufficient height unless the roof is made too flatt. CCC &c., are Cisterns under the back flews into which all the rainwater may be conveyed that falls not only on the Hothous but also from the Gardeners house when built, be drawn out by Cocks in the wall of the Tan bed in the passage B and conveyed there by pipes going from the Cisterns across the Bed'; FF & flew under the Greenhouse'; 'Garden Wall'; and 'A recession in the wall of the

Tan bed in which is the cock for drawing the water out of one of the Cisterns C &.'.
Watermark: R WILLIAMS and Britannia in crested shield
Pen and ink with grey, pink, yellow and brown washes to indicate materials (320 x 405mm)
Scale given
Lit. & repr.: Baggs (1999); Darley (1999), p.105, fig.85.

The drawing shows a glazed timber structure of thirty-one bays built against the north wall of the walled garden, with a secondary pitch to the rear covering a long 'shed'. The central greenhouse is twenty-two feet wide and the flanking hothouses each fifty-two feet long. Although the building described is conventional in form and placement, the scheme is invested with idiosyncratic characteristics that make it unmistakably Soanian. The massive, square-sectioned frame-members betray Soane's interest in ancient, trabeated architecture; the pedimented elevation of the central show-house in particular celebrates the structural power and logic of the post and lintel system. No less typical of his work is the contrast provided by the delicate glazing bars and sliding sash windows of the infilling wall surfaces.

The almost square, clear-span room in the central five-bay greenhouse, with its entrance doorway aligned on the main north-south axis of the walled garden, would have served as a show-house, filled with exotic flowering plants intended to delight and impress visitors.

Heated flues run along the back wall and around the sides and front of the raked beds. The brick vaulted arches shown at far left, which allowed the 'rods' of the vines to pass into the building, extended along the full length of the structure. Archaeological excavation and analysis undertaken by the Cambridge Historic Buildings Group in 1998 demonstrated that the surviving footings and other material evidence correspond in very large measure to this, the last dated design of the sequence.

145 Soane Office. Cross-section through the front part of a Hothouse

Sir John Soane's Museum, 8/3/34
Inscr.: with dimensions
Pencil (365 x 465mm)
Scale given
Watermark: 'B' and fleurs-de-lis

This is a preliminary draft for the Wimpole hothouses. The pitch of the glazed roof is steeper than in the later drawings; Tony Baggs notes that 'on the sketch sections the pitch of the roof is variously shown at 25 and 30 degrees'.[288] At far left is a section of a principal rafter showing the three-tiered sash arrangement, detailed in (*No.141*).

146 Soane Office. Cross-section through the front part of a Hothouse

Sir John Soane's Museum, 8/3/35
Pen and ink, with grey and pink wash and pencil corrections to measurements (380 x 485mm)
Scale given
Watermark: 'B' and fleurs-de-lis

A row, or rather a column, of seven potted pineapple plants is shown in the raked bark bed.

147 Soane Office. Cross-section through a Hothouse

Sir John Soane's Museum, 8/3/36
Inscr.: Dimensions marked
Pen and ink with pink and grey wash (330 x 540mm)
Scale given

This is a finished version of the previous drawing. Verso: A preliminary plan, in pen and ink with grey wash and pencil alterations, for Tyringham, Buckinghamshire, a house designed and built by John Soane for the banker William Praed between 1792 and 1800.

148 End elevation of a double-pitched Glasshouse

British Library, Add. MS 36278 M4
Pencil (286 x 396mm)
Watermark: Britannia within a crowned cartouche, the words 'BRITANNIA', 'DETTINGEN' and 'CULLODEN' in the encircling band.

This unfinished pencil elevation for one end of a double-pitched glasshouse, with an off-centre door, suggests a building of relatively modern design but the paper, at least, with its watermark celebrating George II's military victories at the battles of Dettingen (1743) and Culloden (1746) is of mid-eighteenth century date.

Drawings by John Soane's office for a Castello d'Acqua at Wimpole

Lit.: Wilton-Ely (1969), p.13 and fig.16; Stroud (1979), pp. 758–62; Adshead (2003), pp.15–21.

John Soane's design for a *Castello d'acqua*, or water reservoir, at Wimpole derives from the fantastical neo-classical projects—mausolea, casinos and garden temples—which, like the architects Sir William Chambers and Robert Adam before him, Soane was inspired to invent when confronted in Italy by the remains of classical antiquity. Amongst the unusual fantasy compositions that he produced at the time of his Royal Academy Schools funded tour of that country is a sketch for a *Castello d'acqua* or waterworks, drawn for the annual architectural competition, or *concorso*, staged in Parma in 1780 by the city's art academy, the Accademia di Belle Arti Parmense. Soane's master George Dance junior had won the academy's gold medal, a distinction that Soane must have hoped to emulate. What are probably C.J. Richardson's (1809—72) studies of Soane's original drawings are to be found in the Victoria and Albert Museum.[289]

The Parma building was to have been an elaborate affair with a central, Pantheon-domed reservoir, capable of holding 15,000 hogsheads of water, and a surrounding colonnade. Each of its four projecting wings led to an outlying temple dedicated to one of four river gods, each with its own reflecting pool and fountain. Whilst neither on the monumental scale of the Parma scheme nor as architecturally complex, the Wimpole water reservoir is clearly its humbler offspring. Du Prey suggests that its form derived partly from Soane's earlier scheme (1777) for a mausoleum for his friend James King, who died tragically in a boating accident. It is also loosely related to Soane's 1781 design, of a trefoil plan form, for a mausoleum for William Pitt, 1st Earl of Chatham (1708–78), and conjures up images of the drum-shaped mausolea that the architect admired along the Via Appia. Philip Yorke's commission provided Soane with an opportunity to translate into bricks and mortar, and to find a practical purpose for, what would otherwise have remained a competition exercise, a youthful academic set piece.

Wimpole's *Castello d'acqua* was sited in the gardens just to the north of the medieval road which still passes, east-west, immediately to the north of the parish church. It replaced a square water 'bason' which occupied a site a few yards to the west, and which is shown in a drawing by Henry Flitcroft (*No.55*). Dorothy Stroud notes that this site lay at the southern end of 'Capability' Brown's eastern ride.[290]

On 26 July 1793 Soane recorded in his account book: 'Sent per post to Provis a Plan Elevation & Section of intended Water House on a sheet of foolscap'. The structure was later built by the London bricklayer Thomas Poynder and the plasterer John Bayley. Although the position of the *Castello d'acqua* can be made out on Repton's Red Book plan of 1801 (*No.191*) he makes no

85 The Catalogue

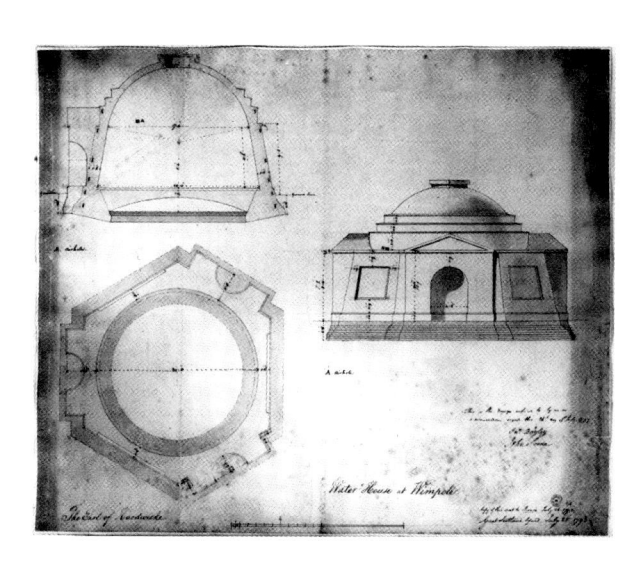

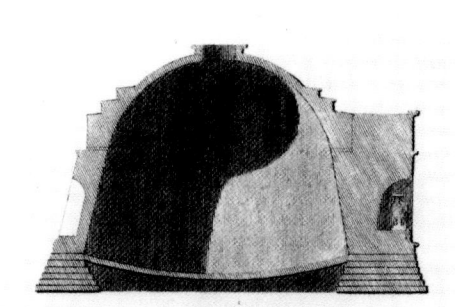

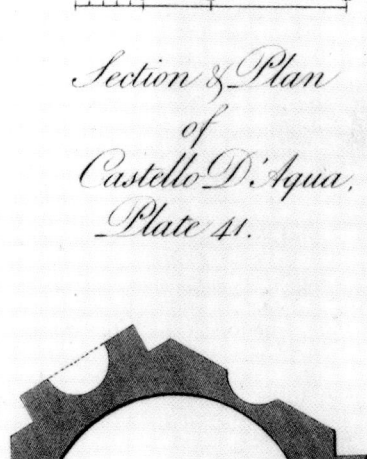

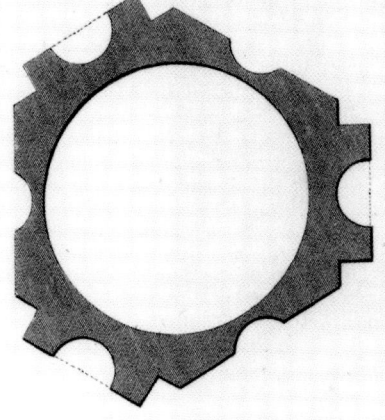

mention of it in his accompanying text. After a visit to Wimpole in 1810, Mary Berry (1763—1852) noted in her *Journal*: 'Began cutting down the trees, and clearing away about the reservoir, the only building in real good taste about this place. It is like a Roman sepulchre, and will look well when no longer choked up with trees—two beautiful yews behind and a fine cedar in front excepted'.[291] The position of the building and the lines of the pipes leading from it to the house are marked on a mid nineteenth-century survey plan (*No.274*), and finally on the Second Series Ordnance Survey map of 1903. The reservoir must have been demolished shortly thereafter. The site was excavated by the Cambridge Archaeology Field Group in July 2002.[292]

A wooden model of the *Castello d'acqua* at Wimpole survives in the Soane Museum.[293] The model is hinged and divides vertically to reveal the reservoir in section.

149 Soane Office. Plan, section and elevations for a water reservoir, 1793

Sir John Soane's Museum, 8/4/9
Pen and ink with grey wash over pencil set-up lines (495 x 520mm)
Lit. & repr.: Adshead (2003), p.18, fig.5.

The reservoir—an idiosyncratic essay in geometry and ornament—is of an unusual hexagonal plan with sides of unequal length; the longer, battered walls containing what might have been intended to be relief panels of neo-classical ornament, while the shorter sides, with shallow triangular pediments capped by palmette *acroteria*, contain semi-circular niches or *loculi*. The shallow, stepped saucer dome with its central oculus, designed to feed the chamber beneath with falling rain-water, derives from that of the Pantheon in Rome.

150 Soane Office. Plan, section and elevation for a water reservoir, 1793

Sir John Soane's Museum, 8/4/10
Pen and ink with pink and grey wash (559 x 681mm)
Inscr.: 'Water House at Wimpole', 'The Earl of Hardwicke', 'Copy of this sent to Provis July 26, 1793. Great Scotland Yard July 25, 1793'. 'This is the design referred to by us in a memorandum signed this 26th day of July 1793'. Dimensions marked.
Lit. & repr.: Adshead (2003), p.18, fig.6.

The dimensions in this more detailed version show that the elegant, bell-shaped, central reservoir was to be 20ft in diameter at ground level, with a 15ft-high dome.

151 John Soane, Castello d'Acqua, 1793

Aquatint (230 x 292mm—plate size)
Plate XLI in *Sketches in Architecture; containing Plans and Elevations of Cottages, Villas and other Useful Buildings, with characteristic Scenery* (London, 1793).
Inscr.: 'Published by L. & J. Taylor, High Holborn, London, Jany 1st 1793'
Lit. & repr. Stroud (1979), p.760, fig.11; Stillman (1988), vol.II, p.512, pl.378; Adshead (2003), p.19, fig.8.

The plate reproduced in *Sketches in Architecture* shows the reservoir set in an idealised, arcadian landscape and is captioned: 'Design for the Castello d'Acqua, now building at Wimpole in Cambridgeshire, a seat belonging to the Earl of Hardwicke. Its exterior representation is that of a mausoleum. The snakes are cut in the solid, and do not project, as shown by mistake in this view'.

The landscape backdrop to this view was interpreted literally in the caption and catalogue to the Royal Academy's 1999 exhibition 'John Soane: Master of Space and Light'. But rather than standing on a wooded hill in the grounds Wimpole's *Castello d'acqua* occupied a flat but strategic site at the western entrance to the Pleasure Grounds laid out by William Emes.

As presented in this view, the building differs from the design drawings and model in that its longer sides are also modelled to provide niches. These are reminiscent of the *loculi* that Soane had used in the deep plinths to the pyramidal extremities of the King mausoleum. The two-handled vessels shown standing on the simple footed plinths in this view are of equivocal meaning—they may serve at once as vases for water bearers and *lachrymae*, symbolic funerary vessels for the catching of tears. Satellite structures—either urns or fountains—are arranged on the radial axes of the pedimented sides.

152 Engraving showing section and plan of the Castello d'Acqua

Sketches in Architecture, plate XXXXI
Engraving (213 x 305mm—plate size)

The plan and section of the Wimpole *Castello d'acqua* is a detail (left-hand side) of the plate XXXXI in Soane's *Sketches in Architecture*. The plate also includes the plan of 'a *Belle-Vue* building, designed by *Sir Sampson Gideon*, now Lord Eardley, and proposed to have been erected at Erith in Kent', and a plan and section for an ice-house.

153 Joseph Michael Gandy (1771—1843)

Sir John Soane's Museum, Volume 69 (formerly Folio D), no.53
Inscr.: 'Jany. 17th. 1800'
Pen and ink with grey wash (232 x 370mm)

Gandy made this powerful wash drawing several years after the completion of the building. Fifteen years later he was to use it as the model for his rendering of the Castello d'acqua in the pictorial tribute to Soane, *A selection of buildings erected from the design of J. Soane Esq. RA between 1780 and 1815*.

Drawings by John Soane's office for cottages and houses on the Wimpole estate

Soane's first designs for estate cottages and houses at Wimpole date from 1793, the year in which he published *Sketches in Architecture, containing Plans and Elevations of Cottages, Villas and other useful buildings with Characteristic Scenery*. Plates II to XI of this volume illustrate designs that are very similar in spirit—if not in their use of materials—to those he proposed for the Earl of Hardwicke's Cambridgeshire estate. In his introduction to the book Soane observed: 'In cottages the rooms are unavoidably small, few in number, and frequently crowded with inhabitants. Their ground floors should be raised, at least, three or four steps from the soil; they should be placed in the most open and airy situations, perfectly dry and warm, built with the best and most durable materials, and well supplied with good water'.

The provision of good estate housing had for some decades been a concern of enlightened landowners and of interest to their architects. Soane's designs were influenced by the standard layouts suggested by Nathaniel Kent, the land agent and agricultural writer. In his 1775 volume *Hints to Gentlemen of Landed Property*, Kent claims that 'cottagers [...] are bred up in greater simplicity, live more primitive lives, more free from vice and debauchery'. Rose-tinted and patronising though these comments may appear to the modern reader, they would have struck a chord both with Yorke and Soane; Kent was writing in the tradition of Enlightenment theorists who praised the virtues of rustic simplicity—a return to the soil was in part a return to Nature. Pierre de la Ruffinière du Prey has demonstrated how, since their first chance meeting amongst the ruined temples of Paestum, to the south of Naples, Yorke and Soane pursued a common interest in primitive architecture.[294] Their search for a rustic estate architecture that satisfied their aesthetic ideals of brute strength and archaic appearance, but that sat happily with an improved, scientific approach to agriculture, is reflected in the farm and cottage buildings erected at Wimpole, as it is exemplified in the celebrated rustic dairy that Soane had previously designed for Yorke's estate at Hammels.

Hardwicke was particularly interested in how 'primitive' building materials might be used to achieve these goals, and Wimpole's model farm buildings are almost unique—as the work of a major English eighteenth-century architect—for being principally constructed in timber.[295] Equally unusual was the use of *pisé* or rammed earth for the walls of Soane's cottages, one of which survives at Wimpole. In his capacity as chairman of the Board of Agriculture, Hardwicke was later to invite to England the French architect François Cointeraux (1740—1830) whose technical publications prompted a revival in the use of *pisé* in France and Germany.[296]

These experiments began for architect and client on the Hammels estate where, in 1784, Soane designed a group of five semi-detached labourers' cottages, each with its own garden, facing onto a semicircular green. Named 'Yorke Place' on Soane's drawings, this ideally planned community anticipates the circular hamlet shown in William Emes's 1790 estate plan for Wimpole (*No.139*).

Soane's subsequent designs for cottages at Wimpole are distinguished by the use of classical elements, such as pediments and centrally placed, monumentally scaled, arched openings that disguise shared entrance lobbies. Although barked columns are not used in the cottage designs as they are in his various dairy proposals, the Primitive is suggested by the use of thatch, swept over distinctive shaped dormers, and *pisé*. Windows filled with leaded quarries, some within lights of Y-tracery (described by du Prey as 'Wyatt-type' windows'), and brick chimneys set at 45°, suggest an antiquarian if not primitive aesthetic.

Soane's assistant David Laing ploughed a similar furrow in his *Hints for Dwellings: Consisting of Original Designs for Cottages, Farm-houses, Villas &c.* (1800)—his aquatint plates offer plans and elevations that are remarkably similar to those that his master designed for Wimpole.

154 Soane Office. Plan and alternative elevations for two cottages and a Sunday School at Wimpole, 1793

Canadian Centre for Architecture, DR 1983: 0854r.
Inscr.: 'The Gable End' and 'Plan of the Ground Floor'. The two variants of the 'Entrance Front' are labelled, and a key—'A for Boys/B for Girls'—is given to indicate the separation of the sexes. 'It is proposed that this Building will make the Cottages, and also serve for the Sunday School, as the Master passes from one room to the other in the dry (thro' the Porch) if so the Porch is ornamental and precludes the necessity of making these Cottages larger'.
Pen and ink with pencil and grey and brown wash (499 x 320mm)
Scale given
Verso: A plan and elevation for another pair of cottages, marked top left with Sir Albert Richardson's collection stamp.
Lit. & repr.: Christie's (1983), p.43, Lot 75.
Exh.: University Art Gallery, Nottingham (1968), cat. no 35.

This design, which Soane explains could serve either for a pair of cottages or for a Sunday School, includes curious, semi-circular, thatched hoods to the round-headed door and two-light, latticed windows, which in elevation lends the drawing a neo-Norman quality. On 20 April 1793, Soane sent Lady Hardwicke three sheets of designs for a Sunday school and cottage.[297]

155 Soane Office. Plans and elevation for a cottage at Wimpole, 1793

Vassar College Art Gallery, Poughkeepsie, New York. Gift of Matthew Vassar. 864.1.213
Inscr.: Signed and dated 'John Soane, April 20 93'. A pencil note in Soane's hand below the elevation reads: 'The Chimney Top in the Position indicated not to be realised'. The alternative plans are marked: 'N°.2' and 'N°.1'. The room functions are given as are the positions of glazed doors.
Pen and ink with watercolour and pencil additions (265 x 203mm)
Scale given along the bottom edge of the surrounding line-wash.

Alternative designs for a pair of thatched cottages. The elevation illustrates the lower plan, 'N°.1', which offers deeper rooms, an improved stair arrangement for the left-hand cottage, and a larger central 'shop'. In both cases the shop is accessible from the kitchen of the right hand cottage. The upper scheme provides an external door to the shop. Noteworthy is Soane's introduction of a glazed inner door to the lobby of one of the cottages and of glazing into the side wall of another. Here even the humble cottage benefits from the architect's interest in how natural light might be introduced to dark spaces—surely a remarkably early instance of the glazed front door.

156 John Soane. Plan and elevation for a cottage at Wimpole, 1793

Sir John Soane's Museum, SM Drawings, Vol.68 (formerly Folio XVII), fo.25
Inscr.: 'The Earl of Hardwick', 'Plan & Elevation of a Cottage', 'Great Scotland Yard April 20 1793', 'N°.3', with the room functions marked.
Pen and ink with watercolour (275 x 220mm)
Scale given along the bottom edge of the surrounding line-wash.

This, marked 'N°.3', is a companion to the Vassar College drawing (*No.155*). It was drawn on the same day, and shows a simpler variant of the two schemes offered there. The entry porch in this proposal is shared by the dwellings to left and right and provides direct access to the central 'shop'.

157 John Soane. Plan and elevation for a pair of cottages, 1793

Sir John Soane's Museum, 64/6/18
Inscr.: 'Plan and Elevation of a Cottage'; 'The Earl of Hardwicke'; and 'Great Scotland Yard April 31 [sic] 1793'
Pen and ink with grey wash and watercolour (276 x 224mm)

This attractive presentation drawing, with the elevation rendered in watercolour against a tree-filled landscape, is for a pair of thatched cottages whose doors share a central, pedimented porch. The fireplace and kitchen oven in each cottage is served by a common stack.

The pencil sketches on the verso include designs for a diagonally braced five-bar gate, what appear to be counterbalanced opening mechanisms, and a two-leaf door with a panel containing sunburst or trophy decoration above. A series of holes along the left-hand margin indicates that the drawing was previously bound into a folio.

But for the position of the stairs, this is very close to the design illustrated as plate VII in Soane's *Sketches in Architecture*, and in the associated plan included in plate X. The published version is shown more conventionally with coursed stonework and quoins, rather than what is here presumably rendered *pisé*.

158 Soane Office. Plans, elevations and sections for a pair of cottages at Wimpole, 1794

Canadian Centre for Architecture, DR1983:0857r
Inscr.: 'Sir John Soane 1st September 1794', 'Cottage at Wimpole built with Clay'. Dimensions marked on plans.
Pen and ink with grey wash and pencil additions (696 x 542mm)
Scale given

The plan form described here is essentially the same as in *No.156* but provides for an altogether larger building. Soane has monumentalised the principal elevation by bringing the central stack forward of the ridge and turning it through 90°; the first-floor windows to either side are also given pointed dormer roofs. In elevation, at least, this two-storey building is very similar to those illustrated in David Laing's *Hints for Dwellings* of 1800. The dramatic long section shows the gathering together of the various chimney flues, the timber construction of the roof, and the bread ovens at either end of the building. The walls, 'Built with Clay', are noticeably thicker in plan than those of *No.160* inscribed 'Built with Brick'. Soane was not knighted until 1831—the inscription is, therefore, clearly not contemporary.

159 John Soane. Plans, elevations and sections for a pair of cottages, 1794

Sir John Soane's Museum, 64/6/21
Pen and ink with grey wash (605 x 468mm)
Inscr.: '[C]ottage at Wimpole built with Clay'. Internal and external dimensions given
Scale given

This is identical to *No.158* except that the shadow projection is drawn as if the light source was reversed.

160 John Soane. Plans, elevations and sections for a pair of cottages, 1794

Sir John Soane's Museum, 64/6/19
Inscr.: 'Cottage at Wimpole Built with Brick'; 'Sep. 1 1794'; dimensions given for rooms, elevations and sections.
Pen and ink with grey wash (405 x 325mm)
Scale given
Watermark: Britannia and CR beneath crown

A variant plan form for a pair of cottages with separate entry lobbies and chimney stacks.

161 John Soane. Plans, elevations and sections for a pair of cottages, 1794

Sir John Soane's Museum, 64/6/20
Inscr.: 'Brick cottage at Wimpole'; 'Sep. 1. 1794'; dimensions given.
Pen and ink with grey wash (405 x 325mm)
Scale given
Watermark: Britannia and CR beneath crown.

This design is very similar to *No.160*. The central ground-floor room, however, is given a fireplace which generates an additional, central stack while the staircases are placed off the entrance lobbies at the front of the building, so producing a different elevation.

162 Soane Office. Ground-floor plan of the Inn at Arrington. No date

Sir John Soane's Museum, 64/6/13
Inscr.: 'Plan of the inn at Arrington'; with names of rooms and dimensions given in Soane's hand
Pen and ink (325 x 405mm)
Scale given
Watermark: Britannia and CM

Folded as a letter, this is a survey drawing of the inn which survives, in altered form, as the Hardwicke Arms, on the east side of the Arrington road, which runs along the west side of the park. Soane occasionally stayed at the inn, which was then known as the Tyger or Tiger. The Tiger Inn appears to have been previously remodeled in 1723. In February of that year John Cossen, Edward Harley's Agent, wrote:

> when there I reviewed the necessary reparations and discoursed John Stevens, and since drew the enclosed Plann I think preferable to ye other and more than 50: less in expence by throwing the Gateway between the design'd building and the Brewhouse, and by so doing the Brewhouses will stand apart from any other building wch yr Lordship did seem to wish for when last there. The Brewhouses y but a weak building wch by thy draft is made less and when repaired may serve that office many years.
>
> If your Lordship be pleased to compare the 2 designs you will find this more convenient in respect to the Cellar &c. because all parts will have a communication within doors wch ever and now is wanting.[298]

As befitted a staging inn along a former Roman road, this plan shows that the Tiger not only had its own brew-house and dairy but stabling for twelve horses and additional loose boxes.

89 The Catalogue

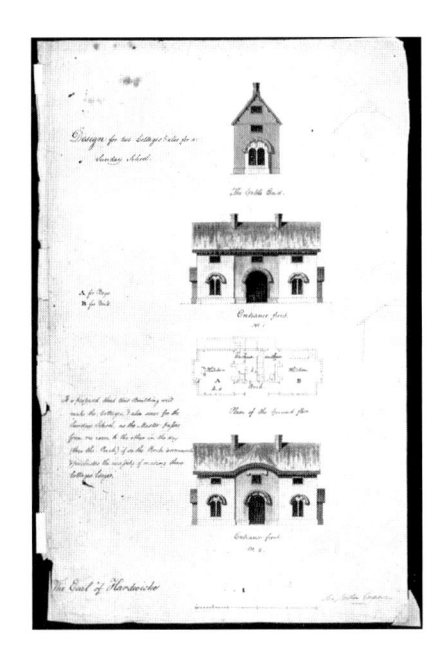

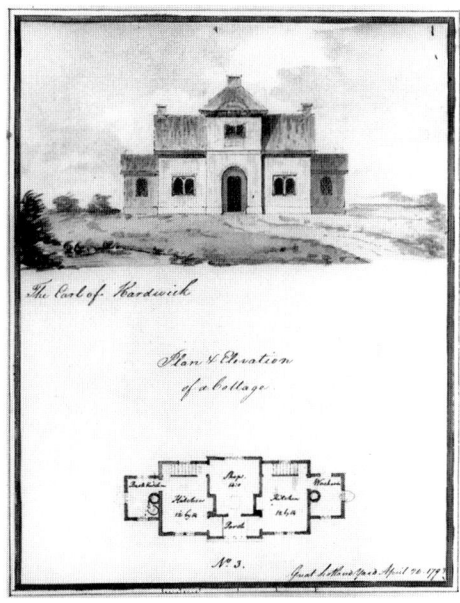

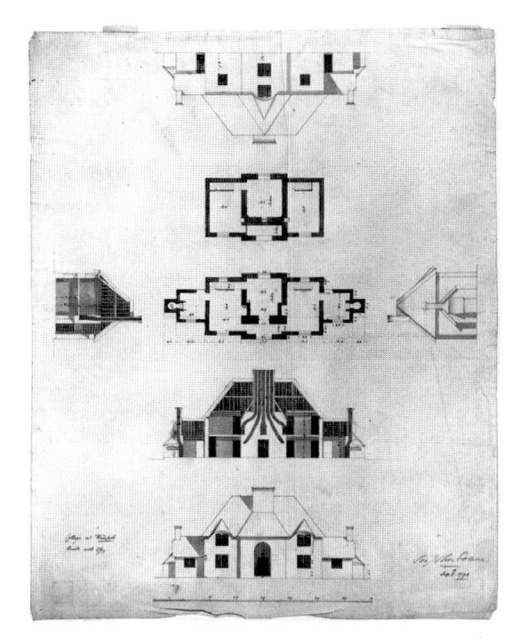

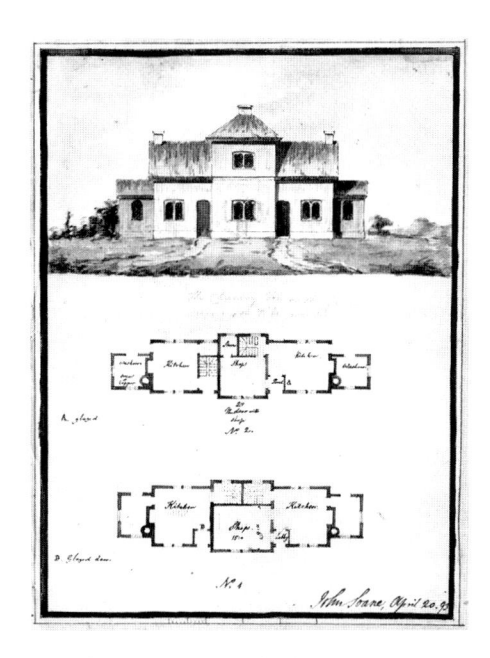

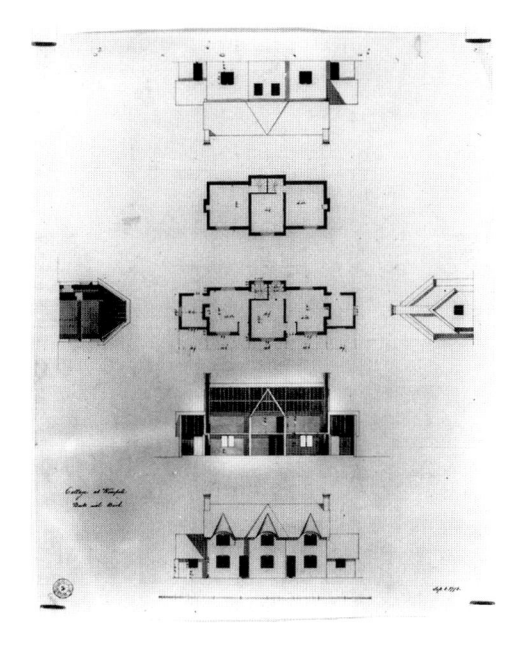

Drawings by John Soane's office for a model farm at Wimpole

The 3rd Earl of Hardwicke was an enthusiastic improving landowner who in 1814 became the president of the Board of Agriculture. His agricultural activities at Wimpole exemplify the principles and practice of the late Georgian 'high farming' movement. Theorists argued that by rationalising land holdings, undertaking enclosure, improving drainage, introducing new crops and rotation systems, experimenting with animal breeding, employing machinery and erecting new, purpose-designed farm buildings, a landowner could solve the problem of inconsistent harvests and poor yields, banishing forever the ancient spectre of famine. By these means, not only might he provide handsomely for his extended household, and send additional crops and produce to market, but his farm could become an exemplar or model for others. Leading landowners who, like Hardwicke, championed this approach in the late eighteenth and early nineteenth centuries included 'Coke of Norfolk', the 1st Marquess of Rockingham, the 5th and 6th Dukes of Bedford, the 3rd Earl of Egremont and the 2nd Marquess of Stafford.[299]

John Britton (1771—1857) and Edward Wedlake Brayley (1773—1854), the authors of the illustrated, multi-volume work *The Beauties of England and Wales*, described Hardwicke's agricultural achievements at Wimpole in the following terms:

> The principal improvements have been effected since the estate came into the possession of the present Earl. Under his direction the gardens and plantations have assumed a new appearance. The inclosures have been considerably extended, and many more acres of land brought into cultivation. His Lordship's farming establishment is on a very extensive scale; and from every improved method in agriculture being judiciously introduced, the produce of his grounds is yearly increasing. The drill husbandry is chiefly employed at Wimpole, and, from various comparative experiments, it has been found to be the most beneficial mode of culture. A new threshing and dressing machine has been lately erected; and the various other inventions to facilitate the labors of the agriculturalist, are in this establishment attended to in proportion to their utility.[300]

Wimpole's overburden of gault clay made for poor drainage and this may have been partly to blame for the outbreak of foot rot amongst the estate's sheep. Hardwicke improved the land by deep ploughing, and by digging and laying an extensive network of ditches and land drains. The diseased sheep were replaced by a new cross-breed, the Leicester-Longhorn; and the park was restocked with deer, for their predecessors had similarly succumbed to disease. Wheat, barley and oats were the main arable crops but Hardwicke also introduced new root and salad crops such as carrots, parsnips, lettuce and radishes.

In 1794, less than a year after the establishment of the Society for the Encouragement of Agriculture—which was to become the Board of Agriculture—Hardwicke set about the planning of a model farm to the north-east of the Hall, beyond the newly built walled garden. Inevitably he called upon John Soane to help him with its design. The new buildings were placed at the centre of the arable and pasture land they were to serve and were arranged around a compact, quadrangular yard in order to ensure the most efficient use of resources and to minimise travel distances.

Soane appears to have laboured over the problem of how best to orientate the farm complex and he experimented with, and then abandoned, plans for an ancillary poultry yard and dairy. The layout of the component parts of the quadrangular plan, however, was established from the first. At the centre of the north range was to be a great barn, the farm's 'engine', where produce was processed and stored and which made possible the over-wintering of animals. Harvested sheaves of cereals could conveniently be brought from the rickyards for threshing, straw could be turned and dried under cover, and the barn's products—fodder and grain—could as easily be taken out to the cow-byres, stables and (first-floor) granaries that flanked the barn in the ranges to east and west.

The provision of well-ventilated shelter was one of the key design criteria for the various animal houses, and Soane plastered them internally to improve insulation. The cows benefited from the relative novelty of stable-like conditions - flagged floors with drainage channels and divisions between stalls, and fixed fodder racks and water troughs - that had previously only generally been afforded to horses. The sties and yards for the pigs were placed deliberately in the north-east corner of the yard in order that their smell could be carried off by the prevailing winds from the south-west. Considering this, it is odd that Soane placed the cow-byre on the west side of the yard and the stables on the east, for horses are notoriously sensitive to smells. A similar planning rationale enabled the chaff from the winnowing process to be blown out of the barn (and the bounds of the yard complex) from doors in its north side.

Soane proposed that a farmhouse should be placed at the centre of the otherwise open south side of the yard. It is unclear whether this was ever built, although a building is marked in this position in Robert Withers's survey drawings *(No.220)* and today the space between byre and stables is occupied by an early nineteenth-century range of working buildings, from whose centre a further spine extends northwards, dividing the yard into two smaller enclosures. Despite these additions and the loss of the north-east range and small, enclosed yards to either end of the barn, the farm today is recognisably that shown in Soane's plans of 1794. In the late 1970s Wimpole's new owner, the National Trust, contemplated the demolition of the then very derelict buildings. Happily, they were recognised as being by John Soane, and one of the finest examples of late eighteenth-century model farm architecture to have survived in the country, and escaped that fate. Du Prey has described the farm buildings as 'rare survivors from the dawn of scientific agricultural technology'.[301]

Soane's ideal plan form was not unique to its age; indeed, the layout is not untypical of those advocated by and illustrated in publications such as *The Annals of Agriculture*, and in any number of pattern books and manuals of agricultural improvement. The use of the Primitive in farm buildings was similarly not entirely new, for overtures of this approach are evident in Daniel Garret's (d.1753) pioneering *Designs and Estimates of Farm Houses* (1747).[302] As we have seen, however, the architectural language of Soane's buildings and the materials he employed were unusual.

163 Plan and elevation for a farmyard, May 1794

Sir John Soane's Museum, 64/6/42
Inscr.: The function of the various spaces is marked
Pen and ink with grey wash (465 x 580mm)

This undated sheet is essentially the same as the presentation drawing dated 15 May 1794 which follows (*No.164*).

164 Plan and elevations for a farmyard, 1794

Sir John Soane's Museum, 64/6/26
Inscr.: 'The Earl of Hardwicke'; 'Plan of a Farm Yard &c.'; 'Lincoln's Inn Fields. May 15th 1794'. The various buildings are dimensioned and their functions indicated.
Pen and ink with grey wash and pencil emendations (417 x 280mm)

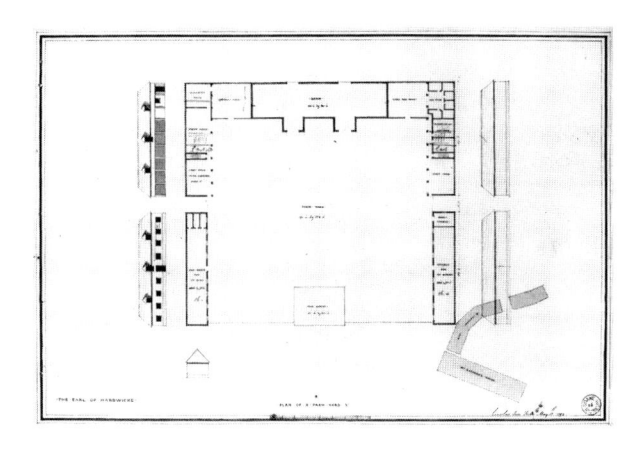

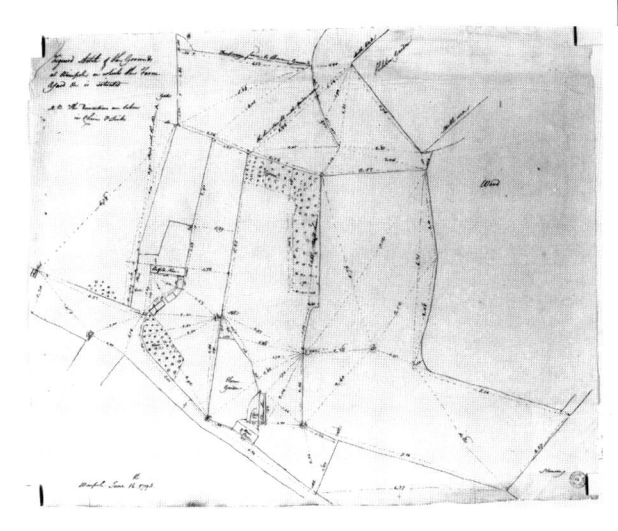

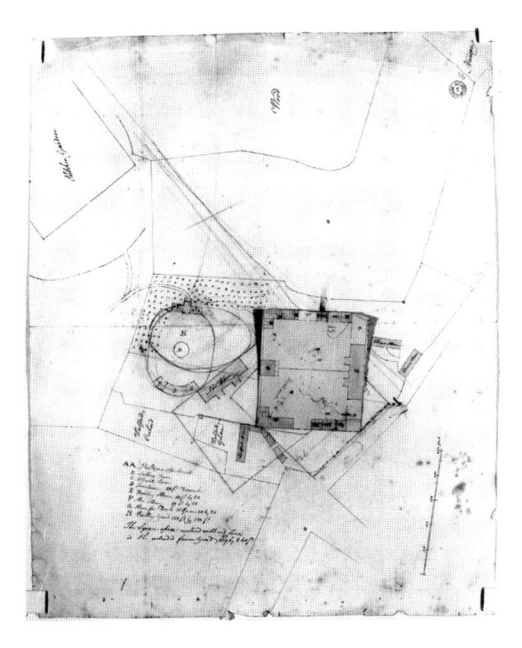

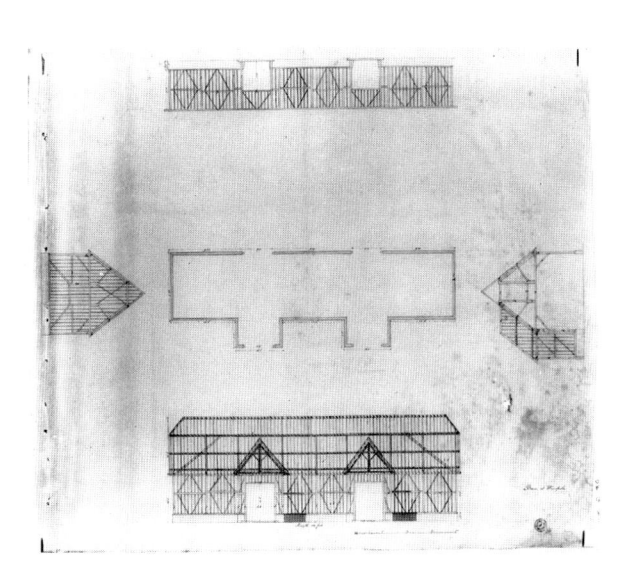

Scale given
Watermark: Fleur-de-lis over shield.
Line wash. Binding holes along left-hand side
Verso: a series of three pencil sketch plans in John Soane's hand, exploring the idea of siting the dairy overlooking both semicircular and oval yards.
Lit. & repr.: Du Prey (1978), pp.28–38, fig.9.

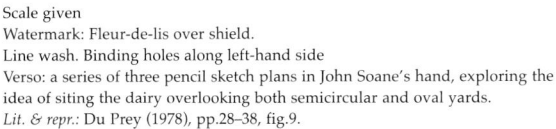

Soane's model farm as it survives today is recognisable from this plan, but various elements have disappeared. The northeast range, which is shown to have comprised 'HOG STIES', 'SLAUGHTER HO. FOR DEER', and a 'CART SHED' is no longer extant. The yard is now enclosed to the south by a range of nineteenth-century buildings, that replace Soane's intended farmer's house. The enclosed 'PASTING YARD' and 'YARD FOR HOGS' to either end of the great barn have also gone, leaving the yard open to the north at these points.

The position of an earlier building, 'MR. RATFORD'S HOUSE', and its outhouses, is shown in outline in order to indicate the siting and orientation of the new buildings. Pencil alterations propose the insertion of cart sheds in the ranges to either side of the great barn.

165 Henry Provis. Annotated survey sketch of the area intended for the proposed farmyard, 1794

Sir John Soane's Museum, 64/6/24
Inscr.: 'Figured sketch of the Ground at Wimpole on which the Farm Yard &c. is situated. NB. the Dimensions are taken in Chains & Links'; 'Wimpole June 16th 1794'. Other annotations give details of existing buildings or explain lines of measurement eg: 'this line straight with Garden Wall' which suggests that the outer wall of the walled garden shown on William Emes's proposal of 1790 (*No.137*) had been built by June 1794.
Pen and ink (475 x 485mm)
Watermark: IV GR under crested cartouche

166 Henry Provis. Survey plan with proposed farmyard superimposed, 1794

Sir John Soane's Museum, 64/6/25
Inscr.: 'The Earl of Hardwicke. Wimpole'; the key reads:
- C   Farm House
- D   Stable for 15 Horses 75^F by 20^F in the Clear
- E   Naggs Stable
- FF   Cart Sheds to hold 8 Carts and 2 Waggons, the Carts to stand two in depth, they must be 20f^t wide in Clear the Waggons being 20f^t long.
- G   Slaughter House for deer
- H   Hog Sties and Yard

I	Straw House
K	Slaughter House for Butchers meat
L	Yard to D^o
M	Barn
N	Cow House for 15 Cows 75^{ft}. by 20^{ft}.
P	Calf Penns
Q	Entrance of Road leading to Kitchen Garden by R
T	Spot mark'd by M^r. Emes for Dairy the front to be in the wood, The Poultry Yard to be an Oval in the open space V behind it.
	Mr. Harvey thinks the Dove Cott may be detatched from the farm Yard
	Hay Lofts over the Stables & Cow Houses
A	Grainery over FI & Store Chamber & over FG

Pen and ink with pencil and grey and sepia washes (405 x 510mm)
Scale given
Watermark: JHL and crowned fleur-de-lis in cartouche over LVG
Binding holes along left hand side
Lit. & repr.: Du Prey (1978), pp.28–38, fig.8.

This drawing must postdate the survey of 16 June. The orientation of the farmyard is as per *No.164*, the drawing of 15 May. The key (T) reveals that the landscape designer William Emes was responsible for suggesting where the dairy should be positioned, against the stand of trees between the 'New Walled Garden' and the farm. It was to be reached by a spur from the path through the pleasure ground, marked 'Walks', to the walled garden. The position of the proposed oval courtyard in front of the dairy is sketched in pencil.

167 Plan for the farmyard superimposed on a survey base, 1794

Sir John Soane's Museum, 64/6/22
Inscr.: 'THE EARL OF HARDWICKE'; (in John Soane's hand) 'July 5, 1794'; positions of 'Mr. Ratford's House', 'Garden' and 'Orchard' are shown together with Mr. Elsom's house and barn, and 'New Kitchen Garden'. The dairy, and the functions of the various other farmyard buildings are given.
Pen and ink with pencil and coloured washes (470 x 590mm)
Watermark: J LARKING, and fleur-de-lis over a heraldic badge, with the letters GR
Binding holes along the left-hand side

This appears to be a presentation copy of *No.166*, but the position and form of the dairy and its associated circular yard has been sketchily pencilled in by John Soane.

168 Henry Provis. Sketch layout of the farmyard, showing alternative orientations, 1794

Sir John Soane's Museum, 64/6/23
Inscr.: Key:
'AA. Poulterers Apartments
B Scalding Room
C Utensil Room
D Fountain 30f^t. Diameter
E Roosting House 40f^t. by 20
F Hen House 20f^t. by 20
G House for Ducks & Geese 20 by 20
H Poultry Yard 150 f^t. by 130 f^t.
The Square space inclosed with red line is the intended farm yard 209 ^{Ft}. by 240 f^t.'
Pen and (black and red) ink with grey and pink washes (458 x 375mm)
Scale given
Watermark: IV and crested cartouche with GR

This drawing, also produced following the survey of 16 June, shows three alternative positions for the orientation of the farmyard, one delineated in red ink and another in the form of a pinned-on flap. None is the same position as indicated in the earlier drawings. The oval poultry yard, with the dairy at one end and the hen and duck houses at the other, is worked up in greater detail than in previous drawings, but clearly the layout of this area and its conjunction with the farmyard complex posed difficulties for Soane's office. John Martin Robinson notes that Samuel Wyatt (1737—1807) designed a semi-circular poultry yard at Winnington Hall, Cheshire, for the 1st Lord Penrhyn.[303]

169 Plan and sections for the Great Barn, 1794

Sir John Soane's Museum, 64/6/46
Inscr.: 'Barn at Wimpole'; 'Length 110 feet'; dimensions given
Pen and ink with grey, yellow and brown washes (525 x 615mm)
Scale given
Binding holes along left-hand side

This beautiful drawing shows the structural and framing timbers of the great barn. The cross-section shows the queen post trusses supporting the roof. It has already been noted that for an eighteenth-century English architect to have used timber in the construction of such a building was unusual. Du Prey observes: 'In so simple a design Soane treads the thin line separating true primitivism from common building practice'.[304] The vast, cathedral-like barn could not be more different to the primitive brick barn 'à la Paestum' that Soane designed for Henry Greswold(e) Lewis at Malvern Hall, Solihull, Warwickshire.

Two doored 'midstreys' or porches on the south side allowed the bringing-in of carts laden with the grain crop at harvest time which, emptied of their cargo, could exit from the opposed doors in the north side. The barn at Wimpole was provided with removable oak threshing floors between the opposed doors; the prevailing wind from the south-west would have ensured that the chaff would have been blown northwards, out of the barn and away from the farmyard. The vast barn provided ample space for the storage of grain.

Drawings by John Soane's office for a dairy and hen house at Wimpole

In 1794 Soane's office produced a number of alternative designs for an ornamental dairy which, as we have seen, was to be sited, following advice from William Emes, on the edge of a wood overlooking an elliptical poultry yard to the south of the home farm complex. The number of variant designs suggests that the architect struggled as much with the building as with its location and orientation. Perhaps it was considered that the scale of the model farm demanded a building of greater size and complexity than the dairy that Soane had successfully designed and built eleven years earlier—at a cost of £550—for Philip and Elizabeth Yorke's estate at Hammels. In comparison with the beauty and sophistication of the Hammels dairy, the Wimpole designs appear both overworked and, in the case of some, overblown. The scheme appears to have remained on the drawing board, although the Countess of Hardwicke certainly had a dairy somewhere for in 1828 she ordered what may have been a replacement set of Wedgwood's Queen's Ware milk pans and cream vases, while a report in the *Cambridge Chronicle & Journal* of 16 July 1819 records that during a visit to Wimpole of the Duke and Duchess of Gloucester and the Princess Sophia Matilda 'the illustrious party particularly noticed Lady Hardwicke's dairy, the neatness and elegance of which strongly reminded us of the royal dairy at Frogmore'. In a journal entry made during her visit to Wimpole in October 1843, Queen Victoria noted that she had 'visited the Dairy, which is very pretty'.[305] In October 1874 Augustus Hare recorded a conversation with Lady Waterford, the 3rd Earl of Hardwicke's granddaughter, who 'talked much of her childhood at Wimpole, the delights of visits to the dairy, and receiving great lunches of brown bread and little cups of cream there'.[306] The present ornamental dairy at Wimpole was not built until 1862.

Soane was sufficiently pleased with the design of the

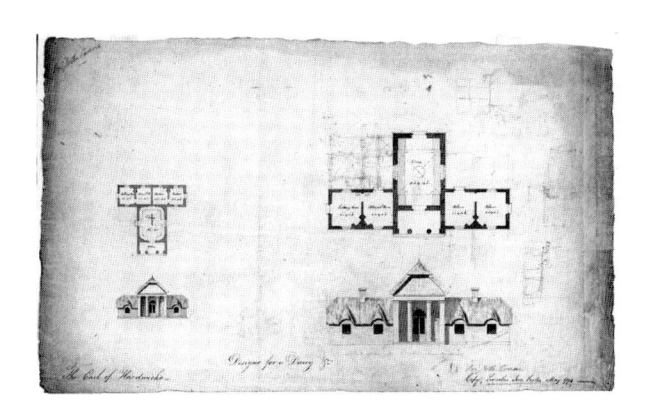

Hammels dairy to include a plan and elevation of it, as plate 43, in *Plans, Elevations, and Sections of Buildings Executed in the Counties of Norfolk, Suffolk, Yorkshire, Staffordshire, Warwickshire, Hertfordshire, et caetera* (1788), with the accompanying description: 'This building is placed near the house, and surrounded with large trees; the fronts are rough casted, and the roof is covered with reeds; the pillars of trees, with the bark on, decorated with woodbines and creepers'. The romantic and intellectual appeal of the Primitive and the associative ideas bound up with a 'Return to Nature' have already been discussed in the context of Soane's cottage and farm architecture. The symbolism of milk, and the dairy as a temple to milk, allowed for further allusions to the primitive rustic. If a return to the soil could be associated with the unsullied lives and virtuous qualities of country folk, unadulterated milk could symbolize the simplicity, wholesomeness and innocence of a lost Arcadian world.

So too was it appropriate for the lady of the household (and her daughters) to oversee the processes undertaken in the dairy—the separation of milk and cream, the making of butter, cheese and junkets—where the strictures of cleanliness were of paramount importance. The addition, in 1783, to Marie-Antoinette's *ferme arrangée* at Versailles of *L'hameau de la Reine*, reflected rather than triggered the cult of the farm as an aristocratic plaything; in England it was already well-established, while in continental Europe, Anglomania saw to its promotion. The Hammels dairy was coeval with that at *Le Petit Hameau*. Two years earlier, in 1781, Soane had designed a dairy for Lady Elizabeth Craven's Fulham property which, although never erected, served as the real progenitor of the Hammels and Wimpole designs. Du Prey notes that Lady Craven had been trained by a Swiss governess in the craft of making butter and cheese, and he speculates that it was her advice that steered Soane towards his pleasing but functional design.[307]

The Hammels solution essentially followed the model designed for Lady Craven—though without its coffered barrel vault which oversailed the main dairy room. The dairy was placed at the back of the building while its entrance hall provided access to an apsidal-ended scalding room to one side, and a tea room (the deliciously named Strawberry Room) on the other. A central fountain and marble table tops helped to keep the room and its all-important milk pans and cream vases at the optimal temperature of 50° F (10° C). Soane records that 'the walls are varnished and decorated, and the windows are of stained-glass in lead work'; varnish and tile work were easily cleaned, while the use of coloured glass helped prevent the heating effect of direct sunlight. The building was thatched, providing excellent insulation, and its interiors were further protected from the sun by a portico whose supporting columns were formed from the barked trunks of elm trees.

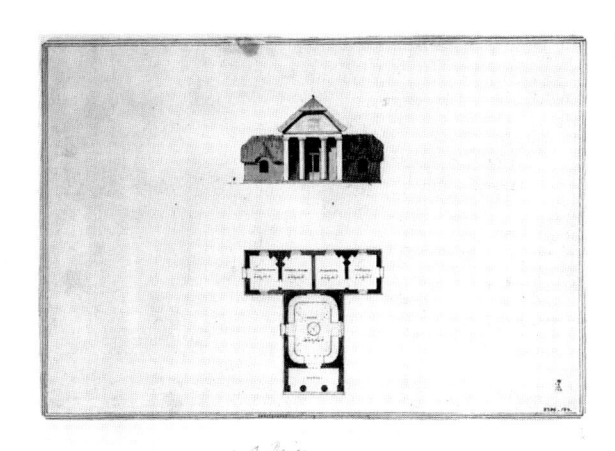

Here was the very embodiment of Abbé Marc-Antoine Laugier's theory of the primitive hut and the origin, as recounted by Vitruvius, of the Doric order, and it is telling that Soane himself explicitly described this building as 'A Dairy in the primitive manner of building'. It has been suggested that the rude, barked architecture illustrated in William Wrighte's *Grotesque Architecture* (1767) may also have provided Soane with a useful starting point for this particular idiom. All this was a far cry from the gauche design for a Moresque Dairy that the young architect had included in his first publishing venture, *Designs in Architecture*.[308]

The attractive bi-exedial form of the Hammels model (illustrated in exquisite watercolour renderings), with the functional scalding room—where utensils were cleaned to prevent bacterial growth—balanced by the decorative tea room where the mistress of the house could entertain, is abandoned in the various Wimpole designs. These incorporate rooms (to which separate, external access is provided) for activities associated with the management of poultry. Here the avian world adulterates the idea of the temple to milk and upsets the architectural poise of Soane's earlier design. But, as John Martin Robinson has noted, the productive poultry house and decorative aviary, like the dairy, 'fell into the woman's field of influence': there was a logic to combining poultry yard and dairy. That this was the Countess of Hardwicke's domain is confirmed by the record, on 4 July 1794, of Soane's Journal No.2:

M[r]. Soane took to Her Ladyship N[o].7 draw[gs].
Viz. 5 plans & elevat[s]. of design for
dairy, on 5 ½ sheets of Royal.
1 Plan, Elevation & Section of design for
Hen Nests […] the General Plan Shew[g].
The farm yard, on 2 sheets of Royal

The following day: 'Meyer de[d]. 2 fair sketches of designs for a dairy on 2 half sheets of royal paper'.

Some twenty five years later the Countess's third daughter, Lady Elizabeth Stuart (1789—1867), was to warn her of the risks to her health of her enthusiasm for the model farm: 'Now pray don't get too keen about cow-houses or hen-houses, and stand in the cold planning improvement'.[309]

In a number of the Wimpole designs, an octagonal plan form is suggested for the dairy room itself—ventilated by high-level therm windows providing the necessary cross-ventilation. In three of these schemes, elevations reminiscent of simple, centrally-planned Romanesque churches are generated; in one a Pantheon-like building; and in another a façade similar in character to the architect's proposals for an entrance screen with flanking lodges. Du Prey notes that although some of these proposals make use of a baseless Doric portico, the Wimpole drawings exhibit a distinct 'diminution of primitivism' when compared to the Hammels design. Soane designed other dairies for the Hon. Lewis Thomas Watson at Lees Court, Kent (1789), and the 1st Marquess of Abercorn at Bentley Priory, Stanmore, Middlesex.

170 Soane Office. Plans and elevations for two alternative Dairy designs, May 1794

Canadian Centre for Architecture, DR 1983:0856
Recto. *Inscr.*: 'The Earl of Hardwicke', 'Designs for a Dairy &c.', 'Copy, Lincoln's Inn Fields May 1794'. The room functions are marked on both plans.
Pen and ink with grey wash and pencil additions (345 x 575mm)

The tri-lobed plan of the Hammels dairy is replaced here by 'T' and inverted T-shaped variants. In both these alternatives the dairy, entered either from the tetrastyle portico or a secondary door, is kept quite separate from the ancillary rooms. On one side are the scalding and utensil rooms for the dairy, and on the other a pair of rooms for the 'Poulterer'. In the right-hand scheme, the ancillary rooms are arranged as pairs in flanking wings, while in the left-hand proposal, drawn to a smaller scale, they are placed in a continuous range along the back of the dairy. The window and door openings are shown protected with what may either be lozenge-camed glazing or wire gauze, commonly used in dairies.

Verso: Plan, elevations and cross-section for a dairy. This is almost identical to the scheme shown on the right-hand side of the recto but may predate it. The sash windows have been scribbled over in pen, in Soane's hand, to indicate alteration to the smaller windows of the presentation version. The long section through the dairy, and the dotted lines on the plan, shows that it was to have had a groin vault rather than the barrel vault of Elizabeth Craven's dairy. Note Sir Albert Richardson's collection stamp at bottom right.

171 Soane Office. Plan and entrance elevation for a Dairy, 1794

Victoria and Albert Museum, 3306.159
Inscr.: 'A Dairy'. The function of the rooms are indicated, and their measurements given
Pen and ink with yellow, pink and grey washes (181 x 268mm)
Scale given and incorporated into the ruled border.
Lit.: Du Prey (1985), p.62.

This proposal for a dairy with a tetrastyle Doric portico and a lower cross-range to the rear of the building containing 'scalding', 'utensil' and 'poulterer's' rooms, is identical to the scheme shown on the left-hand side of *No.170*. The internal walls of the dairy have curved corners, perhaps suggesting that the building was to have been constructed of *pisé*.

Verso: sketches of three plans and elevations for alternative dairy schemes drawn in pencil, pen and sepia ink.

172 Soane Office. Plan and elevation for a Dairy, 1794

Sir John Soane's Museum, vol.59 (formerly fo.IV), 173
Inscr.: 'THE EARL OF HARDWICKE'. 'THE DAIRY' and 'PORCH' labelled.
Pen and ink with watercolour (464 x 285mm)
Scale given, above wash line

The portico, with its garlanded columns and pediment, recalls the barked and festooned dairy design for Hammels. Soane here abandons that T-shaped plan and explores a series of variant schemes generated from a central, octagonal dairy chamber. With a columned portico both at the front and rear of the building, Soane here suggests an unconventional *amphiprostyle* temple.

In 1798 Soane was to design another octagonal dairy, a simple structure built in brick and flint, for Henry Peters at Betchworth Castle, Surrey. Other contemporary dairies were designed using similar plan forms. In 1791, for example, Humphry Repton designed a dairy, poultry yard and farmhouse complex, probably with the assistance of his friend William Wilkins (1751—1815), for High Legh Hall, Knutsford, Cheshire. The dairy room was octagonal in plan with flanking scalding and cheese rooms, and, at the front of the building was placed a 'strawberry room'.[310]

173 Soane Office. Plan and elevation for a Dairy, 1794

Sir John Soane's Museum, vol.68 (formerly fo.XVII), 22
Inscr.: 'THE EARL OF HARDWICKE'. 'THE DAIRY' labelled
Pen and ink with watercolour (465 x 286mm)
Scale given, above wash line

In this variant, an octagonal dairy is capped by a shallow dome which in elevation is seen rising from behind a screen wall, against which a portico is planted. In the watercolour rendering the wings are partially screened by planting. A semi-octagonal verandah has subsequently been sketched in to the rear of the building.

174 Soane Office. Plan and elevation for a Dairy, 1794

Sir John Soane's Museum, vol.68 (formerly fo.XVII), 21
Inscr.: 'THE EARL OF HARDWICKE'; 'Lincoln's Inn Fields'. The room functions: 'THE DAIRY', 'PORCH', 'POULTERER', 'LOBBY', 'UTENSILS'. 'LOGIA', SCALDING ROOM' are labelled.
Pen and ink with watercolour (464 x 285mm)
Scale given, above wash line

In this version it is proposed that the plan of the dairy should be a half-octagon, whose entrance porch takes the form of a great pedimented archway. The elevation, with its flanking pavilions with seats placed in blind arch-headed recesses and links articulated by baseless Greek Doric columns *in antis*, is closely related to Soane's entrance screen designs. A hill, with a lake in the foreground, is shown to the right-hand side of the watercolour rendering.

175 Soane Office. Plan and elevation for a Dairy, 1794

Sir John Soane's Museum, vol.59 (formerly fo. IV), fo.174
Inscr.: 'THE EARL OF HARDWICKE'; 'Lincoln's Inn Fields'. The room functions: 'SCALDING ROOM', 'THE DAIRY', 'LOBBY', 'PORCH', and 'UTENSILS', are labelled, with some rooms dimensioned.
Pen and ink with watercolour (464 x 285mm)
Scale given, above wash line

An altogether more primitive alternative is proposed here. A simple portico is planted against a thatched, windowless range, which screens the octagonal drum of the dairy, lit by semicircular clerestory windows, and capped by a thatched roof and a cross-shaped weathervane.

176 Soane Office. Plan and two alternative elevations for a Dairy, 1794

Sir John Soane's Museum, vol.59 (formerly fo.IV), 172
Inscr.: 'THE EARL OF HARDWICKE'; 'Lincoln's Inn Fields'. The room functions are marked on the plan: 'THE DAIRY', 'SCALDING ROOM', 'POULTERER' and 'PORCH'.
Pen and ink with watercolour (467 x 285mm)
Scale given, above wash line

Here the walls of an octagonal dairy, twenty feet in diameter, are protected from the sun by a deep arcade that wraps around the principal face of the octagon and links with the flanking scalding and poulterer's rooms. But for the wings, the design has echoes of a simple, polygonal, centrally planned Romanesque church. The watercolour rendering is presented as if on a separate sheet of paper, with *trompe l'œil* scrolling corners.

A smaller scaled elevation, placed between the plan and the watercolour, proposes an alternative treatment for the arcade in which the arches are full hemicircles and spring from a low plinth.

95 The Catalogue

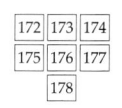

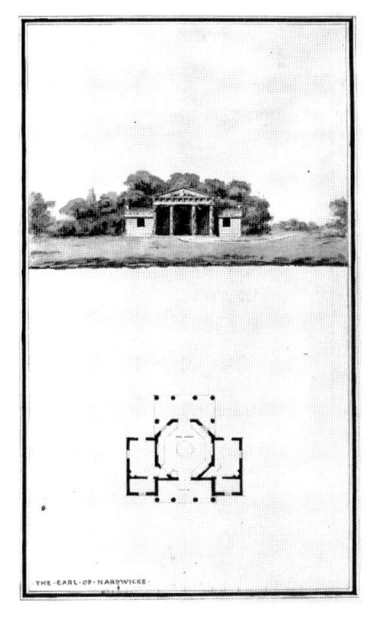

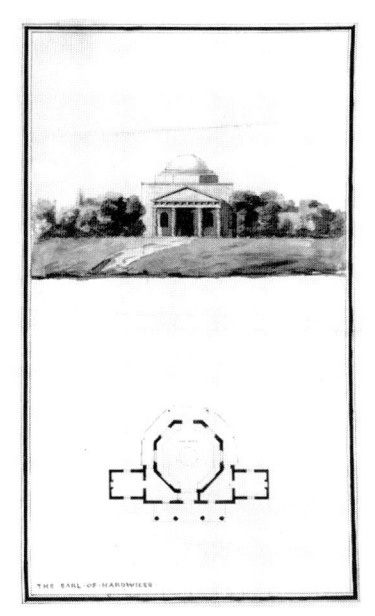

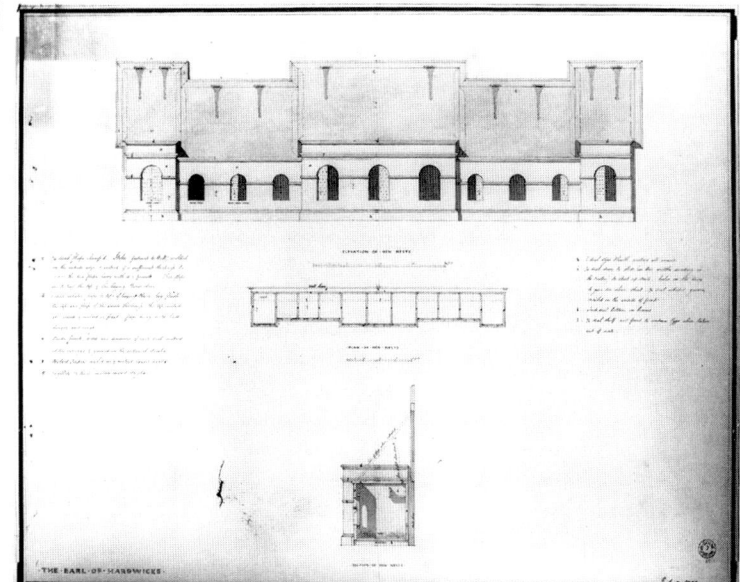

177 Soane Office. Alternative plans and elevations for a Dairy, 1794

Sir John Soane's Museum, vol.68 (formerly fo.XVII), 23
Inscr.: 'THE EARL OF HARDWICKE'; 'Lincoln's Inn Fields'. The room functions are marked on the plan, from left to right:, 'SCALDING ROOM', 'THE DAIRY' 'UTENSILS', SEAT', 'PORCH', and 'POULTERER'. Above the larger plan, in Soane's hand 'Yard'.
Pen and ink with watercolour and pencil additions (468 x 288mm)
Scale given, above washline

Another thatched, 'primitive' variant. Here a simple trabeated arcade, with columns *in antis*, provides an entrance and porch for the dairy, but to either side is planted a broad pier, capped by what appear to be sculptural figures of shaggy-coated cattle.

Interposed between the other drawings, and drawn to a smaller scale, is a plan and elevation for an alternative design of a shallower-roofed dairy, fronted by a longer columnar screen.

On both plans, pencil additions suggest how the planting behind the dairy might be set out.

178 Soane Office. Plan and elevation for a Dairy, 1794

Sir John Soane's Museum, vol.68 (formerly fo.XVII), 24
Inscr.: 'THE EARL OF HARDWICKE'; 'Lincoln's Inn Fields'. The room functions are marked on the plan, left to right: 'SCALDING ROOM', 'THE DAIRY' 'UTENSILS', 'LOBBY' and 'POULTERER'.
Pen and ink with watercolour and pencil additions (468 x 288mm)
Scale given, above washline

Here the octagonal form of the dairy is fully visible. The entrance is via a simple gabled porch, which is reflected in the flanking pavilions. This scheme shares something of the character of Soane's cottage designs for Wimpole.

Pencil emendations to the plan suggest that, following the presentation of this drawing, it was felt prudent to add a verandah or arcade to protect the lower walls of the dairy. Above it is a hastily sketched pencil variant.

179 Soane Office. Plan, elevation and section for a Hen House 1794

Sir John Soane's Museum, 65/1/7
Inscr.: 'THE EARL OF HARDWICKE', 'ELEVATION OF HEN NESTS', 'PLAN OF HEN NESTS', SECTION OF HEN NESTS', and 'July 5, 1794'
'c   […] deal flaps clamp'd..Stiles (fastened to Wall) Molded on the outside edge, & mitred of a sufficient thickness to receive the two flaps hung with 11 x Garnets . These flaps are to keep the top of the laying Places clean.
d   1" deal rebated flaps to tops of laying Places, lay flush the top and flap of the same thickness. The top mitred all round & molded in front..flaps hung with butt hinges and rings
e   Backs, fronts, sides and divisions of inch deal mitred at the external & grooved in the internal angles
f   Molded Impost nail'd on & mitred round angles
g   […] fillets. […] thick, mitred round angles
h   1" deal Ogee Plinth mitred all round
i   […] deal doors to slide (in widths meeting in the center) to shut up nests—holes in the doors to give air when shut—[…] deal rebated groove nailed on the inside front.
k   Inch deal bottom on bearers.
l   […] deal shelf and front to contain Eggs when taken out of nests

Pen and ink with grey and yellow washes (601 x 437mm)
Scale: The elevation and section are drawn to one scale, and the plan to a smaller scale
Lit. & repr.: Robinson (1983), fig. 97; Dean (1999), p.23, fig.1.1.4.

These extraordinary classical nesting boxes, which were to benefit from a complicated arrangement of hinged flaps that could be opened or closed to ventilate or protect the 'laying Places', were designed to stand no more that four feet high. The word Garnet, used in the key, is a contemporary term for a type of T-shaped hinge. Arch-headed doors are shown in various positions—when shut, open and half-open. The section is inscribed: 'Line of flap when extended' and 'Line of flap when opened'. Of this drawing John Martin Robinson has written:

> It is symptomatic of the seriousness with which farm buildings were treated in the late eighteenth century that the august architect of the Bank of England did not consider the design of nesting boxes for hens beneath his attention. His beautifully finished drawings show the timber boxes treated as a symmetrical classical composition sixteen feet long and four feet high with centre, links, and ends, the openings taking the form of semicircular arches. In uncharacteristically light-hearted mood Soane shows in his section a straw nest at the bottom of the box, but no eggs!

Wimpole Architectural Drawings

Drawings by John Soane's office for an entrance screen at Arrington

Following his visit to Wimpole on 22 July 1800, the Rev. James Plumptre noted: 'The entrance into the park is thro' a triumphal arch, having a lodge on each side. The building itself is handsome, but the straight line on the top seemed to want some relief; Horses, cows, deer or sheep, would be more appropriate than Lions or Unicorns, which are usually seen in such places. Deer, of some kind, are the supporters of the Hardwick [sic] arms'. Despite his reservations about the austere character of the design, Plumptre would have seen Soane's screen on the Arrington Road—with its arched entrance and flanking lodges—at its best. Completed in 1796, cracks had already begun to appear in the central arch by 1804, and the structure was eventually demolished and replaced by a gate screen designed by H.E. Kendall (1776—1875) (*Nos.268 & 269*).

The Wimpole entrance screen, which gave access to the park from the west, belongs to a family of Soanian estate gates and lodges. The first of these, which was also the earliest free-standing structure built by the young architect, was likewise commissioned by Philip Yorke; in 1781 Soane designed a pair of simple entrance lodges, with shallow pyramidal roofs and windows framed by giant relieving arches, for his estate at Hammels, Hertfordshire. Three years later came two rather more sophisticated entrance screens for Langley Park, the Norfolk seat of Sir Thomas Proctor-Beauchamp.

Soane's initial proposals for Wimpole combined elements that derive from the two Langley Park screens: the arch from the so-called 'Greyhound Lodges', and the flanking pavilions from the 'Doric Lodges'; the Wimpole design as built was astylar. Soane employed this hybrid design again for the entrance screen at Tyringham, Buckinghamshire, the estate of the banker William Praed. The Tyringham entrance, however, is stripped down to its elemental parts and has been described by Margaret Richardson as a being of a 'reduced primitive order'. Du Prey's conclusion is that 'the Wimpole group fell qualitatively somewhere between them. It lacked the sophistication of Langley, the brute-power of Tyringham and the strength of both'.[311]

In January 1794 Soane had taken with him to Wimpole four sheets of different designs for the 'Lodges at Wimpole, each on ¼ sheet of Imp^l. Paper'. As Dorothy Stroud has noted: 'These all followed the theme of a simple archway spanning the drive and linking the two lodges, the variations being in the application of an Ionic order, or a pediment to the archway, and one of them—with columns—framing the lodge windows'.[312] Work must have begun almost immediately for exactly one month later, Soane's journal records sending Henry Provis 'a Plan of Wall to Lodges for the Digger'.

It was not long, however, before the completed building suffered structural problems. In November 1804 Provis sent Soane an illustrated letter explaining that he had not found 'any memoranda relating to the Foundations of Lord Hardwicke's Lodges', but remembered their depth and the nature of the underlying clay; he explained that a Mr Paddon had contracted for the brickwork.[313] Less than two years later, Lord Hardwicke himself wrote to the architect to alert him to 'the present state of the Lodge which you built for me at this place in the year 1796'. The central arch had cracked, but more seriously one of the flanking lodges had suffered from subsidence and was, therefore, demolished. Soane offered to bear the expense of rebuilding the lodge if it proved that his contractor had been negligent, and Lord Hardwicke's agent explained that it was his master's wish 'to retain the Lodges & Arch according to the original plan'.

180 Soane Office. Elevation for an Entrance Screen, 1794

Sir John Soane's Museum, vol.68 (formerly fo.XVII), 14
Inscr.: 'Lincoln's Inn Fields Jany. 24 1794'
Watercolour over pen and ink (255 x 368mm)

It is likely that this watercolour presentation drawing, in a landscape setting and with a black line wash, is one of the four that Soane took to Wimpole in January 1794. Here the triumphal arch of the greyhound lodges at Langley Park, Norfolk, is combined with flanking pavilions similar to those at the Doric lodge at the opposite entrance to the Langley estate. The three elements are linked by a short section of wall, each with a six-panelled door, to produce a solid screen. The pavilions are defined by baseless Greek Doric columns *in antis*. Soane's 'furniture of death', as Sir John Summerson characterized the architect's quotations from ancient mausolea, is in evidence on the skyline of this group of initial proposals. Here the pavilions are capped with shallow pedimented features with *acroteria* at either end—to all intents and purposes like *sarcophagae*—while the arch is capped with a pair of spiral-fluted drums that recall ancient altars.

181 Soane Office. Elevation for an Entrance Screen, 1794

Sir John Soane's Museum, vol.68 (formerly fo.XVII), 15
Inscr.: 'Lincoln's Inn Fields, Jany. 24 1794'; in pencil to right of arch 'Tendring Hall Cornice'
Watercolour over pen and ink (255 x 368mm)

A section of the deep dentil cornice is crudely sketched in pencil to the left of the arch. Soane first visited Tendring Hall, the Suffolk seat of Admiral Rowley, in May 1784 and was subsequently to build a brick, bow-fronted house there in the Saxlingham and Letton mould. In this variant, the linking walls between pavilions and arch are given round-headed apsidal niches, while the Doric columns are provided with a pronounced batter.

182 Soane Office. Elevation for an Entrance Screen, 1794

Sir John Soane's Museum, vol.68 (formerly fo.XVII), 16
Inscr.: 'Lincoln's Inn Fields. Jany. 24 1794'
Pen and ink with watercolour (255 x 368mm)

This third variant is lighter in effect and proposes open screens of Ionic columns *in antis* between the arch and pavilions. A third pair of columns sits uncomfortably inside the piers of the arch. The pavilions are given pyramidal roofs, topped by chimneys of ancient altar form with *strigilated* decoration, while their windows are set within relieving arches above a blind balustrade.

183 Soane Office. Elevation for an Entrance Screen, 1794

Sir John Soane's Museum, vol.68 (formerly fo.XVII), 17
Inscr.: 'Lincoln's Inn Fields. Jany. 24 1794'
Watercolour over pen and ink (225 x 368mm)

In this compact variant, the lodges abut the sides of the arch and are given hipped roofs. The Ionic order replaces the baseless Greek Doric columns of the first two variants, while *paterae* enrich the frieze.

184 Soane Office. Sections, plan and elevations for an Entrance Screen, 1794

Canadian Centre for Architecture, DR 1983: 0855r
Inscr.: with dimensions and instructions; 'Lodges at Wimpole'; 'Copy of the drawing M^r. Provis took with him March 11th. 1794'; and 'Copy sent to Provis June 18: 1794'
Pen and ink with grey wash and pencil alterations (696 x 542mm)
Lit. & repr.: Christie's (1983), p.43, lot 76, which comprised three drawings.

This drawing, apparently of March 1794, provides a long-

Wimpole Architectural Drawings

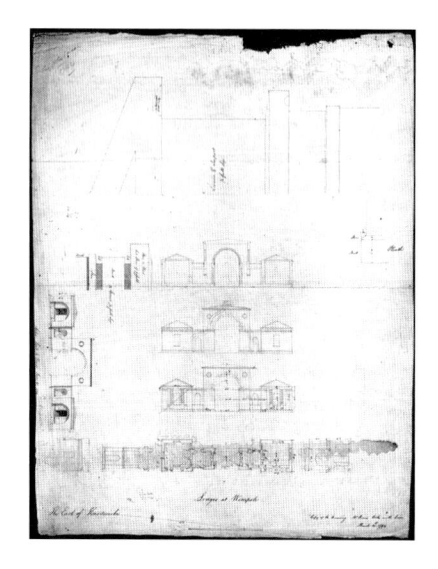

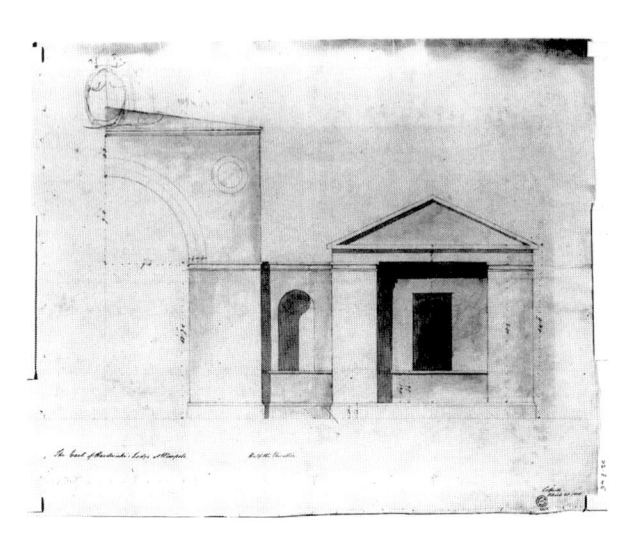

section, plan, and elevations for all four external faces. The scheme, like previous variants, combines the entrance arch of Langley Park's 'greyhound lodges' with the pavilions—with their baseless Greek Doric temple fronts *in antis* framing the windows—of the Doric lodges. An elevation for a simpler astylar alternative has been added at the left-hand side of the sheet, and placed at right angles to the earlier drawings, with the annotation 'copy sent to Provis June 18: 1794'. A detail of the cornice is drawn at half size.

185 Soane Office. Elevation and plan for and Entrance Screen, 1794

Sir John Soane's Museum, vol.68 (formerly fo.XVII), 13
Inscr.: 'THE EARL OF HARDWICKE'
Watercolour over pen and ink (288 x 455mm)

This watercolour elevation of the entrance screen, set in a naturalistic landscape and framed by a wash line, is a presentation rendering of the scheme shown in (*No.184*). *Paterae* are shown in the spandrels of the arch. The plan is dimensioned.

186 Soane Office. Elevation, sections and roof plans for an Entrance Screen, 1794

Victoria and Albert Museum, 3306.166
Inscr.: Dimensions given; 'Section through the Gateway'; 'Plan of End Roofs'; 'Plan of Roof Centre'; Section through the end Room'; and 'Lodge at Wimpole'
Pen and ink with grey and yellow wash (173 x 394mm)
Lit. & repr.: Du Prey (1985), p.63, cat. 142.

This and the following are worked up drawings for the simpler, astylar scheme, shown in outline on the left-hand side of *No.184*, that was finally built. The elevation is as seen from the Arrington Road.

187 Soane Office. Ground plan and three elevations for an Entrance Screen, 1794

Victoria and Albert Museum, 3306.167
Inscr.: Dimensions given; 'Lodges at Wimpole'; 'End Elevation'; 'The dotted line AAAA, shew the Counter Arches in the Foundation, as well as the Arches in the Superstructure'; 'Section at A*'; 'Lodge at Wimpole'; and dated 'Sept. 1st 1794'
Pen and ink with grey and yellow wash (151 x 395mm)
Lit.: Du Prey (1985), p.63, cat.141.

The elevation as seen from the park side.

188 Soane Office. Survey elevation of the right hand side of the Entrance Screen at Arrington, 1818

Sir John Soane's Museum, 62/8/45
Inscr.: 'The Earl of Hardwicke's Lodge at Wimpole', 'Half the Elevation', 'Copied April 28 1818'. Dimensions given.
Pencil and grey wash (550 x 680mm)
Scale given in pencil
Binding holes along left margin

A survey drawing of one half of the entrance screen at Wimpole. A crowned cartouche has been sketched in roughly above the entrance arch.

189 Soane Office. Survey plan of the right hand side of the Entrance Screen at Arrington, 1818

Sir John Soane's Museum, 62/8/46
Inscr.: 'The Earl of Hardwicke's Lodge at Wimpole', 'Half the Plan', 'Copied April 1818'. Dimensions given.
Pen and ink with grey wash and pencil (560 x 679mm)
Scale given in pencil
Binding holes along left-hand margin

Drawings by Humphry Repton (1752—1818) for the Wimpole Red Book, 1801

According to the introduction to his Red Book for Wimpole, Humphry Repton paid his first visit to the Earl of Hardwicke's estate in July 1801, made a second in September, and two months later completed work to the proposals at his house in the village of Hare Street, Essex. The only documentary evidence for Repton's Wimpole commission is the Red Book itself – its text leaves, map and six watercolour plates. The circumstances of Repton's engagement remain uncertain and details of payments made to him appear not to have survived; there is no mention of the commission in Yorke correspondence, and Repton's own account books do not survive for this period. The marginal notes made in the Red Book, most probably by Lord or Lady Hardwicke, are, however, a rare indication of a patron's reaction to the landscape gardener's proposals. Family connections may have been the catalyst for Repton's invitation to Wimpole. In 1792 Repton, assisted by his eldest son, the architect John Adey Repton (1775—1860), produced a Red Book for Port Eliot, Cornwall. His client, Edward Craggs-Eliot, 1st Baron Eliot (1727—1804), was the father-in-law of Caroline Yorke, the step sister of the 3rd Earl of Hardwicke. No doubt Repton's East Anglian base and reputation also made him an attractive choice for the 3rd Earl.

With the help of his wife and various children, Repton produced more than 100 Red Books during his thirty-year career as a landscape gardener. Originally bound in trademark red morocco leather, but long since dismantled, the Wimpole Red Book is typical of this production. The Red Books were a seductive, if formulaic, presentational device whose texts were designed to flatter clients and whose watercolour plates were intended to beguile. Repton's stroke of genius was to provide his illustrations with hinged overlays. The unimproved scene, whose unattractive qualities Repton tended to accentuate, was shown with the flap down; once lifted, Repton's solution was revealed. His principal legacy is this paper world of beautiful manuscript books, together with three published volumes which set out his, often ideologically inconsistent, theories: *Sketches and Hints on Landscape Gardening* (1795); *Observations on the Theory and Practice of Landscape Gardening* (1795); and *Fragments on the Theory and Practice of Landscape Gardening* (1816).

Remarkably few of his proposals were undertaken, and Repton expressed his frustration that they were too often 'a waste of Time'. At Wimpole only a few of his recommendations appear to have been followed up: Brown's belts and carriage-drive were extended to the north east of the park; and the architect-surveyor Thomas West was called in to add a cottage to the rear of James 'Athenian' Stuart's park building, and, it seems, to provide permanent accommodation in the gothic folly. But at Wimpole, as was so often the case, Repton recommended the removal of trees 'by the judicious use of the axe' as well as the planting of new trees, and it is now less easy to determine to what degree his editing of the landscape was effected. In *Observations* he explains something of the palimpsest of planting that he found at Wimpole where the ground had been 'covered in every direction with trees in straight lines, circles, squares, triangles, and in almost every mathematical figure'. He noted that 'The position of all the large trees on the plain near the house' showed the influence of successive planting fashions whose original lines could 'be easily traced by the trees which remain', and that others formed clumps that were 'scattered about like the ghosts of former avenues, or monstrous shapes which could not be subdued' (fo. 124) 'By judiciously removing some hundred trees' he argued 'the place would be made to appear more wooded' (fo.125). Repton was given the opportunity to return to Wimpole in 1809 with John Adey Repton, in order to create a fashionable conservatory, with a glazed roof and semicircular projecting bays, from the carcass of the late seventeenth-century orangery.

The Reptons' work at Wimpole overlapped with Soane's, whose association with the estate stretched from 1790 until the death of the 3rd Earl in 1834. On the various estates where they co-incided Soane and Repton appeared to have tolerated each other's presence rather than engaged in a positive design partnership. Critical of what he saw as Soane's obsession with novelty, 'which he sometimes succeeded in by reversing or turning things topsy turvy', Repton also noted in his memoirs: 'Of his private character I have heard many encomiums, which make me regret we have not been more personally acquainted'.[314] Repton felt that the professional rivalry between the two men had started when Soane 'overturned my beautiful plan for Port Eliot', but generously confides in his memoir: 'We have been sparring with buttons on, and our sharp play does not matter a button'.[315] Repton describes attending one of Soane's lectures at the Royal Academy during which the lecturer attacked the 'pretensions to architecture, of him, whom he was pleased to call the most celebrated of Landscape Gardeners', Repton noted 'I heard myself abused and held up to ridicule without mercy', but at the end of the lecture they shook hands and joked with each other.[316]

190 Anonymous. Map of the Park at Wimpole, 1800

Cambridge University Library, MS Plans 609
Inscr.: 'A Map of the PARK, Pleasure grounds and HOME FARM at WIMPOLE in the County of CAMBRIDGE belonging to the Earl of Hardwicke, 1800'. Various buildings and parcels of land are named. A CUL accessions stamp is dated 11 December 1936.
Pen and ink (319 x 266mm)
Lit. & repr.: Bendall (1992), pl.4.

This appears to be 'the Original Plan' which Repton copied as the base for his Red Book proposals (*No.191*). Sarah Bendall notes that the map's title, while decoratively lettered, is not framed in a cartouche, and suggests that this reflects a late eighteenth-century fashion for restraint and elegance in map design. Because Repton's proposals included the planting of the 'belts' to the north east of the park, beyond Cobb's Wood, in his version of the map he moves the title from top right to top left.

Bendall also notes the 'accompanying terrier [...] gives field names with course of cropping and observations to be filled in'.

191 Map (copy) of the Park at Wimpole, 1801

National Trust WIM/D/484
Inscr.: 'WIMPOLE Park and Farm belonging to the Earl of Hardwicke. Copied from the Original plan in his Lordship's possession'. 'A Scale of Chains'.
Pen and ink with watercolour washes and pencil marginalia (356 x 332 mm)
Beneath the title of the map is a note in red ink: 'I have made use of this Map to explain my opinion. [...] the situation of the trees is inaccurately laid down & many changes seem to have been made since the survey was taken. H. Repton'.
Scale given in chains
Lit. & repr.: RCHME (1968), pl.132; Stroud (1979), p.761, fig.12.

The map from which Repton made this copy is almost certainly that now in the Cambridge University Library, dated 1800 (*No.190*). In his version Repton places the title in the top left rather than top right corner. In the text of the Red Book, under the heading 'Explanation of the Map', Repton repeats his caveat about the accuracy of the map, and provides a key to the coloured washes and lines that he superimposed on it:

> Having availed myself of this map, without making a more accurate survey, to fix the precise situation of the trees and shew the inequalities of the ground, I shall endeavour by difference of colour to explain the general outline of my meaning, altho' this map cannot serve as a measured guide for the detail.

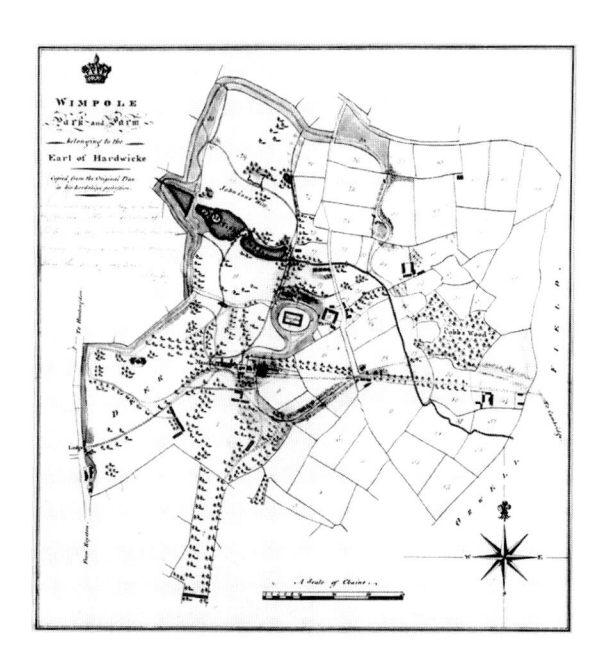

191

The purple washes are woods or trees not before noticed in this map.

The purple strokes are trees inserted where I know there are none at present growing.

The bright green washes are plantations which I suppose to be made for reasons assigned in the preceding pages.

The red strokes are trees or woods which I suppose might be taken away to open views to other woods in the direction of the strokes.

The dark green lines are the courses of the grass Drives which need be only levelled and occasionally mown.

The orange lines are gravel paths proposed to connect (by a dry walk) the beautiful ground about the water with the house and the pleasure ground.

Stephen Daniels explains that although Repton's trade card shows himself as a surveyor, taking a bearing with his theodolite, he 'quickly abandoned instrumental measurement for sketch maps or plans based on existing surveys'.

192 View from the north of the house, with flap, 1801

National Trust WIM/D/485a
Inscr.: Top right 'Nº: 1'
Watercolour (214 x 547mm)
Lit. & repr.: Jackson-Stops (1979:1), p.61; Stroud (1979), figs.9 & 10.

The first plate in the Red Book suggests a dramatic change to the north park as viewed from the house. In the foreground Repton proposes that a flower garden, bounded by railings, should be created within the arms of the projecting library and laundry wings. Repton explains in the accompanying text why he felt it necessary to introduce this proto-gardenesque buffer between house and park: 'It is called natural, but to me it has ever appeared unnatural that a palace should rise immediately out of a sheep pasture'. This view represents a theoretical *volte-face* for in the previous decade Repton had created exactly that relationship at Welbeck Abbey, Nottinghamshire, and at Pretwood, Staffordshire. This change of heart flowed directly from the barbs that had been fired in his direction during the debate of the so-called 'Picturesque Controversy' that was triggered in 1794 by the publication of Sir Uvedale Price's (1747—1829) *An Essay on the Picturesque* and Richard Payne Knight's (1750—1824) *The Landscape: A Didactic Poem*. Repton notes in his memoir that Payne and Knight 'pretended to a new system of taste, in opposition to that introduced by Lancelot Brown, of whom I was accused of being the servile follower'.[317] Repton was eager to flatter these two idealogues, to embrace the newly articulated principles of the Picturesque, and to demonstrate that there was clear blue water between his work and Brown's legacy, but he continued to make recommendations that were, arguably, Brownian in character until the turn of the century.

The proposals set out in the Wimpole Red Book appear to mark an important turning point, at which Repton's practice finally accords with his theoretical stance. In his scheme for the flower garden to the north of the house Repton adopts the unequivocally formal approach that he had previously studiously avoided, and, perhaps encouraged by his new partnership with John Adey, whose association with John Nash (1752—1835) had ended in the previous year, a new interest in antiquarianism is also signalled. Repton proposes in the Wimpole Red Book that an iron rail 'which does not attempt to be concealed' should enclose the garden because, he felt, 'it would surely be unnatural to see deer and flowering shrubs without any line of separation between them', and suggests in this watercolour that the screen should be articulated by regularly spaced urns.

Repton's flower terrace, with its railings, piers and urns was not in fact realised.[318] A marginal note in the Red Book, presumably written by Repton's patron, reads: 'Expensive and the appearance doubtful'. Robert Withers's survey (*No.220*) shows that the line of the present railings screen, placed further to the north than Repton had suggested, was established by 1815. The present railings and piers bear all the hallmarks of H.E. Kendall's work of the mid-nineteenth century.

In the middle ground, beyond the screen intended to separate garden from park, Repton could comfortably revert to a Brownian stratagem. He suggests sweeping away the clump of trees which formed the western side of Robert Greening's 'eyetrap'. Repton felt that the axial view of the Gothic folly on Johnson's Hill—symmetrically framed by these trees—was somewhat contrived. By excising one side of the frame, a more natural effect could be produced. The folly itself, though he could never have dared to recommend its removal, may have offended Repton's sensibilities. Despite describing it as 'one of the best of its kind extant' (perhaps faint praise), more often than not he railed against such structures. In his didactic Preface to *Observations* Repton sets out ten 'Objections' of which 'No.9' reads: 'sham churches, sham ruins, sham bridges and everthing which appears what it is not, disgusts when the trick is discovered' (p. 14). In the Wimpole Red Book he recomments introducing a covered seat in order 'to lead the eye away from the Tower which perhaps at present attracts too much of the attention'. Repton banishes other vestiges of formality such as the statuary to either side of Greening's clump with the lifting of the improving flap. Repton also suggests converting the fields to the north-east into grazed pasture land. In the 'before' view these are, somewhat misleadingly, shown as scrub.

Because of the lie of the land at Wimpole it is not possible, at least from ground level, to see the lakes from the north side of the house. Repton considered this to be a fault whose remedy might be provided by mooring a tall-masted boat on Brown's lower lake, its sails and pennant, visible in the 'after' view at far right, would at least signal the presence of the lakes. This is a typically Reptonian idea; elsewhere he proposed, for example, that the location of a woodsman's cottage might be identified in the landscape by a wisp of smoke produced by a constantly tended fire. Repton's accompanying text reads:

> The principal apartments look towards the north where the view was formerly confined by a regular amphitheatre of trees and shrubs, these have been in a great measure all removed; except a few sickly exotics which mark the danger of partially removing trees that have long protected each other; but tho' the formal semicircle is removed, yet there remain two corresponding heavy clumps, between which is shewn the building on the hill which, I suppose was at one time the only object to be seen beyond this formal inclosure. This building which is one of he best of its kind extant, is now only seen thro' this narrow gap from the centre of the house, while a glimpse of the distant hill and fine shape of ground on which it stands, suggests the propriety of removing one of these clumps and loosening the other.

193 View of the lake-edge with an urn, 1801

National Trust WIM/D/486
Inscr.: 'Nº.II'
Watercolour (214 x 260 mm)
Lit. & repr.: Souden (1991), p.79.

With this view, Repton renders the setting of Brown's artificial lakes even less natural with the introduction of elements from the garden: the neat gravel path at far left, the artfully placed chairs, and the urn and pedestal on the far bank. Perhaps the urn was one of those that Repton intended moving from Greening's 'eyetrap' (*No.78*). He justifies this arrangement as follows: 'There are certain situations in which some object is absolutely necessary to break the monotony of green, and it is no where more desirable than in those dark recesses of water where it may be doubled by reflection. With this view I have supposed a Vase placed in one of the bays—sketch Nº.II—where a Painter's eye will instantly be aware of the great importance which may be derived from an Urn so placed or even a garden chair upon the margin of the water'.

John Peltro (?1760—1808) engraved this view for inclusion in William Peacock's *The Polite Repository* for March 1803 (*No.198*).

194 Proposal for the remodelling of the Hill House, 1801

National Trust WIM/D/488
Inscr.: 'Nº.III'
Watercolour (255 x 290mm)
Lit. & repr.: Stroud (1979), p.759, fig.7; Jackson-Stops (1992), p.88, fig.61; Adshead (2000), p.150–63, fig.7.

In the Red Book text, Repton criticises James 'Athenian' Stuart's design for the Hill House and the way in which it had been constructed, suggesting how the building might be improved:

> The prospect room on the hill is in a state of decay partly from its bad foundation and partly from the absurdity of building a room on Columns for which there is no authority among the ancients. I am the more surprised at this oversight, in an Artist to whom this country must ever be indebted for his valuable and accurate account of Athenian Architecture.

But Repton's criticism went beyond any consideration of architectural precedent, he felt that the building should be given a purpose. Utility was one of Repton's prevailing principles and one that the Picturesque Controversy simply accentuated. He advises:

> This beautiful knoll seems to require a building to be placed upon it, but it is remarkable that either from the swell of the ground or the trees in the valley, there are very few spots from whence the lower part of this building can ever be seen, and consequently the bases of the columns are always invisible, while the heavy mass above seems too mighty for its foundation as

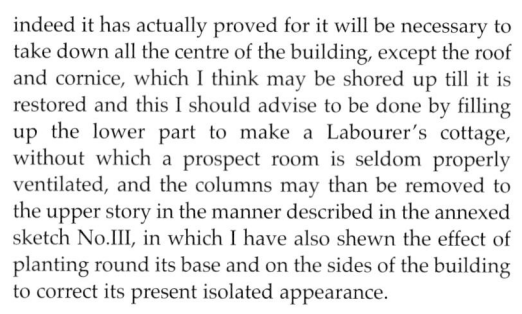

indeed it has actually proved for it will be necessary to take down all the centre of the building, except the roof and cornice, which I think may be shored up till it is restored and this I should advise to be done by filling up the lower part to make a Labourer's cottage, without which a prospect room is seldom properly ventilated, and the columns may than be removed to the upper story in the manner described in the annexed sketch No.III, in which I have also shewn the effect of planting round its base and on the sides of the building to correct its present isolated appearance.

Soane may previously have been called upon to consider the state of this building for in December 1797, he 'survey'd the Summer House' (SM Journal No.3). The proposed remodelling of the central element of Stuart's scheme, although perhaps a fairly standard neo-Palladian arrangement, recalls in a quite striking way the north and south elevations of the water house designed in the 1730s by the amateur architect Henry Herbert, 9th Earl of Pembroke, for the park at Houghton, Norfolk, a building which Repton would certainly have known.[319] Repton's aggrandisement of Stuart's building was also to include the addition of triangular pediments to the first-floor windows. A few years later, Thomas West did prepare drawings for the addition of a cottage to the back of the Hill House, but his plans do not show how it was proposed to treat the front elevation (No.204). The evidence of H.R. Yorke's watercolour of 1836, made from a station point apparently between the columns of the building's ground-floor loggia, strongly suggests that Repton's proposal to replace them with an arcade and to move the columns to the upper floor was not undertaken.

195 View of 'Brick End' Cottages, 1801

National Trust WIM/D/489
Inscr.: 'N°.IV'
Watercolour (212 x 293mm)

The row of cottages shown in this view, known as Brick End, survives in the park at Wimpole to the north of John Soane's model farm. Today it comprises four eighteenth-century semi-detached cottages, with a nineteenth-century house in-filled at the centre. Repton's view, from the south-west, is taken from a point to the north of the walled garden where, according to the 1800 map, a screening plantation should already have existed.

Repton writes: 'There is another row of cottages consisting of a red centre with white wings which would perhaps be sufficiently broken and concealed by planting a few large trees at a proper distance to inclose the yards which are now too often rendered unsightly by linen and other nuisances'. This slightly prissy insistence on screening the workaday is typical of Repton's polite aesthetic which in his earlier Red Books saw him keen to make a distinction between working farm buildings and the dignity of a landscape park. In his Red Book for Courteenhall of 1793 he had gone so far as to suggest that cornfields and cowbyres evoked 'the sordid idea of yielding profit'. In 1804, in the Red Book for Longleat, Repton articulated the principle that he employed at Wimpole, that is: if a building was hidden away it might be 'useful without affecting to be ornamental', but if it was conspicuous 'it should be ornamental'.

Wimpole Architectural Drawings

196 Proposals for 'cottages near the old kennel', 1801

National Trust WIM/D/487
Inscr.: 'N°.V'
Watercolour (213 x 275mm)
Lit. & repr.: Souden (1991), p.89.

These 'before' and 'after' views typify the way that Repton sought to impose polite, gardenesque solutions on buildings that he felt needed improving. Here a red brick house, possibly the one shown on his map at the east end of the lower lake, is lime-washed and its gappy paling fence is replaced by a neat verandah whose posts support a trellised extension to the roof. A vine, wisteria or some other climber is used to quieten the appearance of the building in the landscape, and for the same reason, the white paintwork of the dormer windows—a colour that Repton generally disliked—is subdued. Repton particularly disliked red brick and disguising its gaudy colour and unifying the motley appearance of mixed materials with a render or colour wash is a common theme in many of his Red Books, and one that surfaces too in his published work.

Repton mistakenly referred to this in his text as 'sketch N°.IV': 'There is a view of cottages near the old kennel which with the help of a wash over the bricks and a few laths from the roof may be changed as I have shewn in the sketch N°.IV, and when the ruinous barn and stables &c. are removed this building backed by wood will become as pleasing an object of its kind as the far more sumptuous and costly buildings at the Tower are upon the hill'.

197 Proposals for the south front of the Hall, Church and Stables, 1801

National Trust WIM/D/490
Inscr.: Top right ' N°: VI'; on the verso of the flap: 'These large trees are not supposed to be planted, but are now actually growing on the Spot & by a trifling alteration on the line of the Approach the advantage here shewn may be taken of their present situation'.
Watercolour (212 x 492mm)
Lit. & repr.: Jackson-Stops (1979:1), detail reproduced on front cover; Souden (1991), p.35.

In this proposal Repton addresses three concerns. Firstly, he objected to the difference in colour between the bricks of Henry Flitcroft's central section of the house, James Gibbs's flanking wings, and the outlying survivals from the late seventeenth century—the orangery and service block:

> The principal objection at present arises from the various colours of the different brickwork, because the date of each repair or addition is distinguishable by a different tint in the bricks. I have seen (at Earl Darnley's at Cobham) a large brick house brought to the same tone of colour by sprinkling the walls to imitate the weather stains; but perhaps a general wash of the colour of Sussex or Suffolk bricks would be the more effectual method of reducing the whole mass to uniformity of colour, and it would then be found as I before observed, that the defect of Wimpole is rather in the colouring, than the design of the picture.

Secondly, Repton disliked the piebald effect of Flitcroft's church, which while having a brick carcass is faced with stone at its west end. He cited 'the church near the house which has a white gabel [*sic*] end to a red building' as an example of 'that motley mixture of red and white which is sometimes seen in the same building'. Thirdly, the stables were castigated for their appearance and the way that they impinged on the approach to the house:

> The Stables are at present so ugly and so conspicuous that I do not wonder at the general opinion for their

removal; and without going much further into the detail of British Architecture than my present limits will admit, I am almost afraid to assert that I do not see any necessity for removing the stables, at least till the ground behind them is more worthy to be shewn, and if ever the trees are taken down in the direction marked on the map to let the eye towards the wood on the hill in the corner of the park, the objection to the stables will be far weaker, and in the mean time a few trees planted before the stables, the Church, and the east wing of the house, will connect the whole together and make them less objectionable.

While acknowledging the advantages of approaching a small house obliquely—he credits 'Capability' Brown as having introduced to 'Modern gardening' the 'improvement' of 'shewing two fronts at the same time'—Repton argued that because Wimpole was of such 'great extent with correspondent wings', this would be an inappropriate landscaping strategy. He identified that for the greater part of the drive (from the west side of the park) the house was 'totally hid by trees' but that 'the stables are immediately brought into view'. By a slight alteration of the path of the road, which he indicates on the map, the stables could be hidden instead while 'the house is seen just so much in front as to shew that it consists of a centre and two wings, while the road still goes to its proper object the angle of the house'.

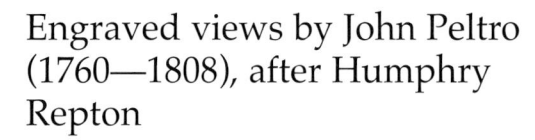

Engraved views by John Peltro (1760—1808), after Humphry Repton

John Peltro engraved the following views for William Peacock's *The Polite Repository, or Pocket Companion*, an almanac-cum-diary which was published annually between the late 1780s and mid 1860s. Between 1790 and 1809 Repton contributed to the production of the Repository, supplying miniature drawings from which Peltro made engravings. It became, in effect, a vehicle for Repton to advertise his work.

In 1805, in an exchange with Richard Payne Knight, in which he sought to demonstrate how wide-reaching his influence had been, Repton wrote 'during the last eighteen years, I have given thirteen designs to an annual work, making 234 views, from each of which I am informed 7,000 impressions have been made'. Repton supplied thirteen designs each year because in addition to the headpiece illustration for each month he produced a view for the frontispiece.

The title page for the 1803 edition explains its purpose and contents as follows: 'Peacock's Polite Repository, or Pocket Companion; containing an Almanack, The Births, Marriages &c., of the Sovereign princes of Europe, Lists of both Houses of Parliament, Officers of State Navy and Army, the Baronetcy of England, and various other articles of Useful Information ornamented with Elegant Engravings and ruled Pages for Occurences, Cash Account &c. &c. to be continued Annually'.

Although many of Repton's views derive from watercolour plates produced for his Red Books, he also produced miniature drawings from which Peltro could work. Nigel Temple explains that these drawings were retained by John Adey Repton rather than by the publisher, and that a small number survive in private collections.[320]

198 View of an urn by the lake, 1803

Victoria & Albert Museum, E.6762-1903
Inscr.: 'Scene at Wimpole, Seat of the Earl of Hardwicke'
Engraving (28 x 58mm)

This view, which was published in The Polite Repository for March 1803, is based on the watercolour 'Nº II' in Humphry Repton's 1801 Red Book for Wimpole.

The view was recycled in the 1827 issue of another pocket-book *The Regent, or Royal Tablet of Memory*, 'Embellished with Twelve views of Gentlemen's Seats, and Monuments, &c.'.

199 View of the Hill House, 1804

Bodleian Library, MS. Eng.misc. g.73, p.10
Inscr.: 'PROSPECT HOUSE, WIMPOLE—Seat of the Earl of Hardwicke'
Engraving (38x57mm)
Lit. & repr.: Carter, Goode & Laurie (1982), p.149; Adshead (2000), pp.150–63, fig.9.

It is not clear whether Repton's proposals to alter the front elevation of Stuart's Hill House were ever undertaken (*No.194*), but this view illustrates how the landscape designer intended it should appear from the south-east. Peltro presumably adapted this from the Red Book plate 'Nº.III'. The engraving was published in the January 1804 edition of Peacock's almanac.

Drawings by Thomas West for the Stables and other estate buildings at Wimpole

William Emes's estate plan of 1790 includes a quadrangular stable block, positioned to the east of the church, of a similar size and plan-form to that which was eventually built by H.E. Kendall; it had perhaps been the 3rd Earl of Hardwicke's intention that John Soane should supply a detailed design for the stables proposed for Emes's site. Two of the following three designs by the Wisbech architect-surveyor Thomas West, drawn fifteen years later, are also for quadrangular stable buildings.

Giles Worsley explains that from the mid-eighteenth century, substantial, detached stables of quadrangular form—once the preserve of royal palaces and the very grandest of aristocratic houses—became 'one of the most familiar images of the Georgian country house' and a 'symbol of the newly dominant landowning classes'.[321] Self-effacing, workaday buildings tucked away in service areas, or stables incorporated in the subsidiary wings of houses (in the correct Palladian manner), were replaced by grandiloquent blocks that held their own in the landscape. Worsley suggests that the arrival of the thoroughbred horse, changes in hunting and racing (which meant that increasing numbers of horses were kept and stabled), and the provision of loose boxes for sick or foaling mares, also influenced changes in late eighteenth- and early nineteenth-century stable design.

In advance of his Wimpole commission, Thomas West, later responsible for the design of the Sessions House in Wisbech (1807), perhaps consulted one of the growing number of architectural pattern books and estate management tutors—such as William Taplin's *The Gentleman's Stable Director; or Modern system of farriery*—that in the late eighteenth century offered the latest advice on the arrangement of the stable. But although West's designs follow the newly established planning convention, the only additional accommodation he offers is for the garaging of coaches and the stabling of the large horses dedicated to pulling them; no increase is made in the number of stalls for the housing of further hacks and hunters. And while his drawings do include stables for 'sick or lame horses', in accordance with the trend of the time, West provides them with no more space than the conventionally stalled animals—indeed his survey of the late seventeenth-century stable range suggests that in the original building the sick or lame horses would have fared better in their wider stalls.

Only in the case of the fourth design (*No.201*, fig.1), where a pair of pavilions at either end of the stable's entrance screen offer accommodation for 'strangers' horses' and 'sick or lame horses', would there have been room for the horses to lie down in greater comfort. West's dedicated stalls cannot properly be described as loose boxes. The architect did take account, however, of another contemporary advance—that of improved ventilation; the two schemes in *No.201* propose that the stables should be ventilated by high-level, semicircular or 'therm'-shaped openings, the upper parts of the blind arches that model the external envelope of the building. This solution meant that the stalls could be properly aired without subjecting the horses directly to a cross-draught.

West's concern with materials is reflected in his comments about the construction details of the two quadrangular schemes (*No.201*, figs.1 & 2):

> Both designs are intended to have Chambers over the Stables and Coach Houses, divided by Stud Partitions, lathed & Plaistered—the Stable walls to be lined with boarded pannels 5 feet high, and from thence to the ceiling plaistered with two coats of mortar—to have cast Iron Hay Racks. The Stable Floors to be paved with Dutch clinkers, the front of the Buildings to the Width of 9 Feet to be paved with pebbles.[322]

Three years earlier, West had designed an addition to James 'Athenian' Stuart's Park Building or Hill House (*No.204*). This and a number of other works on the estate, including the reassessment of Wimpole's stabling needs, followed on from the various architectural recommendations made in Humphry Repton's Red Book of 1801. West's involvement, however, at least on practical estate matters, predated Repton's; in 1800, on the road to Wimpole, the Rev. James Plumptre encountered a 'Mr. West, Engineer of Wisbeach [*sic*], who was inspecting a mill &c., erecting there'.[323] The 'mill' was probably the water-powered threshing mill at Thornberry Hill Farm, completed in 1804 to the designs of a Mr Hume of Midlothian and 'constructed by the Bankers of Wisbech'.

West's other work included the design of a head gardener's house for William Emes's walled garden, and various proposals for farm houses on the estate.

200 & 201 Thomas West. Survey plan, elevation and section of the existing stables with three alternative proposals, 1805

British Library, Add. MS 36278 K.1 & K.2
Pen & ink (K.1 423 x 555mm & K.2 423 x 560mm)
Scale given on both sheets and *Inscr.*: 'Scale of Feet'
A covering letter from the architect (BL Add. MS 36278 K.4) dated 4 May 1805, Wisbech, describes the four figures on these two sheets and those, for various estate houses, on an additional sheet of drawings (K.3).
K.1, fig.1 (at bottom of sheet):
Inscr.:
  'Fig.1', 'Entrance front of the present old Stables', 'Section', and 'Plan'.
  'Reference to Fig.1
  a - Stair-case to the grooms rooms and Hay lofts
  b - Stable for sick and lame horses
  Estimate for taking down &c. £120'

Figure 1 provides a useful survey record of the late seventeenth-century stable block which Kip shows in his engraved bird's-eye view of Wimpole (*No.3*). The stables lay to the south of the medieval church, the long-axis at right angles to the Hall. The only other records of this building are Henry Flitcroft's 'Plan of the Water Pipes and Drains at Wimpole, with the House, Offices, Church etc.' of 1749 (*No.53*); and Humphry Repton's 'before' and 'after' views of the entrance front of Wimpole (*No.197*). Repton's view appears to show a domical roof to the tower over the arched entrance, rather than the pyramidal roof shown in West's survey.

The need to garage coaches rather than stable a large number of additional horses seems to have been the main functional imperative behind West's proposals, though the old-fashioned appearance of the existing building may also have been a factor in its replacement. In his notes on 'The Approach' to the house, Repton inveighs against it: 'The Stables are at present so ugly and so conspicuous that I do not wonder at the general opinion for their removal'. Serious consideration had clearly already been given to the replacement of the stables both in the 1720s, when we know that James Gibbs was paid for a design, and in 1790.

A drawing of a stable range by Edward Stevens (*c.*1744—75), endorsed with the pencil annotation 'Wimpole?', was sold as lot 210 at Sotheby's auction of *Architectural Drawings and Watercolours* on 22 May, 1986; the drawing may be an unexecuted scheme for Wrest Park where Stevens designed a bridge, a cold bath and a garden 'Theatre or Colonnade' for the 2nd Earl of Hardwicke in 1769—70.

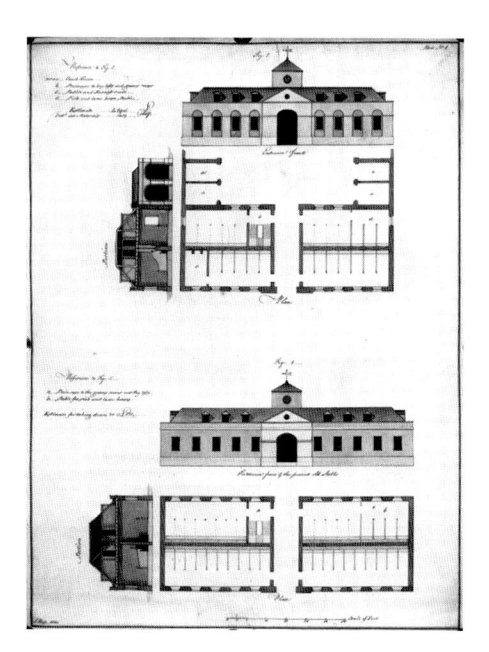

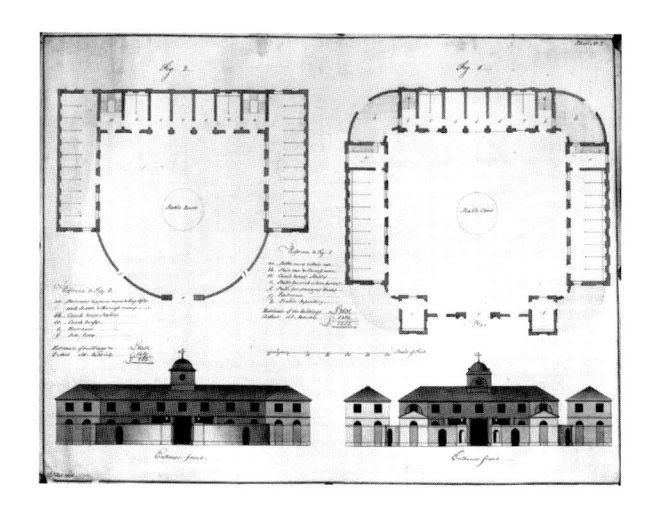

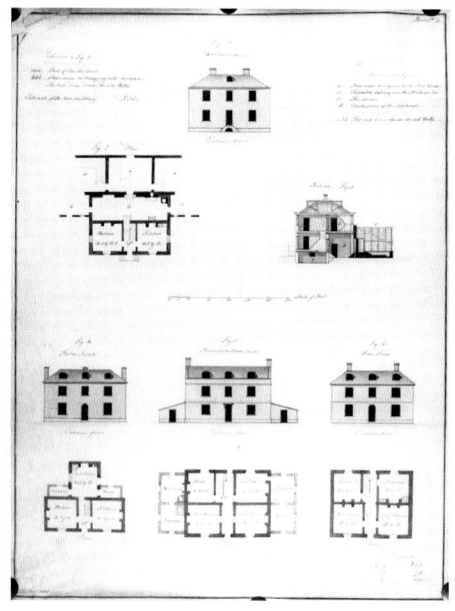

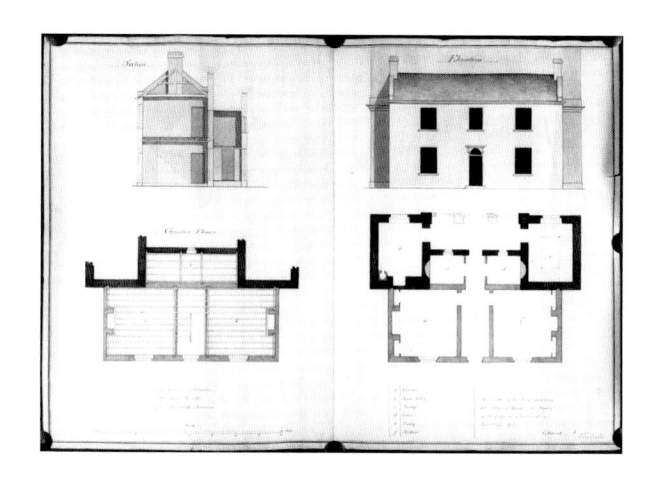

K.1, fig.2 (at top of sheet):
> Inscr.:
> 'Fig.2', 'Entrance Front', 'Plan', and 'Section'
> 'Reference to Fig. 2
> aaaa - Coach Houses
> b - Staircase to hay-lofts and grooms rooms
> c - Saddle and Harness-room
> d - Sick and lame horse Stables
> Estimate   L. 2906 }   £
> Dedt. old Materials   1419 }   1607

Figure 2 proposes the removal of one bay from either end of the stable range and the construction of two short return wings at the back of the building, each of which were to contain a pair of open-fronted coach houses. The front elevation of the stables was also to be remodelled and its ground-floor windows to be set within relieving arches. The roof was to be rebuilt so as to allow better accommodation for the attic hay lofts and grooms' rooms, while its windows were to be changed from pedimented to segmentally-headed dormers. West describes this drawing as follows: 'Figure 2 is an improvement upon the old plan, with a Trunk Roof, with an addition of two Coach Houses upon each Wing—the inside of this stable is intended to be finished upon the same plan as those above described—to enable the Walls of this Stable to support the Weight of the Floor & Roof, they must be one Brick in thickness more than those with single Roofs'.

K.2, fig.1:
> Inscr.:
> 'Reference to Fig.1
> aa – Saddle rooms & Stair-case
> bb – Stair-case & Harness room
> cc – Coach horses Stables
> e - Stable for sick or lame horses
> f - Stable for strangers' horses
> g Entrance
> h - Stable depositary
> Estimate of the buildings -   £ 2631
> Deduct old materials   1419
>   £ 1212'

What may be a circular midden at the centre of the courtyard is inscribed 'Stable Court'.

Of the two drawings on Sheet 2, West wrote: 'In composing these designs I have endeavoured to unite convenience & comfort in the distribution of the different Apartments and Offices. Fig.1 Sheet 2 is a design adapted for an open situation, such as the present stables. Figure 2 is a similar, but contracted plan'.

Wimpole Architectural Drawings

K.2, fig.2:
Inscr.:
'Reference to Fig. 2
aa – Stair-cases to grooms rooms & hay lofts
bb – Coach horse Stables
cc – Coach houses
e - Entrance
f - Side Doors

Estimate of buildings &c -	£ 2351
Deduct - old materials	1419
	£ 932'

202 Thomas West (?). Fragment of a plan for a large, south-facing stable block *c.*1805

National Trust WIM/D/549
Inscr.: 'North Side', and various dimensions given
Pencil and coloured wash with some pen (395 x 320mm)
Scale given
Watermark: BUTTANSHAW 1808

203 Thomas West. Plan, elevation and section for a Gardener's House, and plans and elevations for three Farmhouses, 1805

British Library, Add. MS 36278 K.3
Inscr.: the four designs are annotated, and the work estimated for
Pen and ink with grey wash, existing work indicated in red (420 x 550mm)
Scale given

West describes these designs in the covering letter previously referred to in the context of the stable designs.[324] The three farmhouses—the central, grander building being the 'Steward's, Farm House'—are entirely new schemes. The design for the gardener's house at the top of the sheet, however, incorporates Soane's hot houses and the stove rooms at the centre of the north wall of the walled garden. West's letter provides the following gloss:

> Fig.1, sheet 3 - represents the entrance front of the Gardiner's House, which comprises, two Rooms on the ground Floor, and four Chambers and attic Room above. Fig. 2 is the ground plan, and fig. 3 is a section of the House and Hot House shewing its connection with that Building.
>
> A, represents the present Store Room belonging to the Hot House; over the Stove Room, two Bed Chambers b, are proposed, with a View to enable the Gardiner to overlook his Hothouses and Gardens. C, a Cellar, which will be found useful for many purposes, and, as the foundation of the House on Account of the lightness of the soil, must be nearly the depth required to form the Cellar, it will add very little to the expense of the Building. This and the Farm house I wish to recommend to be covered with Trunk Roofs, which has the preference of all other Roofs for double Building, as having every advantage of the single Roof—gives more Room in the attic Story, and at once covers the whole space of the double Building—in respect of the designs for the Farm House it is only necessary to observe, that there are the same number of Rooms in the upper stories, as are represented in the ground plans.
>
> The following are the estimates for these Buildings—Gardiner's House £565—Farm House Fig:4 £520—Fig:5 £750—and Figure 6 £630.
>
> These buildings are estimated to have inside shutters to all the Windows, and Closets on each side of the fire Place in every Room—In work of this Nature it is not possible to estimate within a few pounds either way—and I am of Opinion that the above Estimates cannot be reduced unless the Buildings are contracted in their dimensions, or the plan proposed for finishing the inside thought unnecessary, by these means the estimates of all the Buildings may be somewhat reduced.

204 Thomas West. Plans, elevation and section for a three-bay addition to the rear of the Park building, 1802

British Library, Add. MS 36278 M.2
Inscr.: The drawing is labelled, with a lettered key indicating the function of the old and new rooms:
'Chamber Floor
a   Common Chamber
b   West Chamber
c   Servants Chamber'
And the ground floor as follows:
'a   Kitchen
b   Back kitchen
c   Pantry
d   Cellar
e   Dairy'
With the further note: 'The Walls of the Park Building are coloured Black - the Walls of the proposed additional new Building Red'. 'Estimate £440'
Pen and ink with red wash (365 x 535mm)
Scale given
Verso: A plan of the joists and rafters, *Inscr.*: 'The Roof in Ledgement'
Lit. & repr.: Adshead (2000), pp.150–63, fig 8.

In his Red Book of 1801, Humphry Repton advised that 'the lower part' of James 'Athenian' Stuart's park building or Hill House should be 'filled up' to 'make a Labourer's cottage'. West's task was to produce an architectural scheme that would translate Repton's advice into bricks and mortar. He proposed a modestly-scaled addition, T-shaped in plan with the downstroke of the 'T' fitting into the open loggia at the rear, or north-facing side, of the building.

West's proposed addition provided a 'kitchen' and 'parlour' to either side of a central stair hall with a 'Common Chamber' and 'Best Chamber' above. Stuart's statuary niches (*No.87*) are here, somewhat ignominiously, incorporated within West's two new service rooms—a pantry and cellar, marked 'c' and 'd'. These niches were redundant, however, for we know from Daintry, Lord Hardwicke's steward, 'that the two statues set up opposite each other within the Piazza, of the Hill Building [...had been] thrown down [...] & demolished', it was thought by one 'Richard Newell a Labourer of Wimpole, a person disordered in his mind'.[325] Nollekens and Scheemakers provided sculpture for a number of Stuart's other garden and park buildings elsewhere. At Wimpole, where Peter Scheemakers and Stuart had collaborated on the design and carving of two family monuments in the church (*No.81*), it seems likely that either the sculptor or his son Thomas furnished this lost statuary.

Squeezed in above the pantry and cellar, but below the oversailing upper floor of the park building, was to be a 'Servants' Chamber'. The diminutive scale of the cottage is revealed in the elevation; its eaves are shown level with the string course which separates the ground and first floors of the park building. A new oven is shown in the eastern room on the ground floor, marked 'Back Kitchen'. The stair in the west room was to become a dairy.

Repton's proposal was to reuse the portico columns for a first-floor loggia which would have been supported by an arcade on the ground floor. It is not clear whether this was ever realised. West's plan does not show the projecting portico on the south side, and it may be that he planned to build the arcade along the line of the two columns *in antis*. This would, however, have made the upper room unsatisfactorily narrow. In order to neaten up the presentation of his drawing, West may simply have chosen not to show the portico; the positions of the four columns of the loggia are marked very roughly in pencil.

Drawings by Humphry Repton and John Adey Repton (1775—1860) for the conservatory at Wimpole

Eight years after the preparation of his Red Book, Humphry Repton returned to Wimpole and, with the assistance of his eldest son John Adey Repton (1775—1860), produced the following designs for the remodelling of the late seventeenth-century orangery at the west end of the Hall. John Adey initially worked in the office of his father's associate John Nash (1752—1835), as his youngest brother George Stanley (1786—1858) was subsequently to do. But from 1800 John Adey worked directly with his father—the partnership between John Nash and Humphry Repton was dissolved in 1802—on the architectural aspects of the country house estates whose gardens he advised on, and it is in this capacity that they worked together at Wimpole in 1809. In 1803, in *Observations*, Repton cites Wimpole as one of a number of large houses 'of the last century' to which 'green-houses were added to conceal offices behind them', noting that 'they either became a wing of the house, or were in the same style of architecture'.[326] He explains too that 'these were all built at a period when only orange trees and myrtles, or a very few other green-house plants, were introduced, and no light was required in the roof of such buildings'. Could he have harboured a hope that within six years he would be invited to alter the building to take account of changed fashion and the needs of newly introduced plants when he added: 'since that period, the numerous tribe of geraniums, ericas and other exotic plants, requiring more light, have caused a very material alteration in the construction of the green-house'.[327]

205 Ground plan, south elevation and section of the Conservatory, 1809

National Trust WIM/D/538; 539 & 540
Inscr.: 'Alteration for the Conservatory at Wimpole for Earl of Hardwicke by H & JA Repton 1809'. The section: 'NB: This West end of the Conservatory is drawn to double the Scale of those below to explain [ie the elevation and plan] better the form of supporting the rafter by Iron'. In pencil: 'Vines or Creepers to be trained on brass wires in festoons from iron braces of the roof'.
Verso: Full size drawing of one of the parapet balusters, with the instructions: 'The distance between each Balluster not to exceed 3½ inches or be less than 2½'.
Pen and ink with pencil (460 x 590mm). The drawing, now in three pieces, was originally folded and posted as a letter.
Scale given
Watermark: RUSE & TURNERS 1807

The drawings show the Reptons' proposed alterations to the late seventeenth-century orangery at the west end of the house. The lowering of the roof involved the removal of the dormered attic storey, which contained servants' bedrooms; the central pediment; and the row of great bas-relief panels on the south side. The Reptons also proposed the glazing of the south pitch of the remodelled roof and the addition of a screening parapet balustrade. This enabled Repton to address his concern about the appearance of glazed roofs; in *Observations* he had argued that 'advantage may be taken of treillage ornaments to admit light, whilst it disguises the ugly shape of a slanting roof of glass', and that by separating a conservatory from a house by a lobby 'its want of conformity to the neighbouring mansion, since it is difficult to make the glass roof of a conservatory architectural, whether Grecian or Gothic' might be ameliorated.[328] Repton's Red Book illustration (Plate VI) of the south front of Wimpole includes an oblique view of the orangery, oddly with the bas-reliefs excised, as if he were then also proposing that the roof—intact with its dormers—should be lowered. This view also suggests its partial screening by planting.

The successive annexation to the house of the eastern end of the orangery by Gibbs and Soane, and the new fenestration of those bays, served to unbalance the south elevation of the building. Similarly, the projecting, pedimented three bays at the centre of the orangery no longer provided a focus for the conservatory. The removal of the pediment would have helped to disguise this asymmetry, and allowed for the glazing of the roof over the remaining eight-bay conservatory.

The plan is squared off at the west end but has an apsidal projection—spanning two bays—marked 'Aviary' on the north side. Pencil additions to the drawing show that Repton and his client later contemplated the possibility of providing a prominent new focus to the old orangery in the form of a top-lit drum, four bays in diameter. A secondary lantern is indicated over the steps leading down from the Bookroom.

The section shows that the new conservatory roof was to be supported by a series of elegant iron trusses containing circular braces. The west end is lit by a simple tripartite window.

206 Ground plan, cross-section and perspective sketch for the remodelling of the orangery, 1809

National Trust WIM/D/537
Inscr. 'Office Copy'. All three drawings have detailed, numbered keys. Verso: 'Plan of Wimpole Greenhouse &ca.'.
Pen and ink with pencil (410 x 520mm)
Scale given
Watermark: EDMEADS & PINE 1808

This plan offers a conservatory of seven bays—rather than the eight shown in the the plan in *No.205*—clear of the steps leading down from the bookroom. In contrast to the other scheme it also proposes a five-sided bay projecting from the west end. At a later point an apsidal projection, apparently containing a small, elliptical pond, has been crudely drawn in at the northern end of the central cross-axis. The drawing appears not to have been completed—the numbers referred to in the key have not been transferred to the plan or sections.

The drawings show an arrangement of banked staging with a path system between. The higher 'Back Benches', on the north side, were intended for 'Orange Trees' while the lower ones were for the display of 'small flowering plants'. The northernmost path, behind the highest row of benches, was to be 'prepared underneath the pavement for Creepers', providing for a hierarchy of planting from front to back.

Beneath the paths it was proposed to run trenches containing two separate flue systems, as the key explains: '10. Front Flue for common use', and '11. Back flue for occasional use to dry up damp &c. in severe long Frosts'.

The 'Cross Section A' and the accompanying key show that the reveals to the windows on the south side, and the brick 'Pilasters' or piers between them were to be covered with trellis work. The key explains: 'Space between Pilasters for basket of plants, underneath prepared for Climbers'. The orangery was to be divided into bays by 'Trellis crossing the House from each Pilaster', and it is this feature which can be seen in Joseph Nash's view (*No.226*)

The 'upper range' of glass in the projecting bay was to be of 'painted glass', and the central window to be 'opened as a French Door'.

207 Cross-section and internal and external elevations of the west end of the Conservatory, 1809

National Trust WIM/D/478
Inscr.: 'Cross Section A', and 'Inside elevation B'. Numbered key, as per the office copy.
Pen and ink with pencil and grey wash (348 x 450mm)
Scale given

This drawing appears to be the presentation drawing of which *No.206* is the office copy, but without the floor plan. Between the cross-section and 'Inside Elevation' (more properly a section and perspective sketch combined) is a pencil perspective of the exterior of the polygonal bay at the west end of the conservatory.

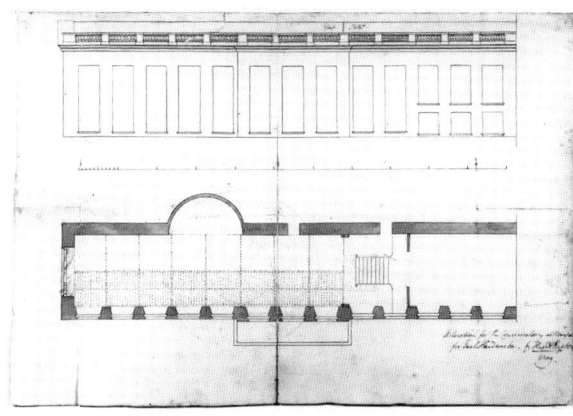

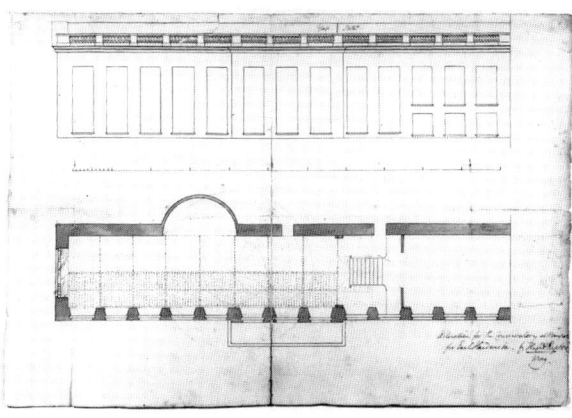

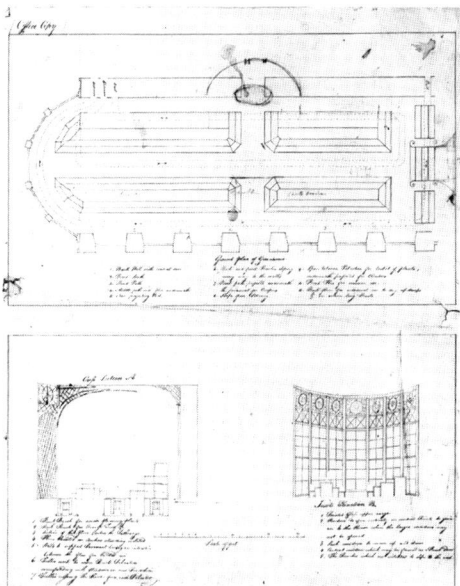

The way that the trellis on the reveals of the piers—with baskets of flowers at their feet—was intended to join the shallow, flat-topped basket arches spanning the conservatory is shown more clearly in this finished drawing than in the office copy.

208 Elevation showing trellising of the north wall and semicircular bay

National Trust WIM/D/479
Inscr.: 'TRELLIS WORK proposed for finishing the Interior COVE of CONSERVATORY'
Pen and ink with grey wash (302 x 388mm)

This presentation drawing shows how trellis work might frame and line the coved projection on the north side of the conservatory. The cove, with its double, glazed door to the gardens at the north side was to provide symmetry to the remodelled building and a focus to the cross-path. The earlier idea that an apse in the north wall might contain an aviary is abandoned here in favour of the practicalities of moving from one part of the garden to another.

209 'Elevation' of the east end of the Conservatory

National Trust WIM/D/480
Inscr.: 'END of the CONSERVATORY with TRELLIS WORK for CREEPERS &c.'
Pen and ink with grey wash (314 x 393mm)
Lit. & repr.: Stroud (1979), p.762, fig.16.

In this exaggerated, one-point perspective, the north and south walls of the first bay of the conservatory are 'folded back'. The flight of steps, with its scrolling ironwork balustrade, leads up to a small landing and two fully glazed doors which communicate with Soane's bookroom. This image complements Joseph Nash's view (No.226) which looks the other way.

The circular and lozenge-shaped decorations on the treillage to either side of the door may be framed mirrors. Below them is staging for the display of potted plants.

The Catalogue

Drawings by John Soane's office for St. Andrew's Church, Wimpole

210 Henry Provis. Plan and internal elevations of the north chapel, May 1793

Sir John Soane's Museum, 47/1/1
Inscr.: 'Plan & section of the Parish church at Wimpole in which are the family Monuments'. 'May 6, 1793. H. Provis'.
Also a key to the monuments:
 'A. Hon.ble Chas York [sic]
 B. Earl of Hardwick [sic]
 C. Hon.ble Cath.n York
 D. Daught.r of Reginald Lygon
 EE. Inscription defaced
 F. Sr. Th. Chichley's Tomb
 GG. Tablets showing who repaired the Church
 HH The Trusses that help to support the roof'
Pen and ink with grey wash (315 x 370mm)
Scale: 1/8 in: 1ft
Watermark: Britannia and Crown

This survey drawing reveals how extensive the rearrangement of the monuments has been since the late eighteenth century. Peter Scheemakers's pyramidal monuments to the 1st Earl of Hardwicke (1764) and the Rt. Hon. Charles Yorke (1770)—marked A and B—are shown in their original positions against the south wall. Scheemakers's third monument (C), to Catharine (Freman), Charles Yorke's first wife, now on the north wall, is recorded here on the east. Sir Thomas Chichley's altar tomb, now against the north wall, is here shown (F), free-standing at the eastern end.

 Provis records three hatchments hanging on the east wall. Their present location is not known but later hatchments for the 3rd Earl of Hardwicke, who died in 1834, can be found hanging in St. Mary's church, Whaddon—to the south of Wimpole—and at Ridge, Hertfordshire.[329]

211 Survey drawing of church and north chapel, showing position of the box pews, 1819

Sir John Soane's Museum, 47/1/3
Inscr.: 'The Earl of Hardwicke', and 'Plan of the Church at Wimpole'
Pen and ink with grey wash (345 x 500mm)
Scale: 1/4 in: 1ft

A comparison of this drawing with Flitcroft's plan 'No.2' (*No.59*) shows that the internal arrangement of the church had changed little during the intervening seventy years. Significantly, however, Flitcroft's 'pentagon pulpit' at the chancel end of the south pews appears to have been swept away. Curiously, the screened lobby entrance in the south-west corner, and staircase leading to the gallery are both absent, nor do they appear on any of Soane's subsequent proposals. But this is true too of the communion table and altar rail which were certainly still in place in 1819. The reveals to the windows in the north chapel appear to have been splayed, perhaps better to light the marble monuments to the Yorkes added by Stuart and Scheemakers.

212 Plan showing proposed alteration to the church, 1819

Sir John Soane's Museum, 47/1/2
Inscr.: 'Plan of Church at Wimpole with proposed alterations. 1819'
Pen and ink with grey and pink wash (505 x 345mm)
Scale: 1/4 in: 1ft

This drawing proposes the opening up of the wall dividing the Chicheley chapel from the body of the church and the insertion of supporting columns *in antis*.

213 Plan showing proposed alterations to the church, 1819

Sir John Soane's Museum, 47/1/4
Inscr.: 'L.I. [ie. Lincoln's Inn] Fields 1819'
Pen and ink with grey and pink wash (510 x 350mm)
Scale: 1/4 in: 1ft
Watermark: Smith & Allnutt 1817

This alternative proposal shows how the wall between the Chicheley chapel and the nave could be breached in two places, the remaining pier obviating the need for columnar supports. The addition of a small chapel, perhaps to house additional family monuments, is suggested at the north-east corner.

214 Longitudinal section showing proposed treatment of north wall of nave, 1819

Sir John Soane's Museum, 47/1/5
Pencil and watercolour (510 x 345mm)
Scale: 1/4 in: 1ft

This drawing is the companion to (*No.213*), above. The scheme shows the north chapel wall breached by two round-headed openings of unequal size, the smaller to the west being balanced by a third arch at the chancel end of the nave, giving access to a new chapel to be built at the north-east corner of the church.

 This scheme was not admired by Lady Hardwicke; on 12 April 1819 she wrote: 'The plan of the Church is not quite to my mind—I confess I should like to see some other Ideas however slightly drawn—the large Arch with the two smaller ones does not please my eye'.[330] She went on to suggest: 'It might be worth considering whether by distributing the seats differently the monuments might not be brought into the church instead of opening to the Chapel—& at the same time not too much diminishing the accommodation'. Two weeks later Soane was told that Lord Hardwicke did not intend to proceed with the alterations to the church, and that work to the plans and estimates could, therefore, be abandoned.[331]

215 Cross-section (south-north) through the church and Chicheley chapel, 1819

Sir John Soane's Museum, 47/1/6
Inscr.: 'Wimpole—1819'
Pen and ink with pink wash (345 x 510mm)
Scale: 1/4 in: 1ft

This section shows the 'Lord's Gallery' in elevation.

216 Plan, 1819

Sir John Soane's Museum, 47/1/7
Inscr.: 'The Earl of Hardwicke'; 'L.I. Fields'; various scribbled dimensions and marginal notes in pencil in Soane's hand
Pen and ink with grey and pink wash and pencil emendations (360 x 490mm)
Scale: 1/4 in: 1ft

This is a copy of *No.213* on which various scribbled alternative arrangements for the placing of monuments and the making and closing of openings have been trialed. The position of the stair to the gallery at the west end is also roughly pencilled in.

217 Long section (west-east) through the church, showing proposed treatment of the north wall, 1819

Sir John Soane's Museum, 47/1/8
Inscr.: 'The Earl of Hardwicke'
Pencil and watercolour (320 x 490mm)
Scale: 1/4 in: 1ft
Slight pencil sketch on verso

This proposal shows alternative, but overlaid, suggestions for the treatment of the opening between the nave and the Chicheley chapel. The underlying drawing is essentially the same as *No.214*, although different wall monuments are illustrated. Sketched crudely over the main round-headed arch is a tripartite columnar screen. This was clearly intended to paraphrase the trabeated gallery at the west end—Ionic columns over a squatter Tuscan base. Scribbled Gothic arches and tracery have been added between the columns of the upper register, creating a mongrel affair that was presumably never intended to be read as one scheme. The pencil oversketch is probably in Soane's hand.

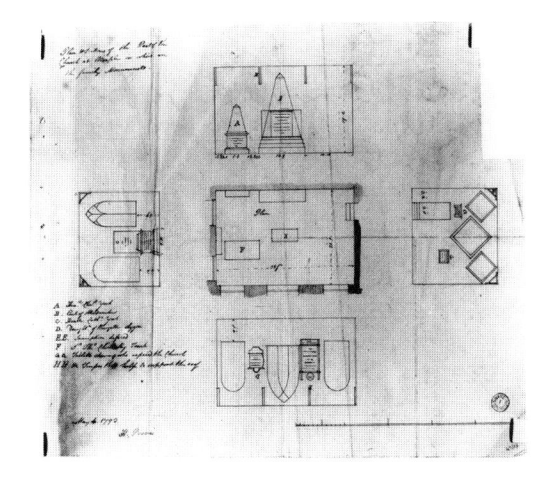

Humphry Repton wrote of Soane: 'I must still maintain his knowledge of Gothic architecture is not more than a certain architect had of natural history, who, when he delivered the plan for a museum, in which he had been desired to prepare receptacles for the three kingdoms of nature viz. animals, vegetables, and fossils, he divided the building into three compartments, and wrote over them England, Ireland and Scotland'.[332]

218 Arthur Patrick Mee (1802—68). A perspective, illustrating a proposal to breach the north wall of the nave, 1819

Sir John Soane's Museum, 47/1/9
Inscr.: 'The Earl of Hardwicke'; 'April 22nd 1819'
Pencil and watercolour (320 x 490mm)
Watermark: J Whatman 1817

This one-point perspective corresponds to the plan at *No.219*. Here a series of three round-headed openings is proposed between nave and chapel, while a fourth communicates with the small additional space proposed at the north-east corner.

219 Plan, 1819

Sir John Soane's Museum, 47/1/10
Inscr.: 'The Earl of Hardwicke'. Pencil annotations in Soane's hand.
Pen and ink with grey and pink washes (360 x 490mm)
Scale: 1/4 in: 1ft

This plan, showing four equally spaced arches in the north wall of the nave, corresponds to the perspective *No.218*. Verso: A very slight sketch plan

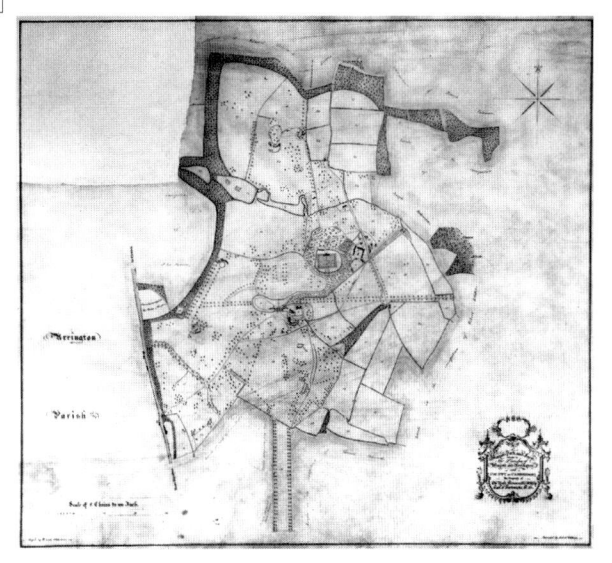

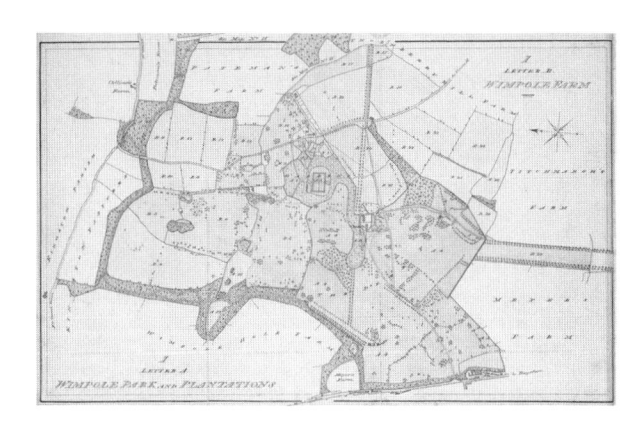

Nineteenth-century maps and plans

220 Robert Withers and Bradbury Last. A survey of the Park at Wimpole, *c*.1815

National Trust WIM/D/560
Inscr.: In a decorative cartouche at bottom right: 'Wimpole Park and Farm situate in The Parishes of Wimpole and Arrington, and COUNTY OF CAMBRIDGE; the Property of The Right Honourable Philip Earl of Hardwicke BT'. 'Scale of 8 Chains to an Inch'. 'Surveyed by Robert Withers', and 'Map'd by B. Last, Whepstead'
Pen and ink with coloured washes (560 x 645mm). The north-west corner is missing.
Scale: 8 chains: 1in
Lit. & repr.: Bendall (1992), p.338 Cat. WMP81501—WMP; Adshead (2000), p.151, fig.1.

This is probably the map that Robert Withers made in 1815 and which he refers to in the introductory comments to the bound volume of fourteen Wimpole estate maps dated 1828 (*No.221*). Of interest here are Stuart's Hill House, shown surrounded by a garden and palisade fence, and the ice-house at the northern end of the 'One and a half Avenue'. The church is not shown in plan and appears to have been sketched in as an afterthought, in its medieval form.

221 (I to XIV) Robert Withers. A survey of the Wimpole Estates of 3rd Earl of Hardwicke, 1828

The Cambridge Collection, Cambridgeshire County Council, COL C43.C32.3
Scale: 'Note. All the Maps in the following Survey are upon a Scale of Twelve Chains to an Inch', ie.1: 9,504
Lit.: Bendall (1992), pp.193–340, Cat. nos.: (I) WMP82801; (II) WMP82802; (III) WMP82803; (IV) WMP82804; (V) WMP82805; (VI) ARR82801; (VII) ARR 82802; (VIII) ARR 82803; (IX) WMP82806; (X) ARR 82804; (XI) WMP82808; (XII) WMP82809; (XIII) WMP82810; (XIV) WMP82811.

A volume of fourteen coloured maps entitled 'Survey of Estates belonging to the Right Honourable Philip Earl of Hardwicke K.G. Situate in the Parishes of Wimpole and Arrington in the County of Cambridge. By Robert Withers. 1815. Reviewed and adjusted 1828'. On 31 December 1827, Withers received £37 3s 'for making ornamental plans for Lord Hardwicke's use'.[333] In September he had received a similar payment for 'making a fair map on Vellum of the Steeple Morden Estate'.
    The volume contains the following maps:
I   'LETTER A -WIMPOLE PARK AND PLANTATIONS'; 'LETTER B – WIMPOLE FARM'
II   'PATEMAN'S FARM'
III   'Part of Kingston Pastures'
IV   'COOMB GROVE farm'
V   'WIMPOLE HOME FARM'
VI   'WRAGG'S FARM
VII   'HAYDON'S FARM'
VIII   'Hardwicke Arms Inn and Farm'
IX   'EIGHT ELMS FARM'
X   'LETTER L - ARRINGTON BRIDGE FARM'; 'LETTER P - THORNBERRY HILL FARM'
XI   'PORTER'S FARM'
XII   'ARBER'S FARM'
XIII   'TITCHMARSH'S FARM'
XIV   'COTTAGES and TENEMENTS IN WIMPOLE and ARRINGTON'

On each plan buildings are coloured red, roads yellow, water blue, arable cultivation brown, and woodland and pasture different shades of green; the names of adjoining farms are given; as are alphanumerical codes that refer to an accompanying terrier which provides details of the field names, acreages and their tenants. The maps are individually catalogued in Bendall (1992). NB. images of maps II to XIV are included on the CD-ROM.

222 A map of the Parish of Arrington, Cambridgeshire, from a corrected survey by Robert Withers of 1828, *c*.1834

Cambridge University Library, MS Plans R.a.7
Pen and ink with coloured washes (1,860 x 990mm)
Scale: 4 Chains to an Inch, ie. 1: 3,168
Lit.: Bendall (1992), p.194, cat. ARR83401

This map may have been drawn up following the death of the 3rd Earl of Hardwicke in 1834. It is coloured, as are other maps by Withers, to denote different land uses. Numbers on the various plots suggest that this map was originally accompanied by a terrier.

WIMPOLE.
Cambridgeshire.

Nineteenth-century topographical views

223 J. Noble. Engraved view of Wimpole after Frederick Nash (1782—1856), 1801

Inscr.: 'WIMPOLE, Cambridgeshire'; 'Engraved by J Noble from a Drawing by F. Nash'; 'For the Beauties of England & Wales'; and 'London, Published by Vernor & Hood, Poultry, Decr. 1.1801'
Engraving (page, 140 x 232mm)

This view, showing Wimpole Hall and the church from the south-west, was engraved for the eighteen-volume work of popular topography, *The Beauties of England and Wales; or, Delineations, topographical, historical, and descriptive, of each county. Embellished with engravings*, published between 1801 and 1815, and jointly edited by the antiquaries and lifelong friends Edward Wedlake Brayley (1773—1854) and John Britton (1771—1857). It first appeared in volume 2 (1801), Cambridge, Cheshire and Cornwall (opposite p.119), and was reused in *Cambridgeshire: or Original Delineations, Topographical, Historical, and Descriptive of That County. The Result of Personal Survey by E.W. Brayley and J. Britton* (1818). Nash also made drawings that were engraved for Britton's *Architectural Antiquities* of 1807.

On 22 June 1801 the Rev. Thomas Sheepshanks (c.1752—1818), who served as the rector of St. Andrew's church between 1794 and 1818, wrote to the Earl of Hardwicke explaining 'A Gentleman of the name of Brayley, and one of the Authors or Editors of a Work called the Beauties of England and Wales, called upon me two Days since with a letter of Recommendation requesting me to furnish him with such Information respecting your Lordship's Seat and Family as may be proper for Communication and Insertion in this Work'.[334]

Brayley was presumably hoping to undertake research for the textual account of Wimpole that would accompany the engraving. He was later to write:

> The grounds in the vicinity of the mansion are rather flat; but from some parts of the Park, the views are extensive and beautiful. Opposite the south front is an avenue of fine trees, about two miles and a half in length. This is crossed by a branch of the river Cam, which flows through this quarter of the grounds. On the north side of the house are three pieces of Water, which greatly contribute to the interest excited by the surrounding scenery; and on a rising ground, an artificial ruin, denominated a Gothic Tower. This, with a heavy and ungraceful building, named the Park House, whose weight has caused the foundation to give way, was erected by the late Lord Hardwicke, who made many alterations in the Park and grounds; but the principal improvements have been effected since the estate came into the possession of the present Nobleman. Under his direction the gardens and plantations have assumed a new appearance.[335]

The untraced view from which this engraving was made was drawn by Frederick Nash (1782—1856), a prolific water-colourist, who served the Society of Antiquaries of London as an architectural draughtsman and lithographer.

224 John Claude Nattes (1765?—1822). A sketch of the ice-house at Wimpole, 1805

Cambridge University Library, SSS.9.6 1458
Inscr.: 'N°.15. 1805 at Wimpole', and, on the paper mount, 'Claude Nattes, del.'
Sepia ink over pencil (166 x 129mm)

Nattes, thought to be a pupil of the Irish landscape painter Hugh Primrose Dean (active 1765—84), made a large number of topographical drawings, which, if not of the highest quality, serve as important records. Amongst the 100 or so views that he produced of the house and gardens at Stowe, for example, can be found details of otherwise little-known corners and obscure details. The Wimpole drawing, made as Nattes was beginning his programme of work at Stowe, is one such, and is the only view to have survived of the thatched ice-house there, whose decaying state may have appealed to the artist. Might the preceding fourteen drawings have also recorded aspects of the Wimpole estate?

The conical thatched roof terminates in a curious polygonal feature, reminiscent perhaps of the ventilators seen on industrial buildings.

This drawing is pasted into a grangerized, or extra-illustrated, copy of the Cambridgeshire volume (vol.II, p.I) of *Magna Britannia: Being a Concise Topographical Account of the Several Counties of Great Britain*, 1806—22, by the Rev. Daniel and Samuel Lysons. The volume, which includes watercolours by Sandars and F. and G. Cordwell, was compiled by Samuel Sandars c.1860—90 and bequeathed to the University Library in 1894.

225 View of the interior of the Gallery at Wimpole, 1819

Private Collection. Current whereabouts unknown
Inscr.: 'Gallery Wimpole 1819'
Watercolour

In his 1979 guidebook Jackson Stops suggested that the Gallery's Ionic columns were probably inserted by H.E. Kendall during his works of the 1840s because, other than their fluting, they so closely resemble those added to Wimpole's Entrance Hall at that date. This watercolour view, however, shows that columns of exactly the same form existed in 1819. The charmingly informal arrangement of disparate furniture suggests, as does the harp and small sets of bookshelves, that the room, which started life as three interconnected cabinets and in which, following its alteration by Flitcroft, housed the cream of the Lord Chancellor's picture collection, succumbed in the early nineteenth century to Picturesque irregularity and a variety of uses. The distinctive spoon backed curricle chair at the centre of the view would at the time have been the height of fashion. The carved pier table and the glass above it at the north end of the room remain in the Gallery today, and, like the upholstered seat furniture, which can now be seen at Lanhydrock, Cornwall, must have survived from the mid-eighteenth century scheme. It is instructive to compare this view with *No.308*.

226 Joseph Nash the Elder (1809—78). Perspective view of the Bookroom, looking west into the Conservatory, c.1830

Private Collection
Inscr.: Signed 'J. Nash'. Verso: A pencil drawing of the Colosseum in Rome
Watercolour over pencil (130 x 190mm)
Lit. & repr.: Sotheby's (1986), lot 308, pp.102–3.

Nash was a watercolour artist and lithographer who specialised in architectural subjects, and is perhaps best known for his publication *The Mansions of England in Olden Times* (3 vols., from 1839). He trained in A.C. Pugin's school of architectural drawing, and later made engravings for him. This undated view, taken from the centre of James Gibbs's ante library, records John Soane's Bookroom and the conservatory beyond it, as remodelled by Humphry and John Adey Repton in 1809. Through these successive works, the late seventeenth-century orangery was transformed into an eight-bay conservatory.

Beyond the red festoon curtain, Nash shows a sequence of basket arches whose spandrels are filled with bracing loops. These correspond with the *treillage* proposed by the Reptons. The iron trusses shown in their design drawings are at a higher level and support the remodelled roof.

Nash's view illustrates very effectively the relationship that Humphry Repton sought to achieve between interior and exterior spaces, and which he discussed in his theoretical publications. It recalls too the vignette of a book-lined 'modern living room' with its view through a glazed door to a conservatory that he reproduces as a didactic contrast to one of an 'ancient cedar parlour' in *Fragments on the Theory and Practice of Landscape Gardening* (1816) (opposite p.58). In the same volume Repton also illustrates, as 'Fragment XXV, *A Plan Explained*—a massively extended sequence of ideal rooms leading from a 'Library or Living Room', via a 'Tribune for Music Books etc.' and a 'Lobby to prevent damp', to an 'Orangerie, Glass roof', and beyond to a flower room, conservatory and aviary—which also shares general characteristics with the arrangement at Wimpole.

227 The Ven., the Hon. Henry Reginald Yorke (1802—71). View from the Hill House towards Arrington, 1836

Private Collection
Signed: 'HRY' and dated 'June 1st 1836'
Pen and ink and watercolour (150 x 180mm)
Lit. & repr.: Christie's (1989), illustrated as lot 134; Adshead (2000), pp.150–63, fig.2; Soros (2006) p.346, fig.7–45.

This drawing is intriguing because it seems to suggest that Repton's proposal (*No.194*) that a rusticated arcade should replace Stuart's columned portico was not executed. But if the building did remain unchanged, it is puzzling that the intercolumniation illustrated here does not correspond with the evidence of either Stuart's design or Lerpinière's engraved view. This discrepancy is most likely the result of artistic licence, which allows a generously framed view of the distinctive tower and flèche of Arrington church. This view appears to describe the same part of the landscape as John Wootton's Hawking scene (*No.40*). The Ven., the Hon. Henry Reginald Yorke held the rectory of Wimpole from 1832 to 1871, a living given to him by his brother the 4th Earl of Hardwicke. He was Archdeacon of Huntingdon from 1856 to 1869 and in 1859 made a canon of Ely Cathedral.

228 Thomas Moule (1784—1851). Engraved map of Cambridgeshire with a vignette of Wimpole

Steel plate engraving (270 x 195mm)

This map of Cambridgeshire was engraved for Moule's *English Counties*, published in parts between 1830 and 1836. In 1837 the parts were brought together in atlas form and published in two volumes by George Virtue as *The English Counties Delineated: or a Topograpical Description of England*, opposite p. 170. The Cambridgeshire plate made a further appearance in James Barclay's *Complete and Universal Dictionary* of 1842.

Typical of Moule's work, the map is embellished with gothic architectural detail, armorial bearings, vignettes of buildings and personages of local historic significance or interest.

The inset view of Wimpole at top right, taken from the south-west, shows the house sandwiched between the steeply roofed, late seventeenth-century orangery wing (left) and the service block (right), remodelled by H.E. Kendall in the mid-nineteenth century, and derives from J. Noble's engraving after Frederick Nash. The Earl of Hardwicke was the Lieutenant of Cambridgeshire at the time of the map's engraving.

229 The Ven., the Hon. Henry Reginald Yorke (1802—71). St. Andrew's. Interior view, looking towards the Chancel, 1839

Parish Church of St. Andrew, on loan to the National Trust, NT WIM/D/635
Inscr.: Signed 'H.Y'. Various annotations by A.C. Yorke on back of frame.
Watercolour (160 x 240mm)
Lit. & repr.: Archer (1985), pp.252–63, fig.4.

Flitcroft's church had been lit by a row of four windows in the south wall of the nave, by one to the north which borrowed light from the 'Chicheley chapel', and by windows, at a higher level, to the gallery at the west end. This watercolour view, made by the rector, records the alterations that were made to this arrangement in 1834—5.[336]

Flitcroft's reredos, which was reflected externally by a blind Venetian window of matching tripartite from (*No.62*), was ingeniously converted to allow the creation of a chancel window into which stained glass was inserted. The Commandments panels, displaced from the central position shown in Flitcroft's section (*No.64*), can be seen hanging to the left of the altarpiece. The eighteenth-century glass in the central light depicts King David playing the Harp, while those which flank it to north and south, of late fifteenth-century date and continental origin, are of Ss. Catherine and Simon. The David panel and the coats-of-arms illustrating Yorke alliances beneath it (Grey, Anson, Heathcote and Freman) were described as being in 'the upper south window' by the antiquary William Cole when he visited the church in July 1777. He thought the glass, which must then have been above the entrance door in the south-west corner, the only elegant element in the church.[337] Michael Archer has attributed it to William Price the Younger (d.1765), who was lauded 'the most ingenious painter and stainer of glass in Europe' by *The Gentleman's Magazine*.[338]

The David panel was removed from the chancel window in 1898 and put into storage in the rectory until 1908 when Philip Yorke II (1849—1922) bought it and the St. Catherine and St. Simon panels for £20 and installed them in the family chapel at Erdigg, Clwyd.

Other alterations evident from this view include the opening up of the wall between the main body of the church and the north chapel, and the consequent re-adjustment of Flitcroft's box pews which Cole had described as 'modern sleeping pews'. H.R.Yorke explains that 'by this addition to the size of the church 100 sittings have been gained & which are declared free and unappointed. The Incorporated Society for the Enlargement Repairing & building of churches & chapels gave £75 towards defraying the expenses'. He also notes that as part of the improvements 'many large family monuments were moved', 'the walls coloured, the pews painted'.

230 John Preston Neale (1780—1847). Engraved view of Wimpole from the south-west

Engraving

John Preston Neale was an architectural designer and engraver of boundless energy who produced a total of 737 plates for his publication *Views of the Seats of Noblemen and Gentlemen in England, Wales, Scotland and Ireland From drawings by JP Neale*, six volumes, London, 1818—23, and a five-volume second series, 1824—9. On other projects he collaborated both with John Britton's publishing partner E. W. Brayley and with the engraver Henry Le Keux (1812—96). Oddly perhaps, although the Earl of Hardwicke subscribed to Neale's *Views*, and his house at Tyttenhanger was included, Wimpole does not appear in any of the volumes, Cambridgeshire being represented only by Earl de la Warr's Bourn House.

231 The Hon. Eliot Thomas Yorke, MP, DL, (1805—85). View of the South Avenue at Wimpole

National Trust WIM/P/108
Pen and ink with watercolour and scratching out (240 x 335mm)
Lit. & repr.: Mallalieu (1979—90), vol. III, p. 288; Sotheby's (1982), p.21, lot 126.
Exh.: The Fine Art Society, London (1974), p.108, cat.103.

This view of Bridgeman's great south avenue is drawn as if from a wide, balustraded terrace. Such a feature never existed here, but it mimics the rather narrower structure found on the north or garden side of the house.

The artist, MP for Cambridgeshire between 1845 and 1865, was the third son of Vice-Admiral Sir Joseph Sydney Yorke (1768—1831), and younger brother of the 4th Earl of Hardwicke. Yorke was taught both by Peter de Wint (1784—1849) and Henry Bright (1810—73). The composition, with its balustraded foreground and consciously placed props—a yellow shawl, blue parasol, open book and red-upholstered chair—recalls Red Book views made by Humphry Repton from the terraces of Woburn Abbey (1805) and Wingerworth (1809).

The picture was acquired by the National Trust in 1982 at Sotheby's sale of British Watercolours and Drawings 1700—1920, lot 126.

232 Anonymous. Sketch of Wimpole Hall and the Gothic Folly

Cambridge University Library, SSS.9.6 drawing 1454
Inscr.: 'Distant View of Wimpole Showing Avenue 3 miles long & Tower behind the house'
Pen and ink (68 x 78mm)

This drawing, like J.C. Nattes's view of the Wimpole icehouse

226	227
228	231
233	232
236	237

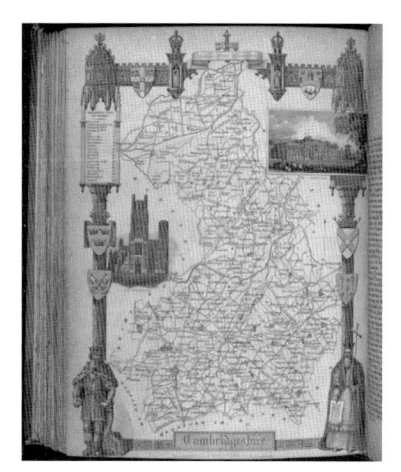

Wimpole Architectural Drawings

(*No.224*) is pasted into Samuel Sandars's grangerized copy of the Cambridgeshire volume of the Lysons' *Magna Britannia*.

233 Anonymous newspaper artist. View of Wimpole from the south-west, 1843.

Engraving (95 x 212mm)

This view, published in *Pictorial Times*, No.33, for Saturday 28 October 1843, p.153, illustrates the arrival of Queen Victoria at Wimpole in a post chaise. Queen Victoria describes these circumstances in her diary:[339]

> At ½ past 4 we left Cambridge in our Postchaise [...] many of the Undergraduates running with us [...] a number of horsemen joined us as soon as we left Cambridge riding with us, pushing & jostling one another, until we reached Wimpole which we did at ½ past 5. Lord Hardwicke received us at the door. The house is large and comfortable, & we were very well lodged, having a Drawing Room on the ground floor, & up a private stairs, a nice bedroom & 2 dressing rooms. I felt somewhat tired and packed up and rested till dinner.

234 Anonymous newspaper artist. View of Wimpole from the south, 1843

Inscr.: WIMPOLE HALL, THE SEAT OF THE EARL OF HARDWICKE
Engraving

235 The Hon. Georgiana Liddell (1822—1905). View of Wimpole Hall from the south-west, after 1843

Royal Collection, RL 20163
Watercolour (297 x 397mm)
Lit. & repr.: Millar (1995), vol.II pp.575–6, cat.3591.

The Hon. Georgiana Liddell, the youngest daughter of Thomas, 1st Baron Ravensworth, was maid of honour to Queen Victoria between 1841 and 1845, and produced a number of watercolours for her. Susan, Countess of Hardwicke (1810—86) was one of Georgiana's older sisters. The Rev. Edward Liddell was rector of St. Andrew's, Wimpole from 1872 to 1876.

This view records the alterations both made to and planned for Wimpole by H.E. Kendall in advance of Queen Victoria's and Prince Albert's visit to Wimpole between 26 and 28 October 1843. Liddell must have had access to Kendall's and Allom's drawings because the Conservatory, though clearly designed by 1843 was not cast in this form until 1870.

Delia Millar gives the provenance of this watercolour as SA II 2, i.e. from Souvenir Album II, for the period 1843—5, one of nine souvenir albums of views complied by Queen Victoria and Prince Albert.

236 After Richard Bankes Harraden (1778—1862). View of the Gothic Folly from the north-east. Early nineteenth century

Author's collection
Inscr.: 'R B Harraden del.'; 'Tower in Wimpole Park'; 'Printed by Engelmann, Graf, [...] & Co.'
Coloured lithograph (paper size 352 x 260mm)
Lit. & repr.: Menuge & Cooper (2001), frontispiece.

This romantic view of the folly, unconventionally seen from within the curtain wall, reveals the true nature of the building—a sham affair with the rear of the tower built from brick rather than the clunch of its fair face. The chickens running free in the foreground add to the sense of picturesque abandonment. Of interest here is the stair and balustraded landing giving access to the raised ground-floor entrance; this is shown as if of stone. Nineteenth-century photographs appear to show a wooden stair.

Richard Bankes Harraden was the son of the Cambridge artist-engraver Richard Harraden (1756—1838). The two men collaborated on the production of *Cantabrigia Depicta* (1809—11), which contained a series of picturesque engravings of the University of Cambridge. R.B. Harraden went on to produce a follow-up volume on the *Costume of the Various Orders in the University* (1803—5) together with various guides to the city.

R.B. Harraden also contributed two engraved vignettes—of Ely and the City of Cambridge—to a *Map of the County of Cambridge, and Isle of Ely* surveyed and published (1821) by R.G. Baker, which was dedicated to the 3rd Earl of Hardwicke.

The 1891 sale particulars for the Wimpole Estate claimed of the 'Wimpole Tower and Ruins: These are very picturesque and occupy an elevated and pleasant position in the Park. A portion of the Tower is now occupied by the Head Gamekeeper on the Estate, and contains 3 Bed Rooms, Sitting Room, Kitchen, and Cellar. In close proximity are the Dog Kennels and Pheasant Aviaries substantially built of brick and slated, with extensive runs and breeding houses. Nag Stable and Poultry House'.

The full name of the printer is indistinct. Adam Menuge notes that this notable firm of London lithographers later traded as Englemann, Graf, Conde & Co.[340]

237 Benjamin Fawcett (1808—93) after Francis Lydon (1836—1917). View of the south front of Wimpole

National Trust WIM/D/442
Inscr.: 'Wimpole Hall'
Coloured xylographic print (woodcut) (131 x 192mm)

This view of the south front of Wimpole, shown at its longest extent, was published in the five-volume topographical survey *The County Seats of the Noblemen and Gentlemen of Great Britain and Ireland* (volumes 1 and 2) and *A Series of Picturesque Views of Seats of the Noblemen and Gentlemen of Great Britain and Ireland, with descriptions and historical letterpress* (volumes 3 to 5), London, 1866—81. The entry on Wimpole appears in volume II, pp.71–2. The views were drawn by the artist Alexander Francis Lydon (1836—1917) and printed from woodblocks cut by the engraver and publisher Benjamin Fawcett (1808—93) of Great Driffield, in the East Riding of Yorkshire, to whom Lydon and his younger brother Frederick were apprenticed. The accompanying text was written by Fawcett's near neighbour and regular collaborator, the Rev. Francis Orpen Morris (1810—93), vicar of Nafferton, who also served as the editor. Printed by the Baxter process, using as many as eight colours, the prints capture something of the quality of watercolour.

The nineteenth-century alterations undertaken by H.E. Kendall are recorded here: the porch and stairs to the main entrance; and the recasting of the conservatory to the west and the service wing to the east.

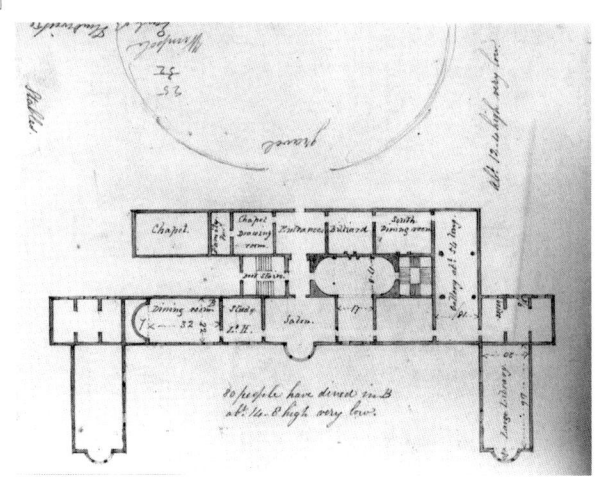

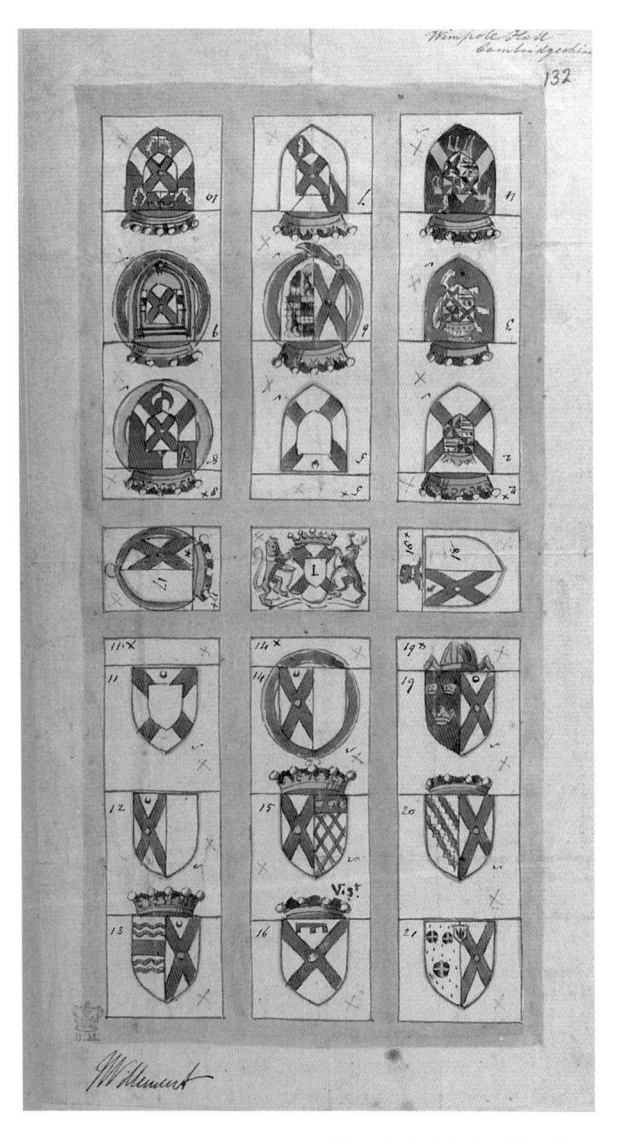

Survey drawing of Wimpole Hall by William John Donthorn (1799—1859)

238 Plan of the principal floor

Royal Institute of British Architects, British Architectural Library, K5/91(a)
Inscr.: 'Wimpole Earl of Hardwicke'; the function of each room is noted, and the dimensions of the gallery, 'large library', Yellow Drawing Room and dining room are given. A marginal note referring to Kenton Couse's dining room reads: '80 people have dined in B abt. 14.8 high, very low'. Another annotation, not clearly related to any one room, reads '12.4 high, very low'
Pencil with sepia wash (150 x 210mm)
Lit.: *Catalogue of the Drawings Collection of the Royal Institute of British Architects, C-F* (1972), p.89.

Trained in the rigorously professional office of Jeffry Wyatt (1766—1840), Donthorn was, like Henry Edward Kendall, a founder member of the Institute of British Architects. He is not recorded as having undertaken any work at Wimpole and the evidence of this and of other drawings by him in the RIBA collection suggests that the architect may have been making a comparative study of country house plans for his own purposes, taking a particular interest in the relative, and appropriate, heights of state rooms. In a survey plan of Blickling Hall, Norfolk, for example, he similarly notes 'Drawing room over Dining 17.3 high' and 'State Drawing room 22 high too high'. When given to the RIBA, Donthorn's drawings were bound in four volumes respectively entitled: 'Classic Mansions'; 'Gothic Mansions'; 'Parsonage Houses'; and 'Plans'. It is thought that he may have intended to publish the drawings arranged in these categories. The Wimpole drawing comes from the fourth volume, 'Plans'.

This drawing is clearly a fairly rapid sketch plan rather than a painstaking measured survey of the type produced for Soane by David Laing and Guibert (*Nos.103–7*), but it is curious that Donthorn here misrepresents Henry Flitcroft's polygonal tower, at the centre of the north front, as a semicircular structure—closer in form to the bombé front which Soane had originally proposed.

Designs for stained glass by Thomas Willement (1786—1871)

239 Design for a laylight decorated with heraldic stained glass, 1838

British Library, Add. MS 34871 fo. 36
Inscr.: 'Wimpole Hall, Cambridgeshire', '132', the glass panels are labelled 1 to 21 (with the central light included, there are 22 panels); signed: 'Willement'
Pen and ink with watercolour and grey wash (275 x 153mm)
Lit.: *A concise account of the principal works in Stained Glass that have been executed by Thomas Willement*, privately printed (1840), p.57.

In the early nineteenth century Thomas Willement played an influential part in reviving medieval methods of assembling stained glass windows from separate pieces of coloured glass, rather than depending, as had generally been eighteenth-century practice, on painting scenes on glass. Active between 1812 and 1865, Willement undertook more than 1,000 commissions. Sucessively heraldic artist to George IV and artist in stained-glass to Queen Victoria, Willement joined with A.W.N. Pugin in 1840 in a not altogether successful partnership; Willement's strengths lay in heraldic rather than figurative work. He also designed wallpapers and encaustic tiles.

This design is for the decoration of the glazed laylight above what is today perhaps misleadingly termed the Back

Staircase at Wimpole. In the 1840 publication *A Concise Account of the principal works in Stained Glass that have been executed by Thomas Willement* this commission is described as being for 'the principal staircase', and it must have been used as such by the family for it led to the Earl and Countess of Hardwicke's apartments, later used by Queen Victoria, at the west end of the house. Soane inserted the staircase in 1793.

According to the *Concise Account*—which repeats the wording of the manuscript 'A chronological list of the principal works on Stained Glass, &c. designed and executed by Thomas Willement of London FSA from the year 1812 to 1865 inclusive'—it was Willement's task in 1838 to provide 'arms of all the various descendents of the family of Yorke, from Philip, the first Earl Hardwicke'.[341] At the centre of the drawing are shown the supporters of the Earls of Hardwicke. Only fragments of this scheme survive at Wimpole. A glazed superstructure above the laylight contains remnants of gas fittings which indicate that the window must have been artificially lit at night.

240 Designs for twenty-one coats-of-arms in stained glass. 1838

British Library, Add. MS 72849 fos.32–5
Inscr.: 'Twenty one Arms in Stained Glass for the Earl of Hardwicke at Wimpole'. Each coat-of-arms is captioned as indicated below.
Pen and ink (each page 333 x 200mm)
Lit.: Hugh Pagan Limited ARCHITECTURE Catalogue No.25, item 129 p.52.

The twenty-one coats-of-arms shown in Willement's watercolour design are drawn in greater detail in four pages of numbered and captioned pen and ink drawings in a manuscript volume entitled 'Armorial Sketch Book of Quartered Coats. From various sources but chiefly from the practice of Thos. Willement F.S.A. London', acquired by the British Library from Hugh Pagan Ltd. in 1996. Each page of the volume is gridded into three columns of two rows, each box containing a coat-of arms; in total the volume contains 400 armorials. The four page entry for the Earl of Hardwicke is preceded by a family tree (fo.31 verso) which shows the interrelationship of the Yorkes and their marital alliances:

fo.32, recto
'1. Philip 1st Earl of Hardwicke and Mary Cocks
 2   Philip 2nd Earl of Hardwicke and Marchioness de Grey
 3   Alexander Baron Home and Amabella Countess de Grey
 4   Lord Grantham and Mary Yorke
 5   Charles Yorke and his first wife Catherine Freeman'
fo.33, recto
'6   Philip 3rd Earl of Hardwicke and Elizabeth Lindsey
 7   Anne Yorke Countess of Mexboro'
 8   Catharine Yorke Countess of Caledon
 9   Elizabeth Yorke and Lord Stewart de Rothsay
 10 Caroline Yorke Viscountess Eastnor
 16 Lord Royston'
fo.34, recto
'11 Charles Yorke and his second wife Agneta Jonson
 12 Charles Philip Yorke and Harriet Maningham
 13 Earl St. Germains and Caroline Yorke
 14 Sir Joseph Sydney Yorke KB and his first wife Elizabeth Rattray
 15 Charles 4th Earl of Hardwicke and Suzanna Liddell
 17 Joseph Yorke Baron Dover KB and Margt. Stocken'
fo.35, recto
'18 John Yorke and Elizabeth Lygon
 19 James Yorke Bishop of Ely
 20 Lord Anson and Elizabeth Yorke
 21 Sir Gilbert Heathcote Bart. and Margaret Yorke'

Sketches by the Hon. Thomas Liddell (1800—56)

The Hon. Thomas Liddell was the second son of Sir Thomas Henry Liddell, 1st Baron Ravensworth (bap.1708, d.1784), and the brother of the Hon. Georgiana Liddell—younger sister of Susan, Countess of Hardwicke, the author of the watercolour view of Wimpole *No.235*.

Sir Howard Colvin explains that, in the later stages of John Nash's protracted rebuilding of Ravensworth Castle, Co. Durham for the 1st Baron Ravensworth, Thomas Liddell first took over the task of superintending the works and subsequently began to make suggestions of his own, designing amongst other things a gate-lodge for the estate. He appears next to have designed a house—Beckett Park, Berkshire (1831)—for his brother-in-law, the 6th Viscount Barrington. In 1835 this amateur architect was appointed to the committee charged with choosing the design for the new Houses of Parliament.

The following sketches for Wimpole were presumably made before 1840 when the architect H.E. Kendall was engaged to modernise the house in advance of Queen Victoria's visit.

241 Sketch proposals for the remodelling of the north and south fronts of Wimpole, before 1840

National Trust WIM/D/475
Inscr.: At top right 'balustrade instead of brickwork over library', and 'Suggestion for improving the front of Wimpole—pilasters in Roman Cement
Pen and ink with pencil (270 x 440mm)

In his drawing of the north front of Wimpole, Liddell proposes applying orders to each storey and semi-circular bows, topped with French domelets, to the northern ends of the library and laundry wings. At the centre of the composition he adds a third domelet to Flitcroft's central, canted bay together with a pierced balcony to the first floor. These arrangements are remarkably similar to those that Liddell proposed in a drawing for the north-west front of The Deepdene, Surrey which Henry Thomas Hope (1808—62) began to remodel within a few years of the death of his father Thomas Hope (1769—1831).[342] David Watkin has likened the balcony proposed for the Deepdene to those used by Charles Barry on the garden front of the Travellers' Club, London.[343]

The verso is inscribed: 'Thomas Liddell'. At the top of the sheet is a proposal to remodel the south front, adding a tetrastyle temple front. At far right is a sketch of what appears to be part of the Chicheley chapel, whose authentic gothic details would have appealed to Liddell. At the centre, a gate screen between piers. At bottom, a sketch, crossed out, of the south front as existing with a building at far right that is remarkably like the stable block that Kendall was later to build (*Nos.272 & 273*).

242 Sketch proposal for the remodelling of the south front of Wimpole, before 1840

National Trust WIM/D/512
Pen and ink (370 x 225mm)
Watermark: J WHATMAN 1833

This is a variant of the sketch on the verso of *No.241*. Liddell shows elaborate parterres to east and west of a semicircular forecourt.

On the verso Liddell has suggested how the east service wing might be rearranged, providing at the east end a courtyard with a stable range to the north and coachhouses to the south. It is difficult to see how such a scheme would not have encroached on the site of the church and churchyard. It is instructive to compare this with Henry Flitcroft's (*Nos.53 & 54*), John Soane's (*No.132*) and George Banyard's (*Nos.309 & 310*) surveys.

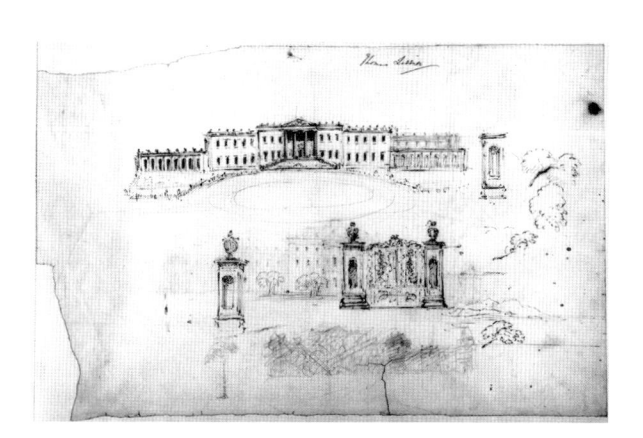

243 Sketch proposal for the remodelling of the north front of Wimpole, before 1840

National Trust WIM/D/515a
Pen and ink (102 x 229mm)

This scheme proposes the addition of towers and domes to the corners of the south front. A pediment is added to a remodelled service wing to the east. The building at far right is presumably intended to be a new stable block.

244 Sketches for a bow window to the Library

National Trust WIM/D/497
Inscr.: 'Library—bookcases painted oak up to cornice line'
Pencil (280 x 220mm)

These sketches appear to propose the replacement of the canted bay at the northern end of the library wing with a semicircular bow, capped by a hemi-dome cupola. The sketch at top right suggests a curtaining arrangement within the bow.

Wimpole Architectural Drawings   120

Drawings by Henry Edward Kendall (1776—1875) for Wimpole Hall

In 1840 Charles Philip Yorke (1799—1873), 4th Earl of Hardwicke, instructed the architect Henry Edward Kendall to rebuild the east service wing of Wimpole. This part of the house had been little altered for more than 100 years. John Soane's survey of 1792 records much the same arrangement as had Henry Flitcroft's survey of c.1742 (Nos.53 & 132). Flitcroft's drawing, in turn, may reflect the late seventeenth-century layout. In 1843, following what must have been the initial phase of Kendall's improvements, Charlotte Elizabeth, Countess Canning (1817—61), a granddaughter of the 3rd Earl of Hardwicke, observed that 'the whole of the bottom of the house has been dug out and it now stands on concrete—the damp and rats are expelled', suggesting that this antiquated part of the building—where provisions were stored and food cooked—had been far from salubrious.[344] Certainly it was unfit to provide for the royal guests that Hardwicke must have anticipated even before he was appointed Lord in Waiting to Queen Victoria in 1841.

In a letter of 7 February 1840, Kendall explains how his design for the remodelled service wing, and proposed alteration of the basement rooms in the main block, would allow for the separation of different departments—the kitchen staff, the 'office domestics', the wash-house and laundry, and the brew-house. Similar attention was paid to the design of the staircases leading to the 'sleeping apartments' of the male and female servants, to ensure 'a complete separation of the sexes'. Kendall estimated that the works to the east wing could be undertaken for 'a sum not exceeding seven thousand pounds', allowing 'for the value of the old materials'.

Kendall argued that the principal elevation of the service wing should take its character from the conservatory wing to the west of the house, which the Reptons had remodelled in 1809. This could be achieved by giving the windows 'a lengthy effect'. The architect went beyond his brief by suggesting that the two wings might be terminated by towers of similar design. The addition of a parapet balustrade to both wings and central block—whose chimneys he thought should be grouped together, as they had been in Sir Thomas Chicheley's house—would further unify the various parts.

To remedy 'the evil of […] the great draft of air in the Principal Hall from the want of a second Door', Kendall proposed the addition of a porch or 'Vestibule occupying the Upper Landing of the approach steps'. In the final line of his letter the architect offered to attend Hardwicke at Wimpole in order to 'give a more detailed explanation of the Design', or to 'make such alterations' as his client saw fit to suggest. As a result of this and subsequent meetings, the scope of Kendall's work must have been considerably extended. A few days after the royal visit to Wimpole, of 26 to 28 October 1843, the Countess Canning noted 'they have really improved the place very much, but there is still a great deal to be done tho' 30,000 £ has been spent on the house alone—& that not in ornamental work but solid repairs—all the office wing is rebuilt in something of the same style but more ornamental, it looks very well and I like all but the chimneys very much'.[345]

Kendall's involvement at Wimpole was to continue until 1852, during which time a good deal more was to be expended on the house. Hardwicke's daughter and biographer, Lady Elizabeth Biddulph of Ledbury, summarised the extent of the works as follows: 'My father made great additions and improvements at Wimpole House. He found it needing repair, and after releading the extensive roof, he built offices on the left side, and later restored the large conservatory on the right, besides entirely rebuilding the stables, and placing the handsome iron gates at the Arrington entrance. A group of sculpture by Foley in the pediment of the stone porch over the front door greatly improved the centre of the house, which was very flat. In round numbers he spent £100,000 in these improvements'.[346] To this list of Kendall's works should be added the almshouses opposite the Arrington gates and various lodges on the estate. Kendall must also have owed to Hardwicke's influence his commission to build a new rectory in the nearby village of Fowlmere, where the incumbent was the Rev. A.C. Yorke.

Kendall's letter makes reference to a number of explanatory drawings, none of which has been traced. The changes that he effected to Wimpole Hall, however, can be read in George P. Banyard's (1880—1948) 1940 survey drawings Nos.309–13, and in his design for the new stable block. Kendall's additions—the remodelled conservatory and the greater part of the east service block—were largely demolished in 1953. The architectural drawings that have survived fall into four groups: plans for the house; designs for the new stables; presentation drawings by Thomas Allom for the conservatory; and proposals for the Arrington gate screen. A further, and probably later, group of drawings, made by the specialist Cambridge wood and stone carvers Rattee and Kett, describe the replacement of various ceilings and the design of new joinery and architectural furniture.

An obituary of H.E. Kendall, published in The Builder on 9 January 1875, provoked a corrective letter, carried in the edition of 16 January, from a 'G.E.' who wrote: 'SIR—In your last issue, your correspondent in noticing the various works carried out by the late Mr. Kendall, has erred in stating that Mr. Kendall built "a fine conservatory at Wimpole". Mr. Kendall rebuilt the east wing of the mansion at Wimpole in 1842. He built a new gateway and park entrance in or about 1849; also new Mansion Stables in 1856, and the Queen's Lodge. The Conservatory at Wimpole was not built by him. G.E.'.[347] 'G.E.' was most probably George Evans, the Wimpole Clerk of Works, who in 1868 drew up proposals to re-gothicise the church (Nos.294–7), and the inference may be that he had been the builder responsible for the recasting of the orangery, undoubtedly to Kendall's plans. That the conservatory was built after the royal visit is corroborated by the evidence of the Countess Canning's description: 'the Greenhouse is dreadfully dilapidated and was made to look as well as could be by the walls being covered with ivy & the whole thing lighted up with coloured lamps'; it may have remained untouched since the Reptons' remodelling some thirty-five years earlier.[348]

It is not clear whether Kendall was involved in the design of the parterre garden to the north of the house, whose planting was described by the American landscape gardener Alexander Jackson Downing (1815—52) following a visit he made to Wimpole in 1850, but the brick piers and iron railings that bound it to the north are characteristic of his work:

Behind the house, and separated from the park by a terrace walk, is a parterre flower garden, lying directly under the windows of the drawing rooms. Like all English flower gardens, it is set in velvet lawn—each bed composed of a single species—the most brilliant and the most perpetual bloomers that can be found. Something in the soil or culture here seems admirably adapted to perfect them, too; for nowhere have I seen the beds so closely covered with foliage, and so thickly sprinkled with bloom. Some of them are made of two new varieties of scarlet geraniums, with variegated leaves, that have precisely the effect of a mottled pattern in worsted embroidery.[349]

The 'union Jack' form of the parterres, evident from aerial photographs and further established through archaeological investigation, was re-established in 1994, and planted with geraniums and permanent bedding of euonymous and hardy fuschias.

245 Plan of the ground floor of Wimpole Hall, 1840

National Trust WIM/D/528
Inscr.: 'Wimpole. The Earl of Hardwicke. Plan of part of Principal Floor. Shewing proposed alterations'. Signed 'H E Kendall'. Each room is labelled.
Pen and ink with coloured washes (420 x 560mm)
Scale: 1in: 1ft
The drawing is holed by pin pricks at the intersection of every line.

The alterations, marked up in red wash, were to include the addition of an entrance porch; the separation of the entrance hall from the ante-chapel (marked as 'inner hall') with a columnar screen; and the subdivision of Kenton Couse's dining room, on the north front, to provide a bedroom with an apsidal-ended dressing room. In the event, but is not clear whether in the 1840s or in 1860, the eighteenth-century dining room was swept away and a new dining room created in its place—which extended one bay further to the east. The present saloon at the centre of the north front is designated here as a billiard room, and Soane's Yellow Drawing Room marked as 'proposed dining room'. In the latter, the head of a small service stair, rising directly from the 'butler's pantry' below, is indicated between the north-facing windows, Kendall proposing optimistically that its position could be hidden from the main body of the room by a sideboard.

246 Plan of the basement floor of Wimpole Hall, 1840

National Trust WIM/D/529
Inscr.: 'Wimpole - The Earl of Hardwicke. Plan of part of Basement Plan shewing proposed alterations'. Signed 'H E Kendall'. The rooms are labelled.
Pen and ink with coloured washes (435 x 600mm)

The few suggested changes to the service rooms at basement level involve the annexation of parts of one room to its neighbour. One example of this is the proposed creation of a room off the butler's pantry at the expense of part of the adjoining 'small beer' store, while another is the creation of a store for faggots off the coal cellar, made possible by reducing the size of the adjoining footman's pantry. The plan also suggests the blocking-up of the interconnection between the housekeeper's room and the chapel to the west.

247 Sketch elevation for a glazed entrance porch. c.1840

National Trust WIM/D/541
Pencil (155 x 228mm)

This rough sketch must surely be by Kendall, for the heavily banded piers topped by urns are the language of his alterations at Wimpole. This appears to be an initial idea for a glazed porch for the entrance in the principal, or south, elevation of the house. The first floor Venetian window at the centre of the three bay break-front is shown immediately above the porch.

Drawings by Henry Edward Kendall (1776—1875) and Thomas Allom (1804—72) for the conservatory

In order that his proposals for the remodelling of the conservatory should be presented in as compelling a way as possible, Kendall employed the architect-artist Thomas Allom to produce a set of seven large watercolour drawings. Allom was an established topographical artist, if slow-starting as an architect, whose dazzling perspectives were frequently exhibited at the Royal Academy. Allom had worked with Kendall as early as 1832—making lithographs of Kendall's designs for Kensal Green Cemetery—and in December 1834 Kendall was a co-signatory of Allom's nomination papers for election to the newly formed RIBA. They became life-long friends, and Allom was to work too with Kendall's son, Henry Edward the younger. Allom also produced presentation drawings for the eminent Victorian architect Sir Charles Barry (1795—1860) and engineer Sir Joseph Bazalgette (1819—91).

248 Interior perspective of the conservatory, looking east, c.1850

National Trust WIM/D/14
Watercolour (850 x 560mm)
Lit. & repr.: Jackson-Stops (1992), pp.126–30, cat. 100; (1991), p.37; Souden (1991), p.37; Brooks (1998), colour plate 3.

This view illustrates how transparent Kendall intended the conservatory to be: wall-high windows were to be inserted on the north side to balance those to the south, and both pitches of the roof were to be glazed. Shown supporting this structure is a series of extraordinarily elaborate hammer-beam roof trusses in a vaguely Jacobethan style. Colza oil lamps hang from the trusses, suggesting that the room was to be used in the evening. At the east end, the entrance into the bookroom is shown with an elaborate, Renaissance-style, shell head.

While this spectacular perspective must have had a seductive effect on Kendall's client, a photograph of the interior taken before the conservatory was demolished shows the degree to which Allom exaggerated the size and impact of the room.

249 Ground plan for the conservatory and garden setting, c.1850

National Trust WIM/D/18
Inscr.: The following spaces are labelled: 'PORTION OF GALLERY'; 'ANTI LIBRARY'; 'LIBRARY'; and 'POTTING GROUND'.
Pen, ink and watercolour (310 x 540mm)
Lit. & repr.: Jackson-Stops (1991), pp.126–30, fig.99; Brooks (1998).

In plan, Kendall's conservatory followed the pattern established by the Reptons' remodelling of 1809, with projecting bows to the west and north, but a square tower was added to the west end. The staged Regency plant stands of the Reptons' scheme are replaced here by deep beds to either side of broad axial paths of decorative tiles. The conservatory is shown surrounded by a raised terrace edged with urns. A lobby immediately to the north of John Soane's bookroom gave access to the walled potting ground to the west of the library wing where plants could be collected by the indoor servants. An ornamental gate, whose counterpart survives to the east of the laundry wing, is shown to the north, on axis with the garden path leading from the northern bow of the conservatory. The architectural bedding and fountain to the north of the tower completes the formal setting provided for the conservatory.

123   The Catalogue

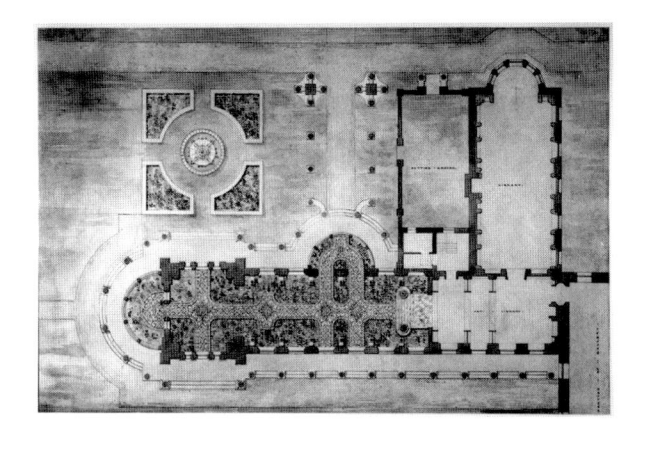

250 South or principal elevation, *c*.1850

National Trust WIM/D/13
Pen, ink and watercolour (512 x 835mm)
Lit. & repr.: Jackson-Stops (1991), pp.126–30, fig.99; Brooks (1998).

But for the addition of the Italianate tower at the west end, the carcass of the building was essentially as left by the Reptons' remodelling—the division between the bookroom and the conservatory marked by a change in fenestration and the move from a slate to a glazed roof.

251 North or garden elevation, *c*.1850

National Trust WIM/D/16
Pen, ink and watercolour (510 x 830mm)
Lit. & repr.: Jackson-Stops (1991), pp.126–30, fig.96; Brooks (1998), fig.30.

This drawing is a not wholly satisfactory combination of elevation (the buildings) and perspective (the foreground elements of the garden setting). To the left is shown the double-height bow at the north end of the library. Immediately to the right (or west) is the elaborate gate which provided access to the walled potting ground to the south. Also shown in elevation are the various architectural features that punctuate the formal gardens to the north of the conservatory: a tiered fountain and two massive brick piers topped with urns.

252 West elevation, *c*.1850

National Trust WIM/D/15
Pen, ink and watercolour (510 x 830mm)
Lit. & repr.: Jackson-Stops (1991), pp.126–30, fig.98; Brooks (1998).

Sizeable trees are shown standing within the walled potting ground to the west of the library wing, which, while attractive ingredients of the perspectivist's art, in reality could never have been allowed to grow to such a scale so close to the house. The side wall to this area also has an elaborate gate in it. The drawing is similarly a hybrid of elevation and perspective.

253 Cross-sections looking east and west, *c*.1850

National Trust WIM/D/17
Inscr.: 'SECTION LOOKING EAST', 'SECTION LOOKING WEST'
Pen, ink and watercolour (510 x 830mm)
Scale: marked along bottom edge

The section on the left-hand side shows the east end of the conservatory and the steps leading up to the level of Soane's bookroom. Above the glazed door is an elaborate shell head. The section to the right illustrates the west end and the interior of its terminal, glazed bow; the Hardwicke arms are shown against the wall beneath the westernmost roof truss.

254 Long section running east to west, *c*.1850

National Trust WIM/D/12
Pen, ink and watercolour (510 x 830mm)

This long section suggests how light the conservatory must have been. It appears that the intention, at least, was that the roof of the tower should be glazed too.

Sketches by Robert William Buss (1804—75) for a pair of decorative paintings in the Yellow Drawing Room

In about 1845, the lunette-shaped wall panels at the north and south ends of the Yellow Drawing Room, left blank by John Soane, were filled with a pair of decorative paintings by R.W. Buss. Highly coloured and somewhat at odds with Soane's neo-classical scheme, the paintings celebrate 'The Origin of Music' (south) and 'The Triumph of Music' (north). Studies and sketches for both compositions survive in the second of a pair of manuscript volumes, dated 1872, that were clearly assembled by the artist as a record of his life's work. The drawings, watercolours and oil sketches are interleaved with Buss's reminiscences. In a section entitled 'Sketches and Studies made for the two pictures at Wimpole', Buss explains the circumstances of his work for the Earl of Hardwicke:

> The dearth of patronage for works of Art consequent upon the movement in Fresco-painting, was of course severely felt by artists: myself among the number. Talking over the distressed state of artists with my excellent and kind friend the Honourable Eliot Yorke, MP for Cambridgeshire, he was induced to speak to his brother the Earl of Hardwicke.
> In a very handsome room at Wimpole used as a concert and drawing-room there were two large compartments left blank by Sir John Soane RA who constructed this room.
> Lord Hardwicke had often thought of having some ornamentation applied to these panels each measuring about 20 feet by 9 feet, having a curved top. The Fresco mode of painting his Lordship considered as a retrograde step in art, however much it might be lauded by Prince Albert and the supporters of that particular mode of execution. He acceded to the proposition that I should be commissioned to paint two subjects for these two panels, stipulating however that they were to be painted in oil.
> Engaged at Wimpole upon a copy of the portrait of the Lord Chancellor Hardwicke a committee of Fine Art was held consisting of Lord and Lady Hardwicke, Archdeacon Yorke, the Honourable Eliot Yorke and myself.

The family committee of taste determined that the pictures should depict the Origin and Triumph of Music, and be painted in oil. Buss explains that 'for convenience' the pictures were painted in London. He adds: 'The studies here collected with the sketches, were then made, the sketches submitted to the family criticism and in due time the pictures were completed. Another experience of the hospitality and kindness of Lord and Lady Hardwicke enabled me to retouch the pictures when placed'.

Buss notes that scaffolding had to be erected to install the paintings, which were the largest he executed, and that he received £45 for each picture, while the expense of the materials – canvas, colours, carpentry and frames—and carriage was borne by the Earl of Hardwicke. Family tradition maintains that some of the putti in the painting at the north end of the room were modelled on Yorke children.

The 'copy of the portrait of the Lord Chancellor' that Buss refers to may either be that after Sir Thomas Lawrence (1769—1830), now in Dublin Castle, or Thomas Hudson (1701—79). Buss also made sketches of the family's private theatricals, which were put on in the gallery at the west end of the house, and from which he developed a pair of oil paintings, 'The Day after the Wedding' and 'Personation'.

Buss, apprenticed initially to his father as an engraver and enameller, worked not only as a portrait painter and copyist but as an illustrator. In the latter capacity he worked for the publisher Charles Knight on editions of Chaucer, Shakespeare and Trollope. It was intended that Buss should complete the illustration of Dickens's serialised *The Pickwick Papers*, following the suicide of Robert Seymour (1798—1836), but, to Buss's lifelong disappointment, Dickens insisted that Hablot Knight Browne should instead succeed Seymour. Buss was one of the unsuccessful, but commended, entrants in various competitions for the fresco decoration in the Houses of Parliament held in the 1840s.

255 Sketch for 'The Origin of Music'

Private Collection
Inscr.: 'ORIGIN OF MUSIC'
Pen and ink

At the centre of the composition, cupids fashion a primitive musical instrument by stringing and plucking the trunk of a twisting olive sapling. Elsewhere cupids experiment with other found objects to create a drum from a great green gourd, a horn from a conch shell and cymbals from the two halves of a coconut.

The painting as executed is very similar to the sketch but for the addition of the putto playing with a goat at left and slight changes in the arrangement of the figures.

256 Two studies of a goat

Private Collection
Watercolour over pencil

One inscribed 'Cashmere goat' and the other 'Rutland'. The head of the cashmere goat was used in a further oil study with a putto and in the executed version of 'The Origin of Music'.

257 Three studies for 'The Origin of Music'

Private Collection
Oil on paper

At far left, a study for the putto blowing a conch shell; at centre, the putto embracing a goat; at far right, the drumming putto.

258 Alternative sketches for the decoration of the 'keystone' above The Origin of Music

Private Collection
Inscr.: 'Design for Pannel [sic] at Wimpole'
Watercolour

These alternative designs for Greek theatre masks wreathed in laurel leaves were clearly intended for the central keystone-shaped panel at the centre of the reeded and stilted arch on the southern wall of the Yellow Drawing Room. The panel is currently blank and it is not clear whether or not this element of the scheme was ever executed. There is no corresponding panel at the northern end of the room, because here the canopy dome opens into the barrel vault. The 'Triumph of Music' decorates the northern end of the barrel vault.

259 Sketch for 'The Triumph of Music'

Private Collection
Inscr.: 'POWER OF MUSIC'

The canvas at the northern end of the room is a fuller segment than that on the fireplace wall. Buss's *mise en scène* shows a group of cupids hanging garlands of flowers around a sculpted term, a personification of music, whose plinth is heaped with musical instruments—a lyre, pan-pipes and a tambour—and a volume of sheet music. On the left a cupid, playing a lyre, sits astride a garlanded lion. In the executed version the term is replaced by a laurel-wreathed bust on an altar-like pedestal carved with a *bukranium* and swags of flowers, while on the right-hand side, a putto *kanephoros* caries a basket of flowers on his head and another wears a helmet and plume.

260 Studies of putti for 'The Triumph of Music'

Private Collection
Oil on paper

These two oil studies are for the cupid that sits on the lion and for the pair of two putti at far right, one of whom carries a basket of flowers on its head, the other wearing a plumed helmet. The late David Yorke maintained that the putto with the basket of flowers was modelled on his great-uncle, Eliot Yorke (junior), while that riding the lion portrayed his great-aunt, Mary Yorke.

261 Studies for the lion in 'The Triumph of Music'

Private Collection
Inscr.: In pencil, 'Study at the Zoological gardens for Ld. Hardwicke's pictures'
Watercolour

These three studies describe the hind-quarters, head and front legs of a lion.

Sketches and drawings by the Hon. Thomas Liddell (1800—56) and Henry Edward Kendall (1776—1875) for entrance gates and lodges

'G.E.', who offered corrections to Kendall's obituary in *The Builder* (see introduction to *Nos.245–7*) tells us that the entrance lodges were built in 1849. The evidence of the block plan dated 1847 (*No.268*) which shows the Arrington Gates in relation to the almshouses on the west side of the road, would appear to corroborate this, while a description in the *Cambridge Chronicle & Journal* for 30 March 1850, p.2, must be of Kendall's long-demolished South Lodge: 'A beautiful new lodge in the later Elizabethan Style has been completed at the Orwell entrance to the park. It is peculiarly chaste in its design and is a very pleasing object on the road'. Is it possible that some of the following ink sketches are initial suggestions by the Hon. Thomas Liddell?

262 Hon. Thomas Liddell (here attrib.) Fragmentary sketch for a gate screen with flanking pavilion, *c.1847*

National Trust WIM/D/515d
Pen and ink (85 x 140mm)

This and the following sketch share design and drawing characteristics with Liddell's suggestions for recasting Wimpole Hall, *Nos.241–4*. A pepper pot pavilion capped by a domelet and an ornate ironwork screen with a gate flanked by stone piers, this sketch is related to the drawing on the verso of *No.264*.

Verso: slight sketch for a small box-shaped pavilion with simple balustrade and window with hood moulding

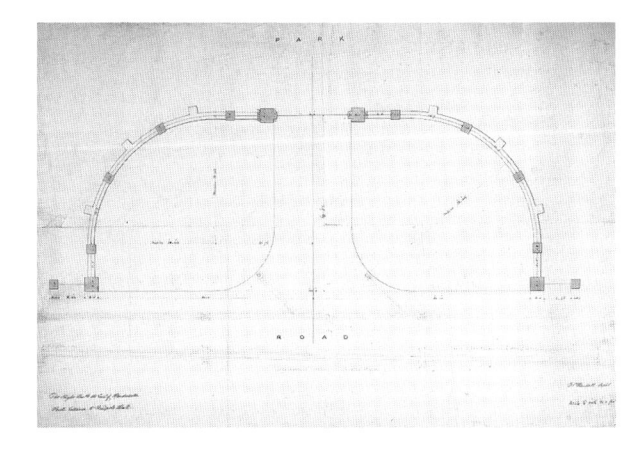

263 Hon. Thomas Liddell (here attrib.) Sketch, elevation and part plan for an entrance gate with flanking lodges, *c.1847*

National Trust WIM/D/514
Inscr.: 'Plan for gate at Wimpole'
Pen and ink (190 x 230mm)

The ornate gate screen is flanked by towers with ogival roofs and adjoining, shallow pitch-roofed pavilions.

264 Hon. Thomas Liddell or H.E. Kendall. Fragmentary sketch for a gate screen with a flanking lodge, *c.1847*

National Trust WIM/D/515b
Pen and ink (110 x 185mm)
Watermark: J WHATMAN 1834

The lodge, a one- and three-storey pavilion with tower in a neo-Tudor style capped by a lattice-work balustrade, is drawn on only one side of the gate. Although this design recalls the style which Kendall had employed in 1830 at the now-demolished Haverholme Priory, Lincolnshire, a slight sketch on the verso for a low gate screen flanked by small, octagonal pepper-pot pavilions with shallow, ogival roofs is related to *No.262*, attributed here to Liddell.

265 H.E. Kendall. Plan and elevation for an entrance screen and lodge, *c.1847*

National Trust WIM/D/593a
Inscr.: 'THE EARL OF HARDWICKE', 'ELEVATION', and 'H E Kendall Arch[t]., Suffolk Street'. The functions of the various rooms in the lodge are marked.
Pencil and watercolour (353 x 524mm)
Scale given. The elevation is drawn at a larger scale than the plan

A small lodge house is hidden behind the screen wall to the right, while the corresponding wall on the left hides a yard. The

Wimpole Architectural Drawings   126

Hardwicke arms are placed in an open arch above the central carriageway. The upper register of the screen walls contain strapwork capped with obelisks in a vaguely Salvinesque style. It seems possible that while the design for this and the following two drawings are Kendall's the watercolour renderings were made by Thomas Allom.

266 H.E. Kendall. Plan and elevation for a gatescreen and flanking lodges at Arrington, *c.*1847

National Trust WIM/D/593b
Inscr.: 'THE EARL OF HARDWICKE', 'ELEVATION', and signed 'H E Kendall, Arch^t., Suffolk Street'. The room functions of the left-hand lodge are given and a 'SUNK AREA' behind the screen wall indicated.
Pencil and watercolour (365 x 526mm)

267 H.E. Kendall. Plan and elevation for a gatescreen and flanking lodges at Arrington, *c.*1847

National Trust WIM/D/593c
Inscr.: 'THE EARL OF HARDWICKE', 'ELEVATION', and signed 'H E Kendall, Arch^t., Suffolk Street'. The room functions of the left-hand lodge are given and a 'SUNK AREA' behind the screen wall indicated.
Pencil and watercolour (356 x 522mm)
Scale given

268 Plan for the Almshouses at Arrington and a Park Entrance opposite, *c.*1847

National Trust WIM/D/543
Inscr.: 'Block Plan of Almshouses', with various pencil annotations and instructions and calculations, some dated May 1847
Pen and ink with pencil annotations (460 x 590mm)
Scale: '1/8 th Scale' ie. 1/8 in: 1ft

This simple layout indicates the intended relationship between the almshouses on the west side of the Arrington Road and the curving gate-screen opposite it on the park side. The existing park boundary wall to north and south of the proposed new entrance was to be retained. This scheme was to provide a single entrance at the centre of the screen; an annotation dated 11 June refers to a 'letter which explains the question of Side Entrance &c.'. The scheme as executed includes a pedestrian gate at the southern end of the screen.

269 Plan for the park entrance at Arrington *c.*1847

National Trust WIM/D/542
Inscr.: 'The Right Honble the Earl of Hardwicke', 'Park Entrance to Wimpole Hall', 'H E Kendall Arch^t.', with dimensions given and the 'Road' and 'Park' sides indicated
Pen and ink with coloured washes and pencil emendations (585 x 850mm)
A plan and longitudinal section of the drainage beneath the road has been added in pencil.
Scale: '1/4 inch to a foot'

Sketches and drawings by the Hon. Thomas Liddell (1800—56) and Henry Edward Kendall (1776—1875) for the stables at Wimpole

'G.E.', writing in *The Builder* in 1875, claimed that the stables at Wimpole were built in 1856, but an inscription cut into the stone plinth to the north, or left, of the building's entranceway reads: 'Built A.D. 1851'. The stables lie to the south-east of the house, some 120 metres to the east of the site occupied by the late seventeenth-century stable range shown in Kip's engraved view (*No.3*). Giles Worsley suggests that in his stable building at Wimpole, H.E. Kendall 'self-consciously set out to rival the great Georgian quadrangles'.[350] As we have seen, despite the evidence that James Gibbs, in the 1720s, and Thomas West, in 1804, designed replacement stables, the 1690s building survived until Kendall demolished it.

Kendall, who in 1836—8 designed a rather more sedate, classical stable block at Aswarby Park, Lincolnshire for Sir Thomas Whichcote, at Wimpole employed a suitably muscular Baroque revival style, with bright red brick and stone dressings that complemented his Italianate extensions to the Hall. The entrance, or western, elevation is the most impressive with its central 'triumphal' arched entrance, sculptural figures on the skyline (the Hardwicke family supporters, the lion and stag), and a two-stage clock tower and cupola above. Worsley likens the clock tower to that atop the entrance portico of St. George's Church (1721—5), Hanover Square, London, by John James (*c.*1673—1746), itself perhaps a paraphrase of the towers of the west front of St Paul's Cathedral.[351] With the exception of the plain northern elevation of yellow brick—that overlooked Wimpole's drying green – the external walls of the stable block are of red brick with stone dressings and are articulated by rusticated pilasters and blind, relieving arches; while the roofline is enriched with ball finials, and the corner pavilions with segmental pediments.

The following drawings describe the initial steps in Kendall's—and possibly Liddell's—design process. The drawings for Kendall's final scheme do not appear to have survived. A survey made ninety years later by the Cambridge architect George P. Banyard, *No.313*, however, provides us with a good impression of how Kendall's design worked.

270 Hon. Thomas Liddell (here attrib.). Sketch elevation for the entrance front of a stable block, before 1851

National Trust WIM/D/515c
Pencil (115 x 185mm)
Watermark: Fragmentary 'J WH [...] TURKE [...]18', ie. Whatman Turkey Mill
Verso, pen and ink sketch for trellis-work plaster detail

Sketch elevation for a stable block; five bays of blind arches, with fanlights, to either side of a pedimented entrance, surmounted by a clock-tower. A balustrade runs the length of the building. This and the following two drawings may be initial sketch proposals by Liddell.

271 Hon. Thomas Liddell (here attrib.). Sketch elevation for the entrance front of a stable block, before 1851

National Trust WIM/D/513
Inscr.: 'Plan for Stables at Wimpole preserving the present line of frontage'
Pen and ink (185 x 225mm)

A more carefully drawn version of *No.270*, with details of a typical arch and balustrade urn. The handwriting appears identical to that on Lidell's, signed, drawings for the house. The neat copperplate of Kendall's letter of 1840 to his client is very different.

272 H.E. Kendall (here attrib.). Elevation for the entrance front of a stable block, before 1851

National Trust WIM/D/530b
Pencil and watercolour (299 x 547mm)

Although related to the previous two sketches (Nos.270 & 271) might this scheme, the blind arches replaced with archaic transomed and mullioned windows, mark a transition of designer from Liddell to Kendall? Clearly of courtyard plan, the opposite range can be seen through the entranceway. In the frieze Kendall has indicated a relief sculpture of a group of horses.

273 H.E. Kendall (here attrib.). Elevation for an entrance gate and wall screening two mansard roofed buildings, before 1851

National Trust WIM/D/530a
Pencil and watercolour (350 x 520mm)
Watermark: J WHATMAN TURKEY MILL

This drawing appears to be for the entrance elevation of a quadrangular stable block whose outer wall screens a pair of buildings with mansard roofs. The wall surface is powerfully modelled, and the rusticated stone piers and contrasting red brickwork is in the same spirit as the stables that were finally built. It seems less likely that it is for an entrance screen with a pair of lodges behind. Pin pricks show that the design has been transferred.

274 Anonymous plan. 1856

Cambridge Records Office, DDCL (P) 260
Inscr.: 'WIMPOLE HALL, THE R^T HON^{BLE} EARL OF HARDWICKE BLOCK PLAN SHEWING EXTERNAL DRAINS From the MANSION, RECTORY and STABLES 1856'.
Pen and coloured inks with various colour washes (888 x 1303mm)
Scale 1in: 24ft.

This block plan shows the house, with the orangery and service wings, its immediate garden setting, the church, and the recently completed stable block. The function of the various buildings and drain and pipe runs are marked. The position of John Soane's *castello d'acqua* is also shown to the north of the church.

More detailed versions of this drawing can be found in the Cambridge Records Office at CL (P) 265 and DDCL (P) 266/14 which include an explanatory key. The latter, endorsed 'Wimpole Drainage. Plan of Hall showing drainage, 1894, also shows the line of a copper pipe running from the Brewhouse to the Ale Cellars in the north range.

Mid-nineteenth-century designs for ceilings, furniture and picture-hanging arrangements by Rattee and Kett

Rattee and Kett's work at Wimpole has traditionally thought to have been executed under H.E. Kendall's direction, in advance of Queen Victoria's visit of 1843, but the evidence of the following drawings suggests that it postdates 1855 and may be part of a subsequent campaign. The ecclesiastical woodcarver and mason James Rattee (1820—55) established a woodcarving business in Sydney Street, Cambridge in 1842 before progressing to a larger workshop on Hills Road in 1850. He worked to the direction of a number of distinguished architects in and around Cambridge, notably Anthony Salvin (1799—1881) on the restoration of the Round Church (1841—3), A.W.N. Pugin (1812—52) on the choir of Jesus College chapel (1846—9), and George Gilbert Scott (1811—78) at Ely Cathedral. It was only after Rattee's death, in 1855, that the firm, 'Wood & Stone Carving Works, Cambridge' was renamed Rattee & Kett. George Kett (1809—72), Rattee's business partner and successor, who worked with Pugin on the Houses of Parliament, was also a Norfolk-born woodcarver. The firm was acquired by the Mowlem group in 1926.

A surviving 'List of Cathedrals, Churches, Chapels, etc. in which messrs. Rattee & Kett have done work (with details of such work)' shows that the firm made successive alterations and repairs to the parish church at Wimpole in 1860, 1871, 1904 and 1922.[352] Details of what works Rattee and Kett undertook in the house, however, are less clear, but it is my suggestion that the following laid-out plans—one of which is watermarked 1856— and ceiling designs are theirs. The authorship and dating of the furniture designs detailed below is more certain for a fair proportion are signed Rattee and Kett and inscribed 1860.

In 1999 a sizeable carved, painted and parcel-gilt sideboard with a marble top was acquired at auction for the Dining Room at Wimpole.[353] It was designed to stand at the east end of Kendall's Dining Room in which position it is shown in *Country Life* photographs of 1927. At the time of the auction it was believed that this and the accompanying side tables that stood to either side of the room's chimneypiece had been designed by the architect as part of Wimpole's remodelling in advance of Queen Victoria's visit of 1843. The inspiration for these Victorian interpretations of neo-Palladian furniture was considered to be a serving table attributed to Henry Flitcroft, possibly carved by Matthias Lock or Sefferin Alken, and shown as such in the 1985 exhibition *The Treasure Houses of Britain*.[354] The emergence from the Rattee and Kett archive of nine sheets of furniture designs for the Dining Room, dated 1860, challenges all these assumptions.

Wimpole Architectural Drawings

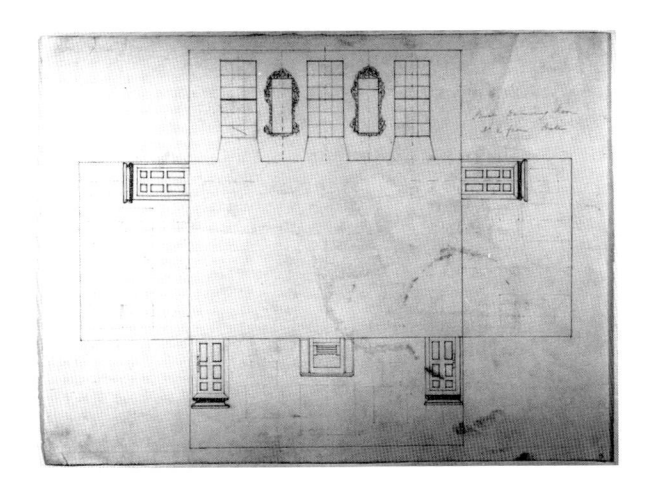

275 Rattee & Kett. Laid-out plan for the South Drawing Room, 1856 or later

National Trust WIM/D/509
Inscr.: In pencil, 'Small Drawing Room N⁰.2 from Hall'
Pen and ink with pencil (297 x 404mm)
Watermark: J WHATMAN TURKEY MILL 1856

What may either be a proposed picture hang, or a record of an existing hang, is shown very faintly in pencil on the south, east and west walls. Two pier glasses are shown on the north wall.

276 Rattee & Kett. Laid-out plan for the Ante-Room. *c*.1856

National Trust WIM/D/508
Inscr.: In pencil, 'Next to Hall'.
Pen and ink with pencil (300 x 486mm)

Laid-out wall plans for the ante-room, to the west of the entrance hall, showing the two windows on the north wall with a pier glass between, a chimneypiece and grate on the south, and door-cases to east and west.

277 Rattee & Kett. Design for the ceiling of the South Drawing Room. *c*.1856

National Trust WIM/D/476(c)
Inscr.: 'Ceiling of South Drawing Room', 'Wimpole Hall', 'Q.ʸ Crest' marked in the roundel at bottom right
Pen and ink (380 x 543mm)

A proposal for a new plaster ceiling for the south drawing room. The fireplace (north) is shown at the bottom of the drawing. This and the following two ceiling designs are in a competent neo-Palladian style and may reflect earlier plasterwork undertaken during Henry Flitcroft's campaign of the 1740s.

278 Rattee & Kett. Design for the ceiling of the Red Room. *c*.1856

National Trust WIM/D/476 (a)
Inscr.: 'Ceiling of Red Room', 'Wimpole Hall'
Pen and ink (374 x 545mm)

A proposal for a new plaster ceiling for the red dining room, now known as the Red Room. The fireplace (south) is marked at the bottom of the drawing.

279 Rattee & Kett. Ceiling design for the Ante-Room. *c*.1856

National Trust WIM/D/476 (b)
Inscr.: 'Ceiling of Anti [sic] Room', 'Wimpole Hall'. Along bottom edge: 'Enriched Cornice same as the other Room'; 'cornice' marked on the other three sides.
Pen and ink (370 x 547mm)

A proposal for a new plaster ceiling for the ante-room.

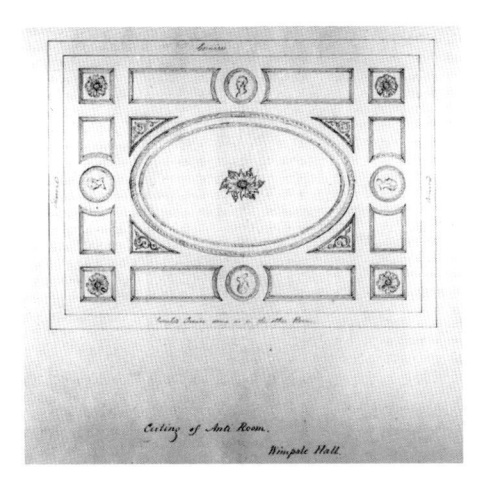

280 Plan and elevations for a draft lobby for the Entrance Hall

National Trust WIM/D/507
Inscr.: '[...] Plan for a Second Door inside the Hall'
Pen and ink with pencil (414 x 544mm)

Proposal for a draft lobby with a shell canopy for the entrance hall. The first part of the inscription, possibly 'W Blaeshy', is indistinct.

281 Rattee & Kett. Design for a glazed cupboard. *c*.1856

National Trust WIM/D/506
Pencil and coloured wash (565 x 425mm)
Watermark: J WHATMAN

A wall-mounted, glazed display cabinet with sliding doors, supported on four brackets with a scrolled pediment decorated with urns at the centre and ends.

282 Rattee & Kett. Three alternative designs for a pier table. *c*.1860

National Trust WIM/D/505
Inscr.: 'For the Right Hon.ᵇˡᵉ The Earl of Hardwicke. Proposed Designs for Hall Table, Wimpole Hall. Scale, 1 inch to the foot'. 'Rattee & Kett, Cambridge'
Pencil (560 x 425mm)
Scale: 1in: 1ft
Watermark: J WHATMAN

Front and side elevations are given for the three alternative designs, which vary in their degree of ornamentation; the third option with a straight, reeded support rather than scrolled leg. This design described as a 'Hall Table' is clearly related to the following designs for side tables for the Dining Room.

283 Plan and elevations for a sideboard for the Dining Room at Wimpole. 1860

Cambridge Records Office, Rattee & Kett Archive, D9 1100
Inscr.: 'Design for SIDEBOARD N⁰ 1'. 'PLAN'. 'Rattee & Kett, Cambridge'. 'SCALE. One Inch to the Foot'.
Pencil, with ink inscriptions (346 x 517mm)
Scale: 1in: 1ft.

The letter B has been addd in pencil at top right. On the wall above the sideboard dotted lines indicate the position of pictures.

At 9ft. rather than 11ft. this is a more compact variant of design A, but it has a much more flamboyant cresting containing the Hardwicke coat-of-arms at the centre with flanking candelabra, and a wine cooler beneath.

284 Plan and elevations for a sideboard for the Dining Room at Wimpole, with two paper flaps. 1860

Cambridge Records Office, Rattee & Kett Archive, D9 855
Inscr.: 'Design for SIDEBOARD Nº 2'. 'PLAN'. 'Rattee & Kett, Cambridge'. 'Scale. One Inch to the Foot'.
Pencil, with ink inscriptions (332 x 492mm)
Scale: 1in: 1ft.

This is the companion drawing to *No.285*. It offers a design for a sideboard 9ft. long, with alternative crestings shown by means of the paper flaps on the two elevations. In the raised position the back cresting is shown with the Hardwicke arms surrounded by a carved mantling, and, in the down position, a simple saltire.

285 Plan and elevation showing two alternative designs for a sideboard for the Dining Room at Wimpole. 1860

Cambridge Records Office, Rattee & Kett Archive, D9 856
Inscr.: 'SIDEBOARDS. Scale, one inch to the foot'. 'A'. Signed and dated 'Feb 5/60 Rattee & Kett, Cambridge', with various annotations.
Pencil, with double ruled border (328 x 465mm)
Scale: 1in: 1ft.
Lit..: Tim Knox, 'National Trust Projects and Acquisitions, 1999—2000', 'A sideboard returns to Wimpole Hall', *Apollo*, April 2000, p.11.

The two alternatives 'half Front Elevation of Nº 1' and Nº 2' are shown to either side of a dotted centre line. The sideboard was to be 3'3" high by 11' long. Marked 'A'.

This is very close to the design of the sideboard as constructed. Designed for the east end of H.E. Kendall's Dining Room, as noted above the sideboard was acquired at auction in 1999.

This is an ornately carved sideboard with cupboards flanked by scrolling volutes at either end. A green man mascaron appears at the centre surrounded by swags and cresting. The back rail is similarly decorated with a mask.

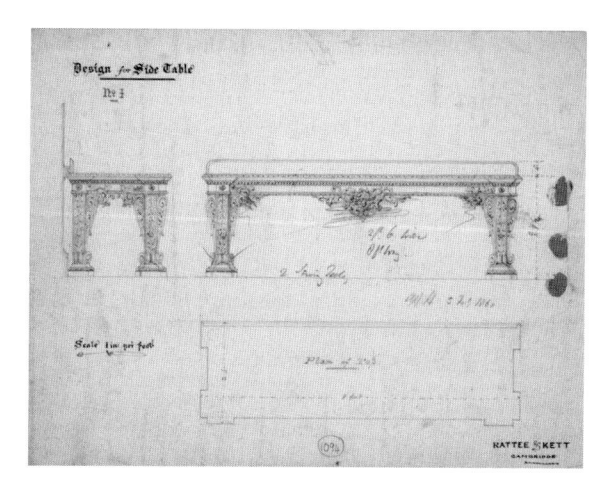

286 Plan and elevations for a sideboard for the Dining Room at Wimpole, with two paper flaps. 1860

Cambridge Records Office, Rattee & Kett Archive, D9 1098
Inscr.: 'Design for Sideboard'. 'Scale One inch pr. foot'. In pencil on the right hand side of the plan: 'Plate Warmer'.
Pencil, with ink inscriptions (320 x 489mm)
Scale: 1in: 1ft.

This is a simpler variant of *No.285*.

287 Plan and elevations for a sideboard for the Dining Room at Wimpole, with two paper flaps. 1860

Cambridge Records Office, Rattee & Kett Archive, D9 1099
Pencil, with brown watercolour wash (344 x 507mm)
Scale: 1in: 1ft

This design is identical to *No.286* with the addition of colour wash and shadow projection.

288 Front and side elevations for a serving table for the Dining Room at Wimpole, with two paper flaps. 1860

Cambridge Records Office, Rattee & Kett Archive, D9 1096
Inscr.: 'Nº 2 Design for Serving Tables. Scale 1inch p: foot'. 'Top 8ft. long x 2.6 wide 2.8 high'. 'Rattee & Kett Cambridge'.
Pencil with ink inscriptions (320 x 490mm)
Scale: 1in: 1ft

289 Elevation for a serving table for the Dining Room at Wimpole, with two paper flaps. 1860

Cambridge Records Office, Rattee & Kett Archive, D9 1097
Inscr.: 'TABLE for END OF ROOM (opposite Side Board) Nº 1'. 'Scale, one inch per foot'. 'Rattee & Kett, Cambridge', with various pencil annotations giving the table's dimensions (7' 6" x 3' x 3'), 'Front Elevation West End of Ding.R' and Appd. H. 5 Feb.1860'
Pencil (225 x 322mm)
Scale: 1in: 1ft.

Wimpole Architectural Drawings

This table with its mask of Hercules draped in the pelt of the Nemean lion which stretches in swags to rings at either end of the frieze corresponds exactly to the table which survives in the Gallery at Wimpole and which has previously been attributed to Henry Flitcroft and Matthias Lock.

290 Elevations and plan for a side table for the Dining Room at Wimpole. 1860

Cambridge Records Office, Rattee & Kett Archive, D9 1095
Inscr.: 'Design for SIDE TABLE'. 'No.b'. 'Scale one inch – 1 foot'. 'Rattee & Kett Cambridge'. 'Plan'. 'Line of Top', and various pencil annotations.
Pencil with ink inscriptions (275 x 341mm)
Scale: 1in: 1ft.

291 Plan and elevations for a sidetable for the Dining Room at Wimpole, with two paper flaps. 1860

Cambridge Records Office, Rattee & Kett Archive, D9 1094
Inscr.: 'Design for Side Table Nº 1'. 'Scale 1in: per foot'. 'Plan of Top'. 'RATTEE & KETT CAMBRIDGE'. Dimensions given. 'App. H. 5 Feb. 1860'.
Pencil with ink inscriptions (271 x 350mm)
Scale: 1in: 1ft

Drawings of the Rectory at Wimpole

292 Ground- and first-floor survey plans of Wimpole Rectory. *c.*1895

Cambridge Record Office, DDL (P) 267/3
Inscr.: 'WIMPOLE RECTORY-CAMBRIDGESHIRE'. Room names indicated.
Pen and ink with pink and blue washes (580 x 522mm)
Scale: 8ft: 1in

These plans describe the double-fronted former rectory which lies to the east of the church. At its core is a medieval timber-framed building, illustrated in Kip's view (*No.*3), but in the 1830s it was encased in white brick in the Tudorbethan style of the day, while the barn immediately to the east was converted to domestic use. Modern date-labels in the two south facing gables to either side of the entrance porch read 'EM 1597' and 'HRY 1833'; these signal the supposed date of the building's construction under the auspices of Edward Marshall, and its modernisation by Henry Reginald Yorke, incumbents who were separated by 240 years of Wimpole's history.[355] Annotations on a photograph of the rectory made by Alexander Campbell Yorke, the rector of Fowlmere—whose rectory was designed by H.E. Kendall—reads 'The Rectory House, as adapted & modernised by my father, 1833 onwards', while his 1914 typescript account 'Wimpole As I Knew It' gives his father's arrival as 1835[356]:

> When my father took possession in 1835 the house consisted of the central block under the two gables, with the room used as a study behind it, and two nurseries that overlooked the yard. The present dining-room was the kitchen. There were thus four rooms on the ground floor, and seven on the upper floor.
>
> The house was in shocking neglect. It was for the most part a Lath and plaster building painted yellow, the plaster in many places fallen away from the laths. Against the east end of the house the old tithe barn leant a decrepit shoulder. Along its front ranged the cart sheds. On its north side lay the little farmyard. As there was no arable glebe, and as tithes in kind had ceased, these buildings were useless.
>
> Yet they were part of the glebe, and therefore had to be maintained and brought under periodical Dilapidations. The difficulty was met by turning the barn into kitchen, scullery, larder and servants' hall; and upstairs, the nurseries and laundry. By a slight enlargement of the back he made room to construct a back staircase of the same measurements as the front, in order that the servants might find no excuse for using the front stairs when about their work. Then as Cambridgeshire mud is a caution, he threw out the back hall, with its two upper floors, to save the front hall from dirty feet. The offices were built round the old farm yard. Such is the genesis of the house. The conversion of the cart sheds into the 'covered way' was the contrivance of which my father seemed to be proudest.

293 The Hon. Eliot Thomas Yorke, MP, DL (1805—85). Watercolour view of the Rectory at Wimpole from the south-west, after 1835

National Trust WIM/P/107
Watercolour (240 x 320mm)

This view shows the easternmost of the rectory's two gables, bearing the date panel marked 1833 and the timber-framed wing to the east which provided a kitchen, servants' hall, laundry and nursery. This range was probably demolished by the Bambridges; a single-storey wing, fronted by a modern evocation of Henry Reginald's 'covered way', was built on the same site by the National Trust in 1996. The rectory complex now serves as a restaurant for visitors to Wimpole. An elaborate parterre garden, also recorded in late nineteenth-century photographs, is shown in the foreground. Yorke provided illustrations for George T. Lowth's, *The Wanderer in Western France* (1863).

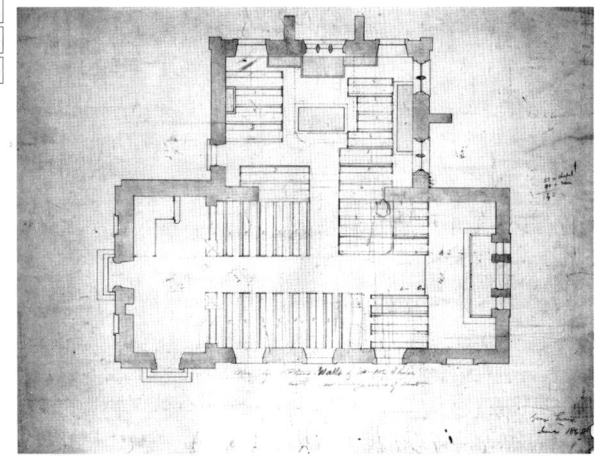

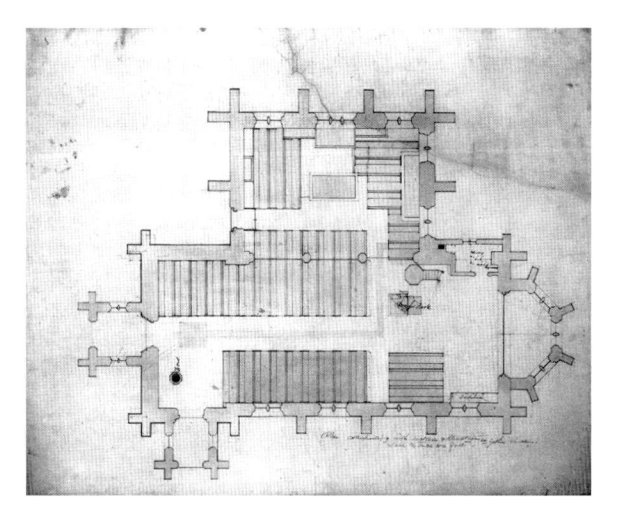

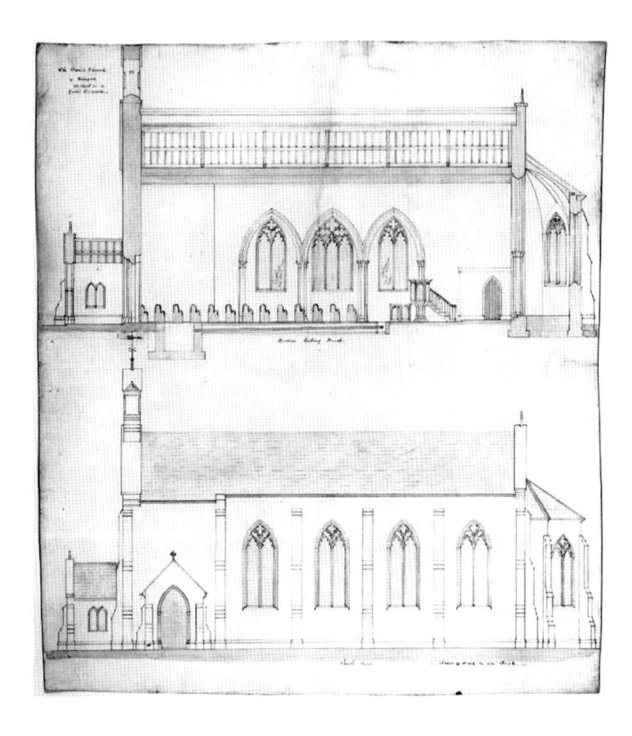

Drawings by George Evans for the remodelling of the Church

The Wimpole parish records show that the church was repaired and altered on a number of occasions during the nineteenth century: in 1834 a new entrance was made to the Chicheley chapel from the main body of the church, monuments were moved, and Flitcroft's formerly blind east window was opened and filled with painted glass.[357] The drawings below, made by the Wimpole Clerk of Works George Evans, describe a major, unexecuted scheme of 1868. In the event, the building was remodelled in a lesser way than is proposed in these drawings between 1887 and 1890 by the Royston mason and contractor W. Whitehead.

A.C.Yorke's typescript memoir of 1914 sheds further light on the Victorian changes that were contemplated and made to St. Andrew's:

> The embellishment of the Church was often discussed in my hearing. One drastic proposal was to pull it down, retain the Chicheley Chapel as a family Valhalla, and build a new church near the Lodge on Wimpole Road. [...] The plan ultimately adopted used also to be discussed, and Mr. Erant [sic], the Clerk of Works, prepared plans before 1873. If only a real Church architect had been called in, he might have advised treatment like that of a Renaissance College Chapel, and so have saved us from the present mongrel anachronism.

294 Survey plan of the church, 1868

National Trust WIM/D/564c
Inscr.: 'Plan of Present Walls of Wimpole Church, with new arrangement of seats'. 'George Evans June 1868'. Some dimensions in pencil.
Pen and ink with grey wash and pencil additions (470 x 660mm)
Scale: 1/4 in: 1ft

This survey drawing includes proposals to reorganise the pews in the north chapel. Postcard views of the 1920s show that this scheme was followed exactly, providing a very crowded result in the Chicheley chapel with the pews squeezed in amongst the monuments. Mrs Bambridge removed the seating in the reordering of the church that she undertook with the help of Professor, Sir Albert Richardson (1880—1964).

In addition, Whitehead replaced Flitcroft's round-headed windows in the south wall of the nave, moved and cleaned various monuments, placed columns with naturalistically carved capitals under the gallery, whose woodwork he repaired, laid a new York-stone pavement to the nave and a black and red Minton tile floor to the chapel.

295 Plan for the remodelling of the church, 1868

National Trust WIM/D/564b
Inscr.: 'Plan corresponding with Sections & Elevations see Gothic Elevations'. 'Scale 1/4 Inch to a Foot'. A font is marked at the west end, and new sedilia, and vestry indicated at the east.
Pen and ink with grey and brown washes. Pencil inscriptions (520 x 660mm)
Scale: 1/4 in: 1ft

This scheme for the re-gothicising of Flitcroft's church was to have included the addition of a polygonal apse at the east end, porches to the west and south doors, a vestry to the north east, and the planting of buttresses against the external walls. Evans also proposed the addition of a polygonal pulpit and a desk. None of this work was undertaken in Whitehead's remodelling of 1887—90, but for £10 he did replace the columns supporting the gallery at the west end, carving capitals with fern, oak, thorn and columbine decoration.

Wimpole Architectural Drawings

296 South elevation and west-east section for the proposed remodelling, 1868

National Trust WIM/D/564a
Inscr.: 'The Parish Church of Wimpole Restored as a Gothic Church'. 'Section looking north', 'South Front' and 'Scale 4 Feet to and Inch'.
Pen and ink with coloured washes (590 x 670mm)
Scale: 1/4 in: 1ft

The drawing shows the replacement of Flitcroft's austere round-headed windows and bellcote with gothic alternatives (No.61). Evans's design for the south windows of the nave, with *mouchette* tracery over a pair of trefoil-headed lights, was followed in Whitehead's remodelling some twenty years later, which work was estimated at £90. The four windows were also provided with 'new wrot-iron [sic] patent Casements' for £6.

297 West elevation and north-south section through chapel and nave, 1868

National Trust WIM/D/564d
Inscr.: 'George Evans Clerk of Works Wimpole Office 1868'. 'West Front' and 'Section looking East'. In pencil: a circular window above the west porch 'this should be a rose window decorated style'; and on the east windows of the north chapel 'In Memoriam late Countess of Hardwicke' and 'Memorial Honourable Rector Yorke'. The levels of the existing and proposed floor levels are indicated.
Pen and ink, with coloured washes and some pencil additions and inscriptions (420 x 670mm)
Scale: 1/4 in: 1ft

In 1887 it was decided that the west end of the church, with its bell-cote, should remain as Henry Flitcroft had designed it.

Drawing for a glasshouse range

298 Boulton & Paul. Plan, section and perspective sketch for a range of glasshouses and cold-frames, 1907

Cambridge Records Office, CL(P)271/2
Inscr.: 'ALTERATION TO HORTICULTURAL BUILDINGS AT WIMPOLE, CAMBS'. Stamped: 'BOULTON & PAUL Ltd. HORTICULTURAL BUILDINGS NORWICH'
Pen & ink with watercolour (372 x 692mm)
Scale: 1/8 in: 1ft. (plan & section; 1/16 in: 1ft.(block plan).

These horticultural buildings were to be sited opposite the bothy ranges to the north of walled garden laid out by Emes and built by Soane.

Drawings by Reginald Francis Guy Aylwin (b.1877) for Wimpole Hall

It appears from the evidence of these drawings that in 1935 the Yorke family considered seriously a return to the seat which the 5th Earl of Hardwicke's bankruptcy had caused to be transferred to the Robartes bank some forty years previously. The first five of this set of nine drawings—N°.1 appears to be missing—are surveys of the house, whilst the remainder comprise 'Alterations for Philip Yorke Esq'. Philip Grantham Yorke (1906—74) suceeded his uncle as the 9th Earl of Harwick in 1936. Each drawing—a dyeline reproduction of a pen and wash original—is marked: 'R F G Aylwin. Arch^t, 17 Buckingham S^t, Adelphi, W. C. 2'. The surveys are inscribed 'Nov. 1935', and the proposals 'Dec. 1935'. All the drawings are to a common scale, an 'Eighth of an inch to a foot', and measure 420 x 755mm. The areas subject to alteration are colour-washed.

The proposals, which were not executed because in 1938 the house was bought by Capt. and Mrs Bambridge, were radical and would not only have seen the destruction of much of the most interesting of Sir John Soane's work within the main body of the house but also the wholesale removal of the flanking wings to east and west. The scheme suggested three major changes to the house: firstly, the separation of the northern, barrel-vaulted arm of the Yellow Drawing Room—which was to be retained as a double-height space—from the southern part of the room, whose east and west halves were to have been given over to lavatories and bathrooms. The space directly below Soane's lantern, was to have been translated into an open courtyard or 'area'. The opening that this brutal intervention would have made between the roofs of the double pile was intended to light a service passage running east-west through the centre of the Yellow Drawing Room at ground, and a reinstated first-floor, level.

299 Part survey of the basement floor, 1935

National Trust WIM/D/563a
Inscr.: 'Wimpole Hall. Part Survey 1935', 'N° 2/2191', 'Basement Plan'
Dyeline
Scale: 1/8 in: 1ft

300 Survey plan of the ground floor, 1935

National Trust WIM/D/563b
Inscr.: 'Wimpole Hall. Part Survey 1935', 'N° 3/2192', 'Ground Floor Plan'
Dyeline

The house is shown essentially as it is now, with the exception of the glazed screen placed between the Ionic columns which stand on the threshold of the entrance hall and inner hall.

301 Part survey of the first floor, 1935

National Trust WIM/D/563c
Inscr.: 'Wimpole Hall. Part Survey 1935', 'N° 4/2193'
Dyeline

302 Part survey of the second floor, 1935

National Trust WIM/D/563d
Inscr.: 'Wimpole Hall. Part Survey 1935', 'N° 5/2194', 'Second Floor Plan'
Dyeline

303 Proposal for the alteration of the basement floor, 1935

National Trust WIM/D/565a
Inscr.: 'Wimpole Hall Alterations for Philip Yorke Esq.', 'Basement Plan', 'N°6/2195'
Dyeline

Apart from the continuation down to basement level of the light well created by the removal of the south-eastern section of the Yellow Drawing Room, the main changes proposed in this plan are at the east end of the central block. On the south front of the house external steps are shown, providing access to the western end of the basement-level chapel—this presumably for estate staff. The entry was to have been protected by an internal draft-lobby. The boiler room beneath the mezzanine warming room of Soane's bath, which is adjacent to the Chapel entrance, was to be converted to a sacristy. The lamp room to the east of the removed bathroom is marked 'Housekeeper', the then housekeeper's room to the west of the chapel becoming the 'servants' hall'. Further minor changes to the layout of the service rooms to the north of the proposed new light-well 'area' are indicated.

304 Proposal for the alteration of the ground floor, 1935

National Trust WIM/D/565b
Inscr.: 'Ground Floor Plan', 'N° 7/2196'
Dyeline

As indicated above, Aylwin's proposal involved the destruction of the southern half of the Yellow Drawing Room and its replacement with a cloakroom, substantial light-well and service corridor which would have connected Soane's stairs to the west with the inner hall to the east. The proposed subdivision of the state dining room was undertaken in a modified form for the Bambridges by the architect Trenwith Wills, see *No.314*. The provision of what appears to be an external staircase, marked 'Trades Entrance', at the east end of the house and the proposed blocking up of the doorway and lobby between the gallery and book room at the north-west corner of the central block of the house, suggests that Aylwin intended to demolish wholesale the library wing to the west and Kendall's service wing to the east.

305 Proposal for the alteration of the first floor, 1935

National Trust WIM/D/565c
Inscr.: 'First Floor Plan', 'Nº 8/2197'. Some pencil annotations, suggesting alternative uses of some of the minor spaces.
Dyeline

The alterations proposed here are almost wholly associated with the provision of additional bathrooms and lavatories and with the lighting of the central part of the house, with new windows giving onto the three light-wells it was proposed to form or enlarge between the two 'piles' of the house. What are now known as Mrs. Bambridge's Dressing Room and Bedroom at the centre of the south front are marked as 'Own' dressing room and bedroom.

306 Proposal for the alteration of the second floor, 1935

National Trust WIM/D/565d
Inscr.: 'Second Floor Plan', 'Nº 9/2198'
Dyeline

Twentieth-century topographical views

307 Algernon Newton, R.A. (1880—1968). View of the north façade of Wimpole Hall, 1940

National Trust WIM/P/89
Signed and dated: 'an 1940'
Oil on canvas (75 x 121cm)
Exh.: Newton exhibited a view of Wimpole at the Royal Academy in 1938, no.407.

Algernon Newton is perhaps best known for painting urban scenes—deserted streetscapes and canal-side buildings—and landscapes.

During a ten year period between *c*.1935 and 1945 Newton expanded his repertoire to include country house 'portraits'—a genre, that together with Rex Whistler (1905—44), he helped to revive for a twentieth-century audience. This series included views of Castle Howard, Carclew (Cornwall), Stowe and Ditchley Park. The Wimpole view belongs to that group, and clearly it was a subject that he painted on at least two occasions.

308 William Bruce Ellis Ranken (1881—1941) Watercolour view of the Gallery at Wimpole, 1937

National Trust WIM/P/88
Signed and dated: WBER 1937
Watercolour (790 x 570mm)

A member's back label for the Royal Institute of Painters in Watercolours is inscribed: 'The drawing Room, Wimpole Hall, Cambridgeshire. WBE Ranken, 14 Cheltenham Terrace', the location of the artist's London studio, off Chelsea's King's Road near that of his friend and near contemporary John Singer Sargent (1856—1925). W.B.E. Ranken trained at the Slade School of Art and worked in oils, watercolours and occasionally pastel, painting interiors (especially of country houses), portraits and still lifes for English and American high society. Amongst his patrons in the United States of America can be counted members of the Vanderbilt and Whitney families.

This view of the ground-floor gallery at Wimpole, looking north, has been taken from almost exactly the same station point as the anonymous view of 1819 (*No.225*) and records the furnishing arrangements that the 2nd Lord Robartes must have found himself with when he acquired Wimpole from the 5th Earl of Hardwicke, in his capacity as chairman of the Agar-Robartes Bank to which the earl was massively in debt. It was presumably Captain and Mrs Bambridge, who rented the house from 1936, who commissioned this watercolour rather than Gerald Agar Robartes, 7th Viscount Clifden, who inherited Wimpole in 1930. The eighteenth-century seat furniture—armchairs and sofas—is now at Lanhydrock, Cornwall.

Survey drawings by George Philip Banyard (1880—1948) of the Hall and stables

Banyard, who established his Cambridge practice in 1910, initially concentrated on domestic commissions but during World War I worked with the Royal Engineers on the construction of camps and hospitals. The scope of his work later developed to include the design and alteration of commercial buildings, such as shops, factories and garages, and the building of schools. Amongst his better known buildings in Cambridge can be counted the department store Eaden and Lilley and the town's two cinemas.

309 Survey plan of the ground floor, 1940

National Trust WIM/D/568a
Inscr.: 'SURVEY OF WIMPOLE HALL, CAMBRIDGESHIRE'; 'GROUND FLOOR PLAN'; and 'Surveyed & Drawn by George P. Banyard, FRIBA, Cambridge Feb. Mar. 1940'. The room functions are marked. Against the conservatory at the west end of the house is the legend: 'Base stone inscribed REBUILT 1870'
Pen and ink with blue wash (1,540 x 710mm)
Scale: 'EIGHT FEET TO ONE INCH'

This and the following survey drawings provide the only record of the internal layout of Kendall's service block to the east, which included a 'brewery' in the north-east corner. It shows too how a large 'boiler chamber' and various other outbuildings had been erected in Kendall's walled potting yard which sat against the west side of the library (and whose western wall was then blind). This presumably had to be done with the arrival of a central heating system in 1895.

The conservatory and 'potting yard' to the west, and the majority of the service wing to the east, have been crossed out in blue pencil with the notes 'pulled down' and 'All this pulled down'.

310 Survey plan of the basement floor, 1940

National Trust WIM/D/568b
Inscr.: 'SURVEY OF WIMPOLE HALL, CAMBRIDGESHIRE'; 'LOWER GROUND FLOOR PLAN'; and 'Measured & Drawn by George P. Banyard, FRIBA, Cambridge Mar.—April 1940'. The room functions are marked.
Pen & ink (1,100 x 600mm)
Scale: 'EIGHT FEET TO ONE INCH'

135 The Catalogue

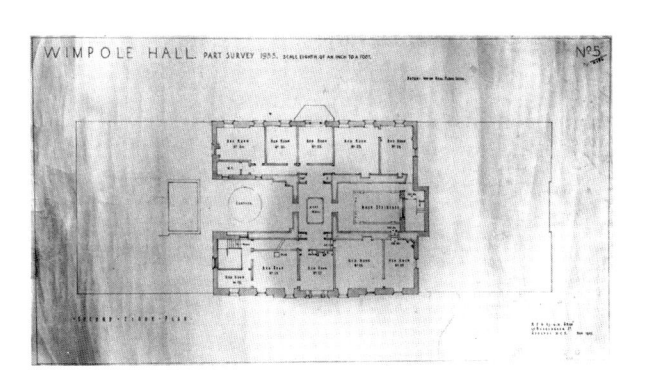

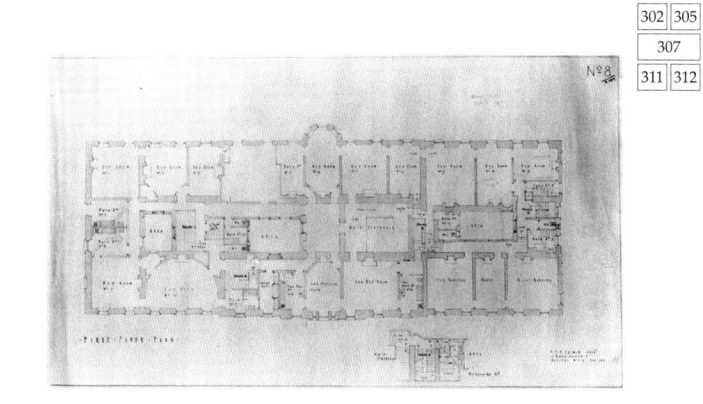

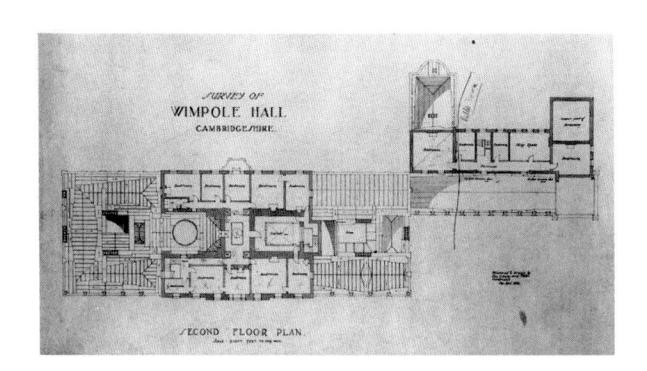

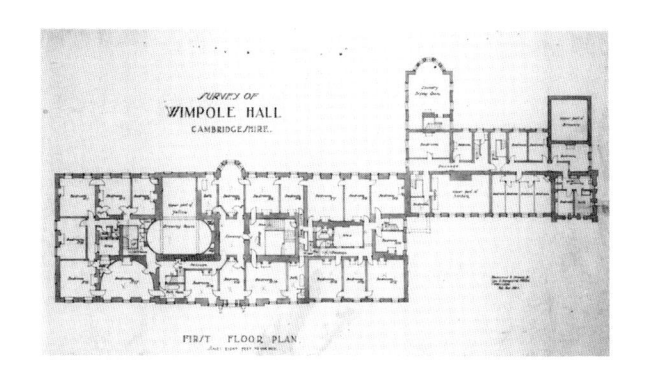

Recorded here are the wine cellars beneath James Gibbs's library that the poet Alexander Pope had joked about in correspondence with Edward Harley: 'I wish a small Cellar of Strong beer were somewhere under the Library, as a proper (brown) Study for the Country-Gentlemen; while the Cantabrigians are imployed above'.[358]

The bedrooms shown to the west of a stud and matchboard partition in the room at the south-west corner of the plan—immediately to the left of John Soane's 'Deed Room'—are subdivisions of Kendall's Steward's Room.

311 Survey plan of the first floor, 1940

National Trust WIM/D/568c
Inscr.: 'SURVEY OF WIMPOLE HALL, CAMBRIDGESHIRE'; 'FIRST FLOOR PLAN'; and 'Measured & Drawn by George P. Banyard, FRIBA, Cambridge Feb. Mar. 1940'. The room functions are marked.
Pen and ink (1,100 x 600mm)
Scale: 'EIGHT FEET TO ONE INCH'

This plan shows that the kitchen in Kendall's east service wing was a double-height space.

312 Survey plan of the second floor, 1940

National Trust WIM/D/568d
Inscr.: 'SURVEY OF WIMPOLE HALL, CAMBRIDGESHIRE'; 'SECOND FLOOR PLAN'; and 'Measured & Drawn by George P. Banyard, FRIBA, Cambridge Mar.—April 1940'. The room functions are marked.
Pen and ink (1,100 x 600mm)
Scale: 'EIGHT FEET TO ONE INCH'

This plan shows that the brewery in the north-east corner of Kendall's service wing was a triple-height space.

313 Survey plans of the Stable Block, 1940

National Trust WIM/D/568e
Inscr.: 'SURVEY OF WIMPOLE HALL, CAMBRIDGESHIRE, STABLE & GARAGE BLOCK'; 'GROUND FLOOR PLAN' and 'FIRST FLOOR PLAN'; and 'Measured & Drawn by Geo. Banyard FRIBA, Cambridge May 1940'. The room functions are all marked.
Pen and ink (1,025 x 645mm)
Scale: 'EIGHT FEET TO ONE INCH'

This drawing records the ground and first floor plans of the quadrangular stable block erected by H.E. Kendall in 1851. It has been suggested that the grooms' cottages in the four corners of the ground floor may be have been inserted between 1851 and 1940. In the west range, the coach house has given way to 'Garages', with an ancillary space dedicated to 'Chauffeurs'. The chauffeurs were a reality; in the late 1920s the Bambridges were described as 'travelling through England in great pomp in an enormous motor full of luggage, with chauffeur and a Spanish valet in gorgeous footman's livery and yellow waistcoat'.

Drawing by Trenwith Wills (1891—1972) for Wimpole Hall

314 Ground-floor plan with proposed alterations

National Trust WIM/D/590
Inscr.: 'Wimpole Hall Cambridgeshire Proposed Alterations', 'Drawing No.3', 'Ground Floor Plan', 'Trenwith Wills F.R.I.B.A. 24, Yeoman's Row, Brompton Road, London S.W.3 May 1941'.
Blueprint, with pencil and coloured pencil additions and annotations (600 x 1070mm)
Scale: '1" to 8'0"'

This scheme is illustrative of the reductive way in which great country houses were adapted during the inter- and post-war years in order to serve changing needs; in the case of Wimpole, a very small household. With his partner, the Hon. Gerald Wellesley, later 7th Duke of Wellington, Wills built up a country house practice specialising in just such adaptations and alterations.

The Bambridges used the small room on the north front of the house to the east of the saloon as their dining room rather than H.E. Kendall's great dining room. Trenwith Wills subdivided the latter to provide, from west to east: a servery, pantry, and kitchen with larder. This solution is almost identical to that which R.F.G. Aylwin had suggested in December 1935 (*No.304*) The partition walls were to support a false ceiling which, until its removal by the National Trust in 1979, hid the ornate mid-nineteenth century plasterwork above. The drawing shows that it was the architect's intention to encase the dining room fireplace behind a breeze-block partition. The fireplace, the dado panelling, the doorcases and some of the other architectural elements of the room were, however, unfortunately stripped out and disposed of—presumably at the time when Wills's proposals were effected.

The drawing also describes the re-facing of the east and west ends of the building, which was necessitated by the truncation of the east service wing and the demolition of the conservatory to the west. A garage, accessed from the east service courtyard, was also formed in the laundry wing.

This scheme must have been drawn after 1939, when Wills became a Fellow of RIBA, and presumably after 1940 when George Banyard undertook a survey of Wimpole Hall for the new owners, the Bambridges (*Nos.309–13*). Banyard's survey record shows the great dining room intact.

Drawings by Sir Albert Richardson (1880—1964)

315 Plan and internal elevation of St Andrew's Church, 1960

Bedfordshire & Luton Archives & Records Services, RGH6/3/5
Inscr.: 'Wimpole Church, Cambridgeshire', '57/2', 'May 1960', and 'Proposed method of strengthening of Chapel Roof'. 'Sir Albert E. Richardson, PPRA & E.A.S. Houfe F/FRIBA, 20 Church Street, AMPTHILL—Bedfordshire & London'. Notes on materials are also given.
Pen and ink on tracing paper (505 x 755mm) with pencil additions.
Scale: 'One Inch equals Eight Feet'

The scheme proposes the narrowing of the opening between the main body of the church and the chapel to the north, in order to carry the south ends of the roof trusses in the chapel. The wooden beam previously spanning the larger square-headed opening is marked as 'decayed', and the concrete beam above it as 'partly decayed'.

Richardson's watercolour view of the wall between the Chicheley chapel and the main body of the church (*No.316*) corresponds to this proposal to reduce the size of the opening.

Richardson designed Captain Bambridge's gravestone in the churchyard at Wimpole. Despite a brief falling out when Mrs Bambridge learned that Richardson had suggested in Cambridge circles that the University might acquire Wimpole Hall for educational purposes, Richardson was a regular visitor to the house. In his biography, Simon Houfe describes Mrs Bambridge falling on any slight drawing that the professor made on these occasions 'begging off him some little sketch he had made from the dregs of the teacup.'[359]

137 The Catalogue

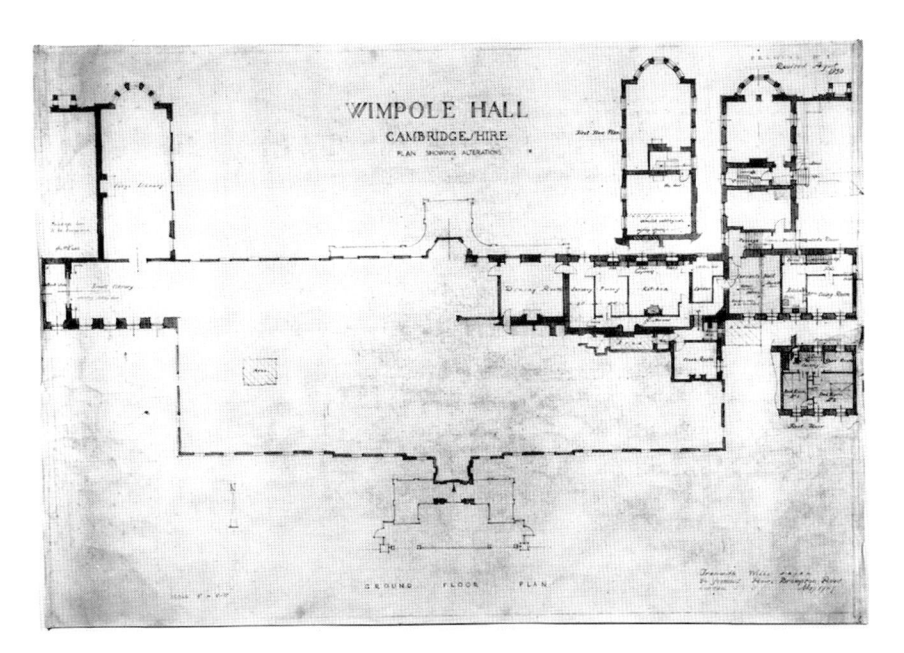

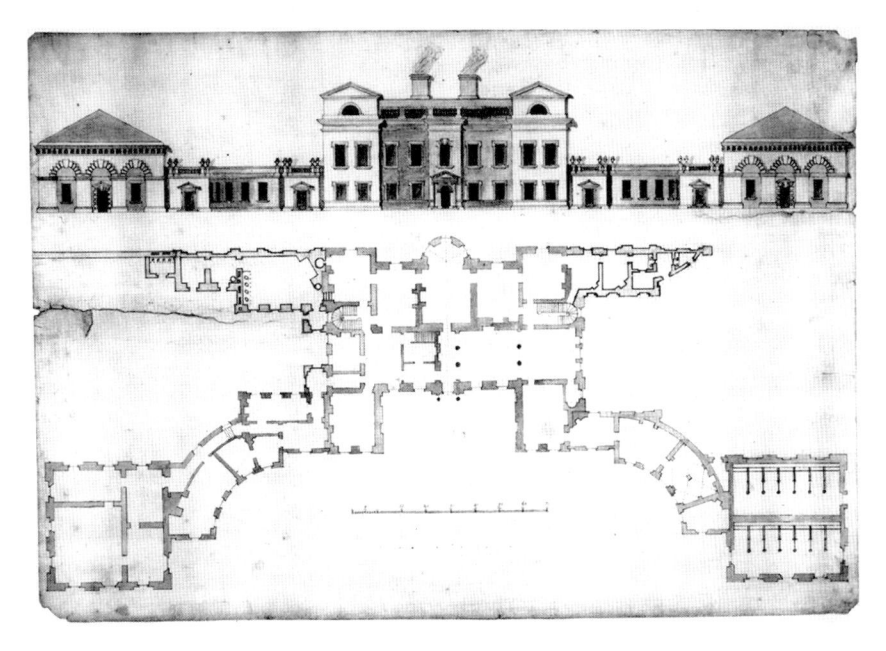

316 Sketch of the interior of St Andrew's Parish Church, 1960

National Trust WIM/D/545
Inscr.: Signed and dated '26 May AER 1960'
Watercolour (575 x 385mm)

A view from the south-east towards the Chicheley chapel. It is not clear whether the images of The Holy Family and The Crucifixion shown hanging to either side of the basket-arched opening between the nave and chapel are proposals by Richardson, or records of paintings, or textiles, that have since been lost.

Miscellaneous architectural drawings at Wimpole

317 Kenton Couse (1721—90). Principal elevation and ground floor plan of Normanton Park, Rutland showing proposed additions, c.1763

National Trust WIM/D/553
Sepia ink with grey wash (535 x 370mm)
Scale given

Normanton Park was designed by Henry Joynes (*c.* 1684—1754), and built between *c*.1735 and 1740, for Sir John Heathcote, the son of the wealthy merchant Sir Gilbert Heathcote (1651?—1733) who was both a co-founder of the new East India Company and the Bank of England and who was repeatedly satirised by Alexander Pope. In the poet's *Moral Essays* he wrote:

> The grave Sir Gilbert holds it for a rule,
> That every man I want is knave or fool.

The H plan house with its four outlying towers—antiquated in conception but dressed in neo-Palladian guise as a Roman *villa rustica*—at the centre of this drawing is Joynes's work. Joynes's design recalls Lord Burlington's Tottenham Park, Wiltshire (1721), designed for Lord Bruce, and Sir Thomas Robinson's Rokeby Park, Yorkshire (1725).

Kenton Couse remodelled Normanton Park for another Sir Gilbert Heathcote between 1763 and 1767. He here proposes the addition of flanking pavilions—the right one providing stabling—and quadrant links containing offices. He also suggests the addition of further offices and service rooms to either side of the rear range. The highlighting of the new work with a strongly inked outline is unfinished. Couse's additions are, in elevation, strikingly Burlingtonian in style, presumably in an attempt to marry with Joynes's Palladianism. The drawing shows that the bow at the centre of the rear façade predates the further additions made to the house by Thomas Cundy senior (1765—1825) and junior (1790—1867).

Couse perhaps brought this drawing to Wimpole for his own reference, or to show his new clients. Couse, who first worked at Wimpole as Henry Flitcroft's assistant designed a new Dining Room, in the neo-classical style, for the house in 1778 (*No.98*). The Normanton drawing may alternatively have been lent by Sir Gilbert Heathcote who was Philip Yorke's brother-in-law and who coincidentally bought the 1st Lord Hardwicke's Grosvenor Square house when he died in 1764.

After the auction of its contents in 1925, Normanton Park was earmarked to be 'sold for demolition', and demolition was its fate after first suffering a fire. Fifty years later its site and 6,000 acre estate, together with the villages of Emphinham and Edith Weston, were drowned beneath Rutland Water which, with a capacity of 900 million gallons, remains the largest man-made lake in Western Europe. Only the estate church, a bizarre sight, 'waist deep' in the banked gravel of the artificial shoreline, and the stable block survive above the level of the reservoir.

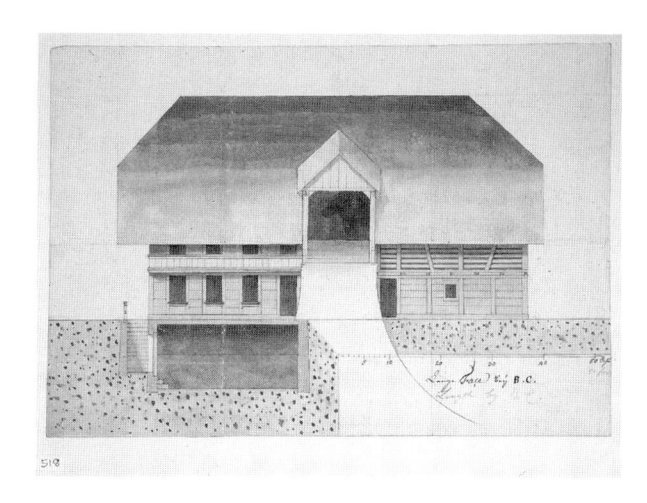

Drawings of a Swiss Barn lent to John Soane

Lit. & repr.: Du Prey (1979), pp.28–38, fig.12.

A letter from John Soane of September 1800 reveals that he borrowed the following group of drawings from Philip Yorke; the architect was sufficiently impressed by them to make his own reference copies.[360] The drawings describe a complicated late-eighteenth-century Swiss farm building that incorporates a barn, stabling, a house, and pig sties. Both lateral and vertical separation of the various functions is ingeniously achieved. The agricultural activities are restricted to one end of the building with stabling beneath a first floor barn, accessible via a great ramp. This ramped access artificially enables the planning advantages that the Lake District's 'Bank Barns' exploit from their naturally sloping sites.

It is tempting to speculate whether this Swiss design influenced the architecture of Soane's model farm at Wimpole, for the elevation of the long side of the building (*No.318*)—in particular its massive roof, entrance porch, and its use of timber boarding as a cladding material—bears a family resemblance to the Great Barn there. The date of Soane's correspondence, however, perhaps suggests that the loan of the drawings rather reflects the continuing fascination of architect and client in finding a simple, 'classical' vernacular appropriate for agricultural buildings. The drawings reinforce the evidence of Hardwicke's interest in the use of timber construction in farm buildings of Continental Europe. Wimpole's farm complex had been designed in 1794 and it seems unlikely that so meticulous a figure as Soane would have retained the drawings for six years before returning them.

Translations of the German inscriptions and annotations on all five drawings, have been added in pencil. These anonymous drawings are in pen and ink, with coloured washes denoting the different materials and are drawn to approximately $1/8$ in.: 1ft - the translator at least has clearly taken the scale as such.

318 Elevation and part section.

National Trust WIM/D/518
Inscr.: 'Length by BC'
Pen and ink, with coloured washes (280 x 370mm)

Elevation, 'BC', of the long side of the building (see corresponding plan, *No.321*) showing the ramp to the upper or 'garrett' floor. The drawing includes a section, on the left, of the brick-lined cellar beneath the 'house'.

The massive, steeply pitched roof, the porch that provides access to the upper level, and the building's horizontal boarding are all features that are reflected in Soane's designs for the buildings of Wimpole's model farm.

319 'Front' elevation and part section

National Trust WIM/D/556a
Inscr.: 'Front'
Pen and ink with coloured washes (275 x 300mm)

The elevation 'AB'—marked on the corresponding plan (*No.321*)—of the symmetrical, five-bay, three-storied façade to the farmhouse, with a cross section showing the access to the cellars beneath.

The elevation also shows the first floor balconies, protected from heavy snows by pronounced, overhanging eaves, on the side walls of the house. The entrance door, giving access to the 'hausgang', a spine passageway, is placed at the centre of the façade. The side of the ramp (with its door to the pig-sties beneath) is shown on the right.

320 Cross section

National Trust WIM/D/556b
Inscr.: Variously, the function of each room marked.
Pen and ink with coloured washes (270 x 295mm)

On the ground floor, this stepped cross section shows the stairs within the house (on the left hand side) and the bulkhead boarding to the passage end of the stables (on the right) with the storage space of the barn above. In an ingenious way even the space beneath the ramp, revealed in this section, has been used—for a pair of 'hog-styes'.

321 Ground Floor Plan.

National Trust WIM/D/519
Inscr.: The room functions again translated in pencil and the overall dimensions of the building given—'Long 74 feet', 'Whole Breadth 40 feet'.
Pen and ink with coloured washes (280 x 355mm)

At the house end of the building the rooms, four per floor, are arranged to either side of a wide central passage, which meets a narrower, staired, service passage that crosses the building at the stable end.

322 First Floor Plan.

National Trust WIM/D/520
Inscr.: Variously, again the room functions given and translated, and on what are clearly first floor balconies, 'Berceau, probably the projection of the Roof', and 'Berceau, Trellis'.
Pen and ink with coloured washes (270 x 330mm)

Yorke Family Tree

Owners of Wimpole are set in **BOLD CAPITALS**
* indicates monument in Wimpole Church
' sons of 3rd Earl:
Philip, Viscount Royston (1784–1808)
Charles (1787–91)
Charles James, Viscount Royston (1797–1810)
Joseph John (1800–01)

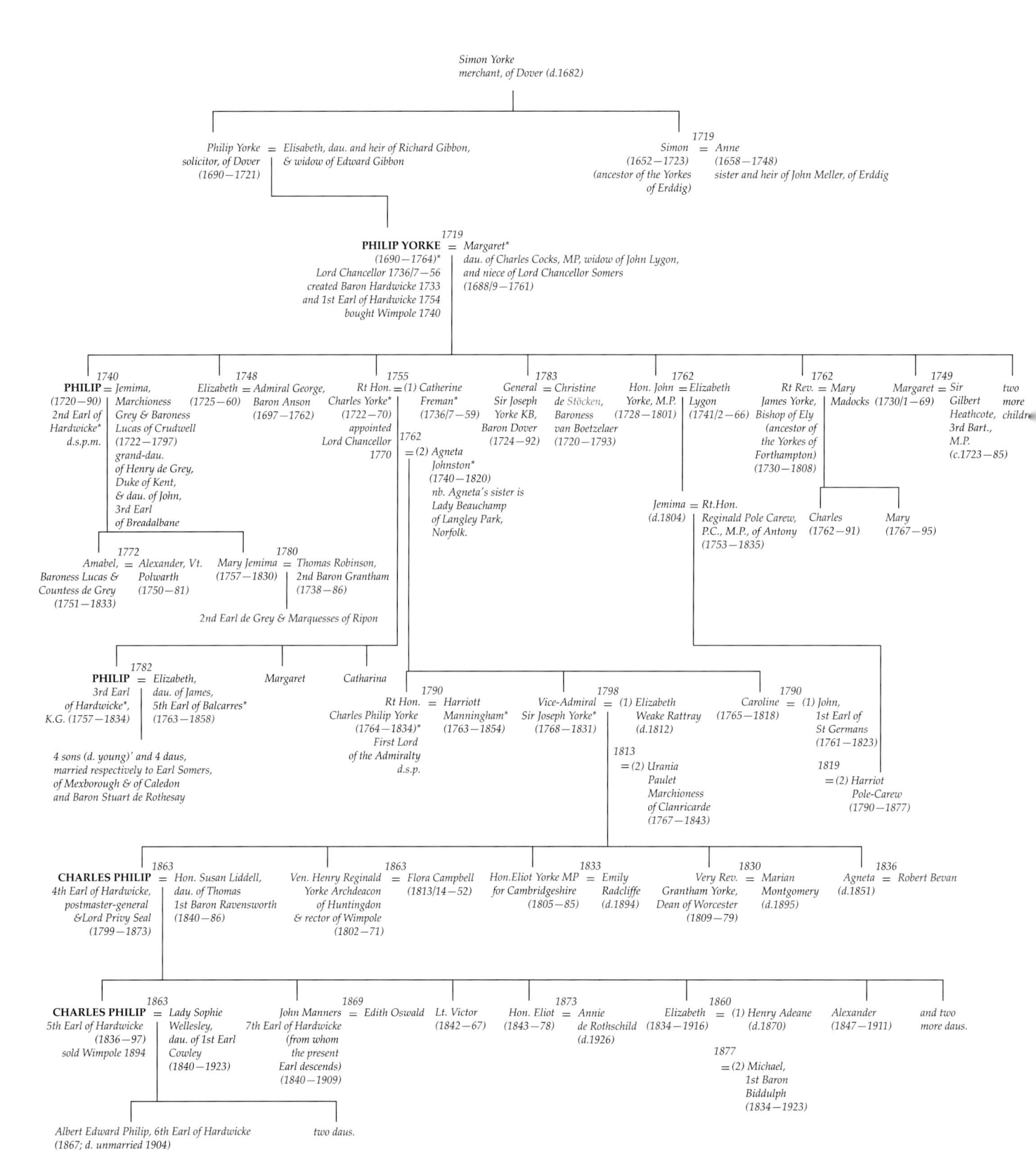

Simon Yorke
merchant, of Dover (d.1682)

Philip Yorke = *Elisabeth, dau. and heir of Richard Gibbon,*
solicitor, of Dover   *& widow of Edward Gibbon*
(1690–1721)

1719
Simon = *Anne*
(1652–1723)   *(1658–1748)*
(ancestor of the Yorkes   *sister and heir of John Meller, of Erddig)*
of Erddig)

1719
PHILIP YORKE = *Margaret**
(1690–1764)*   *dau. of Charles Cocks, MP, widow of John Lygon,*
Lord Chancellor 1736/7–56   *and niece of Lord Chancellor Somers*
created Baron Hardwicke 1733   *(1688/9–1761)*
and 1st Earl of Hardwicke 1754
bought Wimpole 1740

1740	1748	1755	1783	1762	1762	1749	
PHILIP = *Jemima,*	*Elizabeth* = *Admiral George,*	*Rt Hon.* =(1) *Catherine*	*General* = *Christine*	*Hon. John* = *Elizabeth*	*Rt Rev.* = *Mary*	*Margaret* = *Sir*	*two*
(1720–90) *Marchioness*	*(1725–60)* *Baron Anson*	*Charles Yorke** *Freman**	*Sir Joseph* *de Stöcken,*	*Yorke, M.P.* *Lygon*	*James Yorke,* *Madocks*	*(1730/1–69)* *Gilbert*	*more*
2nd Earl of *Grey & Baroness*	*(1697–1762)*	*(1722–70)* *(1736/7–59)*	*Yorke KB,* *Baroness*	*(1728–1801)* *(1741/2–66)*	*Bishop of Ely*	*Heathcote,*	*childre*
Hardwicke* *Lucas of Crudwell*		*appointed*	*Baron Dover* *van Boetzelaer*		*(ancestor of*	*3rd Bart.,*	
d.s.p.m. *(1722–1797)*		*Lord Chancellor*	*(1724–92)* *(1720–1793)*		*the Yorkes of*	*M.P.*	
grand-dau.		*1770*			*Forthampton)*	*(c.1723–85)*	
of Henry de Grey,		1762			*(1730–1808)*		
Duke of Kent,		=(2) *Agneta*					
& dau. of John,		*Johnston**		*Jemima* = *Rt.Hon.*			
3rd Earl		*(1740–1820)*		*(d.1804)* *Reginald Pole Carew,*	*Charles* *Mary*		
of Breadalbane		*nb. Agneta's sister is*		*P.C., M.P., of Antony*	*(1762–91)* *(1767–95)*		
		Lady Beauchamp		*(1753–1835)*			
		of Langley Park,					
		Norfolk.					

1772	1780		
Amabel, = *Alexander, Vt.*	*Mary Jemima* = *Thomas Robinson,*		
Baroness Lucas & *Polwarth*	*(1757–1830)* *2nd Baron Grantham*		
Countess de Grey *(1750–81)*	*(1738–86)*		
(1751–1833)			

2nd Earl de Grey & Marquesses of Ripon

1782
PHILIP = *Elizabeth,*   *Margaret*   *Catharina*
3rd Earl   *dau. of James,*
of Hardwicke*,   *5th Earl of Balcarres**
K.G. (1757–1834)   *(1763–1858)*

4 sons (d. young)' and 4 daus,
married respectively to Earl Somers,
of Mexborough & of Caledon
and Baron Stuart de Rothesay

1790	1798	1790	1836
Rt Hon. = *Harriott*	*Vice-Admiral* =(1) *Elizabeth*	*Caroline* =(1) *John,*	*Agneta* = *Robert Bevan*
Charles Philip Yorke *Manningham**	*Sir Joseph Yorke** *Weake Rattray*	*(1765–1818)* *1st Earl of*	*(d.1851)*
(1764–1834)* *(1763–1854)*	*(1768–1831)* *(d.1812)*	*St Germans*	
First Lord	1813	*(1761–1823)*	
of the Admiralty	=(2) *Urania*	1819	
d.s.p.	*Paulet*	=(2) *Harriot*	
	Marchioness	*Pole-Carew*	
	of Clanricarde	*(1790–1877)*	
	(1767–1843)		

1863	1863	1833	1830
CHARLES PHILIP = *Hon. Susan Liddell,*	*Ven. Henry Reginald* = *Flora Campbell*	*Hon.Eliot Yorke MP* = *Emily*	*Very Rev.* = *Marian*
4th Earl of Hardwicke, *dau. of Thomas*	*Yorke Archdeacon* *(1813/14–52)*	*for Cambridgeshire* *Radcliffe*	*Grantham Yorke,* *Montgomery*
postmaster-general *1st Baron Ravensworth*	*of Huntingdon*	*(1805–85)* *(d.1894)*	*Dean of Worcester* *(d.1895)*
&Lord Privy Seal *(1840–86)*	*& rector of Wimpole*		*(1809–79)*
(1799–1873)	*(1802–71)*		

1863	1869		1873	1860		
CHARLES PHILIP = *Lady Sophie*	*John Manners* = *Edith Oswald* *Lt. Victor*	*Hon. Eliot* = *Annie*	*Elizabeth* =(1) *Henry Adeane*	*Alexander*	*and two*
5th Earl of Hardwicke *Wellesley,*	*7th Earl of Hardwicke* *(1842–67)*	*(1843–78)* *de Rothschild*	*(1834–1916)* *(d.1870)*	*(1847–1911)*	*more daus.*
(1836–97) *dau. of 1st Earl*	*(from whom*	*(d.1926)*	1877		
sold Wimpole 1894 *Cowley*	*the present*		=(2) *Michael,*		
(1840–1923)	*Earl descends)*		*1st Baron*		
	(1840–1909)		*Biddulph*		
			(1834–1923)		

Albert Edward Philip, 6th Earl of Hardwicke   *two daus.*
(1867; d. unmarried 1904)

Wimpole Architectural Drawings

Bibliography
Published in London, unless otherwise indicated.

Adshead, 1996:
David Adshead, 'Wedgwood, Wimpole and Wrest: the landscape drawings of Lady Amabel Polwarth', *Apollo*, vol.CXLIII, no.410 (New Series), April 1996, pp.31-6.

Adshead, 1998:
David Adshead, 'The design and building of the Gothic Folly at Wimpole, Cambridgeshire', *The Burlington Magazine*, vol.CXL, no.1139, February 1998, pp.76-84.

Adshead, 2000:
David Adshead, 'A Modern Italian Loggia at Wimpole Hall', *The Georgian Group Journal*, vol.X, 2000, pp.150-63.

Adshead, 2002:
David Adshead, 'A Noble Musæum of Books': A View of the Interior of the Harleian Library at Wimpole Hall?', *Library History*, vol.18, no.3, November 2002, pp.191-206.

Adshead, 2003:
David Adshead, 'Like a Roman Sepulchre':John Soane's design for a *Castello d'acqua* at Wimpole, Cambridgeshire, and its Italian origins', *Apollo*, vol.CLVII no.494 (New Series), April 2003, pp.15-21.

Allen, 1985:
Brian Allen, 'Thornhill at Wimpole', *Apollo*, vol.CXXII, no.283 (New Series), September 1985, pp.204-11.

Aldrich, 1990:
Megan Aldrich (ed.), *The Craces: Royal Decorators 1768—1899* (Brighton, 1990).

Andrews, 1935:
C.B. Andrews (ed.), J. Byng, 'Tour in the Midlands, 1790', *The Torrington Diaries: containing the tours through England and Wales […] between the years 1781 and 1794*, 3 vols. (1935).

Archer, 1985:
Michael Archer, 'Stained Glass at Erdigg and the work of William Price', *Apollo*, vol.CXXII, no.284 (New Series), October 1985, pp.252-63.

Baggs, 1999:
Tony Baggs, *The Green Houses in the Walled Garden at Wimpole Hall, Cambridgeshire*, a Cambridge Historic Buildings Group report, July 1999.

Baggs, 2004:
Tony Baggs, 'The Hearth Tax and the Country House in 'Old' Cambridgeshire', *Proceedings of the Cambridge Antiquarian Society*, XCIII, 2004, pp.151-8.

Batey, 1999:
Mavis Batey, *Alexander Pope: The Poet and the Landscape* (1999).

Beaman & Roaf, 1990:
Sylvia P. Beaman and Susan Roaf, *The Icehouses of Britain* (1990).

Beard, 1981:
Geoffrey Beard, *Craftsmen and Interior Decoration in England 1660—1820* (1981).

Bendall, 1992
Sarah A. Bendall, *Maps, Land and Society: a history, with a carto-bibliography of Cambridgeshire estate maps, c.1600—1836* (Cambridge, 1992).

Biddulph, 1910:
Lady Elizabeth Biddulph of Ledbury, *Charles Philip Yorke, 4th Earl of Hardwicke, Vice-Admiral RN: A Memoir* (1910).

Bignamini, 1988:
Ilaria Bignamini, 'George Vertue, Art Historian and Art Institutions in London, 1689—1768: A study of Clubs and Academics', *The Walpole Society*, vol.LIV (Oxford, 1988)

Bold & Chaney, 1993:
John Bold and Edward Chaney (eds.), *English Architecture Public and Private: Essays for Kerry Downes*, (1993).

Bolton, 1923:
Arthur T. Bolton, *The Works of Sir John Soane, FRS, FSA, RA (1753—1837)*, The Sir John Soane Museum Publication Nº.8 (1923).

Bowden Smith, 1987:
Rosemary Bowden Smith, *The Water House, Houghton Hall, Norfolk*, English Garden Features, 1600—1900, No.1 (1987).

Britton & Brayley, 1801—16:
John Britton & E.W. Brayley, *The beauties of England and Wales; or Delineations, topographical, historical, and descriptive, of each county. Embellished with engravings* 18 vols. (1801—16).

Bristol, 2000:
Kerry Bristol, 'The Society of Dilettanti, James 'Athenian' Stuart and the Anson family', *Apollo*, vol.CLII, no.461 (New Series), July 2000, pp.46-54.

Brooks, 1998:
Diana Brooks, *Thomas Allom (1804—1872)* (1998), catalogue to accompany an exhibition at the RIBA Heinz Gallery, London, 26 March—9 May 1998.

The Builder, 1875:
The Builder, vol.XXXIII, 1875.

'J.L.C.', 1962:
'250 years of English Watercolours', *Country Life*, vol. CXXXII, no.3425, 25 October, 1962.

Carter, 1753:
Edmund Carter, *The History of the County of Cambridge from the earliest accounts to the present time* (Cambridge, 1753).

Carter, Goode & Laurie, 1982:
George Carter, Patrick Goode & Kedrun Laurie, *Humphry Repton Landscape Gardener 1752—1818*, exh. cat. (Norwich, 1982).

Cavendish-Bentinck, 1937:
William John Arthur Charles James Cavendish-Bentinck, 6th Duke of Portland, *Men, Women and Things: Memories of the Duke of Portland* (1937).

Chase, 1943:
Isabel Wakelin Urban Chase, *Horace Walpole: Gardenist. An edition of Walpole's 'The History of Modern Taste in Gardening' with an estimate of Walpole's contribution to Landscape Architecture* (Princeton, N.J., 1943).

Cocke, 1984:
Thomas Cocke, *The Ingenious Mr. Essex, Architect 1722—1784*, exh. cat., Fitzwilliam Museum (Cambridge, 1984).

Cointeraux, 1790:
François Cointeraux, *Ecole d'architecture rurale et économique* (Paris, 1790).

Collard, 1990:
Frances Collard, 'A Design For Library Steps by Henry Keene', *Furniture History*, vol.xxvi (1990), pp.34-38.

Collins, 1752:
Arthur Collins, *Historical collections of the noble families of Cavendish, Holles, Vere, Harley and Ogle, with the lives of the most remarkable persons […] The lives of the Earls of Oxford.*[etc.] (1752).

Colvin, 1952:
Howard Colvin, *Architectural Drawings in the Bodleian Library* (1952), Bodleian Picture Book no.7.

Colvin, 1976:
Howard Colvin (ed.), *The History of the King's Works*, vol. V, 1660—1782 (1976).

Colvin, 1995:
Howard Colvin, *A Biographical Dictionary of British Architects 1600—1840*, 3rd ed. (New Haven & London, 1995).

Colvin & Moggridge, 2006:
Colvin and Moggridge Landscape consultants, 'Wimpole Park and Estate Cambridgeshire - Conservation Plan (Filkins Lechlade, 2006).

Croft-Murray, 1962:
Edward Croft-Murray, *Decorative Painting in England 1537—1837*, 2 vols. (Feltham, 1962 & London, 1970).

Cruickshanks, Handley & Drayton, 2002:
Eveline Cruickshanks, Stuart Handley & D W Hayton (eds.), *The History of Parliament: House of Commons 1690—1715* III Members A-F, (Cambridge, 2002).

Daniels, 1999:
Stephen Daniels, *Humphry Repton: Landscape gardening and the Geography of Georgian England* (New Haven & London, 1999).

Darley, 1999:
Gillian Darley, *John Soane: An Accidental Romantic* (New Haven & London, 1999).

Darley, 2002:
Gillian Darley, 'The surprising discretion of Soane and Repton', *The Georgian Group Journal*, vol.XII, 2002, pp.38-47.

Dean, 1999:
Ptolemy Dean, *Sir John Soane and the Country House Estate* (Aldershot, 1999).

Dean, 2006:
Ptolemy Dean, *Sir John Soane and London*, (Aldershot, 2006).

Defoe, 1927:
Daniel Defoe, *A Tour Thro' the whole Island of Great Britain*, 2 vols. (1927).

Desmond, 1994:
Ray Desmond (ed.), *Dictionary of British and Irish Botanists and Horticulturists, including Plant Collectors, Flower Painters and Garden Designers* (1994).

Dickins & Stanton, 1910:
Lilian Dickins and Mary Stanton (eds.), *An Eighteenth-Century Correspondence - Being the letters of Deane Swift - Pitt - The Lyttletons and the Grenvilles - Lord Dacre - Robert Nugent - Charles Jenkinson - The Earls of Guildford, Coventry, & Hardwicke - Sir Edward Turner - Mr. Talbot of Lacock and others, To Sanderson Miller, Esq., of Radway* (1910).

Du Prey, 1982:
Pierre de la Ruffinère du Prey, *John Soane, The Making of an Architect* (Chicago & London, 1982).

Du Prey, 1978:
Pierre de la Ruffinière du Prey, 'John Soane, Philip Yorke and their Quest for Primitive Architecture', *National Trust Studies*, 1979 (1978), pp.28-38.

Du Prey, 1985:
Pierre de la Ruffinière du Prey, *Sir John Soane*, Catalogues of Architectural Drawings in the Victoria and Albert Museum (1985).

Du Prey, 1989:
Pierre de la Ruffinière du Prey, 'The *Bombé*-Fronted Country House from Talman to Soane' in *The Fashioning and Functioning of the British Country House*, Studies in the History of Art 25, National Gallery of Art, Washington (1989), pp.29-49.

Eden, 1995:
Christine Eden, Archaeological investigations at the Old Rectory (Marshall and Yorke Cottages) Wimpole Hall, Cambridgeshire (Cambridge, 1995).

Ellison, 1975:
David Ellison (ed.), Alexander Campbell Yorke, *Wimpole as I knew it* (Bassingbourn, 1975).

Ellison, 1981:
Susan Ellison (ed.), *Wimpole Amuses Victoria* (Orwell, 1981).

Elrington, 1973
C.R. Elrington (ed.), *Victoria County History: Cambridgeshire and the Isle of Ely*, vol.v (Oxford, 1973).

Erskine, 1916:
Mrs. Steuart Erskine (ed.), *Twenty Years at Court. From the Correspondence of the Hon. Eleanor Stanley, maid of honour to her late Majesty Queen Victoria, 1842—1862* (1916).

Evans & Rose, 2000:
Nesta Evans & Susan Rose (eds.), *Cambridge Hearth Tax Returns, Michaelmas 1664*, The British Record Society Hearth Tax Series, vol.1, Cambridge Records Society vol.15, in association with The University of Surrey, Roehampton.

Friedman, 1984:
Terry Friedman, *James Gibbs* (New Haven, 1984).

Garnier, 2006:
Richard Garnier, 'Alexander Roos (*c*.1810—1881)', *The Georgian Group Journal*, vol.XV (2006), pp.11-68.

Garrett, 1747:
Daniel Garrett, *Designs and Estimates of farm-houses, etc. for the County of York, Northumberland, Cumberland, West-moreland and Bishoprick of Durham* (1747).

The Gentleman's Magazine:
Vols. XLIX & LX.

Gibberd, 1913:
J.E. Gibbert 'A Century at Wimpole Hall', *The Country Home*, pp.263-70.

Gibbs, 1728:
James Gibbs, *A Book of Architecture* (1728).

Gibbs, 1981:
Julian R. Gibbs, 'Wimpole Hall', *The Kipling Journal*, June 1981, pp.14–17.

Gilbert, 1978:
Christopher Gilbert, *Furniture at Temple Newsam House and Lotherton Hall: a catalogue of the Leeds collection*, 2 vols. (Bradford, 1978)

Girouard, 1978:
Mark Girouard, *Life in the English Country House* (New Haven & London, 1978).

Godber, 1968:
Joyce Godber, 'The Marchioness Grey of Wrest Park, Bedfordshire', *Proceedings of the Bedfordshire Historical Records Society*, vol.47, 1968.

Goldsmith, 1770:
Oliver Goldsmith, *The Deserted Village, A Poem* (1770).

Gore & Carter, 2005:
Ann Gore and George Carter (eds.), *Humphry Repton's Memoirs* (Norwich, 2005).

Gough, 1792:
Richard Gough, 'Description of the old Font in the Church of East Meon, Hampshire, 1789; with some Observations on Fonts', *Archaeologia or Miscellaneous Tracts relating to Antiquity*, vol.X (1792), pp.183–209.

Goulding, 1936:
Richard W. Goulding, *Catalogue of the pictures belonging to His Grace the Duke of Portland, K.G at Welbeck Abbey, 17 Hill Street, London, and Langwell House* (Cambridge, 1936).

Graves, 1906:
Algernon Graves, *The Royal Academy of Arts: A Complete Dictionary of Contributors and their work from its foundation in 1769 to 1904*, 4 vols. (1906).

Gunnis, 1968:
Rupert Forbes Gunnis, *Dictionary of British Sculptors 1660–1851* (2nd edn. 1968).

Gunther, 1928:
R.T. Gunther (ed.), *The Architecture of Sir Roger Pratt* (Oxford, 1928).

Hambly, 1988:
Maya Hambly, *Drawing Instruments 1580–1980* (1988).

Hare, 1893:
Augustus John Cuthbert Hare, *The Story of Two Noble Lives: Being memorials of Charlotte, Countess Canning, and Louisa, marchioness of Waterford*, 3 vols. (1893).

Hare, 1896—1900:
Augustus John Cuthbert Hare, *The Story of My Life*, 6 vols. (1896—1900).

Harris, 1990:
Eileen Harris, *British Architectural Books and Writers 1556–1785* (Cambridge, 1990).

Harris, 1960:
John Harris, *English Decorative Ironwork from Contemporary Source Books: 1610–1836* (1960).

Harris, 1979:
John Harris, 'Newly Acquired Designs by James Stuart in the British Architectural Library, Drawings Collection', *Architectural History*, volume 22: 1979, pp.72–77.

Harris, 1982:
John Harris, *William Talman: maverick architect* (1982).

Harris & Jackson-Stops, 1984:
John Harris and Gervase Jackson-Stops (eds.), *Britannia Illustrata:Knyff & Kip* (1984).

Harris, 1985:
John Harris, 'Harley, the Patriot Collector', *Apollo*, vol.CXXII, no.283 (New Series), September 1985, pp.198–203.

Harris, 1987:
Leslie Harris (ed. Gervase Jackson-Stops), *Robert Adam and Kedleston: The making of a Neo-classical Masterpiece* (1987).

Hawkes, 1964:
William Hawkes, 'Sanderson Miller 1716—80 Architect', unpublished dissertation, University of Cambridge, 1964.

Hawkes 2005:
William Hawkes (ed.), *The diaries of Sanderson Miller of Radway: together with his memoir of James Menteath*, The Dugdale Society, vol. 41 (Stratford-upon-Avon, 2005)

Hayden, 1985:
Peter Hayden, 'British Seats on Imperial Russian Tables', *Garden History*, vol.13, no.1, Spring, 1985, pp.17–32.

Haylett, 1992:
Elizabeth Haylett, 'The Changing Plan of the English Country House and its relationship to Social Life - The Wimpole Example', unpublished dissertation, submitted to the Department of Architecture, University of Cambridge, 1992.

Hewlings, 1981:
Richard Hewlings, 'Ripon's Forum Populi', *Architectural History*, vol.24 (1981), pp.39–52.

Heyworth, 1989:
P.L. Heyworth (ed.), *Letters of Humfrey Wanley: palaeographer, Anglo-Saxonist, librarian, 1672—1726* (Oxford, 1989).

Historic Manuscripts Commission:
Bath iii; Egmont, ii; Portland, v & vii.

The Horticulturist, 1850:
The Horticulturist, October 1850, vol.V.

Houfe, 1980:
Simon Houfe, *Sir Albert Richardson: The Professor* (Luton, 1980).

Hunt & Willis, 1975:
John Dixon Hunt & Peter Willis (eds.), *The Genius of The Place: the English Landscape Garden 1620—1820* (1975).

Hussey, 1927 (1 & 2):
Christopher Hussey, 'Wimpole Hall I and II, Cambridgeshire: The Seat of The Hon. Gerald Agar-Robartes', *Country Life*, LXI, no.1583, 21 May and no.1584, 28 May 1927, pp.806–13 & 844–51.

Hussey, 1967 (1, 2 & 3):
Christopher Hussey, 'Wimpole Hall—The Home of Mrs. Bambridge—I, II, & III', *Country Life*, CXLII, no.3691, 30 November, no.3692, 7 December & no.3693, 14 December 1967, pp.1400-4, 1466-71, & 1594-7.

Ingamells, 1997:
John Ingamells, compiled from the Brinsley Ford Archives, *A Dictionary of British and Irish Travellers in Italy 1701–1800* (New Haven & London, 1997).

Jackson-Stops, 1971
Gervase Jackson-Stops, 'English Baroque Ironwork - I: The sources of Tijou's Designs', *Country Life*, CXLIX, no.3842, 28 January 1971, pp.182-3.

Jackson-Stops, 1979 (1):
Gervase Jackson-Stops, *Wimpole Hall*, National Trust guidebook (1979).

Jackson-Stops, 1979 (2):

Gervase Jackson-Stops, 'Exquisite Contrivances, The Park and Gardens at Wimpole—I', *Country Life*, CLXVI, no.4287, 6 September 1979, pp.658–61.

Jackson-Stops, 1985:
Gervase Jackson-Stops (ed.), *The Treasure Houses of Britain: Five Hundred Years of Private Patronage and Art Collecting* (New Haven & London, 1985).

Jackson-Stops, 1992:
Gervase Jackson-Stops, *An English Arcadia: Designs for Gardens and Garden Buildings in the Care of the National Trust 1600–1990*, exh. cat. (1992).

Jacques, 1983:
David Jacques, *Georgian Gardens: The Reign of Nature* (1983).

Joll, 2002:
Evelyn Joll, *Cecil Higgis Art Gallery: Watercolours and Drawings* (Bedford, 2002).

Kip & Knyff, 1707:
Leonard Knyff and Jan Kip, *Britannia Illustrata, or Views of Several of the Queens Palaces also of the Principal Seats of the Nobility and Gentry of Great Britain* (1707).

Nouveau Théâtre de la Grande Bretagne: ou description exacte des palais de la Reine, et des maisons les plus considerables des Seigneurs & des Gentilhommes de la Grande Bretagne

Les Delices de la Grand' Bretagne, et de l'Irlande, où sont exactement décrites les antiquitez, les provinces, les villes [...] la religion, les mœurs des habitans..[etc.] (Leyden, 1707), published by Pieter Van der Aa.

Knox, 2000:
Tim Knox, 'National Trust Projects and Acquisitions, 1999—2000', 'A sideboard returns to Wimpole Hall', *Apollo*, April 2000, p.11.

Laing, 1800 :
David Laing, *Hints for Dwellings: Consisting of Original Designs for Cottages, Farm-houses, Villas &c.* (1800).

Laing, 1991:
Alastair Laing, 'Every Picture Tells a Story', *Country Life*, CLXXXV, no.12, 21 March 1991, pp.110-3.

Laird, 1999:
Mark Laird, *The Flowering of the Landscape Garden: English Pleasure Ground, 1720–1800* (Philadelphia, 1999).

Langley, 1740:
Batty Langley, *The City and Country Builder's and Workman's Treasury of Designs: or, the art of drawing, and working the ornamental parts of architecture* (1740).

Lees-Milne, 1962:
James Lees-Milne, *Earls of Creation: Five Great Patrons of Eighteenth-Century Art*, (1962). See chapter IV, 'Edward Harley, 2nd Earl of Oxford (1689—1741)', pp.173-271.

Legh, 1917:
Evelyn Legh, *The House of Lyme from its foundation to the end of the eighteenth century [...] Illustrated* (1917).

Legh, 1925:
Evelyn Caroline Legh, Baroness Newton, *Lyme Letters 1660–1760* (1925).

Lewis, 1865:
Lady Theresa Lewis (ed.), *Extracts of the Journals and Correspondence of Miss Berry from the year 1783 to 1852*, 3 vols. (1865).

Lewis, 1937—83:
W.S. Lewis (ed.), *The Yale Edition of Horace Walpole's Correspondence*, 48 vols.(New Haven & Oxford, 1937—83).

Liddell, 1911:
A.G.C. Liddell, *Notes from the Life of an Ordinary Mortal* (1911).

Little, 1955:
Bryan Little, *The Life and Work of James Gibbs 1682–1754* (1955).

Llanover, 1861:
Lady Llanover (ed.), *The Autobiography and correspondence of Mary Granville Mrs. Delaney*, 3 vols. (1861).

Louw, 1981:
H.J. Louw, 'Anglo-Netherlandish architectural interchange c.1600—c.1660', *Architectural History*, vol.24, 1981, pp.1–23.

Lycett, 1999:
Andrew Lycett, *Rudyard Kipling* (1999).

Maguire, 1992:
Alison Maguire, with contributions by Howard Colvin, 'A collection of seventeenth-century architectural plans', *Architectural History*, vol.35 (1992), pp.140-82.

Mallalieu, 1979—90:
H.L. Mallalieu, *The Dictionary of British Watercolour Artists up to 1920*, 3 vols. (Woodbridge, 1979—90).

Menuge & Cooper, 2001:
Adam Menuge & Anwen Cooper, *The Gothic Folly, Wimpole Park, Wimpole, Cambridgeshire*, an Architectural Investigation Report, English Heritage (2001).

Meyer, 1974:
Arline Meyer, *British Sporting Painting, 1650–1850*, Hayward Gallery, 1974–5

Meyer 1984:
Arline Meyer *John Wootton, 1682–1764, Landscapes and Sporting Art in Early Georgian England*, exh. cat., The Iveagh Bequest, Kenwood House, London, 4 July–30 September 1984.

Meyer, 1985:
Arline Meyer, 'Wootton at Wimpole', *Apollo*, vol.CXXII, no.283 (New Series), September 1985, pp.212-9.

Meyer, 1988:
Arline Meyer, 'Sir William Musgrave's 'Lists' of portraits, with an account of head-hunting in the eighteenth-century', *The Walpole Society*, vol.LIV (Oxford, 1988)

Millar, 1995:
Delia Millar, *The Victorian watercolours and drawings in the collection of Her Majesty the Queen*, 2 vols. (1995).

Needham, 1934:
Francis Needham (ed.), *A Collection of Poems by Several Hands, Never before Published*, Welbeck Miscellany, No.2 (1934).

ODNB.
Oxford Dictionary of National Biography (Oxford, 2004).

Palmer, 1935 (1):
William Mortlake Palmer, *William Cole of Milton* (Cambridge, 1935).

Palmer, 1935 (2):
William Mortlake Palmer (ed.), *John Layer (1586–1640) of Shepreth, Cambridgeshire: A seventeenth-century local historian*, Cambridge Antiquarian Society, Octavo Series No.LIII (1935).

Parry, 1986:
Eric Parry, 'Inspired Alterations and Additions to a Country House—Wimpole Hall', Masters of Building Series, *The Architectural Journal*, March 1986, pp.36–55.

Pattison & Garrow, 1998:
Paul Pattison and D. Garrow, *Wimpole Park, Cambridgeshire*, a RCHME report (1998).

Pattison & Barker, 2003:
Paul Pattison and Louise Barker, *Wimpole Park, Cambridgeshire*, English Heritage Archaeological Investigation series 15/2003.

Pevsner, 1970:
Nikolaus Pevsner, *The Buildings of England: Cambridgeshire* (2nd edn., 1970).

Phibbs, 1980:
John L. Phibbs, 'Wimpole Park, Cambrideshire' (1980). An unpublished survey report, commissioned by the National Trust.

Pitt, 1753:
Revd. Christopher Pitt, Revd. Joseph Warton et. al. (transls.), *The works of Vergil in Latin and English*, 4 vols. (1753).

Pollard, Hooper & Moore, 1974:
E. Pollard, M.D. Hooper & N.W. Moore, *Hedges* (1974).

Pope, 1731:
Alexander Pope, *Of false taste; an epistle to the Right Honourable Richard Earl of Burlington. Occasioned by his Publishing Palladio's Designs of the Baths, Arches, and Theatres, &c. of Ancient Rome* (1731).

Raeburn, 1995:
Michael Raeburn, Ludmila Voronikhina & Andrew Nurnberg (eds.), *The Green Frog Service* (London & St. Petersburg, 1995).

RCHME, 1968:
Royal Commission on Historical Monuments of England, *West Cambridgeshire*, 1968.

Redway, 1931:
W.F. Redway (ed.), *Documents of Catherine the Great* (Cambridge, 1931).

Repton, 1795:
Humphry Repton, *Sketches and Hints on Landscape Gardening* (1795).

Repton, 1803:
Humphry Repton, *Observations on the Theory and Practice of Landscape Gardening* [etc.] (1803).

Repton, 1816:
Humphry and John Adey Repton, *Fragments on the Theory and Practice of Landscape Gardening* [etc.] (1816).

RIBA, 1972:
Catalogue of the Drawings Collection of the Royal Institute of British Architects, C-F (Gregg International Publishers Ltd, 1972), p.89.

Richardson & Stevens, 1999:
Margaret Richardson and MaryAnne Stevens (eds.), *John Soane Architect: Master of Space and Light* (1999), exh. cat., Royal Academy of Arts, London, 11 September—3 December 1999.

Roberts, 1997:
Jane Roberts, *Royal Landscape: The Gardens and Parks of Windsor* (New Haven & London, 1997).

Robinson, 1976:
John Martin Robinson, 'Model Farm Buildings of the Age of Improvement', *Architectural History*, vol.19 (1976).

Robinson, 1983:
John Martin Robinson, *Georgian Model Farms: A Study of Decorative and Model Farm buildings in the Age of Improvement, 1700–1846* (Oxford, 1983).

Root, 1978:
Arnold Root, 'The Wimpole Landscape', unpublished dissertation, submitted to the Department of Architecture, University of Cambridge, April 1978.

Roscoe, 1987:
Ingrid Roscoe, 'James "Athenian" Stuart and the Scheemakers Family: A Lucrative Partnership between Architect and Sculptors', *Apollo*, vol.CXXVI, no.307 (New Series), September 1987, pp.178–84.

Roscoe, 1999:
Ingrid Roscoe, 'Peter Scheemakers', *Walpole Society*, vol. 66 (1999), pp.243-4.

Rowe, 1998:
Anne Rowe, 'Country House chameleon: The story of Hamels Mansion', *Hertfordshire's Past*, Issue 43/44 - Summer 1998, pp.44-54.

Saunders, 1997:
Ann Saunders, 'Lord Harley and his Friends', *Westminster History Review*, I (1997).

Schumann-Bacia, 1991:
Eva Schumann-Bacia *John Soane and The Bank of England* (New York, 1991).

Sherburn, 1956
George Sherburn (ed.), *The correspondence of Alexander Pope*, 5 vols. (Oxford, 1956).

Sigwalt, 1990:
Philippe Sigwalt, 'Sir John Soane's Lectures at the Royal Academy of Arts'. Unpublished thesis, submitted to the Architectural Association School of Architecture, 1990. The third part of this addresses 'Wimpole Hall according to Soane's teaching'.

Soane, 1778:
John Soane, *Designs in Architecture; consisting of plans, elevations, and sections, for temples, baths, casinos, pavilions, garden-seats, obelisks, and other buildings* (1778).

Soane, 1788:
Plans, Elevations, and Sections of Buildings Executed in the Counties of Norfolk, Suffolk, Yorkshire, Staffordshire, Warwickshire, Hertfordshire, et caetera (1788).

Soane, 1793:
Sketches in Architecture; containing Plans and Elevations of Cottages, Villas and other Useful Buildings, with characteristic Scenery (1793).

Soros, 2006:
Susan Weber Soros (ed.), *James "Athenian" Stuart: The Rediscovery of Antiquity* (New Haven & London, 2006).

Souden, 1991:
David Souden, *Wimpole Hall*, National Trust guidebook (1991).

Sparrow, 1922:
W. Shaw Sparrow, *British Sporting Artists* (1922).

Stewart, 1996:
David Stewart, 'Political Ruins: Gothic Sam Ruins and the '45', *The Journal of the Society of Architectural Historians*, vol. 55, no.4 (December 1996), pp.400-11.

Stillman, 1988:
Damie Stillman, *English Neo-classical Architecture*, Studies in Architecture Volume XXVI, 2 vols. (1988).

Stroud, 1962:
Dorothy Stroud, *Humphry Repton* (1962).

Stroud, l979:
Dorothy Stroud, 'The Charms of Natural Landscape, The Park and Gardens at Wimpole II', *Country Life*, CLXVI, no.4288, 13 September, 1979, pp.758-62.

Stukeley, 1743—52:
William Stukeley, *Palaeographia Britannica or Discourses on Antiquities in Britain* (1743—52).

Summers, 1985:
Peter Summers (ed.), *Hatchments in Britain, vol.6, Cambridgeshire, Essex, Hertfordshire, Huntingdonshire and Middlesex* (London & Chichester, 1985).

Surtees, 1975:
Virginia Surtees, *Charlotte Canning: lady-in-Waiting to Queen Victoria and Wife of the first Viceroy of India 1817—1861* (1975).

Surtees Society,
The Family Memoirs of the Rev. William Stukely, M.D, and the Antiquarian and other Correspondence of William Stukeley, Roger & Samuel Gale etc., 3 vols., The Surtees Society, vol. LXXVI (1883), vol.II.

Taylor 1997:
Alison Taylor, *Archaeology of Cambridgeshire, vol. 1: South West Cambridgeshire* (Cambridge, 1997).

Taylor 1995:
Christopher C. Taylor, 'Dispersed settlement in nucleated areas', *Landscape History* 17, 1995.

Temple, 1988:
Nigel Temple, 'Humphry Repton, Illustrator, and William Peacock's "Polite Repository" 1790—1811', *Garden History*, vol. 16, no.2 (Autumn, 1988), pp.161-73.

Temple, 1993:
Nigel Temple, *George Repton's Pavilion Notebook: a catalogue raisonné* (Aldershot, 1993).

Tijou, 1693
Jean Tijou, *A Newe Booke of Drawings Invented and Desined by John Tijou* (1693)

Tipping, 1908:
Avery Tipping, 'Wimpole Hall, Cambridgeshire: A Seat of Viscount Clifden', *Country Life*, vol.XXII, no.580, 15 February 1908, pp.234-41.

Turnbull, 1955:
E. Turnbull, 'Thomas Tudway and the Harleian Collection', *The Journal of the American Musicological Society*, vii (1955), pp.203-7.

Wainwright,1997:
Angus Wainwright, 'Looking for the Peasants under the Park', *The National Trust: Views*, No.26, Spring 1997, pp.14-6.

The Walpole Society:
'Vertue Note Books I', vol.XIX, (Oxford, 1930); 'Vertue Note Books III', vol.XXII (Oxford, 1934); vol.XXIV (for 1935—6) (Oxford, 1936); 'Vertue Note Books V', vol.XXVI (Oxford, 1938); 'Vertue Note Books, vol.VI', vol.XXX (for 1948—50) (Oxford, 1955).

Ward-Jackson, 1958:
Peter Ward-Jackson, *English Furniture Designs of the Eighteenth Century* (1958).

Wareham & Wright, 2002:
A.F. Wareham & A.P.M. Wright (eds.), *Victoria County History: Cambridgeshire and the Isle of Ely*, vol.X (Oxford, 2002).

Waterson, 1980:
Merlin Waterson, *The Servants' Hall: The Domestic History of a Country House* (1980).

Watkin, 1968:
David Watkin, *Thomas Hope 1769—1831, and the Neo-Classical Idea* (1968).

White,1987:
Roger White (ed.), *Georgian Arcadia: Architecture for the Park & Garden. An exhibition to mark the Golden Jubilee of the Georgian Group*, Colnaghi, 14 Old Bond Street, London, 22 July—15 August, 1987.

Williamson, 1909:
George Williamson, *The Imperial Russian Service* (1909).

Williamson, 1995:
Tom Williamson, *Polite Landscapes - Gardens & Society in Eighteenth-Century England* (Stroud, 1995).

Willis, 1977:
Peter Willis, *Charles Bridgeman and the English Landscape Garden*, Studies in Archtiecture, Volume XVII, ed. Anthony Blunt, John Harris and Howard Hibberd (1977); *Reprinted with supplementary plates and a catalogue of additional documents, drawings and attributions* (Newcastle upon Tyne, 2002).

Willis, 1993:
Peter Willis, 'Charles Bridgeman and the English Landscape Garden: New Documents and Attributions', *English Architecture Public and Private: Essays for Kerry Downes*, ed. John Bold and Edward Chaney (London and Rio Grande 1993), pp.246-64.

Wilton-Ely, 1968:
John Wilton-Ely, *Architectural Drawings from the Collection of Sir Albert Richardson*, Nottingham University Art Gallery, l968.

Wilton-Ely, 1969:
John Wilton-Ely 'The architectural models of Sir John Soane: a catalogue', *Architectural History*, vol.12, 1969.

Woodward, 1999:
Christopher Woodward, 'Dancing Soane: The Yellow Drawing Room at Wimpole Hall', *Apollo*, vol.CXLIX, no.446 (New Series), April 1999, pp.8-13.

Worsley, 1995:
Giles Worsely, *Classical Architecture in Britain: The Heroic Age* (New Haven & London, 1995).

Worsley, 2004:
Giles Worsley, *The British Stable* (New Haven & Yale, 2004).

The Wren Society:
The Wren Society, vol.XII (1935); vol.XVII (1940).

Wright, 1962:
C.E. Wright, 'Portrait of a Bibliophile VIII: Edward Harley, 2nd Earl of Oxford, 1689—1741', *The Book Collector*, xi, no.2 (Summer, 1962), pp.158-74.

Wright & Wright, 1966:
C.E. & Ruth C. Wright (eds.), *The diary of Humfrey Wanley: 1715—1726*, 2 vols. (1966).

Wrighte, 1767:
William Wrighte, *Grotesque Architecture* (1767).

Young, 1995:
Hilary Young (ed.), *The Genius of Wedgwood* (1995).

Yorke, 1913:
Philip C. Yorke (ed.), *The Life and Correspondence of Philip Yorke, Lord Chanellor Hardwicke*, 3 vols. (Cambridge, 1913).

'J', 1931:
'J' [probably Margaret Jourdain], 'Furniture at Wimpole Hall', *Country Life*, LXX, no.1819, November 28th, 1931, pp.590-1.

Exhibition catalogues

London, 1951:
English Landscape Gardening of the Eighteenth and early Nineteenth Centuries, The Hayward Gallery, London, 1951, The Arts Council of Great Britain.

Bedford, 1959:
Water-Colours and Drawings in the Cecil Higgins Collection, Cecil Higgins Museum Bedford (Bedford, 1959).

Cambridge, 1978:
'An Exhibition of Old Cambridgeshire Maps from Cambridge, East and South Cambridgeshire, selected from Maps in the County Record Office Shire Hall' (Cambridge, 1978).

Cambridge, 1984:
Thomas Cocke, *The Ingenious Mr. Essex, Architect 1722—1784*, Fitzwilliam Museum (Cambridge, 1984).

London, 1962;
Watercolours and Drawings from the Cecil Higgins Art Gallery, Bedford, Thomas Agnew & Sons, Ltd, 43 Old Bond Street, London, 23 October—17 November 1962.

London,1974—5:
Arline Meyer, *British Sporting Painting, 1650—1850*, Hayward Gallery, 1974—5.

London, 1984:
John Wootton, 1682—1764, Landscapes and Sporting Art in Early Georgian England, exh. cat., The Iveagh Bequest, Kenwood House, London, 4 July—30 September 1984.

London, 1987:
Roger White, *Georgian Arcadia—Architecture for the Park & Garden*. An exhibition to mark the Golden Jubilee of the Georgian Group, Colnaghi, London, 22 July—15 August, 1987.

London, 1999:1
Visions of Ruin: Architectural fantasies & designs for garden follies, The Soane Gallery, Sir John Soane's Museum, 2 July—8 August 1999.

London, 1999:2:
Margaret Richardson and MaryAnne Stevens (eds.), *John Soane Architect: Master of Space and Light* (1999), Royal Academy of Arts, London, 11 September—3 December 1999.

London, 2001:
David H. Solkin (ed.), *Art on the Line; The Royal Academy Exhibitions at Somerset House 1780—1836* (New Haven & London, 2001). Exhihibtion at the Courtauld Institute Gallery.

Norwich, 1965:
English Watercolours from the Cecil Higgins Art Gallery, Bedford, Castle Museum Norwich, July 1965.

Nottingham, 1968:
John Wilton-Ely, *Architectural Drawings from the Collection of Sir Albert Richardson*, Nottingham University Art Gallery (l968).

Reading, 1965:
English Watercolours from the Cecil Higgins Art Gallery, Bedford, Reading Museum and Art Gallery, 30 January—20 February 1965.

Auction Catalogues

Christie's, 1983:
Important Architectural Drawings and Watercolours including The Sir Albert Richardson Collection, Christie, Manson & Woods Ltd., sale catalogue, 30 November, 1983.

Christie's, 1989:
British Drawings and Watercolours, including Architectural Drawings, Christie, Manson & Woods Ltd., sale catalogue, 19 December 1989.

Christie's, 1999:
The Collection of Maureen, Marchioness of Dufferin and Ava, Christie, Manson & Woods Ltd., sale catalogue, 25 March, 1999.

Sotheby's, 1982:
British Watercolours and Drawings 1700—1920, Sotheby's, sale catalogue, 21 January 1982.

Sotheby's, 1986:
Victorian Drawings and Watercolours, Architectural Drawings and Watercolours, Sotheby's sale catalogue, 22 May, 1986.

Notes

1. Gervase Jackson-Stops, *An English Arcadia: Designs for Gardens and Garden Buildings in the Care of the National Trust: 1660—1990* (1992). The exhibition was circulated in the USA by the American Architectural Foundation.
2. See Gervase Jackson Stops, 'The Cliveden Album: drawings by Archer, Leoni and Gibbs for the 1st Earl of Orkney', *Architectural History*, vol.19 (1976), pp.5-16; *idem.*, 'The Cliveden Album II: nineteenth-century and miscellaneous drawings' *Architectural History*, vol.20 (1977), pp.65-78; John Maddison, 'Architectural drawings at Blickling Hall', *Architectural History*, vol.34 (1991), pp.75-135; and Geoffrey de Bellaigue (General ed.), Alastair Laing, Martin Meade, J.W. Niemeijer, Christopher White, Michael Jacobs, Karin Wolfe and Michael Snodin, *Waddesdon: Catalogue of Drawings for Architecture, Design and Ornament*, 2 vols. (2006).
3. Eric Parry, 'Inspired Alterations and Additions to a Country House—Wimpole Hall', Masters of Building Series, *The Architectural Journal*, March 1986, pp.36-55.
4. Christopher Hussey, 'Wimpole Hall—I, Cambridgeshire: the Seat of the Hon. Gerald Agar-Robartes', *Country Life*, LXI, no.1583, 21 May 1927, p.806.
5. Gervase Jackson-Stops, *Wimpole Hall*, National Trust guidebook (1979); David Souden, *Wimpole Hall, Cambridgeshire* (1991).
6. Henry Chichele, Archbishop of Canterbury (1362—1443) acquired the Manor of Wimpole in 1428, and during the next 250 years the Chichele family, subsequently Chicheley, consolidated its Cambridgeshire landholdings, gradually buying up the lesser, outlying manors in the parish.
7. BL, Add. Ch. 44821.
8. I am grateful to John Harris for drawing this to my attention. See 'Merly Library: A Catalogue of the well known and celebrated library of the late Ralph Willett Esq.'. The auction was held by Legh and Sotheby Booksellers, 145 The Strand, London on 6 December 1813 and over the following sixteen days. The drawings, making up lot 2744, were bought by one 'Booth', who also acquired the previous lots 2740 'A Parcel for Monuments, Domes &c. *by Sir Inigo Jones*' and 2743 'Thirteen Plans and Designs for Greenwich Hospital *by Sir C. Wren*'.
9. William Mortlake Palmer (ed.), *John Layer (1586—1640) of Shepreth, Cambridgeshire: A seventeenth-century local historian*, Cambridge Antiquarian Society, Octavo Series No.LIII (1935). Palmer identifies seven different MS versions of Layer's History which he lists A to I.
10. *Ibid.*, p.111. The 'extraordinary curious neat house' is referred to in version G, Bod. MS. Gough, Camb. 19, p.130—Dr. Charles Mason's fair copy.
11. Wimpole might more properly be described as having a triple-pile plan for, like Hugh May's (1621—84) Eltham Lodge, London (1663—4), but unlike Belton House, Lincolnshire (1685—8), a narrow range sandwiched between the two principal piles accommodated the main and secondary staircases.
12. Lady Evelyn Caroline Legh Newton, Baroness Newton, *Lyme Letters 1660—1760* (1925), p.9.
13. S.L. Sadler, 'Sir Thomas Chicheley (1614—1699)', *Oxford Dictionary of National Biography* (Oxford, 2004), pp.396-7 Hereafter *ODNB*.
14. Andrew Thrush, 'Sir William Russell (c.1575—1654)', *ODNB*, pp.355-6 Francis Russell's son John married Frances, Oliver Cromwell's daughter, and his daughter Elizabeth married Henry Cromwell. Although Sir William Russell, who as Treasurer to the Navy Board on two occasions effectively bankrolled the British Navy, was briefly imprisoned by Charles I in 1642, he was later treated with disdain by Parliament.
15. See *Calendar of Committee for Compounding, Cases 1643—46* (1890), p.1,437, '6th August 1646, THOS. CHICHELEY, Wimpole, Co. Cambridge, 'Begs to compound on Oxford Articles for delinquency. Sat in the Assembly there [vol. 192, p.868]; 5th December, 'Fine at 1/10, £1,985 10s 8d [vol.3, p.316]. Thomas Chicheley's mother, Lady Dorothy Chicheley, had had her goods removed and been assessed for £150 three years earlier in 1643—see *Calendar of Committee for Advance of Money*, 3 parts (1888), part 1, p.223.
16. Nesta Evans & Susan Rose (eds.), *Cambridge Hearth Tax Returns, Michaelmas 1664*, The British Record Society Hearth Tax Series, vol.1, Cambridge Records Society vol.15, in association with The University of Surrey, Roehampton (2000), p.xviii. For a table giving the 1662 and 1664 entries for 'Wympole' see p.318. The 1664 return for Cambridgeshire is at NA E179/84/437.
17. 11 January 1656 Thomas Chicheley, son of Thomas Chicheley, was baptised in the church at Wimpole.
18. R.T. Gunther (ed.), *The Architecture of Sir Roger Pratt* (Oxford, 1928), pp.61-62.
19. Newton (1925), *op.cit.*, p.4.
20. Henry B. Wheatley (ed.), *The Diary of Samuel Pepys, M.A. F.R.S. Clerk of the Acts and Secretary to the Admiralty*, 9 vols.(1893—9), vol. viii, p. 96, September 2—4, 1667.
21. Newton (1925), *op.cit.*, p. 32, letters of 1 and 8 January, from Richard Legh to his wife Elizabeth at Lyme Park, Cheshire. Lyme Park is now in the care of the National Trust.
22. Wheatley (1896), *op.cit.*, vol.vii, pp.358-9, March 10–12, 1668.
23. Newton (1925), *op.cit.*, p.13.
24. *Ibid.*, pp.113–4. Mrs. Langley was Sir Thomas Chicheley's Housekeeper and her husband, Thomas Langley, his Private Secretary.
25. *Ibid.*, p.114.
26. *Ibid.*, pp.205–6.
27. Maya Hambly, *Drawing Instruments 1580—1980* (1988).
28. Standard reference works include: W.A. Churchill, *Watermarks in Paper in Holland, England, France, Etc., in the XVII and XVIII Centuries and their interconnection* (Amsterdam, 1935); and Edward Heawood, *Watermarks Mainly of the seventeenth and eighteenth centuries* (Hilversum (Holland), 1950), issued as vol.I of *Monumenta Chartæ Papyraceæ: or Collection of Works and Documents illustrating the History of Paper* (General ed., E.J. Labarre).
29. John L. Phibbs, 'Wimpole Park, Cambridgeshire' (1980), an unpublished survey report, commissioned by the National Trust. The earliest record of there being a park at Wimpole is 1302.
30. Angus Wainwright, 'Looking for the Peasants under the Park', *The National Trust: Views*, no.26, Spring 1997, pp.14–16.
31. C.R. Elrington (ed.), *Victoria County Histoy: Cambridgeshire and the Isle of Ely*, vol.v (Oxford, 1973), p.272 (hereafter *VCH*).
32. A.F. Wareham & A.P.M. Wright (eds.), *VCH, A History of the County of Cambridge and the Isle of Ely*, vol x (Oxford, 2002), explain that Chicheley took over more than 1,000 acres of

33 allotments in and around Soham, Cambridgeshire that had been assigned to the Bedford Level Adventurers in the 1630s.
33 Sarah A. Bendall, *Maps, Land and Society: a history, with a carto-bibliography of Cambridgeshire estate maps, c.1600—1836* (Cambridge, 1992).
34 Daniel Defoe, *A Tour Thro' the whole Island of Great Britain*, 2 vols. (1927), vol. I, p.88.
35 University of Nottingham, Hallward Library, Department of Special Collections and Manuscripts, The Portland (London) Collection (hereafter UN, PLC) 1/420. Letter from John Cossen to Edward Harley, 2nd Earl of Oxford, 26 September 1723.
36 Wilton MSS diaries, Wilton House Archives, Wiltshire and Swindon Record Office (hereafter WSRO), Matthew Decker, 'Account of a Journey into East Anglia' made between 21 June and 12 July 1728.
37 *Historical Manuscripts Commission* (hereafter HMC), Egmont, ii, p.206, letter of 24 June 1701.
38 HMC, Portland, v, p.341, letter of 26 September 1713.
39 I am grateful to John Martin Robinson for elucidating the heraldry (left to right): 1. Cutler – *Azure* three dragons' heads erased *Or*. A chief. The crest comprises a dragon's head erased holding a laurel spray in its mouth; 2. Robartes, for the 2nd Earl of Radnor. Robartes – *Azure* three estoiles *Or*. A chief. Impaled with Culter, as above, for his wife Elizabeth. Supporters two goats ducally gorged. Earl's coronet; 3. Boulter for John and Edmund Boulter – Boulter is not officially recorded; Harley, for the 2nd Earl of Oxford. Harley – *Or* a band cortise *Sable*, impaled with Holles *Ermine* two piles in point *Sable* (for his wife Henrietta). Supporters two angels. Earl's coronet.
40 For a fuller account of these complexities see: Eveline Cruickshanks, Stuart Handley & D. W. Hayton (eds.), *The History of Parliament: House of Commons 1690—1715*, III, Members A-F, 'Boulter, Edmund', (Cambridge, 2002), pp.276-8.
41 *Ibid.*, p.277.
42 D.W. Hayton 'Sir John Cutler (1607/8—1693)', *ODNB*, p.841-3.
43 James Lees-Milne, *Earls of Creation: Five Great Patrons of Eighteenth-Century Art*, (1962), p.179.
44 *The Wren Society*, vol. XVII (Oxford, 1940), pp.9-10, letter from James Gibbs to Edward Harley, 23 November 1714. More than twenty years later Gibbs appears to have refaced Harley's townhouse - 'Draughts for the Front of Dover Street House, by Mr. Gibbs, 1737', see BL, Add. MS 18240, fo.36.
45 *The Wren Society* (1940), *op.cit.*, p.10.
46 C.E. and Ruth C. Wright (eds.), *The diary of Humfrey Wanley: 1715—1726*, 2 vols. (1966), vol. I, p. xvi.
47 Souden (1991), *op.cit.*, p.12.
48 P.L. Heyworth (ed.), *Letters of Humfrey Wanley: palaeographer, Anglo-Saxonist, librarian, 1672—1726* (Oxford, 1989), p.361. Letter of 30 November 1716.
49 *Ibid.*, p.361.
50 Wright & Wright (1966), *op.cit.*, vol.I, p.xxvii, fn.7.
51 HMC, Portland, v, p.562, letter of 17 August 1718.
52 Heyworth (1989), *op.cit.*, pp.395-6. Letter from Humfrey Wanley to Arthur Charlett, Master of University College, Oxford, 14 June 1719.
53 *Ibid.*, p.398, letter to Arthur Charlett, 20 June 1719.
54 *The Wren Society* (1940), *op.cit.*, p.10, a receipt dated 24 July 1719, extracted from 'My Lord Harley's accompt'. The account is now at BL, Add. MS 70376, fos.136-42.
55 HMC, Portland, vii, p.259, letter from Dr William Stratford to Edward, Lord Harley, 28 August 1719.
56 *The Wren Society* (1940), *op.cit.*, p.11. Alastair Laing has suggested to me that 'beard earth' might mean 'burnt earth', ie. 'fired earth' or terracotta.
57 UN, PLC 1/443, 26 February 1724; 1/450, 2 June 1724; and 1/456, 18 June 1724.
58 Richard Hewlings, 'Ripon's Forum Populi', *Architectural History*, vol.24 (1981), pp.39-52.
59 Remarkably, another perspective on Sir Matthew Decker's visit survives, this recorded by John Cossen who arranged for the grandee's party to be met at Royston: 'he brot. em thro' Whadden by ye Bason and up ye Avenue thro' ye Great Gates up to ye Hall Door. The Library were made indifferent clean and Sr. Matthew wth his Family went thro' the House spoke in ye praise of every thing but much admired ye Chappele and Library he gave Barbara a Crown, he did not go into ye Garden saying he see them out of ye Windows in ye House' (UN, PLC 1/163).
60 Victoria & Albert Museum (hereafter V&A), 86NN2 (MS/1912/1255) fo.102. John Harris has observed that drawings in the same volume showing Chiswick as an ideal house rather than a villa suggests that this is a copy ms and must have been made earlier than the cover date of 1728.
61 George Sherburn (ed.), *The correspondence of Alexander Pope*, 5 vols. (Oxford, 1956), vol.III (1729—35), pp.114-5, Letter from Alexander Pope to the 2nd Earl of Oxford, assumed to be June 1730.
62 *Ibid.*, pp.135-6. 'Curlls' is a punning reference to Pope's adversary of twenty years, the bookseller, Edmund Curll (1675—1747), whom Pope pilloried in *The Dunciad* and to which Curll responded in *The Curliad*.
63 *Ibid.*, pp.146-7, Letter from the 2nd Earl of Oxford to Alexander Pope, 10 November 1730.
64 Sir John Soane's Museum (hereafter SM), Vol.26, Gibbs MS, fo.91. Fos.83-102 comprise 'A short account of Mr. James Gibbs Architect and of several things he built in England &c. after his return from Italy, Memorandums, &c.'.
65 'Vertue Note Books, vol.VI', *The Walpole Society*, vol.XXX (for 1948—50) (Oxford, 1955), pp.63-4.
66 Terry Friedman, *James Gibbs* (New Haven, 1984); John Harris 'Harley the Patriot Collector', *Apollo*, vol.CXXII, no.283 (new Series), September 1985, pp.198-203, fig.8; Parry, (1986), *op.cit.*, pp.36-55, fig.8; and Souden (1991), *op.cit.*, p.12.
67 UN, PLC 1/689.
68 BL, Add. MS 15776, fos.43-5.
69 *The Wren Society* (1940), *op.cit.*, pp.10-1, an extract from 'My Lord Harley's accompt'.
70 Thornhill also worked at Cannons, painting the saloon and staircase.
71 HMC, Bath, iii, p.498
72 *Ibid.*, p.499
73 For a full account of St. Luke's Club see Ilaria Bignamini, 'George Vertue, Art Historian and Art Institutions in London, 1689—1768: A study of Clubs and Academics', *The Walpole Society*, vol.LIV (Oxford, 1988) pp.2–18.
74 Tate, T10437. The meetings and feasts were more commonly held in London taverns.
75 HMC, Bath, iii, p.500.
76 The three versions are at BL, Lansdowne MSS, MS 846, fos.165-6; and Portland literary collection, UN, Pw V, 416-7. One of the Portland versions was published as 'A Hue and Cry' by Sir James Thornhill in Francis Needham (ed.), *A Collection of Poems by Several Hands, Never before Published*, Welbeck Miscellany, no.2 (1934), pp.53-6, and reprinted in *The Wren Society* (1940), *op.cit.*, pp.11-3.
77 BL, Lansdowne MSS, MS 846 fos.187-8, emended to fos.165-6.
78 HMC, Portland, vii, p.295.
79 BL, Add. MS 36258. Thomas Tudway (d.1726) was University Organist at Cambridge and acted as an agent for Edward Harley, buying music manuscripts on his behalf. See E. Turnbull, 'Thomas Tudway and the Harleian Collection', *The Journal of the American Musicological Society*, vii (1955), pp.203-7.
80 An oil portrait of Tudway also hung in the ante-library at Wimpole, see 'Vertue Note Books, vol.IV', *Walpole Society* vol.XXIV (for 1935—6) (Oxford, 1936), p.56.
81 UN, PLC 1/367, 14 January 1722; 1/378, 29 July 1722; 1/402, April 1723; 1/401, 28 April 1723; and 1/467, 3 August 1724.
82 'Vertue Note Books, vol.I', *Walpole Society*, vol.XIX, (Oxford,

83 1930), p.138.
83 *HMC*, Portland, vii, p.299.
84 'Vertue Note Books, vol.III', *Walpole Society*, vol.XXII (Oxford, 1934), p.80.
85 Mr Ford auctioned the prints on 16 March, and the books on 18 and 19 March. See: 'A Catalogue of the Entire Large and Valuable Collection of Prints, Drawings And Books of Prints of Mr. George Vertue, Engraver' (V&A National Fine Art Library, II RC Q 25).
86 V&A, 86NN2 (MSC/1912/1255), fos.102–3.
87 BL, Add. MS 15776, fo. 43, 'An Account of the Journey Mr. Hardiess & I took in July 1753'.
88 *The Gentleman's Magazine*, LX, November 1790, p. 992, cited in Brian Allen, 'Thornhill at Wimpole', *Apollo*, vol.CXXII, no.203 (New Series), September 1985, pp.204–11, fn.11.
89 BL, Add. MS 15776, fo.43, July 1753.
90 Scottish Record Office, MS 8968.
91 WRSO, 2057/F5/2, see fn.36.
92 V&A, 86NN2 (MSL/1912/1255) fo.103—diary 1728—30).
93 BL, Add. MS 35679, fo.73.
94 Eileen Harris, *British Architectural Books and Writers 1556—1785* (Cambridge, 1990), p.210.
95 UN, PL E3/1/1/8.
96 The complexities of whether the fourth virtuoso was John Wootton or the medallist and seal-engraver Charles Christian Reissen (c.1680—1725), and of the authorship of the verses, are explained in Peter Willis, 'Charles Bridgeman and the English Landscape Garden: New Documents and Attributions', John Bold and Edward Chaney (eds.), *English Architecture Public and Private: Essays for Kerry Downes*, (London & Rio Grande, 1993), pp.262–3.
97 Wright & Wright (eds.) (1966), *op.cit.*, vol. I, p. 87. Bridgeman made more than a dozen visits to the Library between February 1720 and April 1725. On 6 July Wanley noted ruefully 'Mr. Bridgeman came & promised to send me another dosen of Black-Lead-pencils; but they came not'; and on 30 June, somewhat huffily, 'Mr. Bridgeman's man disturbed the books', *ibid*. pp.119 & 359; for Charles Bridgeman Senior, who appears to have died at Wimpole in 1726, see Peter Wilis, *Charles Bridgeman and the English Landscape*, 2nd edn. (Newcastle-upon-Tyne, 2002), p.26, fn.7.
98 Bridgeman was Henry Wise's partner from 1726 to 1728 (replacing Joseph Carpenter), before taking sole responsibility for the royal gardens, albeit under the 'Cognizance' of Charles Dartiquenave, the Surveyor of Gardens and Water.
99 Willis (2002) *op.cit.*, p.25.
100 Isabel Wakelin Urban Chase, *Horace Walpole: Gardenist. An Edition of Walpole's* 'The History of the Modern Taste in Gardening', *with an Estimate of Walpole's Contribution to Landscape Architecture* (Princeton, N.J., 1943), pp.24–5. Quoted in Willis (2002) *op. cit.*, p.18.
101 Stephen Switzer (?1682—1745), a friend and colleague of Bridgeman's, credits instead the architect Sir John Vanbrugh with what may, ironically, be a French or Italian introduction.
102 Chase (1943) *op.cit.*, p.24.
103 *HMC*, Bath, iii, p.499, letter from Matthew Prior to Edward, Lord Harley, 18 March 1721.
104 Phibbs (1980), *op.cit.*, p.17, explains that because of the sheer number of trees required the elms were of necessity a mixture of approximately one-third *Ulmus procera* and two-thirds *Ulmus carpinifolia*.
105 In 1725 Bridgeman drew up a related proposal for Sir John Curzon at Kedleston; in this a tree-lined canal—rather than an avenue—is interrupted by a circular basin. See Leslie Harris (ed. Gervase Jackson-Stops), *Robert Adam and Kedleston: The making of a Neo-classical Masterpiece*, (1987), p.66, cat.52.
106 *HMC*, Portland, vii, p.293–4, letter from Dr. William Stratford to Edward, Lord Harley, 5 April 1721.
107 *Ibid*.
108 *The London Journal*, CXV, 7 October 1721, also relayed in MS form—see: BL, Add. MS 39814, fo.299. The discovery was recycled in Edmund Carter, *The History of the County of Cambridge from the earliest accounts to the present time* (Cambridge, 1753), p.304: 'the said Earl [of Oxford] digging canals at Wimple, found many bodies & rusty pieces of iron, the remains of some battle'.
109 UN, PLC 1/375, letter from John Cossen to Edward Harley, 2nd Earl of Oxford, 11 April 1722. Cossen wrote from the village of Norton, on the Welbeck estate, and must be describing work at Worksop Manor for Thomas Howard, 8th Duke of Norfolk (1683—1732). The digging of Norfolk's canal appears to have been overseen by 'Bridgeman's foreman', see: UN, PLC 1/381, 18 August 1722.
110 UN, PLC 1/381, letter from John Cossen, to Edward Harley, 2nd Earl of Oxford, Wimpole, 30 August 1722.
111 UN, PLC 1/394, letter from John Cossen to Edward Harley, 2nd Earl of Oxford, Wimpole, 10 March 1722/23.
112 UN, PLC 1/441, letter from John Cossen to 2nd Earl of Oxford, Wimpole, 18 February 1724.
113 Sherburn (1956), *op.cit.*, vol.II, p.260, letter from Oxford to Pope, Wimpole, 25 September 1724.
114 *Ibid.*, vol. II, pp.263-4, letter of 8 October 1724. Pope was later to explain to Oxford: March 1725/6, Pope to Oxford: 'I have just turfed a little Bridgmannick Theatre myself'.
115 *Ibid.*, vol.II, p.317, Pope to Oxford, letter of 7 September 1725.
116 Child's branch of Williams & Glyn's Bank Ltd., London, Edward Harley's MS Accounts, Ledger 1688—1732.
117 Sherburn (1956), *op.cit.*, vol.II, pp.376-7, letter of 22 April 1726.
118 Willis (2002) *op.cit.*, pp.73–6.
119 *Ibid.*, pp.30–1.
120 Phibbs (1980), *op.cit.*, p.15.
121 Lady Theresa Lewis (ed.), *Extracts of the Journals and Correspondence of Miss Berry from the year 1783 to 1852*, 3 vols. (1865), vol.II, p.401, Journal entry for 4 November 1801.
122 UN, PLC 1/419.
123 Arline Meyer, 'Wotton at Wimpole', *Apollo*, vol.CXXII, no.283 (New Series), September 1985, p.212.
124 BL, Add. MS 39167, fo.73.
125 The reference is to Jacques Courtois (1621—76), the émigré Jesuit artist from the Franch Comté (formerly part of the medieval Duchy of Burgundy), who was known in Rome as 'Il Borgognone', the French for which is 'Le Bourgnignon'. He was best known for his battle-pieces.
126 The wash drawing, possibly intended as a sketch for a painting of the Virtuosi for Wimpole Hall, is in the Leonora Hall Gurley Memorial Collection, Art Institute of Chicago.
127 Meyer (1985), *op.cit.*, p.214
128 I have found no documentary evidence of there having been a menagerie at Wimpole, although Jackson-Stops (1992), *op. cit.*, p.17, notes: 'The memory of the one at Wimpole is kept alive only by the pub known as the *Tiger* in Arrington, which backed on to the section of park where the animals were kept'. The *Tiger* or *Tyger*, was renamed *The Hardwicke Arms* with the arrival of the Yorke family.
129 'Vertue Note Books vol.III', *Walpole Society* (1934), *op.cit.*, p.34, quoted in Meyer (1985), *op.cit.*, pp.212-9, fn.27.
130 William John Arthur Charles James Cavendish-Bentinck, 6th Duke of Portland, *Men, Women and Things: Memories of the Duke of Portland* (1937), p.95: see also: Richard W Goulding, *Catalogue of the pictures belonging to His Grace the Duke of Portland, K.G at Welbeck Abbey, 17 Hill Street, London, and Langwell House* (Cambridge, 1936).
131 Arline Meyer, *British Sporting Painting, 1650—1850*, Hayward Gallery, 1974—5; and *idem. John Wootton, 1682—1764, Landscapes and Sporting Art in Early Georgian England*, exh. cat., The Iveagh Bequest, Kenwood House, London, 4 July-30 September 1984, no.9, ill. on p.38.

132 UN, PLC 1/384.
133 BL, Add. MS 36228, fo.168.
134 CRO, R92141 Cp 17.
135 Geoffrey Beard, *Craftsmen and Interior Decoration in England 1660—1820* (1981), p.242-4.
136 *Ibid.*, pp.241-2.
137 H. M. Colvin (ed.), *The History of the King's Works*, vol. V, 1660—1782 (1976). In Appendix C—Principal Craftsmen and others employed at Somerset House between 1776 and 1795 - John Devall is listed as Mason and from 1790 John Devall & Son; in Appendix D John Devall is recorded as Sargeant Plumber from the 7 May 1742 to his death in 1769.
138 BL, Add. MS 35367, fo.17.
139 BL, Add. MS 35679, fo.69, letter from Henry Flitcroft to Baron Hardwicke, Whitehall, September 23 1752.
140 RA, CP 43/191, cited in Jane Roberts, *Royal Landscape: The Gardens and Parks of Windsor* (New Haven & London, 1997), p.38.
141 BL, Add. MS 5823, fo.135.
142 BL, Add. MS 35679, fo.76.
143 BL, Add. MS 35679, fo.104.
144 BL, Add. MS 35679, fo.135.
145 BL, Add. MS 35635, fos.274 & 280.
146 Sir John Summerson, *Architecture in Britain 1530—1830* (3rd edn., 1983), p.157; John Harris and Gordon Higgott, *Inigo Jones: Complete Architectural Drawings* (New York, 1989), p.298.
147 H.J. Louw, 'Anglo-Netherlandish architectural interchange c.1600—1660', *Architectural History*, vol.24, 1981, pp.1–23.
148 Giles Worsely, *Classical Architecture in Britain: The Heroic Age* (New Haven & London, 1995), pp.7-9.
149 Royal Collection, RL: 17937.
150 CRO, R 92141 Cp 17.
151 Lady Llanover (ed.), *The Autobiography and correspondence of Mary Granville Mrs. Delaney*, 3 vols. (1861), vol.III, p.462.
152 See BL, Add. MS 35679, fos.l3-6, 20, 28, 53, 54 & 69.
153 BL, Add. MS 35679, fos.13-5.
154 CRO, P l79/1/1 Registers, fo.63.
155 Ely Diocesan Record, D3/1a/68.
156 BL, Add. MS 35591, fos.421-9.
157 Staffordshire Record Office (hereafter SRO) D615/P (S)/1/3/7, letter of 13 June 1749: 'The next business of importance is the Painting upon Brick, which M[r]. Flitcroft has already rouched for [...] The use of Sand is apprehended to be in order to give it more the appearance of Stone; as to the Church at Wimpole it is not to undergo the operation 'till the next year, it being neccessary that the Brick-work should have been finished a sufficient time first'. See also Lady Anson's letter of 4 June 1749, SRO D615/P (S)1/3/6A.
158 Michael Archer, 'Stained Glass at Erdigg and the work of William Price', *Apollo*, vol. CXXII, no.284 (New Series), October 1985, p.256.
159 Nikolaus Pevsner, *The Buildings of England: Cambridgeshire* (2nd edn., 1970), p.493.
160 CUL, Add. 5819.
161 HRO, D/ECd E73, Bill no.87a.
162 HRO, D/ECd E73, 1830 Bill no.5.
163 Letter from Horace Walpole to Richard Bentley, Arlington Street, September 1753 W.S. Lewis (ed.), *The Yale Edition of Horace Walpole's Correspondence*, vol.35 (New Haven & Oxford, 1973) p.148.
164 Warwick Record Office (hereafter WRO), CR 125B/348, letter from Sir George Lyttleton to Sanderson Miller, London, 1 June 1749.
165 WRO, CR 125B/788, letter from 1st Earl of Hardwicke to Sanderson Miller, Powis House, 15 March 1750.
166 BL, Stowe MS 753, fo.146v., letter from Sanderson Miller to Charles Lyttleton, Gosfield, 16 September 1750.
167 Bedfordshire Record Office (hereafter BRO), Lucas MSS, L30/21/2/7, letter from Lady Amabel Yorke, later Polwarth, to Miss Catherine Talbot, 30 October 1767.
168 BRO, L/30/11/122/26, Letter from Marchioness Grey to her daughter Lady Amabel, 1 October 1772.
169 Jackson-Stops (1992), *op.cit.*, p.86.
170 Thomas Cocke, *The Ingenious Mr. Essex, Architect 1722—1784*, exh. cat., Fitzwilliam Museum. (Cambridge, 1984), p.5, notes that James Essex was encouraged by his friend Richard Gough, the Secretary of the Society of Antiquaries of London, in the study of Crowland Abbey—see: 'Mr. Essex's Observations on Croyland Abbey and Bridge' in *Bibliotheca Topographica Britannica*, xxii (1784), pp.177-204.
171 BRO, L/30/9/97/32, letter from Agneta Yorke to Lady Grey, 7 September 1774.
172 BRO, L/30/9/111/138, letter from Mary Yorke to Lady Grey.
173 C.B. Andrews (ed.), J. Byng, 'Tour in the Midlands, 1790', *The Torrington Diaries: containing the tours through England and Wales [...] between the years 1781 and 1794*, 3 vols (1935), vol. II, p.239. Byng was an admirer of genuine, medieval ruins whether abbeys or castles.
174 CUL, Add. MS 5189: J. Plumptre: *A journal of a Tour to the Source of the River Cam made in July 1800*.
175 WRO, CR 125B/168 & CR 125B/741.
176 *The Annual Register, or a View of the History, Politics and Literature for the year 1775*, vol.xviii (1776), p.196.
177 William Hawkes, 'Sanderson Miller 1716—80 Architect' unpublished dissertation, University of Cambridge, 1964, p.5, fn.17. It is possible that Lord Hardwicke also sent a copy to Horace Walpole, for on 16 July 1777 Walpole wrote from Strawberry Hill: 'Mr Walpole returns Lord Hardwicke the volume of letters with many thanks, and as many for the print, which he admires extremely, and the design. He does not like the verses less, which are very just.' See Lewis, *op.cit.*, vol.41 (1980), p.364.
178 HMC, Dartmouth Report 15, app. I, 1896, pp.238-9.
179 *The Gentleman's Magazine* vol.XLIX, p.150.
180 *The Family Memoirs of the Rev. William Stukely, M.D, and the Antiquarian and other Correspondence of William Stukeley, Roger & Samuel Gale etc.*, 3 vols., The Surtees Society, vol. LXXVI (1883), vol.II, p. 51, letter of 8 September 1747 (Diary, vol. vi, 86).
181 BL, Add. MS 35591, fo. 421.
182 Ray Desmond (ed.), *Dictionary of British and Irish Botanists and Horticulturists, including Plant Collectors, Flower Painters and Garden Designers* (1994), p.295. Nothing is known of Richard Greening, a fourth son.
183 David Jacques, *Georgian Gardens: The Reign of Nature* (1983), p.70.
184 BL, Add. MS 33074, fo.104, Letter from Thomas Pelham-Holles, 1st Duke of Newcastle to his wife. I am indebted to Sophie Chessum for this information.
185 Roberts (1997) *op.cit.*, p.38; Roberts explains, p.43, that Thomas Greening was paid £3,000 for work at Windsor between 1747 and 1748, while smaller payments were made to 'Robert Greening and Company'.
186 BL, Add. MS 35679, fos.73–5. The underlining is original.
187 Jackson-Stops (1992), *op.cit.*, p.44. In fact he gives George Shenstone in error for William Shenstone.
188 BL, Add. MS 35679, fo.67, Wimpole, 23 September 1752, 'Instructions for Mr Bird from Robert Greening'.
189 *Ibid.*
190 *Ibid.* By 'tan' Greening means crushed oak bark bought from a tannery—see the account of John Soane's designs for hothouses below (*Nos.140–7*).
191 BL, Add. MS 35679, fo.71, 'Directions for Mr. Moses at Wimple, Oct[r]. 30th: 1752 RG'.
192 BL, Add. MS 35679, fo.91, letter from John Bird to 1st Earl of Hardwicke, 4 August 1753.
193 BRO, L30/9a/6/p.117, letter from Jemima, Marchioness Grey to Miss Mary Talbot, Wimpole, 20 September 1753.
194 BL, Add. MS 35679, fo.96, 17 January 1754.

195 BL, Add. MS 35679, fo.96, 17 January 1754.
196 BL, Add. MS 35679, fo.102, letter from 1st Earl of Hardwicke at Powis House, to John Bird at Wimpole, 8 March 1754.
197 BL, Add. MS 35679, fo.104, letter from 1st Earl of Hardwicke at Powis House, to John Bird, 23 March 1754.
198 BL, Add. MS 35679, fo.193, letter from John Bird at Whaddon, to 1st Earl of Hardwicke, 17 March 1757.
199 BL, Add. MS 35679, fo.67.
200 BL, Cole MSS, Add. MS 5848, fos.428–30.
201 Stuart and Thoms Scheemakers worked together on Dr. Ralph Freman's monuments at Braughing church, Hertfordshire and on Joseph Cockes's and Mrs. Mary Cockes's monuments at Eastnor, Hertfordshire—all of whom were relatives of the Yorke family.
202 In the same year Brown acted as a go-between during the sale of the the 1st Earl of Hardwicke's house in Grosvenor Square, London to Lord Exeter—see Dorothy Stroud, 'The Charms of Natural Landscape, The Park and Gardens at Wimpole II', *Country Life*, CLXVI, no.4288, 13 September, 1979, p.758.
203 BRO, 9a/9 fo.125, letter from Jemima Marchioness Grey to Catherine Talbot, Wimpole, 19 September 1767.
204 BRO, L30/21/27, letter from Lady Amabel Yorke to Catherine Talbot, 30 October 1767.
205 BL, Add. MS 69795, fo.20.
206 I am grateful to John Drake for this suggestion.
207 Oliver Goldsmith (1730?—74), *The Deserted Village, A Poem* (1770), p.15, Mavis Batey has argued that the poem describes the 'improvements' made by the 1st Earl of Harcourt and Lancelot Brown at Nuneham Courtenay, Oxfordshire which saw the destruction of the Domesday village of Newnham. See also Wainwright (1997), *op.cit.*, pp.4–16.
208 Brown's account book is in The Lindley Library, The Royal Horticultural Society, for Wimpole see fo.59; HRO, D/Ecd F81; and Hoare's Bank Archive, Ledgers D (1766—69) and E (1769—73).
209 CRO (Huntingdon), 2268/1 Wood & Ingram, Ledger for 1748—84, pp.120-1. I am grateful to John Drake for furnishing me with these details.
210 E. Pollard, MD Hooper, and NW Moore' *Hedges* (1974), p.46; Wood and Ingram, Ledger for 1748—84, p.131.
211 BRO, L30/9/97/13, letter from Agneta Yorke to Marchioness Grey, 21 October 1770.
212 BRO, L 30/9/97/20, letter from Agneta Yorke to Marchioness Grey, 13 October 1771.
213 BL, Add. MS 35629, fo.92. Letter from Robert Plumptre, DD., to 2nd Earl of Hardwicke, 22 May 1781.
214 BL, Add. MS, 35607, fo. 234.
215 BL, Add. MS, 35695, fo.243.
216 Andrews (1935), *op.cit.*, vol. II, p. 239.
217 J. Britton and E.W. Brayley, *The Beauties of England and Wales; or, Delineations, topographical, historical, and descriptive, of each county. Embellished with engravings*, 18 vols. (1801—16), vol. II, p. 125.
218 CUL, Add. MS 5819, 'A Journal of a Tour to the Source of the River Cam made in July 1800 by Walter Blackett Trevelyan Esq[r], A.B. of S[t].John's College and the Rev[d]. James Plumptre, A.M. Fellow of Clare Hall, Cambridge'.
219 HRO, D/ECd F82 to F84.
220 CUL, W.M. Palmer collection B.51.
221 BL, Add. MS 35695 fo. 348.
222 Rev. Christopher Pitt (ed.), *The works of Vergil in Latin and English*, 4 vols. (1753), pp.262–3.
223 HMC, MSS Dartmouth, Report 15, appendix I, 1896, 238-9.
224 See particularly: George Williamson, *The Imperial Russian Service* (1909); Peter Hayden, 'British Seats on Imperial Russian Tables', *Garden History*, vol. 13, no.1. (Spring, 1985), pp.17–32; Michael Raeburn, Ludmila Voronikhina & Andrew Nurnberg (eds.), *The Green Frog Service* (London & St. Petersburg, 1995); and Hilary Young (ed.), *The Genius of Wedgwood* (1995).
225 Wedgwood Archive, Keele University Library, E32-5184, excerpt from the title page of Bentley's *Catalogue and General Description*.
226 Letter from Catherine the Great to Voltaire, 25 June/6 July 1772, sent from Peterhof: W.F. Redway (ed.), *Documents of Catherine the Great* (Cambridge, 1931), p.163, cited in Young (1995), *op.cit.*, p 140, fn.17, the fuller original reads: 'J'aime à la folie présentement les jardins à l'anglaise, les lignes courbes, les pentes douces, les étangs en forme de lacs, les archipels en terre ferme, et j'ai un profound mépris pour les lignes droites, les allées jumelles. Je hais les fontaines quie donnent la torture à l'eau pour lui faire prendre un cours contraire à sa nature; les statues sont reléguées dans les galleries, les vestibules, etc.; en un mot, l'anglomanie domine dans ma plantomanie'.
227 Wedgwood Archive, E25-18455, letter from Josiah Wedgwood to Thomas Bentley, 9 April 1773.
228 Wedgwood MS E25–18487, letter from Wedgwood to Bentley 14 August 1773, cited in Michael Raeburn 'The Frog Service and its sources', Young (1995), *op.cit.*, p.142, fn.25
229 A note was placed to this effect in *The Public Advertiser* for 1 June 1774: Malcolm Baker, 'A Rage For Exhibitions—The Display and Viewing of Wedgwood's Frog Service', Young (1995), *op.cit.*, pp.118–27.
230 BRO, L30/11/122/60, letter from Marchioness Grey to Lady Amabel Polwarth, 19 June 1774.
231 *Ibid*.
232 BRO, L 30/9/60/35, letter from Lady Amabel Polwarth to Marchioness Grey, 19 June 1774.
233 Wedgwood Archive, E32-5184. The cost of printing and translation amounted to £9 14s 0d.
234 BL, Add. MS 35695 fos. 57, 66, 68 & 71.
235 HRO, D/Ecd F82, entries for 27 February 1776 and 12 December 1777
236 North Yorkshire County Record Office, archive of Worsley of Hovingham, letter from Kenton Couse to Thomas Worsley, 31 August 1777, ZON 13/3/215.
237 Elizabeth P. Biddulph of Ledbury, *Charles Philip Yorke, Fourth Earl of Hardwicke Vice-Admiral RN: A Memoir* (1910), p.163.
238 HRO, D/Ecd. F82, F83 and F84.
239 HRO, D/Ecd. F106.
240 BL, Add. MS 35695, fos. 89, 101 & 102.
241 W.M. Palmer, *William Cole of Milton* (Cambridge, l935), p. 77.
242 BL, Add. MS 5848, fos.428–30. On 29 August 1778 William Cole wrote to Horace Walpole from Milton: 'I never could bring myself to pay the usual homage in fashion here, to go and dine at Wimpole. [...] there is something very forbidding [in t]he manner of his Lordship that I could never persuade myself to pay court to a person whom I could not honour', see Lewis, *op.cit.*, vol.2 (1937) p.113.
243 BL, Add. MS 35687 fo.290, 7 October 1806.
244 *Ibid.*, fo.299, 6 November, 1806.
245 See Arline Meyer, 'Sir William Musgrave's 'Lists' of portraits with an account of head-hunting in the eighteenth-century', *The Walpole Society*, vol.LIV (Oxford, 1988), pp.454–502.
246 Du Prey (1978), *op.cit.*, p.28; Souden (1991), *op.cit.*, p.29; Dean (1999), *op.cit.*, p.67; and Darley (1999), *op.cit.*, p.38.
247 BL, Add. MS 35378, fo.305v, letter from Philip Yorke to Philip Yorke, 2nd Earl of Hardwicke, 31 January 1779.
248 Darley (1999), *op.cit.*, p.37, provides a measure for the difference in their status, explaining that Soane's stipend from the Royal Academy amounted to £60 per annum while Yorke, who was far from extravagant, spent £204 2s 8d and £54 19s 8d respectively in January and February 1779.
249 Biddulph (1910), *op.cit.*, p.163. Letter from Caroline Yorke to Lady Beauchamp, 1781.
250 Margaret Richardson and MaryAnne Stevens (eds.), *John Soane Architect: Master of Space and Light* (1999), exh. cat., Royal Academy of Arts, London, 11 September—3 December 1999, cat. no.49. The model is now on display at Wimpole.
251 SM Journal No.2, fos.243, 244, & 245.

252 Souden (1991), *op.cit.*, p.31.
253 Pierre de la Ruffinère du Prey, *John Soane, The Making of an Architect* (Chicago & London, 1982), pp.124–5.
254 V&A 3436.188. Du Prey (1985), *op. cit.*, p.53, suggests that Soane may have been influenced by 'the decadently lavish Parisian baths that were all the rage among French courtesans and rich nobles'.
255 Elizabeth Cartwright-Hignett, *Libi at Aynhoe: Victorian life in an English Country House* (1989), p.117. The watercolour is dated 8 May 1847.
256 I am particularly grateful to Susan Palmer for her advice on the question of hands in Soane's Office.
257 SM Journal No.I, fo.164.
258 Darley (1999), *op.cit.*, p.5.
259 Ptolemy Dean, *Sir John Soane and London* (Aldershot, 2006), p.213.
260 Christopher Hussey, 'Wimpole Hall—The Home of Mrs. Bambridge—III', *Country Life*, CXLII, 14 December 1967, p.1596.
261 SM Account Book Wimpole 1791—4, fo.43.
262 *Ibid.*, fos.72 & 130.
263 BL, Add. MS 35628, fo.149. Letter from the Rev. Plumptre to the 2nd Earl of Hardwicke, 4 May 1772.
264 BRO, L30/11/240/53.
265 Sir John Summerson, 'Soane: the Man and the Style', in *John Soane* (New York & London, 1983), p.13.
266 Sir John Summerson, *Georgian London* (revised ed., 1970), p.157.
267 Darley (1999), *op.cit.*, p.22.
268 BRO, Lucas MSS, L30/9/97/129.
269 Pierre de la Ruffinière du Prey, 'The *Bombé*-Fronted Country House from Talman to Soane' in *The Fashioning and Functioning of the British Country House*, Studies in the History of Art 25, National Gallery of Art, Washington (1989), pp.29–49.
270 Dean (1999), *op.cit.*, pp.69–70.
271 Nicholas Savage, 'Exhibiting Architecture: Strategies of Representation in English Architectural Exhibition Drawings, 1760—1836', in David H. Solkin (ed.) *Art on the Line: The Royal Academy Exhibitions at Somerset House 1780—1836* (New Haven & London, 2001), p.208.
272 Megan Aldrich (ed.), *The Craces: Royal Decorators 1768—1899* (Brighton, 1990), p.9.
273 HRO, D/Ecd. F101.
274 SM Journal, No.2, fo.144.
275 BRO, l30/11/240/53.
276 SM Journal, No.2, fo.141.
277 Biddulph (1910), *op.cit.*, pp.163–4.
278 Mark Girouard, *Life in the English Country House* (New Haven & London, 1978), p.230.
279 Dean (2006), *op.cit.*, pp.213–4.
280 SM Journal, No.2, fo.243.
281 Merlin Waterson, *The Servants' Hall: The Domestic History of a Country House* (1980), pp.138–9.
282 I am grateful to Keith Goodway for suggesting these family connections.
283 BL, Add. MS 35378, fos.395-6, letter from 'Southill, November 12, 1779'.
284 BL, Add. MS 35378, fo.397, 18 November 1779, London.
285 Keith Goodway, 'William Emes (1729/30—1803), *ODNB*, vol.18, p.404.
286 BL, Add. MS 35629, fo.158. Letter from Robert Plumptre, DD., to the 2nd Earl of Hardwicke, Sunday 11 May 1783.
287 SM Account Book, Wimpole 1791—4, fos.30–3
288 Tony Baggs, *The Green Houses in the Walled Garden at Wimpole Hall, Cambridgeshire*, a Cambridge Historic Buildings Group report, July 1999, p.4.
289 V&A 3307.1-9 & 20.
290 Stroud (1979), *op.cit.*, p.760.
291 Lady Theresa Lewis (1865), *op.cit.*, vol.II, p.446, *Journal* entry for 8 December 1810.
292 Cambridge Archaeology Field Group, Excavation Report, forthcoming.
293 SM, M1148.
294 Pierre de la Ruffinière du Prey, 'John Soane, Philip Yorke and their Quest for Primitive Architecture', *National Trust Studies 1979* (1978).
295 John Martin Robinson, *Georgian Model Farms: A Study of Decorative and Model Farm Buildings in the Age of Improvement 1700—1846* (Oxford, 1983). Robinson explains that the use of timber was very much more common on the continent.
296 Cointeraux discussed the use of *pisé* in a number of publications but his most influential, translated into German, was *Ecole d'architecture rurale et économique* (Paris, 1790).
297 SM Journal 2, fo. 245.
298 UN, PLC 1/392, 28 February 1723.
299 John Martin Robinson, 'Model Farm Buildings of the Age of Improvement', *Architectural History*, vol.19, 1976, p.17.
300 Britton & Brayley (1801—16), *op.cit.*, vol.II (1801), pp.125-6.
301 Du Prey (1978), *op.cit.*, p.28.
302 Garrett's publication, *Designs and Estimates of farm-houses, etc. for the County of York, Northumberland, Cumberland, Westmoreland and Bishoprick of Durham* (1747), was the first such pattern book to focus exclusively on the design of farmhouses.
303 Robinson (1976), *op.cit.*, p.21.
304 Du Prey (1978), *op.cit.*, p.86.
305 Wedgwood Archive, H20—23357: 'Lady Hardwicke wishes Edward Cole to Shew this letter to Messrs. Wedgewood [*sic*], and request of them to send down four of the largest size of Milk-pans at 12 Sh. each to be sent by the waggon, Wimpole, Nov. 6. 128'. I am grateful to Patricia Ferguson for drawing this to my attention. Wedgwood illustrated this range in his *Catalogue of Useful Wares*, 1774. The Royal Archives, Windsor Castle, Queen Victoria's Journal for Saturday 28 October 1843.
306 Augustus J.C. Hare, *The Story of My Life,* 6 vols. (1896—1900), vol.4, p.252.
307 Pierre de la Ruffinière du Prey, *Sir John Soane*, Catalogues of Architectural Drawings in the Victoria and Albert Museum (1985), p.31.
308 John Soane, *Designs in Architecture; consisting of plans, elevations, and sections, for temples, baths, casinos, pavilions, garden-seats, obelisks, and other buildings* (1778).
309 Augustus J.C. Hare, *Two Noble Lives: Being memorials of Charlotte, Countess Canning, and Louisa Marchioness of Waterford*, 3 vols. (1893), vol.i, p.112, Letter from Lady Elizabeth Stuart to the Countess of Hardwicke, 20 November, 1820.
310 Nigel Temple, *George Repton's Pavilion Notebook: a catalogue raisonné* (Aldershot, 1993), pp.45-6.
311 Du Prey (1985), *op.cit.*, p.63.
312 Stroud (1979), *op.cit.*, p.761.
313 SM Priv. Corr. XIII G3, letter of 7 November 1804. The saga of the entrance lodges continues in SM Corr XIII G4, G5, G6 and G8 in a series of letters, several illustrated with rough survey sketches, between Lord Hardwicke, his agent and architect. A further sheet of such sketches can be found at SM vol.42, 153 (formerly Original Sketches).
314 Ann Gore and George Carter (eds.), *Humphry Repton's Memoirs* (Norwich, 2005), p.137-8.
315 *Ibid.* See also: Gillian Darley, 'The surprising discretion of Soane and Repton', *The Georgian Group Journal*, vol. XII (2002), pp.38-47.
316 *Ibid.*
317 Gore and Carter (2005), *op.cit.*, p.141.
318 Dorothy Stroud, *Humphry Repton* (1962), Appendix I, 'List of works by Humphry Repton, p.174, mistakenly claims that it was.
319 Rosemary Bowden-Smith, *The Water House, Houghton Hall, Norfolk*, English Garden Features, 1600—1900, No.1, (1987).
320 Nigel Temple, 'Humphry Repton, Illustrator, and William Peacock's "Polite Repository" 1790—1811', *Garden History*, vol.

321 Giles Worsley, *The British Stable* (New Haven & London, 2004), pp.124-8.
322 BL Add. MS 36278 K.4, covering letter from Thomas West, 4 May 1805.
323 CUL MS Add. 5819, fo.66.
324 BL, Add. MS 36278 K.4.
325 BL, Add. MS 35695, fo.348, letter of June 1788.
326 Humphry Repton, *Observations on the Theory and Practice of Landscape Gardening* (1803), p.104.
327 *Ibid.*, p.104.
328 *Ibid.*, pp.104-5.
329 Peter Summers (ed.), *Hatchments in Britain, vol. 6, Cambridgeshire, Essex, Hertfordshire, Huntingdonshire and Middlesex* (London & Chichester, 1985) pp.22 & 106.
330 SM Priv. Corr. XIII G 12.
331 Gore and Carter (2005), *op.cit.*, p.138
332 SM Priv. Corr. XIII G 31.
333 HRO, D/Ecd E64, Wimpole No.2 General Cash Book 1820—27.
334 BL, Add. MS 35687, fo. 120v.
335 Britton & Brayley, *op.cit.*, vol II (1801), p 125.
336 Yorke also described these improvements in the Parish Records CRO, P 179/1/2 p.34.
337 BL, Cole MS Add MSS 5848 fos.428-30.
338 Archer (1985), *op.cit.*, p.257
339 Queen Victoria's diary for 25 October 1843, reproduced in the *Orwell Bulletin*, March 1980.
340 Adam Menuge and Anwen Cooper, *The Gothic Folly, Wimpole Park, Wimpole, Cambridgeshire*, an Architectural Investigation Report, English Heritage (2001) p.38, fn.27.
341 BL Add. MS. 52413, fos. 18 & 113.
342 This and a drawing for the entrance front are misattributed, to Henry Thomas Hope and Alexander Roos, respectively, in David Watkin, *Thomas Hope, 1769—1831, and the Neo-Classical Idea* (1968), pl.86, and Richard Garnier, 'Alexander Roos (c.1810—1881)', *The Georgian Group Journal*, vol. XV (2006), pp.11-68, figs.11 & 12.
343 Watkin (1968), *op.cit.*, pp.184-5.
344 Quoted in Delia Millar, *The Victorian watercolours and drawings in the collection of Her Majesty the Queen*, 2 vols. (1995), vol.II, p.576.
345 Hare (1893), *op.cit.*, vol.i, pp.269-70, letter from Viscountess Canning to Lady Stuart de Rothesay (at St. Petersburg), from Grosvenor Square, London, 31 October 1843. Different parts of this letter, with variations in transcription, are reproduced in Virginia Surtees, *Charlotte Canning: lady-in-waiting to Queen Victoria and wife of the first Viceroy of India 1817—1861* (1975), it appears too to be the same partially quoted in Millar (1975).
346 Biddulph (1910), *op.cit.*, p.299. The sculpture group, of two figures, representing *Charity*, was carved by John Henry Foley (1818—74).
347 *The Builder*, Vol. XXXIII, 9 January, 1875, p.33; and 16 January, p.60.
348 Surtees (1975), *op.cit.*, p.120. This improvised stage-management clearly tricked the reporter from the *Cambridge Chronicle* whose article for 4 November 1843 noted: 'The ante-library opens with immense plate-glass doors upon the conservatory. The conservatory was brilliantly illuminated with variegated lights, and the effect when viewed from the darkened library was enchanting. Her Majesty, who remained some time contemplating the scene, appeared greatly to admire it'.
349 'Mr. Downing's Letters from England', *The Horticulturist*, October, 1850, vol.V, no.4, pp.156-60, University of East Anglia, Microfiche, LAC 30987-91.
350 Worsley (2004), *op.cit.*, p.260.
351 *Ibid.* This similarity was also observed by A.C.Yorke, CUL, Palmer B51, 1914, p.6: 'ugly as they are, and with the early Victorian bad taste of popping St. George's Hanover Square, tower on top of coach-houses and horse-stalls'.
352 CRO, Rattee & Kent Achive, R100/9.
353 Christie's, King Street, London, 25 March 1999, Lot 377.
354 Gervase Jackson-Stops (ed.), *The Treasure Houses of Britain: Five Hundred Years of Private Patronage and Art Collecting* (New Haven & London, 1985), pp.234–5, cat.155.
355 For an analysis of this building see the report: Christine Eden, Archaeological investigations at the Old Rectory (Marshall and Yorke Cottages) Wimpole Hall, Cambridgeshire (Cambridge, 1995).
356 CUL, Palmer B51, 1914. Campbell's amusing account of the estate was published as David Ellison (ed.), Alexander Campbell Yorke, *Wimpole as I knew it* (Bassingbourn, 1975).
357 CRO, P/179, l560—1968.
358 Letter, probably of June 1730, Longleat Portland Papers, xii.
359 Simon Houfe, *Sir Albert Richardson: The Professor* (Luton, 1980), p.159.
360 BL, Add. MS 35644, fo.30.

Appendix

The following list of nineteenth and early twentieth century drawings for farm and other estate buildings, which are not included in the catalogue or illustrated on the CD-Rom, includes a small number from the National Trust's Bambridge Collection at Wimpole but the majority, formerly on deposit in the Cornwall Record Office, are now in the Cambridge Record Office. In 1894 the 2nd Lord Robartes took over the house and estate at Wimpole, in his capacity as Chairman of the Agar-Robartes Bank, in satisfaction of the 5th Earl of Hardwicke's bankruptcy, but only three years later, he inherited the title 6th Viscount Clifden and moved to Lanhydrock, Cornwall, the family's main seat. The Wimpole estate was thereafter managed, by his Agent S.W. Jenkins, from Cornwall and work commissioned from Cornish engineers such as J.W. Jenkins. Lanhydrock was given to the National Trust by the 7th Viscount Clifden in 1953. The author of many of these drawings is not known and not all are dated; as far as is possible they have been listed in chronological order.

E B Metcalfe. Plan, section and elevation of a Malting House. 1809.
National Trust WIM/D/544

Robert Withers. Plan for the conversion of a Bullock Shed to a Maltings. 1830.
National Trust WIM/D/546

William Chadwick Mylne. Design for a bridge. 1834
National Trust WIM/D/592

Cotton and Haller. Design for a 16ft. cattle bridge with three alternative designs for gating the ends
National Trust WIM/D503

(?)Thomas Savell. Sketch plans and elevations for a pair of cottages
National Trust WIM/D/498

Thomas Savell. Ground and first floor plans, and alternative elevations for a 'Tudor' lodge on Croydon Road, Arrington. 1856
National Trust WIM/D/542; 548a; & 548b

'T.H.A.' Plans, elevations and sections for a pair of cottages in Wimpole Valley. 1895
Cambridge Record Office, DDCL(P) 267/2; & 272/2

Plan and elevations for buildings at River Cam Farm, Wimpole
Cambridge Record Office, R93/62 (DDCL(P)386/3)

Plan, elevations and sections for a Schoolroom
Cambridge Record Office, R93/62 (CL(P)271/11)

Elevation and plan for alterations to Kingston Pastures Farm. 1895
Cambridge Record Office, CL(P) 269/7; & DDCL (P) 267/8

Plan and elevation for a sluice gate at Avenue Farm, Shingay. 1895
Cambridge Record Office, CL (P) 269/10

Sketch plan for additions to the Gardener's ('Burgess's) house, Wimpole. 1895
Cambridge Record Office, CL (P) 272/12

Sidney French. Designs for schools and teachers' houses at Arrington, Wimpole and Whaddon
Cambridge Record Office, CL(P) 266/11; 272/14; 13; & 17

Plan and elevation for new farm buildings at Morden
Cambridge Record Office, CL(P) 273/11

Plan, elevations and sections for new farm buildings at Wimpole Lodge
Cambridge Record Office, CL(P) 273/9

Sketch plan, elevation and section for new farm buildings at Wraggs Farm, Arrington
Cambridge Record Office, CL(P) 273/19

William Bain & Co. Plans and sections for a Sawing Shed for the Woodyard at Wimpole
Cambridge Record Office, CL(P) 270/21; 272/7
One of the drawings is stamped William Bain & Co., Lochrin Iron Works, Coatbridge

William Bain & Co. Designs for iron gates
Cambridge Record Office, CL(P) 269/2; & 273/18

Plans, elevations and section of constructional detail for new farm buildings at Church Farm Arrington. *c.*1895
Cambridge Record Office, CL(P) 273/2

Plan and elevation for new farm buildings at Hoback Farm. *c.*1895
Cambridge Record Office, CL(P) 270 (8)

Plans, elevations and sections for new farm buildings at Holbins Farm, Great Eversden
Cambridge Record Office, CL(P) 386/2

Detail of staircase for a farm house at Guilden Morden
Cambridge Record Office, DDCL(P) 266/5

Sketch plans and section for two covered yards on the Wimpole estate.
Cambridge Record Office, CL(P) 269/13

Jones and Attwood, heating engineers. Floor plans, specification and estimate for providing 'heating apparatus' to Wimpole. 1895
Cambridge Record Office, CL (P) 269/4; 269/11; 269/12; 270/11; 272/1; 272/6
The specification provided for forty-five cast iron 'ornamental radiators of neat appearance'. Additional radiators were fitted in the Conservatory and the library.

Jones and Attwood. Proposed addition of hot water pipes to John Soane's hothouses. 1895
Cambridge Record Office, DDCL (P) 266/4

Outline plan of Wimpole Hall, showing St. Andrew's parish church, the castello d'acqua and the position of drains and pipe runs
Cambridge Record Office, CL(P) 273/3

'J.H.S.' Sketch plan of 'Old Reservoir' and elevation of 'overflow gate' at Wimpole
Cambridge Record Office, CL(P) 273/14
'T.H.A.' Elevations for a range of buildings at Shingay Gate Farm. 1896
Cambridge Record Office, R93/62 (DDCL(P)386/5); & 272/2

Plan showing field drainage on Shingay Gate Farm. 1897
Cambridge Record Office, CL(P) 271/8

Plan of Cobbs Wood Farm
Cambridge Record Office, CL(P) 271/9

Plan of Manor Farm, Shingay
Cambridge Record Office, CL(P) 271/12

J. W. Jenkin & Son. Plan and sections for an underground water reservoir at Wimpole. 1898
Cambridge Record Office, R93/62 DDCL (P) 386/4; 386/7; & 386/8
Designed by J. W. Jenkin & son, Civil Engineers, Liskeard, Cornwall, this covered, concrete walled structure, designed to accommodate 50,000 gallons of water, still stands on the brow of the hill to the north-west of the Hall. It was intended that rainwater draining from the curved, corrugated iron roof should help to keep the reservoir full. Water seems also to have been sent up to it from 'the pumping station', presumably that which stood between the Upper and Lower lakes.

J. W. Jenkin & Son. Plans, elevation and section for alterations to Wimpole Lodge
Cambridge Record Office, CL(P) 269/15; 270/7; 270/23; & 272/9

Scales and Robins, Builders. Plan and part elevation of Wimpole Lodge showing proposed additions and alterations
Cambridge Record Office, CL(P) 266/10; & 268/12

Sketch plan of barn and implement shed for South Farm, Shingay. 1899
Cambridge Record Office, DDCL(P) 267/5

S.W. Jenkin. Site plan for The Mission Room, Shingay
Cambridge Record Office CL (P) 269/3; 269/8; with additional tracing copies of both

Thomas H Porter (d.1902). Plans, elevations and section for a Bake House at Great Eversden. 1900
Cambridge Record Office, R93/62 (DDCL(P)271/10)

'J.H.J'. Alterations proposed to cottages at New Wimpole. 1902
Cambridge Record Office, CL(P) 270/20

Cockett and Nash, Architects, Royston. Plans for proposed alterations to a house at Arrington Bridge
National Trust WIM/D/504

Alexander Paul MacAlister & Edwin James Tench (b. 1875). Plans and elevations for alterations to the Hardwicke Arms. 1905
Cambridge Record Office, CL(P) 270/22; 271/3; 271/4; 271/5; 271/6; & 217/7

Plans and elevations for alterations and repairs to Hoback farmhouse, Wimpole. 1910
Cambridge Record Office, DDCL(P) 266/8

Index

Page numbers in **bold** indicate a catalogue entry; page numbers in *italic* indicate an illustration

Alken, Sefferin 38
All Souls College chapel, Oxford 24
Allom, Thomas, Wimpole conservatory **122**, *123*, **124**, *pl.11*, *pl.13*
architectural pattern books 105
Arrington, Cambs.,
    inn **88**
    map **112**
Artari, Giuseppe 38
Aylwin, Reginald Francis Guy, Wimpole drawings **133–4**, *135*

Bagutti, Giovanni 23, 38
Bambridge Collection 12
Bambridge, Capt. 133
Bambridge, Mrs Elsie 12, 77, 133
Banyard, George Philip, Wimpole survey drawings **134**, *135*, **136**
Basire, James, St. Andrew's Church **67**
bathhouses 68
Beauties of England and Wales (ed. Brayley and Britton) 113
Bentley, Thomas, Frog Service 63, 65
Berain, Jean, I 28
Berry, Mary 33
Bickham, George 63
Bird, John 53, 54, 56
Boulter, Edmund 17
Boulton & Paul Ltd **133**
Boydell, John 63
Brayley, Edward Wedlake 113
Bridgeman, Charles 29, 30
    Wimpole Park 14, 16, 30, **31–4**, *32*, *pl.1*
Brompton Park nursery 31
Brown, Lancelot 'Capability' 47, 52, 81, 101
    landscaping for Wimpole 57, 58, *58*, **59–60**
Buck, Nathaniel 63
Buck, Samuel 63
Buss, Robert William, Wimpole Yellow Drawing Room paintings **124–5**, *125*

Cambridge, University of, Senate House 23
Cambridgeshire map **115**, *116*
Cannons House, Edgware 24
Carpentière, Andries 28
Catherine the Great, Empress of Russia 63
Chatelain, Jean-Baptiste-Claude 63
Chawner, Thomas
    Wimpole **74**, *75*, **76**, **77–8**, *77*
Chicheley Chapel *see* St. Andrew's Church
Chicheley, Sir Thomas 10, 11, 14, 40, 41
chimneypieces, New Cavendish St, London **79**, *80*
Clifden, 6th Viscount *see* Robartes, 2nd Lord
Cossen, John 30–1
Couse, Kenton 39
    Normanton Park plan *137*, **138**
    Wimpole dining room 41, **66**, *66*
Cutler, Sir John 17

Dahl, Michael 36
dairies 93
Dall, Nicholas 63
Decker, Sir Matthew 19
Defoe, Daniel 14
Delany, Mary 43
Devis, Anthony 63
Donthorn, William John, Wimpole survey drawing **118**, *118*
Down Hall, Essex 25, 31

Emes, William 81
    Wimpole Park **81**, *pl.3*
Essex, James 47, **48**
Evans, George, Wimpole St. Andrew's Church **132–3**, *132*

farms, model 90 *see also under* Wimpole
Fawcett, Benjamin, view of Wimpole **116**, *117*
Flitcroft, Henry, drawings for Wimpole
    Gothic eyecatcher **48**, *48*
    ice-house **46**, *46*
    park **42–3**, *43*
    St. Andrew's Church 43, **44–5**, *44*, *45*, 110, 132, 133
    surveys 22, 23, 38–9, *39*, **40–2**
Foley, John Henry 154
Fougereau, Jacques 25
    Wimpole sketches 19, 28, **35**, *35*
Frog Service 63–5 *see also under* Wimpole

Gandy, Joseph Michael, Wimpole Castello d'Acqua **85**, *86*
gardeners, Royal 14, 30
Gibbs, James 17, 18, 19
    A Book of Architecture 19, 23, 28
    monuments 19, 28–9
    Wimpole chapel 24, **25–6**, *25*
    Wimpole garden **28**, *28*, *29*
    Wimpole Hall 17, 18, 19, **20–3**, *20*, *22*
    Wimpole orangery **19–21**, *20*
    Wimpole urns **28–9**, *29*
Godfrey, Richard 63
Goeree, Jan, Wimpole Hall view **16**
Greening, John 52
Greening, Robert 39, 40, 46, 51, 52
    Drawings for Wimpole **52–4**, *55*, **56–7**
Greening, Thomas, junior 52
Greening, Thomas, senior 52
Grey, Jemima, Marchioness (Countess of Hardwicke) 47, 54, 57, 63
Guibert, John, Survey drawings of Wimpole 16, 22, **69**, *69*

Hagley, Worcs. 47, 48, 60
Hammels, Herts. 68, 81, 92, 93, 97
Hardwicke Arms *see* Arrington inn
Hardwicke, Earls of *see* Yorke
Hardwicke, Jemima, Countess of *see* Grey, Jemima, Marchioness
Hare, Benjamin 14
    map of Wimpole Estate **14**, *15*
Harleian Library 17–8
Harley, Edward, 2nd Earl of Oxford and Mortimer 17, 20, 24, 31

Catalogue of Collections frontispiece **36**, *37*
    portrait **36–8**, *37*
Harley, Robert, 1st Earl of Oxford and Mortimer 17
Harraden, Richard Bankes, Wimpole Gothic Folly **116**, **117**
Heathcote, Sir Gilbert 138
Holles, Henrietta Cavendish, Countess of Oxford 17, 20, 34, **35**
Holles, John, 1st Duke of Newcastle 17

ice-houses 46 *see also under* Wimpole

Jeans, Thomas, Wimpole plan **80**
Jones, Inigo 24, 40, 41
Joynes, Henry 138

Keene, Henry, Wimpole library steps **52**, *52*
Kendall, Henry Edward 97, 121–2
    Wimpole conservatory **122**, *123*, **124**, *pl.11*, *pl.13*
    Wimpole entrance **126–7**, *126*, *pl.14*
    Wimpole stables 127, **128**, *128*
Kent, Nathaniel, *Hints to Gentlemen of Landed Property* 87
Kett, George 128 *see also* Rattee & Kett
Kerrich, Thomas 67
Kip, Johannes
    Britannia Illustrata 16
    Wimpole Hall view 14, *15*, **16–7**, 30, 105
Kirkhall, Edward, Wimpole urns **28**, *29*
Knyff, Leonard, *Britannia Illustrata* 16

Laguerre, Louis 24
Laing, David
    Hints for Dwellings 87
    Wimpole survey drawings 16, **69**, *69*
landscape gardening 30
Langley, Batty 16, 56
Langley Park, Norfolk 97
Last, Bradbury, map of Wimpole **112**, *112*
Layer, John 10, 14
Le Neve, Peter 16
Lerpinière, Daniel, Wimpole Hill House **61**, **62–3**
Liddell, Hon. Georgiana, view of Wimpole **117**, *pl.12*
Liddell, Hon. Thomas, sketches of Wimpole **119–20**, *120*, **126**, *126*, *127*, *128*
London, George 14, 30
Lydon, Alexander Francis, view of Wimpole **116**, *117*
Lysons, Daniel, *Magna Britannia* 67
Lysons, Samuel
    Magna Britannia 67
    Wimpole St. Andrew's Church 67
Lyttleton, Sir Thomas 47

Mansfield, Isaac 23
Marshall, Edward 131
Mortin, Jean de 14
Mason, James 63
Mee, Arthur Patrick, Wimpole St. Andrew's Church **218**, *218*
Miller, Sanderson 40, 47, 48
    Wimpole Gothic Folly **49–50**, *49*
Milles, Jeremiah 23, 25
Mills, Peter 41
Milton House, Northants. 41
Moule, Thomas, map of Cambridgeshire **228**, *229*

Nash, Frederick 113
Nash, Joseph (the elder), Wimpole Book Room **114**, **116**, *pl.8*
Nattes, John Claude, Wimpole ice-house **113–4**, *114*
Neale, John Preston, view of Wimpole **115**
Newton, Algernon, view of Wimpole **134**, *135*
Noble, J., view of Wimpole **113**, *113*
Normanton Park, Rutland **137**, *138*

Oxford, Earls of *see* Harley

Peckitt, William 67
Peltro, John, view of Wimpole 101, **104**, *104*
plaster-carvers 23
Plumptre, Rev. James 46, 60, 62, 97, Wimpole St. Andrew's Church **66**, **67**
Plumptre, Robert 59
Polwarth, Lady Amabel (née Yorke) 47, 48, 58
    Frog Service **63–4**, *64*, **65**
    Wimpole view **59**, 60
Pope, Alexander 17, 18, 19, 24, 31, 58
Pratt, Sir Roger 11, 41
Provis, Henry, drawings for Wimpole
    farmyard **91–2**, *91*
    hot house **82**
    St. Andrew's Church **110**, *111*

Radnor, 2nd Earl of *see* Robartes, Charles Bodville
Ranken, William Bruce Ellis, Wimpole gallery **134**, *pl.15*
Rattee, James 128 *see also* Rattee & Kett
Rattee & Kett, Wimpole designs 128, **129–31**, *129*, *130*
Repton, Humphry 33, 99, 111, 114
    Red Books 99
    Wimpole conservatory **108–9**, *109*, *pl.7*
    Wimpole Red Book drawings 99, **100–4**, *100*, *102*, *103*, *pl.4*, *pl.5*, *pl.6*
Repton, John Adey 99, 100, 101, 108
    Wimpole conservatory **108–9**, *109*, *pl.7*
Rhodes, David 65
Richardson, Sir Albert, Wimpole St. Andrew's Church **136**, *137*, **138**
Robartes, Charles Bodville, 2nd Earl of Radnor 11, 16, 17
Robartes, 2nd Lord 155
ruins, sham *see* Wimpole Gothic Folly
Russell, Sir William 10

Savile, Hon. Anne 10–1
Scheemakers, Peter 57, 110
    monuments for St. Andrew's Church **55**, **57**, 110
Serlio, Sebastiano 40
Seward, Henry Hake, Wimpole plan **80**
Soane, Sir John 23, 68, 87, 100, 111, 138
    Wimpole Book Room **70**, *70*, *71*
    Wimpole estate cottages **87**, **88**, *89*
    Wimpole dairy and hen house **92–6**, *95*, *96*
    Wimpole Yellow Drawing Room 71, **74**, *75*
Soane, Sir John, office, chimneypieces **79**, **80**
Soane, Sir John, office, drawings for Wimpole
    Book Room 70, *70*, *71*
    Castello d'Acqua **84**, *85*, **86**
    entrance screen **97–9**, *98*
    estate cottages **87–8**, *89*
    hothouse **82–4**, *83*
    inn at Arrington **88**
    model farm **90–2**, *91*
    plans and surveys **69**, *69*, **77–80**, *77*, *79*
    St. Andrew's Church **110–1**, *111*
    Yellow Drawing Room **72–4**, *73*, *75*, **76–7**
Sparrow, S. 63
St. Andrew's Church, Wimpole 39, 43, **44–5**, *44*, *45*, **55**, **57**, **66**, **67**, 103, *103*, **104**, **110–1**, *111*, **132–3**, *132*, **136**, *137*, **138**, *pl. 10*
St. Bartholomew's Hospital, London 25
St. James's Palace Queen's Chapel, London 24
St. Mary-le-Strand, London 24, 26
St. Paul's Cathedral 11
stables 105 *see also under* Wimpole
Stone, Nicholas 40, 41
Stringer, Samuel 63

Stuart, James 'Athenian' 48
    Wimpole Frog Service *64*, **65**
    Wimpole Hill House 60, *61*, **62–3**
Stukeley, William
    Palaeographica Britannica 51
    Wimpole topographical drawings **51**, *51*
Swiss barn **138–9**, *138*

Talman, William, Wimpole orangery **19–21**, *20*
Thornhill, Sir James 24, 25
    Wimpole chapel 24–5, *25*, **26–7**, *26*, *27*
Tiger Inn *see* Arrington inn
Tijou, Jean, Wimpole gate screen **14**, *15*
Tyringham, Bucks. 97

Vertue, George 19
    frontispiece **36**, *37*
    portrait and Wimpole library **36**, *37*
    Wimpole façade and font **36**, *37*
Vivares, François 63

Walpole, Horace 30, 36
Wanley, Humfrey 17, 18, 36, 38
Wedgwood, Josiah, Frog Service **63–4**, *64*, **65**
Welbeck Abbey, Notts. 17, 19
West, Thomas, Wimpole stables and estate buildings **105–7**, *106*
Willemont, Thomas, Wimpole stained glass **118–9**, *118*
Wills, Trenwith, plans of Wimpole **136**, *137*
Wimpole
    almshouses **127**
    architectural style and influences 11, 40, 41
    Book Room 23, **70–1**, *70*, 114, **116**, *pl.8 see also* Wimpole library
    Castello d'Acqua 84, *85*, **86**
    ceilings *22*, **23**, **129**, *129*
    chapel 24–5, **25–7**, *25*, *26*, *27*
    Chinese Bridge *12*, 43, *64*, **65**
    church *see* St. Andrew's Church
    conservatory **108–9**, *109*, **122**, **123**, **124**, *pl.7*, *pl.11*, *pl.13*
    construction 10, 14, 40, 41
    dairy and hen house 92–3, **94–6**, *95*
    dining room **66** *66*
    entrance gates and screens **14**, *15*, **16**, **97–9**, *98*, **126–7**, *126*, *pl.14*
    estate buildings **87–8**, *89*, **102**, *102*, **103**, **106**, **107**, 155–6
    farm, model **90–2**, *91*, 138
    fish-ponds 14, 31
    Frog Service 48, *64*, **65**, 92
    furniture **52**, *52*, 128, **129**, **130–1**, *130*
    gallery **114**, *114*

gardeners 46, 54, 55
gardens 28, *28*, **29**, 34, **35**, *35*, 39, **51**, *51*, 52–4, **55**, **56–7**
glasshouses **133** *see also* Wimpole hothouses
glaziers 44–5
Gothic Folly *12*, 47, **48–50**, *48*, *49*, *64*, **65**, **115**, *116*, **117**
Great Staircase **22–3**, *22*
Hearth Tax 10, 14
hen house *see* Wimpole dairy and hen house
Hill House 48, 60, *61*, **62–3**, *64*, **65**, **101–2**, *102*, **104**, *104*, 105, **106**, *107*
hothouses **82–4**, *83*, 107
ice-houses 39, **46**, *46*, **113–4**, *114*
lakes and reservoirs **42–3**, *43*, *64*, **65**, **101**, *102*, **104**, *104*, *pl.5*
landscaping 14, 16, 30–1, 53, 57, 58, 99–100, 101
library 17, 19, 21, 23, 36, **37**, **120** *see also* Wimpole Book Room
maps **14**, *14*, *15*, **65**, **100**, *100*, **112**, *112*, *pl. 4*
nineteenth-century topographical views **113–7**, *113*, *114*, *116*
orangery **19–21**, *20*
owners 10, 11, 12, 16, 17, 133
Park 30, **31–3**, *32*, **42–3**, *43*, 57, **58**, **59–60**, 81, **100**, *100*, *pl.2*, *pl.3*, *pl.4*
plunge bath 68
Prospect House *see* Wimpole Hill House
rectory **131**, *131*
Red Book 99, **100–4**, *100*, *102*, *103*, *pl.4*, *pl.5*, *pl.6*
spillway **43**, *43*
stables **103–4**, *103*, **105–7**, *106*, **127–8**, *128*
stained glass **118–9**, *118*
twentieth-century topographical views **134**, *135*
workmen 38–9, 46
Yellow Drawing Room 71, **72–7**, *73*, *75*, 124, **125**, *125*

Wise, Henry 14, 30
Withers, Robert, Wimpole map **112**, *112*
Woollett, William 63
Wootton, John, topographical paintings of Wimpole Park 34, **35**
Wray, Mary, view of Wimpole **60**
Wrest Park, Beds. 40, 57
Wrighte, William 93

Yorke, Lady Amabel *see* Polwarth, Lady Amabel
Yorke, Charles Philip, 4th Earl of Hardwick 121, 124
Yorke, Charles Philip, 5th Earl of Hardwicke 133
Yorke, Eliot Thomas, views of Wimpole **115**, *116*, **131**, *131*, *pl.9*
Yorke, Henry Reginald, views of Wimpole **114–5**, *116*, *pl.10*
Yorke, Philip, 1st Earl of Hardwicke 38
Yorke, Philip, 2nd Earl of Hardwicke 47, 57
Yorke, Philip, 3rd Earl of Hardwicke 68, 81, 90